NEW YORK

THE

MISSION BOOK:

A MANUAL OF

INSTRUCTIONS AND PRAYERS

ADAPTED TO PRESERVE

THE FRUITS OF THE MISSION.

DRAWN CHIEFLY FROM THE

WORKS OF ST. ALPHONSUS LIGUORI.

New and Improved Edition.

New York:
D. & J. SADLIER & CO., 31 BARCLAY ST.

MONTREAL:—COR. OF NOTRE DAME & FRANCIS XAVIER STS

The "Mission Book" has received the commendation of many distinguished Prelates in Europe, as a work eminently fitted for the instruction of the faithful, and the promotion of solid piety. We cheerfully permit its publication.

✠ JOHN,
ARCHBISHOP OF NEW YORK.

NEW YORK, *September 8th* 1858

Table of Movable Feasts.

Year of our Lord.	Dominical Letter.	Golden Number.	The Epact.	Septuagesima Sunday.	Ash Wednesday.	Easter Sunday.
1875	c	14	xxiii	Jan. 24	Feb. 10	Mar. 28
1876	b A	15	iv	Feb. 13	Mar. 1	April 16
1877	g	16	xv	Jan. 28	Feb. 14	April 1
1878	f	17	xxvi	Feb. 17	Mar. 6	April 21
1879	e	18	vii	Feb. 9	Feb. 26	April 13
1880	d c	19	xviii	Jan. 25	Feb. 11	Mar. 28
1881	b	1	*	Feb. 13	Mar. 2	April 17
1882	A	2	xi	Feb. 5	Feb. 22	April 9
1883	g	3	xxii	Jan. 21	Feb. 7	Mar. 25
1884	f e	4	iii	Feb. 10	Feb. 27	April 13
1885	d	5	xiv	Feb. 1	Feb. 18	April 5
1886	c	6	xxv	Feb. 21	Mar. 10	April 25
1887	b	7	vi	Feb. 6	Feb. 23	April 10
1888	A g	8	xvii	Jan. 29	Feb. 15	April 1
1889	f	9	xxviii	Feb. 17	Mar. 6	April 21
1890	e	10	ix	Feb. 2	Feb. 19	April 6
1891	d	11	xx	Jan. 25	Feb. 11	Mar. 29
1892	c b	12	i	Feb. 14	Mar. 2	April 17
1893	A	13	xii	Jan. 29	Feb. 15	April 2
1894	g	14	xxiii	Jan. 21	Feb. 7	Mar. 25
1895	f	15	iv	Feb. 10	Feb. 27	April 14
1896	e d	16	xv	Feb. 2	Feb. 19	April 5
1897	c	17	xxvi	Feb. 14	Mar. 3	April 18
1898	b	18	vii	Feb. 6	Feb. 23	April 10
1899	A	19	xviii	Jan. 26	Feb. 15	April 2
1900	g	1	xxix	Feb. 11	Feb. 28	April 15
1901	f	2	x	Feb. 3	Feb. 20	April 7

Table of Movable Feasts.

Year of our Lord.	Ascension Day.	Whit Sunday.	Corpus Christi,	Sundays after Pentecost.	First Sunday of Advent.
1875	May 6	May 16	May 27	27	Nov. 28
1876	May 25	June 4	June 15	25	Dec. 3
1877	May 10	May 20	May 31	27	Dec. 2
1878	May 30	June 9	June 20	24	Dec. 1
1879	May 22	June 1	June 12	25	Nov. 30
1880	May 6	May 16	May 27	27	Nov. 28
1881	May 26	June 5	June 16	24	Nov. 27
1882	May 18	May 28	June 8	26	Dec. 3
1883	May 3	May 13	May 24	28	Dec. 2
1884	May 22	June 1	June 12	25	Nov. 30
1885	May 14	May 24	June 4	26	Nov. 29
1886	June 3	June 13	June 24	23	Nov. 28
1887	May 19	May 29	June 9	25	Nov. 27
1888	May 10	May 20	May 31	27	Dec. 2
1889	May 30	June 9	June 20	24	Dec. 1
1890	May 15	May 25	June 5	26	Nov. 30
1891	May 7	May 17	May 28	27	Nov. 29
1892	May 26	June 5	June 16	24	Nov. 27
1893	May 11	May 21	June 1	27	Dec. 3
1894	May 3	May 13	May 24	28	Dec. 2
1895	May 23	June 2	June 13	25	Dec. 1
1896	May 14	May 24	June 4	26	Nov. 29
1897	May 27	June 6	June 17	24	Nov. 28
1898	May 19	May 29	June 9	25	Nov. 27
1899	May 11	May 21	June 1	27	Dec. 3
1900	May 24	June 3	June 14	25	Dec. 2
1901	May 16	May 26	June 6	26	Dec. 1

PREFACE

TO THE

NEW AND IMPROVED EDITION OF THE MISSION BOOK.

THIS little volume, called the "Mission-Book,' is intended as a companion to the Sermons and Instructions of the Mission. Its object is to aid those who attend the Mission to make it well, and to help them, after the Mission is over, to remember the sacred truths they have heard, to practice the good resolutions they have made, and to preserve the gifts of grace they have received. The want of such a little Manual for the Mission was long felt by missionaries laboring in Europe; and they accordingly prepared one, which has been from time to time, published in different languages, and with such variations as were thought suitable and proper. It has had a wide circulation, and has carried with it a great blessing in several different countries, and particularly in Austria, Bohemia, Belgium, Holland, and France. The English Mission-Book was prepared some years ago, on the basis of the German edition, but it was entirely remodelled and enriched with much additional matter, in order to make it more useful to Catholics in the United States. Since that time it has been occasionally revised and corrected anew, and it has now once more been subjected to a careful revision, and improved by the addition of much interesting and useful matter.

In this little book you will find, dear Christian Reader, a plain and simple compendium of the instructions of the Mission, in the form of Instructions on the Sacraments and Christian Duties, Meditations, and Spiritual Readings on the great truths of religion. You will find also the forms of private and public devotion, which are commonly contained in a Prayer-Book. Thousands of Catholics in this country, have, within a few years past, found this little book next to the Mission itself, a most precious and a most efficacious means of grace, for themselves and for their families. Use it then, diligently, for the sake of your eternal salvation. Use it also for the salvation of your children and those intrusted tc your care, and for the salvation of others, especially for those who are uninstructed, who are careless of their religion, and who are living sinful lives. In this way you may save your own soul, and rescue the souls of many others from eternal perdition.

EXPLANATION OF THE MISSION: THE WAY TO MAKE IT WELL, AND HOW TO PRESERVE ITS FRUITS.

A Mission is a series of Spiritual Exercises given publicly in a Church for several days, or for one or more weeks in succession. These exercises include daily Mass and Benediction, with other public Prayers, Sermons, and Instructions, and the administration of the sacraments of Penance, and the Holy Eucharist. Its end is to enlighten and instruct the mind, to excite the conscience, to inflame the will, and to renew the whole inward and outward life, by the solemn truths, and wholesome doctrines of religion. The Papal Benediction is usually given at the close of the Mission, by special authority of the Holy See, and those who receive this Benediction can gain a Plenary Indulgence, if they have attended the exercises, and have made a good confession and communion. There is a partial indulgence of two hundred days attached to each one of the exercises of the Mission. If the mission continues for ten days, another Plenary Indulgence granted to all those who perform the Spiritual Exercises for ten days may be gained.

In order that a Mission should succeed well, it is very necessary that it should be announced to the people two weeks before the opening, and that they should be urged and exhorted to attend the Exercises. It is a most salutary practice to offer up public prayers with them during the interval, for its success, and to request them to say certain special prayers for the same intention, every day in private.

When the Mission is opened in a Parish, all should hail it as a singular and special blessing from Heaven. The Mission is usually opened on a Sunday and the first Sermon is preached at High Mass.

In this Sermon you will hear the nature and advantages of the Mission, and the way to make the Mission well, fully explained. Let every one, therefore, make it a point to attend the Introductory Sermon. After this you should attend all the Exercises—the Evening Sermons and Morning Instructions—diligently to the end. Without this constant attendance it will be impossible for you really to gain the fruits of the Mission. Even if you live at some distance from the church, make the sacrifice and attend the Exercises. It is but once perhaps in your life that you will be invited to do it, and the great good which you will gain is worth any sacrifice and any labor. How many who come in from the remote parts of the parish just as the Mission is closing are sent away unheard, or if they are permitted to receive the Sacraments, are deprived of all the Special Graces and Blessings of the Mission!

Besides attending the exercises, you must from the beginning break off every habit of mortal sin, avoid all bad company, and shun all dangerous places and occasions of sin.

You must also pray fervently in church and at home, that you may make the Mission well. Perhaps your eternal salvation depends on it and the everlasting destiny of your soul may be decided now.

And then, dear Christian, after you have made the Mission well, and have obtained its precious graces, you must take care that you do not fall into the fatal mistake of supposing that you have no more to do—that the grace of the Mission will of itself keep you from falling, and secure your eternal Salvation.

If you have made the Mission well, you have only taken the first step of a long journey, and made a good beginning in the great work of your salvation, which must employ your whole lifetime. The Mission is no substitute for the good works of the Christian Life, by which a sinner can escape hell and gain heaven, without a solid and lasting conversion. If your good resolutions pass away with the excitement of the Mission—if, after the Mission you again allow years to pass in the neglect of your Easter Duty; if you neglect Mass on Sundays; if you relapse into habits of vice, and violate anew the vows of your baptism, which you have ratified at the foot of the cross—

your salvation will be in the greatest danger. Watch over yourself then most carefully, employ all diligence, all zeal in maintaining in your heart the fruits of the Mission, and in order to preserve them until the end of your life, use faithfully the following means of perseverance:—

HOW TO PERSEVERE IN THE GRACE OF GOD AFTER THE MISSION.

1. *You must avoid the occasions of sin.* Evil company and dangerous amusements are the great highways to sin and hell. In your baptism you promised to renounce the devil and all his pomps. Renounce, therefore, now and for ever, the ball, the dancing party, the theatre, the circus, the tavern-bar, the liquor-shop, and every place of temptation. Above all, abandon for ever the person whose company has already proved dangerous to your purity. "He that loveth danger shall perish in it." Eccli. iii. 27.

2. *You must read good books.* What was it in the Mission inspired you with so many holy thoughts—with such noble resolutions? Was it ot the Word of God, chasing away from your mind the false maxims of this world, and filling it with the eternal truths of faith? Lay aside then the foolish romance, the dangerous novel, and the silly tales of the newspapers, and occupy your minds every day with useful and holy reading, such as the Lives of the Saints, the works of St. Alphonsus, and other devout writers of the Catholic Church, and above all the Gospels the New Testament, which contain the life of

our Lord Jesus Christ on earth, his holy lessons to man, and the history of his death.

3. *You must frequent the Sacraments.* Confession and communion are fountains of grace, which God has placed at our doors for common use. Without confession your conscience will soon become hardened, blinded, and loaded with guilt. The Body and Blood of Christ is the food of the Christian's soul. Without frequent communion that soul will faint for want of nourishment, and fall into sin. How many die to the grace and friendship of God from pure starvation, because they let months and months go by without communion. The Saviour of the world says, that unless you eat his flesh and drink his blood, you shall have no life in you. S. John, vi. 54. Resolve then to receive this Bread of Heaven at least once in the month.

4. *You must pray.* "Without me," says Jesus Christ, "you can do nothing." S. John, xv. 5. You cannot do any thing whatever for your soul's good; you cannot take a single step in the way of salvation without the grace of God, and that grace you must obtain by prayer. "If any of you want wisdom, let him ask of God, who giveth to all abundantly." S. James, i. 5. Be constant, therefore, in the habit of prayer. Say every day without fail, your morning and evening prayers. Be present not only at the Mass on Sundays and Holy days, as the Church commands, but as often as you can on the week days also, and pray devoutly then. Pray especially in the moment of temptation, before the evil thought has time to

gain strength, and God will always give you the victory. The promise of final perseverance and of salvation, is to those who are constant and persevering in prayer: "And it shall be that every one that shall have called upon the name of the Lord, shall be saved." Joel, ii. 32.

Often then, dear Christian, recall to mind the graces given to you during the Mission; and renew the firm resolution to put in practice the above means so necessary to preserve them. Do not doubt that all those graces were obtained for you by the intercession of the Blessed Virgin, and that she may help you to keep them, offer to her the following petition:

PRAYER FOR PERSEVERANCE.

Oh! Mary, Mother of God, and my own beloved Mother! I cast myself at thy feet to thank thee for all the graces which thou hast obtained for me during the Holy Mission. How sweet it is to remember all those eternal truths which enlightened my mind, inflamed my heart, and taught me to prepare for death and judgment! How joyful was that moment when first I resolved to change my life, and keep the commandments of God! How great the peace of my heart after I had made that sincere confession of all my sins! Never shall I forget that delightful hour, when I recommended my soul and salvation to thy motherly care;—that solemn hour also when I renewed the vows of my baptism, and then received the Papal Benediction, with the plenary Indulgence of the Church. How happy would be, could I persevere in that same state of life until the last breath of life! But, alas! the world is full of dangers. Satan is seeking always to ensnare my soul, and the frailty of the human heart is so great! Oh! no, Mother of God! I cannot persevere by my own strength. I should fall into mortal sin; and, oh! if that sin should be my last, and remain unforgiven!

Therefore, oh! Mother of God, take my heart into thy keeping, and maintain me in these my firm resolutions. Never will I sin any more. Never will I utter sinful words, never follow dangerous amusements, keep evil company, or expose my soul to the occasions of sin; never more will I neglect prayer, or the sacraments of the Church, and so lose again all the fruits of my conversion. Now I am a child of God. Jesus Christ, thy divine Son, is my friend, the angels are my companions. Oh! Holy Lady! am I not a dear child of thine? Keep me ever in thy loving heart. Maintain these resolutions in my soul. Pray for me, thy child, to Jesus thy divine Son; and should Satan ever come to seduce my soul, then will I pray to thee.

Oh! Mother, help me, watch over me, support me; never let my soul be separated from Jesus Christ, thy Son and my Redeemer. *Amen.*

USEFUL TABLES

Festivals of Obligation.

The Movable Feasts are:

EASTER SUNDAY, WHIT-SUNDAY, and ALL SUNDAYS in the year. The ASCENSION and CORPUS CHRISTI.

The Immovable Feasts are:

Jan. 1. THE CIRCUMCISION.
Jan. 6. THE EPIPHANY.
Mar. 25. THE ANNUNCIATION.
Aug. 15. THE ASSUMPTION.
Nov. 1. ALL-SAINTS.
Dec. 25. CHRISTMAS.

N. B.—In the dioceses of New Orleans, St Louis, Mobile, Vincennes, Dubuque, Little Rock, and Chicago, the CIRCUMCISION, EPIPHANY ANNUNCIATION, and CORPUS CHRISTI are not festivals of obligation.

Days of Fasting.

1. THE FRIDAYS IN ADVENT.
2. EVERY DAY IN LENT, Sundays excepted.
3. THE EMBER-DAYS, which occur four times in the year; viz., the Wednesdays, Fridays, and Saturdays,—immediately after the First Sunday in Lent,—in Whitsun-week,—immediately after the 14th of September, immediately after the Third Sunday of Advent.
4. THE VIGILS OF CERTAIN FEASTS; viz., of Whit-Sunday, of the Assumption, of All-Saints, and of Christmas.

N. B.—When a fasting-day falls upon a Sunday, it is kept on the Saturday before. To fast consists in abstaining from flesh-meat, and eating only one full meal in the day, which must not be before noon. Besides this, a collation or light refreshment is allowed in the evening. All who have completed their twenty-first year are obliged to observe the fasts of the Church until the age of sixty, unless exempted for some legitimate cause.

In the above-mentioned dioceses of New Orleans, St. Louis, &c., &c., the Friday of the Ember-days is the only Friday in Advent on which there is an obligation to fast.

Days of Abstinence.

1. THE SUNDAYS IN LENT.
2. ALL FRIDAYS, except when Christmas falls upon a Friday.

N. B.—A day of abstinence is that on which we are not allowed to eat flesh-meat. All who have attained to the age of reason are obliged to observe these days.

The Ordinary Prayers.

The Prayers, &c., of most necessary and common use will be found as follows:

GENERAL DEVOTIONS.

Prayers for Daily Devotion.

HOW TO PRAY.

"*Before prayer prepare thy soul, and be not as a man that tempteth God.*"—Eccli. xviii. 23.

Prayer is the lifting up of the mind and heart to God, and constitutes one of the first duties of a true Christian. There are two different kinds of prayer, namely, mental and vocal.

MENTAL PRAYER, or MEDITATION, is when we pray silently in our hearts, without using any set form of words, or speaking with the voice.

VOCAL PRAYER is that which is uttered by the voice, and commonly is made according to some form; in other words, it is to say, or recite prayers.

To make our prayers good and pleasing in the sight of God, they must be offered:

1. With a pure heart, or at least a sincere desire to obtain a pure heart through penance. "*The Lord is far from the wicked: and he will hear the prayers of the just.*" Prov. xv. 29.

2. A lively faith. We ought to have a firm and childlike trust in God, that he will grant our prayers, if what we ask is really for the good of our souls. "*Let him ask of God, but let him ask in faith, nothing wavering, for he that wavereth is like a wave of the sea that is moved and carried about by the wind. Therefore let not that man think that he shall receive any thing of the Lord.*" St. James, i. 5.

3. Profound humility. "*He hath had regard to the prayer of the humble, and he hath not despised their petition.*" Ps. ci. 18.

4. Earnest attention. "*I cried with my whole heart, hear me, O Lord!*" Ps. cxviii. 145.

5. Unwearied patience. We must not leave off praying, even if our prayer is not heard at once. "*The continual prayer of a just man availeth much.*" St. James, v. 16.

MORNING DEVOTIONS.

"*The wise man will give his heart to resort early to the Lord that made him, and he will pray in the sight of the Most High: he will open his mouth in prayer, and make supplication for his sins.*" Eccli. xxxix. 6, 7.

If you would spend a holy day, dear Christian, you must begin it in a holy way.

As soon therefore as you awake, and it is time to get up, raise your thoughts immediately to God, make the holy sign of the cross, dress quickly, fall upon your knees, and begin to pray.

I. Thank God that he has again permitted you to see another day, and guarded you against every evil during the night.

II. Ask him with childlike confidence to keep you, during the day, from sin, and every other evil.

III. Offer to him all your thoughts, words, and actions of the day, uniting them to the sufferings and death of Jesus Christ.

IV. Make a firm resolution to commit no sin during the whole day. Be on guard especially against your most frequent and besetting sin. Consider well all the dangers and occasions of sin, which you are likely to meet with, and reflect upon the means by which you may escape from them. Make a firm resolution to resist manfully every temptation which may fall in your way, and ask of God the necessary grace to do so.

All this can be done inwardly in your own heart, without any sound of your voice, or motion of your lips; but if you find it easier to recite vocal prayers, you can make use of the following form.

MORNING PRAYERS.

IN the name of the Father, and of the Son, and of the Holy Ghost. Amen.

THANKSGIVING.

O MY God! I adore thee, and I love thee with my whole heart. I thank thee for all the benefits which thou hast granted me, and especially for having protected me so mercifully this night.

PRAYER FOR NECESSARY GRACE.

O MY Jesus! bear me in thy hands this day. Mary, holy Virgin! may I find shelter under thy protecting mantle. And do thou, O heavenly Father! help me for the love of Jesus and of Mary. My Guardian Angel, and all my patron Saints, help me by your holy prayers.

GOOD INTENTION.

TO thee, my God, I offer all that I shall do, all that I may suffer during the day which is now begun. I unite all my actions and sufferings to the sufferings of Jesus and Mary, and I make the intention now to gain all the indulgences to which I may be entitled, for any good works of mine this day.

RESOLUTION.

MY God! I firmly resolve to fly from sin, and I implore thee for Jesus' sake to grant me the grace of perseverance. And especially I am resolved that in every trial, taking refuge in thy holy will, the prayer of my heart shall be, "O Lord! thy will be done!"

Here set before your mind the labors, and other occupations in which you are likely to be engaged throughout the day. Consider well how you can order all your affairs for the honor of God, and the good of your neighbor. Call to mind your usual faults, also the dangers and the occasions of sin to which you will be exposed, and make the firm resolution to guard yourself carefully against these temptations and occasions; and especially against that one which you know to be the greatest and most dangerous of all. Say then, with a sincere heart:

O MY God! I am resolved to avoid this sin of —— above all others, and with the greatest care, and to be on my guard against this dangerous occasion ——.

Then recommend yourself to the intercession of Mary, to all the Saints, and to your holy Guardian Angel.

O MOST Holy Mary, Mother of God! and all ye blessed Saints of Paradise, pray to God for me, that I may not offend him to-day by any sin. And thou, Holy Angel, who art given to me by God for my Guardian, keep me this day from falling into any deliberate sin.

Then recite with the greatest possible devotion and attention the following prayers:

THE LORD'S PRAYER.

OUR Father who art in heaven! hallowed be thy name. Thy kingdom come: thy will be done on earth, as it is in heaven. Give us this day our daily bread: and forgive us our trespasses, as we forgive them that trespass against us. And lead us not into temptation, but deliver us from evil. Amen.

HAIL MARY.

HAIL Mary, full of grace! Our Lord is with thee. Blessed art thou amongst women, and blessed is the fruit of thy womb, Jesus. Holy Mary, Mother of God, pray for us sinners, now, and at the hour of our death. *Amen.*

THE CREED.

I BELIEVE in God the Father Almighty, Creator of heaven and earth; and in Jesus Christ his only son our Lord, who was conceived by the Holy Ghost, born of the Virgin Mary, suffered under Pontius Pilate, was crucified, dead and buried. He descended into hell: the third day he arose from the dead: he ascended into heaven, and sitteth at the right hand of God, the Father Almighty; from thence he shall come to judge the living and the dead. I believe in the Holy Ghost, the holy Catholic Church, the com munion of Saints, the forgiveness of sins, the resurrection of the body, and the life everlasting. *Amen.*

Afterwards recite three Hail Marys more in honor of the purity of the Blessed Virgin Mary. "Hail Mary," &c. Then make the following Acts of Faith, Hope, and Charity, which should be done also before you go to sleep at night.

ACT OF FAITH.*

O MY God! who art the infallible Truth! I believe all that the Holy Church proposes to my belief, because thou hast revealed it to her. I believe that thou art the Creator of all things, that thou givest during eternity Paradise as a recompense to the just, and punishest sinners in Hell. I believe that thou art one Essence in three Persons, namely: the Father, the Son, and the Holy Ghost. I believe the incarnation, passion, and death of Jesus Christ. I believe, in fine, all that the Holy Church believes. I thank thee for having made me a Christian, and I protest that I will live and die in this holy faith.

ACT OF HOPE.

O MY God! Confiding in thy promises, because thou art faithful, powerful, and mer-

* According to a concession of Pope Benedict XIV., granted in December, 1754, an indulgence of seven years and seven quarantains (280 days) may be gained by devoutly repeating these acts. If recited daily for a month, with confession and communion made in the course of the same month, a plenary indulgence is gained.

ciful, I hope through the merits of Jesus Christ, for the pardon of my sins, final perseverance and the eternal glory of Paradise.

ACT OF CHARITY.

O MY God! I love thee with all my heart, and above all things, because thou art infinitely good, and worthy of infinite love, and for love of thee I love my neighbor as myself.

ACT OF CONTRITION.

O MY God! I am heartily sorry for all my sins, because by them I have lost heaven, and deserved the fire of hell, but more than all because I have offended thee, O my God, who art infinitely good, and worthy of all my love; but now I am firmly resolved, by the help of thy grace never to sin against thee any more, and to avoid all the occasions of sin.

N. B.—It is a most profitable exercise for those whose way of life allows of it, to make at least a quarter of an hour's meditation after their morning prayers. For this purpose you can make use of any approved book of Meditation or pious reading, as for example, one of those devout little works composed by St. Alphonsus Liguori, "The Way of Salvation," "The Clock of the Passion," Preparation for Death," &c., &c., or read a chapter from the celebrated "Following of Christ," by Thomas à Kempis. In case you have none of these books, endeavor to reflect upon something you remember of the passion of Christ, something which shows how much he suffered for sinners, and how much he loved them; apply it to yourself, and try to find some good lesson or some holy resolution to put in practice.

HOW TO PASS THE DAY IN A HOLY MANNER

I.

Wherever you go, whatever you do, be always like one who walks in the presence of God. Remember that he is present everywhere, that his eye follows you everywhere, and that he knows your most secret thoughts.

II.

Begin every thing you undertake with a good intention, and keep in mind the words of the Apostle: "*Whether you eat or drink, or whatever else you do do all for the glory of God.*"—1 *Cor.* x. 31.

AT WORK.

Before you begin your work, say—"All for thee, O Lord—O my Jesus, all for thee!"

IN TEMPTATION.

When you are tempted to anger, say—"O my Jesus, give me patience! Bless me, Mary, my Mother!"

If wicked thoughts come in your mind, say quickly—"Jesus and Mary, help me!" Repeat the Hail Mary, or some other prayer, until you have banished them.

AT THE ANGELUS.

When the bell rings for the "Angelus," at morning, noon, and evening, remember how the Son of God became man in the womb of Mary, and say as follows:

The Angel of the Lord declared unto Mary,
And she conceived of the Holy Ghost.
Hail, Mary, &c.

Behold the handmaid of the Lord.
May it be done unto me according to thy word.
Hail, Mary, &c.

And the Word was made flesh,
And dwelt among us.
Hail, Mary, &c.

Prayer.

POUR forth, we beseech thee, O Lord, thy grace into our hearts, that we, to whom the incarnation of Christ thy Son was made known by the message of an angel, may, by his passion and cross, be brought to the glory of his resurrection, through the same Christ our Lord. *Amen.*

[Whoever says the Angelus daily at the sound of the bell, for a whole month, and in the course of the same month goes to confession and communion, gains a plenary indulgence. *Benedict XIII.*]

BEFORE MEALS.

Before meals, say—"Bless us, O Lord, and these thy gifts which we are about to receive from thy bounty, through Christ our Lord. *Amen.*"

AFTER MEALS.

After meals, say—"We give thee thanks, Almighty God, for all thy benefits, who livest and reignest world without end. *Amen.*

"May the souls of the faithful departed rest in peace! *Amen.*"

EVENING DEVOTIONS

"*O Lord, stay with us, because it is towards evening, and the day is now far spent.*"—St. Luke, xxiv. 29.

Having begun the day well by prayer, let prayer also sanctify the close. Remember that you are now one day nearer to eternity. Who knows if God will not call your soul this very night before his judgment seat?

It is a most excellent practice in a Christian family to say the evening prayers in common, for they bring a great blessing upon the house. "*Where two or three are gathered together in my name,*" says Jesus Christ, "*there I will be in the midst of them.*" Ought not so kind a promise from our Lord to make us love to pray together?

The evening devotions should consist, at least, of the following parts:

I. Thank God for all the mercies he has shown you during the day past.

II. Pray the Holy Ghost to enlighten you, that you may see and be sorry for the sins which you have committed during the day, and that you may do better for the future.

III. Examine your conscience diligently. Consider how you have passed the time from morning until evening: in what you have done wrong: what has been the nature of your thoughts, words, and actions examine especially how you have put in practice the good resolution which you made in the morning.

IV. Excite in your heart a true sorrow for your sins, and for your neglect (if any) in keeping the good resolution you made.

V. Make once more a firm resolution to amend your life, and ask God to give you his grace that you may do so. And do all this, as if the last night of your life had come.

NIGHT PRAYERS.

In the name of the Father, &c. Amen.

THANKSGIVING.

O GREAT and Almighty God! I kneel before thee to thank thee with my whole heart for all the favors which thou hast bestowed upon me this day; for my food and drink, my health, and all my powers of body and soul. I thank thee for all thy holy lights and inspirations, for thy care and protection, and for all those other mercies which I do not think of now, or which I do not know how to value as I ought. I thank thee for them all, O heavenly Father, through Jesus Christ thy Son, our Lord.

PRAYER FOR LIGHT.

O ALL-WISE and all-seeing God; thou who dost always look upon my actions, and count all my steps, from whom no thought is hid, enlighten my understanding that I may clearly see what evil I have done this day, and what good I have left undone: move my heart that I may sincerely repent and amend.

Ask yourself then seriously and carefully the following questions, by way of an

EXAMINATION OF CONSCIENCE.

Have I not sinned this day—

In thought? By willingly entertaining some unchaste, uncharitable, or covetous thoughts?

In word? By using immodest language—uttering oaths—curses—lies—passionate, slanderous, profane, or irreverent words? Have I given scandal so?

In action? By being idle?—slow and impatient about my work? Have I not been in evil or dangerous company? Done any immodest action? Been too free in my manners? Been rude, cross, or disobedient towards my parents or superiors? Been unkind, insolent, malicious, cruel, or unjust towards my neighbor? Have I given any bad example to my children, my servants, my neighbors?

By omission? Have I refused or neglected to do any act of charity? Been watchful over my children and others depending upon me, and careful for their salvation? Have I omitted my prayers, my penance, or some other duty?

Finally, examine whether you have kept the resolution you made in the morning. If not, consider well what was the cause of your fall, and seek out the means to preserve you from falling in future. For be assured that your whole Christian perfection depends upon this diligent examination of conscience.

Having finished this examination, say with all your heart the following

CONTRITE PRAYER.

O FATHER, infinitely good and merciful! I have offended thee again to-day. Is this the thanks I owe thee for so many and so great favors? Alas! I confess my guilt. I am not worthy to be called thy child. But still, O heavenly Father, thou art infinitely good and merciful: therefore I return to thee with confidence, and on my knees, and in sorrow, I pray thee to pardon all my sins which I have committed this day, and all the sins of my whole life. From the bottom of my heart I repent, and am sorry for them, not only because I have deserved punishment, but because through them, O my God, I have displeased thee, my best and dearest friend, and my Sovereign good. O that I had never offended thee! O that I could make amends for what I have done!

GOOD RESOLUTION.

I AM seriously resolved to make a sincere confession of all my sins, and that soon; to shun all the occasions of sin; to fulfill all my duties perfectly from this time forward, and to die rather than to be guilty of any mortal sin, and before all and with all my power I will endeavor to overcome that sin which I commit the most: (*name it.*) With all my heart I forgive all my enemies: pardon me also, O God of mercy! Grant me thy powerful assistance that I may lead a holy life, and remain faithful to thee until death.

Recommend yourself now to the protection of Mary, and of all the Saints and Angels of God, saying:

O LORD, I beseech thee, visit this house, and drive far from it all the snares of the enemy. May thy holy Angels dwell in it to keep us all in peace, and let thy blessing be upon us always, through Jesus Christ thy Son our Lord.

Blessed Virgin Mary, after God my only hope! holy Guardian Angel! thou my patron Saint and protector, and all ye blessed Saints of God! pray for me during my life and in the hour of my death.

Pray now for the living and the dead.

BLESS, O Lord, all my relations and acquaintances, benefactors, friends, and enemies. Protect and bless our holy Father, Pope (Pius IX.), all the Bishops and Priests of thy holy Church, my Pastor, my Confessor, and all my superiors, both spiritual and temporal. Help the poor, and all who are afflicted, prisoners and travellers, the sick and the dying; convert all sinners, and heretics; enlighten the infidels, and the heathen.

O merciful God! have pity also on the poor souls in purgatory: put an end to their sufferings, and bring them to eternal rest.

Then say the *Lord's Prayer*, the "*Hail Mary*," and the *Creed*, as in the morning. Repeat also the three *Acts of Faith, Hope, and Charity* (page 18), and say afterwards:

MY God! I thank thee for having brought me safely through this day and I implore thee to watch over me also during this night, and to preserve me from every sin. I dedicate to thee all my sleep, that with every breath I draw, I may praise thee, thank thee, and love thee as the Saints do in Paradise. *Amen.*

Go to bed now, with holy thoughts, or repeating with your lips some short fervent ejaculations of love, and continue thus until you fall asleep. If you awake in the night, lift up your thoughts immediately to God, that no evil imaginations may enter your mind, and if they should, say promptly.

O Jesus! O Mary! No, no, I will die rather than do, or wish, or even think of such a thing! In the name of the Father, and of the Son, and of the Holy Ghost. Amen.

Devotion at Holy Mass.

"*From the rising of the sun even to the going down, my name is great among the Gentiles; and in every place there is sacrifice, and there is offered to my name a clean oblation: for my name is great among the Gentiles, saith the Lord of Hosts.*" —Malach. i. 11.

INSTRUCTION.

Of all the blessings and treasures which Jesus Christ has bequeathed to his holy Church, the august Sacrifice of the Mass is the greatest, most precious, and holiest. The Holy Mass is the sacrifice of the body and blood of Jesus Christ, which is offered to the heavenly Father on our altars under the species or appearances of bread and wine. It was instituted by Our Blessed Lord himself, in order to represent and continue that sacrifice which he made on the cross at Calvary. The sacrifice on the cross was made in a manifest and bloody manner; the sacrifice of the Mass is made in a mysterious and unbloody manner. In a mysterious manner: that is to say, when Christ is offered in the Mass, we cannot see him with our eyes as the Jews saw him on the cross, his body, and his wounds, and his blood, but all we can see is that humble appearance of bread and wine under which he hides himself now from our sight. It is made in an unbloody manner: that is to say, in the Mass our Lord does not die again, his life is not taken as formerly by the shedding of his blood. Although he is really present on the altar, he is there as a living victim, his death is only represented. Since his resurrection he is our living Lord, and cannot die again. "*Christ being risen from the dead dieth no more: death hath no more dominion over him.*"

Jesus Christ, dying once on the cross, offered himself up for us to his heavenly Father: "*He has blotted out our sins by his blood that was shed for us, and by his painful death,*" and thus he hath reconciled us to his Father. But in order to leave us a perpetual memorial of this, his great love, at that last supper which he partook with his disciples, he took bread in his holy hands, and after giving thanks to God, broke it, and gave it to them to eat, saying, "*This is my body which is given for you; do this for a commemoration of me.*" Also he took the chalice, and said, "*This is the chalice, the new testament in my blood which shall be shed for you.*"—St. Luke, xxii. 19, 20.

By these words, "*Do this in commemoration of me,*" Jesus gave to his Apostles, and their successors, the Bishops and Priests of the Church, the power to change the bread and the wine into his most holy Body and Blood. The Priest blesses the bread and wine as Christ did; he speaks over them the same words of consecration which Christ spoke; and thus the bread and wine are changed now on the altar, as they were at the last supper, into the Body and Blood of Jesus Christ. As Jesus Christ sacrificed himself on the cross to his heavenly Father for our sins, so here on the altar he offers himself up to the same heavenly Father, by the hands of the Priest.

After the consecration which the Priest makes by saying over the bread and wine the same words which Jesus Christ said at the last supper, there is no longer any bread and wine on the altar, but the true and living Jesus Christ, at the same time God and man, really present, although hidden under appearances of bread and wine.

The Priest offers up Jesus Christ to his heavenly Father, in the name of the holy Catholic Church, and the prayer of the Church, together with the pious desires and prayers of the faithful, is united with this holy sacrifice. It is Jesus Christ rather who upon the altar offers himself up, and prays for us, and we may confidently hope, that what we cannot obtain from God by our prayers alone, we can obtain through the Holy Mass, in which Jesus Christ himself prays for us, and with us.

It is an excellent practice, therefore, for those who can, to be present daily at this most holy sacrifice, of which St. Augustine says: "*One who devoutly hears holy Mass will fall into no mortal sin, and will obtain the pardon of his venial sins.*" I say it is good to be present every day: for to hear Mass on Sunday or a Holy day is, of course, not only good, but a necessary duty; and to be absent without a strong reason, is a mortal sin. Be present, then, as often as you can, and while the sacrifice goes on, imagine yourself standing near the Saviour when he celebrated his last supper with his disciples; or, if you please, on Mount Calvary, at the foot of the cross, upon which he offered himself to his heavenly Father for the sins of the world.

In order to have a part in the merits of the holy Sacrifice of the Mass, either you must follow the actions and prayers of the Priest, especially at the three principal points; namely, at the Offertory, the Consecration and the Communion; or make a meditation upon the passion of Christ; or you may make use of devout prayers as you find them in your prayer-books; or you may say the Rosary-beads in the meanwhile; or in fine, make use of any other devout exercise best suited to your own feelings of devotion, uniting all the while your intention to the intention of the sacrificing Priest.

PRAYER BEFORE MASS.

ALMIGHTY, infinite and holy God! Behold me here before thine altar, a poor wretched mortal, who am come to take my part in this precious sacrifice of the Holy Mass. Of every sacrifice this one alone is worthy of thine infinite Majesty, because it is here thine only and eternal Son is offered up as the victim. In union with that most pure and perfect will with which that beloved Son has given himself to be a sacrifice for us, I offer this holy Mass in adoration of thy holy Name, in thanksgiving for all thy past mercies, and in satisfaction for my many sins. offer it, moreover, that I may obtain all those graces which I need for my salvation, and a blessing upon my daily life. (*Here you may call to mind any special favor which you desire to ask of God.*) I offer it, also, for the help and consolation of all those for whom I am in duty bound to pray, and for those who desire or need my prayers the most; for those who are living (*name them if you like*) and for those who are dead (*name them*).

O God! prepare my heart, purify my mind, blot out all my sins, that I may assist as I ought at this most Holy Sacrifice.

PRAYERS FOR MASS.

✠

When the Priest at the foot of the altar begins the Ma with the sign of the cross, bless yourself at the sam time, call to mind for a moment your sins, and then recite with him also the "CONFITEOR," thus:

I CONFESS to Almighty God, to blessed Mary ever Virgin, to blessed Michael the Archangel, to blessed John the Baptist, to the holy Apostles Peter and Paul, to all the Saints, and to you, Father, that I have sinned exceedingly in thought, word, and deed, through my fault, through my fault, through my most grievous fault, (*here strike your breast three times:*) therefore I beseech the blessed Mary ever Virgin, the blessed Michael the Archangel, the blessed John the Baptist, the holy Apostles Peter and Paul, all the Saints, and you, Father, to pray to the Lord our God for me.

Pray then for pardon, thus:

MAY God have mercy on me, forgive my sins, and lead me on to eternal life. May the Almighty and Merciful God grant me the pardon, absolution, and remission of my sins. *Amen.*

At the "KYRIE ELEISON" repeat in your own language,

LORD, have mercy on us! Christ, have mercy on us! Lord, have mercy on us!

At the "GLORIA IN EXCELSIS," repeat that beautiful hymn of the Angels, as follows:

GLORIA in excelsis Deo, et in terrâ pax hominibus bonæ voluntatis. Laudamus te, benedicimus te, adoramus te, glorificamus te. Gratias agimus tibi propter magnam gloriam tuam, Domine Deus, Rex cœlestis, Deus Pater omnipotens. Domine Fili unigenite Jesu Christe. Domine Deus, Agnus Dei, Filius Patris, qui tollis peccata mundi, miserere nobis. Qui tollis peccata mundi, suscipe deprecationem nostram. Qui sedes ad dexteram Patris, miserere nobis. Quoniam Tu solus sanctus, Tu solus Dominus, Tu solus altissimus Jesu Christe, cum Sancto Spiritu, in gloriâ Dei Patris. *Amen.*

GLORY be to God in the highest! and on earth peace to men of good will We praise thee, we bless thee, we adore thee, we glorify thee, we give thanks to thee because of thy great glory, O Lord God, Heavenly King, God the Father Almighty. O Lord Jesus Christ the only begotten Son: O Lord God, Lamb of God, Son of the Father, who takest away the sins of the world, have mercy on us. Thou that takest away the sins of the world, receive our prayers. Thou that sittest at the right hand of the Father, have mercy on us. For thou only art holy. Thou only art the Lord. Thou only, O Jesus Christ, with the Holy Ghost, art most high in the glory of God the Father. *Amen.*

After the "Gloria," the Priest turns to the people and pronounces the salutation.

Dominus vobiscum. The Lord be with you.

To which the Acolyte replies for the people,

Et cum spiritu tuo.	And with thy spirit.

Then, as if to invite the whole congregation to unite their intentions to his own intention, the Priest says OREMUS. Let us pray. Then follows the *Collect*, that is to say, the collection, because the Priest gathers together the desires and prayers of all present, and as a mediator offers them to God in the name of all the Faithful. Repeat here the following prayer:

THE COLLECT.

ALMIGHTY and Eternal God! hear the prayer of thy people, and turn not away from us thy most holy countenance on account of our sins. Graciously listen to the prayers of thy servant, the Priest, who prays for the salvation of thy people, and through thy mercy grant that we may obtain what we confidently ask of thee; through Jesus Christ our Lord. *Amen.*

THE EPISTLE.

Then follows the Epistle. It consists commonly of a portion from the writings of the Prophets or Apostles. While this is read, you can repeat the following prayer:

O MY God! I adore thy Holy Spirit, who has spoken by thy Prophets and Apostles, and still speaks through the holy Church. I receive with humility all the commandments and instructions which the holy Church gives me through her Priests. Grant, O God, that I may always believe what thy Church teaches, and do what she commands; through Jesus Christ our Lord. *Amen.*

THE GOSPEL.

When the book is carried to the other end of the altar, stand up while the Priest is reading the Gospel, and pray thus:

O DIVINE Saviour, how great was thy love to come thyself upon the earth to be our teacher, and show us the way to heaven. Grant me this grace, that I may listen with humility to all the truths which thou hast preached; enlighten my mind that I may understand them; renew my heart that I may love and follow them. Grant me thy divine assistance that I may never be ashamed of thy holy Gospel, but confess the same always in words as well as in works; who livest and reignest, world without end. *Amen.*

THE CREED.

While the Priest is repeating the "Credo," remain standing, and recite it also with him, as follows:

CREDO in unum Deum, Patrem omnipotentem, factorem cœli et terræ, visibilium omnium et invisibilium.

Et in unum Dominum Jesum Christum, Filium Dei unigenitum, et ex Patre natum ante omnia sæcula; Deum de Deo, lumen de lumine, Deum verum de Deo vero; genitum non factum, consubstantialem Patri, per quem

I BELIEVE in one God, the Father Almighty, Maker of heaven and earth, and of all things visible and invisible.

And in one Lord Jesus Christ, the only begotten Son of God, and born of the Father before all ages; God of God; Light of Light; true God of true God; begotten, not made; of the same substance with the Father; by

omnia facta sunt. Qui, propter nos homines, et propter nostram salutem, descendit de cœlis; et incarnatus est de Spiritu Sancto, ex Mariâ Virgine; ET HOMO FACTUS EST.* Crucifixus etiam pro nobis, sub Pontio Pilato passus, et sepultus est. Et resurrexit tertiâ die, secundum scripturas; et ascendit in cœlum; sedet ad dexteram Patris; et iterum venturus est cum gloriâ judicare vivos et mortuos; cujus regni non erit finis.

whom all things were made. Who for us men, and for our salvation, came down from heaven, and became incarnate by the Holy Ghost of the Virgin Mary, AND WAS MADE MAN.* He was crucified also for us, suffered under Pontius Pilate, and was buried. And the third day he rose again according to the Scriptures, and ascended into heaven, and sitteth at the right hand of the Father. And he is to come again with glory to judge the living and the dead, of whose kingdom there shall be no end.

Et in Spiritum Sanctum, Dominum et vivificantem, qui ex Patre Filioque procedit; qui cum Patre et Filio simul adoratur, et conglorificatur; qui locutus est per prophetas. Et unam sanctam Catholicam et Apostolicam Ecclesiam. Confiteor unum Baptisma in remissionem peccatorum. Et expecto resurrectionem mortuorum, et vitam venturi sæculi. *Amen.*

And in the Holy Ghost, the Lord and Life-giver, who proceedeth from the Father and the Son; who, together with the Father and the Son, is adored and glorified; who spoke by the Prophets. And one Holy, Catholic, and Apostolic Church. I confess one baptism for the remission of sins; and I look for the resurrection of the dead, and the life of the world to come. *Amen.*

* Kneel in reverence of Christ's Incarnation.

THE OFFERTORY.

Here follows the *Offertory;* that is to say, the bread and wine which are to be changed into the most holy Body and Blood of our Saviour, are offered to God. Say the following prayer:

RECEIVE, O Father, infinitely holy, almighty and eternal God, this offering which thy Priest presents to thee for us. I believe most firmly and surely that it will soon be changed into the true body and true blood of Christ. Receive this offering, O heavenly Father, for the glory of thy most holy name, for the pardon of my sins, in thanksgiving for all thy mercies bestowed on me, and that I may obtain new graces still, especially those which are most necessary to my salvation; and also for all my superiors, both spiritual and temporal; for my friends and my enemies, and for all Christians, living and dead. *Amen.*

The Priest presently turns to the people, and says, "ORATE FRATRES, *Pray, my brethren.*" By this, he asks those present to pray with him, that this sacrifice may be pleasing to God. Then say:

MAY the Lord receive this sacrifice from thy hands, to the praise and glory of his own name, and also for our benefit, and that of all his holy Church.

THE PREFACE.

The Preface is the introduction to the Canon of the Mass The Priest says, in a loud voice "*Per omnia sæcula sæculorum: World without end:*" which are the last words of the SECRET, or *silent prayer*, which he has just been saying. He then begins the Preface with the following appeals to the devotion of the people, in whose name the Acolyte duly replies:

P. Dominus vobiscum.	P. The Lord be with you.
A. *Et cum spiritu tuo.*	A. *And with thy spirit.*
P. Sursum corda.	P. Lift up your hearts.
A. *Habemus ad Dominum.*	A. *We do lift them up to the Lord.*
P. Gratias agamus Domino Deo nostro.	P. Let us give thanks to the Lord our God.
A. *Dignum et justum est.*	A. *It is meet and just.*

The Priest then goes on with the Preface. Unite with him in the same prayer of praise and thanksgiving, and say:

IT is truly meet and just, right and salutary, that we should always, and in all places, give thanks to thee, O holy Lord, Almighty Father, Eternal God, through Christ our Lord: by whom the Angels praise thy Majesty, the Archangels adore it, the Powers tremble before it, the heavens, and the Virtues of heaven, and the blessed Seraphs, also, with united exultation praise it. We pray thee let our voices ascend with theirs to thee, while with the deepest awe we confess, and cry (SANCTUS), Holy! holy! holy! Lord God of Sabaoth! Heaven and earth are full of thy glory! Hosanna in the highest! Blessed is he that cometh in the name of the Lord. Hosanna in the highest!

After the Sanctus, repeat the following words which are nearly the same as those with which the priest begins now,

THE CANON.

WE earnestly pray and beseech thee, most merciful Father, through Jesus Christ our Lord, that thou wilt accept and bless these gifts, these offerings, this unspotted sacrifice. We offer them, first, for the holy Catholic Church, that thou wilt be pleased to keep it in peace, to protect, unite, and govern it throughout the whole world: together with thy servant N——, our Pope, and N——, our Bishop, and all the true believers and followers of the holy Catholic Faith.

MEMENTO FOR THE LIVING.

BE mindful, O Lord, of thy servants—

[Here pray for those of your friends still living, whose welfare you wish to recommend to God in this holy Sacrifice.]

Be mindful, also, of all here present, whose faith and devotion are known to thee, for whom we offer this sacrifice of praise, or who offer it up for themselves, their families and friends. We pray for the safety of their souls, for their final perseverance and eternal happiness; and in fine, we recommend all their desires to thee, the living, true and everlasting God.

At the same time, we honor the memory of the ever glorious and immaculate Virgin Mary, the Mother of our Lord and God Jesus Christ; and also of thy blessed Apostles, and all thy holy Martyrs and Saints who have lived and died in this holy faith which we profess, and this only church in which we live. For the sake of their merits and their prayers, grant us in all things thy help and protection, through the same Christ our Lord. *Amen.*

We beseech thee, also, O Lord, graciously to accept this sacrifice at the hands of us, thy servants, and of thy whole family; bless the days of our life with thy holy peace, save us from everlasting damnation, and may we be counted ever among the number of thy elect, through Christ our Lord. *Amen.*

O God, may this offering be blessed, and in every way acceptable and agreeable to thee; and for our salvation's sake be changed into the Body and Blood of thy beloved Son, our Lord Jesus Christ. *Amen.*

At the CONSECRATION, represent to yourself, in a lively manner, Christ as at the last supper, when he took bread in his holy hands, blessed it, and said, "*This is my Body which is given for you;*" and when he took also the cup of wine, saying, "*This is the chalice of my Blood.*" Cherish and cling to this article of your faith, that Jesus Christ, who died for you on the cross, is really, truly, and substantially present, as soon as the Priest pronounces the sacred words of consecration. With firm faith, and deep humility pray to your Saviour and say,

WHEN THE SACRED HOST IS ELEVATED.

I BELIEVE, O Jesus, that thou art truly present here, as God and Man, under the form of bread. I adore thee with the deepest reverence, as my Lord and my God. O Jesus, may I live for thee only! may I die for thee gladly! O Jesus, living or dying, let me be thine!

AT THE ELEVATION OF THE CHALICE.

O MY Saviour, I believe that thou art here. I believe that thy most precious Blood, which was poured out once upon the Cross for a sacrifice to atone for our sins, is substantially present in this cup, under the appearance of wine. Ah! holy blood of my Redeemer, I beseech thee, wash and purify me from all my sins.

After consecration, say with the Priest:

BEING mindful, therefore, O Lord, of Jesus Christ thy Son, our Lord, of his blessed passion his resurrection from the dead, his glorious ascension into heaven, we offer before the throne of thy most excellent majesty, of thy gifts and presents, a holy, pure, and unspotted Host, the holy bread of eternal life, and the chalice of everlasting salvation.

Be pleased to look upon them with a propitious and benignant countenance, and graciously accept them as thou didst accept the gifts of thy just servant Abel, the sacrifice of the Patriarch Abraham, and the holy sacrifice, the unspotted gift which was offered to thee by thy High Priest Melchisedech. Prostrate here before thee, O Almighty God, we beseech thee, command these offerings to be brought up to thine altar on high, into the sight of thy Divine Majesty, that all who partake of the most sacred Body and Blood of thy Son at this altar, may be filled with every heavenly grace and blessing, through the same Christ our Lord. *Amen.*

MEMENTO FOR THE DEAD.

BE mindful likewise, O Lord, of thy servants, N—— and N——, who are gone before us with the sign of faith, and rest in the sleep of peace. (*Here make mention of those departed friends whom you wish to recommend especially to the mercy of God, that their sufferings may be lessened, or that they may be taken from their place of torment to the abode of eternal bliss.*) To these, O Lord, and to all who sleep in Christ, grant, we beseech thee, a place of refreshment, light, and peace, through the same Christ our Lord. *Amen.*

To us, also, sinners though we are, yet thy servants, and trusting in the multitude of thy mercies, deign to grant some part and fellowship with thy holy Apostles and Martyrs, with John and Stephen, Matthias, Barnabas, Ignatius, Alexander, Marcellinus, Peter, Felicitas, Perpetua, Agatha, Lucy, Agnes, Cecilia, Anastasia, and with all thy Saints: Into their company we beseech thee graciously to admit us, not weighing our merits, but thine own mercy, through Christ our Lord; by whom, O God, thou dost create, sanctify, quicken, bless, and impart all these thy good gifts to us. By him, therefore, and with him, and in him, to thee, O God, Almighty Father, together with the Holy Ghost, be all honor and glory, world without end. *Amen.*

PATER NOSTER.

Here, with the Priest, repeat the "Lord's Prayer," Our Father who art in heaven, &c. Then offer the following petition:

WE beseech thee, O Lord, to deliver us from all evils, past, present, and to come, and through the intercession of the blessed and glorious Mary, ever Virgin, Mother of God, of the holy Apostles Peter and Paul, of Andrew, and of all the Saints, mercifully grant peace in our days, that we, through the help of thy mercy, may be always free from sin, and safe from every trouble, through the same Jesus Christ thy Son, our Lord. *Amen.*

When the Priest breaks the sacred Host and drops a particle of it into the chalice, say with him,

MAY this commingling and consecration of the Body and Blood of our Lord Jesus Christ, become to us who receive it the source of eternal life. *Amen.*

AGNUS DEI.

At the "Agnus Dei," strike your breast three times, an pray to Jesus, the incarnate Lamb of God, for the pardon of your sins, saying with the Priest,

LAMB of God, who takest away the sins of the world, *have mercy on us!* Lamb of God, who takest away the sins of the world, *have mercy on us!* Lamb of God, who takest away the sins of the world, *give us peace.*

O Lord Jesus Christ, who hath said to thy Apostles, "Peace I leave with you, my peace I give to you," look not upon my sins, but upon the faith of thy Church, and be pleased to keep her according to thy will in peace and unity.

O Lord Jesus Christ, Son of the living God, who, according to thy Father's will, and by the co-operation of the Holy Ghost, hast given life to the world through thine own death, deliver me by this thy most sacred Body and Blood from all my sins, and from every evil. Make me cling to thy commandments always, and never let me be separated from thee.

If during the Mass, or after it, you receive holy communion, you may repeat with the Priest the following additional prayer:

O LORD Jesus Christ, let not this communication of thy Body, which, all unworthy as I am, I venture to receive, turn to my judgment and condemnation, but rather through thy tender compassion become my safeguard both of body and soul, and a merciful remedy; O thou who livest and reignest with the Father, and the Holy Ghost, one God, world without end. *Amen.*

THE COMMUNION.

At the sound of the little bell, when the Priest takes the sacred Host in his hand, before his own communion, strike your breast three times also, repeating with him each time:

LORD! I am not worthy that thou shouldst enter under my roof, but only speak the word, and my soul shall be healed.

If you do not receive holy communion in reality, you can at least make a spiritual communion, uniting yourself in desire with the Priest and the others who do communicate. Or if you are so unfortunate as to be in mortal sin, and unworthy of communion, you should make an act of regret at your unworthiness. See Spiritual Communion, page 114.

THE LAST COLLECT.

After the communion, while the Priest is repeating the Collect, pray as follows:

ALMIGHTY God! I thank thee with my whole heart for all the mercies and benefits thou hast bestowed on me, but above all that thou hast given thy Son Jesus Christ to be the propitiation for our sins, and his Body and Blood for the nourishment of our souls. O merciful God, watch over me, and forbid that I should ever assist at this holy Sacrifice in an irreverent manner, or receive unworthily this most sacred food; through the same Jesus Christ our Lord. *Amen.*

At the ITE MISSA EST, and the BENEDICTION of the Priest, say,

MAY this service which is now ended be pleasing to thee, O most holy Trinity, and grant that the sacrifice here offered by thy servant the Priest, may be acceptable in thy sight, and may bring reconciliation and salvation to me, and to all for whom it has been offered: through Christ our Lord. *Amen.*

May the Almighty God, ✠ Father, Son, and Holy Ghost, bless us now and evermore. *Amen.*

THE LAST GOSPEL.

At the last Gospel, stand up, and say,

JESUS! eternal Word of the Father, thou didst become man for love of us. I adore thee. I trust in thee. I love thee. Thou didst come into the world to show us the way of eternal life. Guide me, O Thou who art the true light of the world, that I may not wander in the darkness of this life, but according to thy light lead a holy life, and die a blessed death.

PRAYER AFTER HOLY MASS.

O MOST merciful God, I thank thee for having permitted me to take part in this holy sacrifice. Pardon me all my faults, my coldness, and my distraction. I make the firm resolution to sin no more, but to be so watchful over all my thoughts, words, and actions, that I may not lose the fruits of this holy sacrament. Grant me every necessary grace, that I may sanctify myself in this world, and possess thee eternally in heaven. *Amen.*

EJACULATIONS.

I adore thee every moment, O Living Bread of Heaven, Great Sacrament!

Jesus, Heart of Mary, I pray thee send thy blessing on my soul.

Holiest Jesus! loving Saviour! I give thee all my heart.

The same Pope Leo XII., by the same Rescript, granted—

THE INDULGENCE OF 100 DAYS to every one who says the above Ejaculations with contrition, adding the following:

May all know, adore, and praise every moment, always, the most holy and most divine Sacrament.

MASS FOR THE DEAD.

[The prayers given in this Method are compiled from the Missal, the Breviary, the Ritual, and the works of St. Alphonsus Liguori.]

AT THE BEGINNING OF MASS.

✠

DELIVER me, O Lord, from eternal death in that tremendous day, when the heavens and the earth shall be shaken, when thou shalt come to judge the world with fire. Seized am I with trembling, and I fear for that approaching trial, and that wrath to come. O! that day, that day of wrath, of calamity and misery, that great and bitter day indeed, when thou shalt come to judge the world with fire.

Eternal rest give them, O Lord: and let perpetual light shine on them: may they rest in eace. *Amen.*

THE CONFITEOR.

I CONFESS to Almighty God, to blessed Mary, &c.

As in the other Mass. Pray, then, for pardon, thus:

May God have mercy on me, forgive my sins, nd lead me to eternal life! May the almighty and merciful God grant me the pardon, absolution, and remission of all my sins!

THE INTROIT.

When the Priest mounts the steps of the Altar, imagine you hear the poor souls in Purgatory repeating the following verses, as if to implore your prayers:

HAVE pity on me, have pity on me, at least you, my friends, because the hand of the Lord hath touched me. My flesh is consumed, my bone hath cleaved to my skin, and nothing but lips are left about my teeth. Have pity on me, have pity on me, at least you, my friends. Job xix. 21. (*Then pray.*) Eternal rest give them, O Lord: and let perpetual light shine on them. May they rest in peace. *Amen.*

KYRIE ELEISON.

LORD, have mercy on them!
Christ, have mercy on them!
Lord, have mercy on them! } Repeat each three times.

THE COLLECT.

O GOD, the Creator and Redeemer of all the faithful, give to the souls of thy servants departed the remission of all their sins, that through the help of pious supplications, they may obtain the pardon which they have always desired: Who livest and reignest, world without end. *Amen.*

THE EPISTLE.

IN those days, the most valiant Judas, having made a gathering, sent twelve thousand drachms of silver to Jerusalem, for sacrifice to be offered for the sins of the dead, thinking well and religiously concerning the resurrection. (For if he had not hoped that they that were slain should rise again, it would have seemed superfluous and vain to pray for the dead.) And because he considered that they who had fallen asleep with godliness, had great grace laid up for them. It is, therefore, a holy and wholesome thought to pray for the dead, that they may be loosed from sins.—2 Mach. xii.

(Gradual.)—Grant to them eternal rest, O Lord; and may perpetual light shine on them. The just shall be in everlasting remembrance: he shall not fear the evil hearing.—Ps. cxi.

(Tract.)—Release, O Lord, the souls of all the faithful departed from the bonds of their sins; and by the assistance of thy grace, may they escape the sentence of condemnation, and enjoy the bliss of eternal light.

Here, sometimes, is said the following hymn: when you perceive it is not said at the altar, you may pass it over also, and go on to the Gospel.

DIES IRÆ.

Nigher still, and still more nigh,
Draws the Day of Prophecy,
Doom'd to melt the earth and sky.

MASS FOR THE DEAD.

O, what trembling there shall be
When the world its Judge shall see,
Coming in dread majesty!

Hark, the trump with thrilling tone,
From sepulchral regions lone,
Summons all before the throne.

Time and Death it doth appall,
To see the buried ages all
Rise to answer at the call.

Now the books are open spread;
Now the writing must be read,
Which condemns the quick and dead:

Now, before the Judge severe,
Hidden things must all appear;
Naught can pass unpunish'd here.

What, shall guilty I then plead?
Who for me will intercede,
When the saints shall comfort need?

King of dreadful Majesty!
Who dost freely justify,
Fount of Pity, save thou me!

Recollect, O Love divine!
'Twas for this lost sheep of thine
Thou thy glory didst resign:

Satest wearied seeking me,
Sufferedst upon the Tree:
Let not vain thy labor be.

Judge of Justice, hear my prayer.
Spare me, Lord, in mercy spare!
Ere the Reckoning-day appear.

Lo! thy gracious face I seek!
Shame and grief are on my cheek;
Sighs and tears my sorrows speak.

Thou didst Mary's guilt forgive,
Didst the dying thief receive,
Hence doth hope within me live.

Worthless are my prayers, I know,
Yet, O cause me not to go
Into everlasting woe.

Sever'd from the guilty band,
Make me with thy sheep to stand,
Placing me on thy right hand.

When the cursed in anguish flee
Into flames of misery;
With the Blest then call Thou me.

Suppliant in the dust I lie!
My heart a cinder, crush'd and dry;
Help me, Lord, when death is nigh!

Full of tears, and full of dread,
Is the day that wakes the dead,
Calling all, with solemn blast,

From the ashes of the past.
Lord of mercy! Jesus blest!
Grant the Faithful light and rest.

THE GOSPEL.

AT that time, Jesus said to the multitude of the Jews: 'Amen, amen, I say unto you that the hour cometh. and now is, when the dead shall hear the voice of the Son of God, and they that hear shall live. For as the Father hath life in himself, so hath he given to the Son also to have life in himself; and he hath given him power to do judgment, because he is the Son of man. Wonder not at this, for the hour cometh wherein all that are in the graves shall hear the voice of the Son of God; and they that have done good, shall come forth unto the resurrection of life; but they that have done evil, unto the resurrection of judgment.—*St. John*, v.

THE OFFERTORY.

O LORD Jesus Christ, King of Glory! deliver the souls of all the faithful departed from the flames of hell, and from the deep pit. Deliver them from the lion's mouth, lest hell swallow them, lest they fall into darkness; and let thy standard-bearer, St. Michael, bring them into the holy light, which thou hast promised of old to Abraham and his posterity. We offer thee, O Lord, a sacrifice of praise and of prayer: accept it on behalf of the souls we commemorate this day, and let them pass from death to life.

Here make an offering, also, of your own death and sufferings in union with the Holy Sacrifice, thus:

O MY God, I offer thee, also, the hour of my death, and all the pains I am destined to suffer from this moment until my last breath. Give me strength to bear them with perfect conformity to thy will. I cheerfully offer thee, moreover, all the pains which thou shalt prepare for me in purgatory. It is just that the fire should punish in me all the insults I have offered to thee. O holy prison, when shall I find myself shut up in thee, secure of never again being able to lose my God? O holy fire, when wilt thou purify me from so many stains, and render me worthy to enter the Land of bliss? I offer all these pains to thy glory, uniting them with the bitter pains of Jesus' passion. Eternal Father! I sacrifice to thee my life, and my whole being. I entreat thee to accept this my sacrifice, in union with, and through the merits of, this great sacrifice of Jesus Christ thy Son. *Amen.*

Almighty God, who art the guardian of souls, the safeguard of salvation, and the confidence of all believers: look mercifully down upon us, and through the merits of thy dear Son, whose sacred Body we offer in this sacrifice, bless the graves of our departed friends, that those mortal bodies which there repose, after the course of this life is ended, may with their happy souls at the great judgment day, be found worthy to participate in the rewards of eternal life.

Enter not, O Lord, into judgment with these thy servants, for with thee shall no man be justified, except through thee the remission of all his sins shall be accorded. We beseech thee, therefore, let not the sentence of thy justice lie heavy upon those whom the earnest prayer of Christian faith recommends to thee; but rather, by the succor of thy grace, may they be found worthy to escape the avenging judgment, who were signed with the seal of the Holy Trinity while they lived.

Graciously regard, O Lord, these gifts which we offer thee for the souls of the faithful departed, that by celestial remedies made pure, they may repose in thy compassionate mercy. Through Jesus Christ thy Son, our Lord. *Amen.*

When the Priest, turning towards the people, says, "ORATE FRATRES, PRAY, MY BRETHREN," answer:

MAY the Lord receive this sacrifice from thy hands, to the praise and glory of his holy name, for the salvation of our souls, and for the repose of the faithful departed.

The Secret.

LOOK favorably down, O Lord, we beseech thee, upon this Sacrifice which we offer for the souls of thy departed servants, that as thou wast pleased to bestow on them the merit of Christian faith, thou mayest also grant them its reward, through Jesus Christ thy Son our Lord *Amen.*

THE PREFACE.

IT is truly meet and right, just and salutary, that we should always and everywhere give thanks to thee, O Holy Lord, Almighty Father, Everlasting God, through Christ our Lord; who by dying hath destroyed death for us, and rising again hath renewed our life; and who hath left us this tremendous sacrifice as a propitiation for our sins, and for the sins of the Faithful departed. Mercifully grant, therefore, that they, for whom it is offered this day, may speedily be released from all their sufferings, and find eternal rest and perpetual light with thee in Paradise; that there we, with them, may praise and celebrate thy Majesty, in company with all the Angels and Archangels, the celestial Powers, the blessed Seraphs, and the whole Host of heaven, who chant thy glory, evermore repeating: HOLY! HOLY! HOLY! is the Lord God of Armies! the heavens and the earth are full of thy glory! Hosanna in the highest! Blessed is he who cometh in the name of the Lord! Hosanna in the highest!

THE CANON.

WE therefore suppliantly beseech thee, O Father of mercies, through Jesus Christ thy Son, our Lord, graciously to accept and bless this holy Sacrifice, which we offer thee; for the peace and prosperity of the Holy Catholic Church, for thy servant our Father, Pope N——, for our Bishops and clergy, and for all thy faithful Catholic people; for the living, that they may prepare for death, and for the dead, that they may obtain eternal rest.

MEMENTO OF THE LIVING.

BE mindful, O Lord, of thy servants, N— and N—, (*Here pause and recommend to God any living friend for whom you feel urged to pray during this Mass,*) and of all those friends who are very near and very dear to me, and of all those who have asked for, or desire my prayers, or for whom I ought especially to pray; and so direct and strengthen them by thy holy grace, during life, that at the hour of their death the enemy may not prevail against them; through Jesus Christ our Lord.

O Almighty and Merciful God! who hast bestowed on the human race both the means of salvation and the gift of eternal life, look graciously upon us thy servants, and cherish these souls which thou hast created, that in the hour of our departure, being free from the stain of sin, we may merit to be borne upwards by the hands of the holy Angels to thee, our Creator.

Accept, O Lord, we beseech thee, this Sacrifice, which we offer thee for the souls of the faithful departed, and grant to us also, who still remain, the grace of a happy death, that by it being purged of all our faults, we who in this life are afflicted by the scourges of thy dispensation, may receive our eternal rest in the life to come.

When the first sound of the bell announces that the Priest is about to begin the consecration, say:

O GOD, may this offering be blessed, and in every way acceptable and agreeable to thee: and for our salvation's sake, and for the comfort of departed souls, be changed into the Body and Blood of thy dear Son our Lord Jesus Christ. *Amen.*

THE CONSECRATION.

At the elevation of the Sacred Host, profoundly bowing, say:

HAIL! true Body of Jesus Christ, my Saviour! O bless and sanctify my soul! (*Then add:*) Give them eternal rest, O Lord.

At the elevation of the chalice, say:

HAIL! true Blood of Jesus my Redeemer! O wash me pure from all my sins! (*Then add:*) Give them eternal rest, O Lord. May they rest in peace.

AFTER THE CONSECRATION.

COMMEMORATING, therefore, O Lord, the blessed passion of Jesus Christ thy Son our Lord, his resurrection from the dead, and his glorious ascension into heaven, we offer before the throne of thy most excellent Majesty, in behalf of these departed souls, whom thy justice still detains in the pains of temporal punishment, this most holy, pure, and unspotted victim, the holy Bread of eternal life, and the chalice of everlasting salvation.

A special Memento of the dead.

BE mindful especially, O Lord, of thy servants N—— and N——, who are gone before us with the sign of faith, and rest in the sleep of peace. (*Here make mention of those departed friends whom you wish in particular to recommend to the divine mercy.*) To these and to all who sleep in Christ, grant, we beseech thee, a place of refreshment, light, and peace; through the same Christ our Lord. *Amen.*

Grant, O Lord, to thy servants departed, that they may not receive a return of punishment for their deeds, who in desire were observers of thy will; and that as here true faith has joined them to the company of thy faithful, so there thy mercy may associate them to the choir of Angels.

O God, whose attribute it is always to show mercy, and to spare, we humbly beseech thee for the souls of thy faithful servants, whom thou hast called out of this world, that thou wouldst not deliver them into the hands of the enemy, nor forget them until the end, but command them to be received by the holy Angels, and so be led to Paradise, their true country; that as they have believed and hoped in thee, they may not suffer the pains of hell, but possess everlasting joys.

O God, the light of faithful souls, be present to our supplications, and grant to all thy servants and handmaids whose bodies rest in Christ, a seat of refreshment, a blissful rest, and the light of glory.

We humbly pour our prayers to thee, O Lord, for these thy servants, beseeching thee, that whatever guilt they may have contracted through human frailty, thou wilt mercifully pardon, and place them in the seat of those happy souls whom thou hast redeemed: through Jesus Christ our Lord.

To us also, sinners though we are, yet thy servants, and trusting in the multitude of thy mercies, deign to grant some part and fellowship with all thy saints: Into their company we beseech thee graciously to admit us, not weighing our merits but thy mercy: through Christ ou Lord. *Amen.*

PATER NOSTER.

Repeat with the Priest, "*Our Father who art in heaven,*" &c.; and then offer the following petition:

DELIVER, O Lord, I beseech thee, the souls of thy servants from all sorrow and suffering and bring them to the participation of thy heav enly joys, and through the intercession of the blessed and glorious Mary, ever Virgin, Mother of God, of the Holy Apostles Peter and Paul, and Andrew, and of all the Saints, mercifully grant to me also the pardon of my sins, grace to the remnant of my days, and peace in the hour of my death, that so through the help of thy mercy, in the awful hour of judgment I may stand before the face of my accusing enemy without alarm: Through Jesus Christ thy Son our Lord. *Amen.*

AGNUS DEI.

At the "*Agnus Dei,*" pray thus:

Lamb of God, who takest away the sins of the world! *grant them rest.*

Lamb of God, who takest away the sins of the world! *grant them rest.*

Lamb of God, who takest away the sins of the world! *grant them eternal rest.*

O LORD Jesus Christ, Son of the living God, who, according to thy Father's will, and by the co-operation of the Holy Ghost, hast given life to the world through thine own death, deliver me by this, thy most sacred Body and Blood, from all my sins, and from every evil: make me cling to thy commandments always, and never let me be separated from thee.

O Almighty and Merciful God! I beseech

thee, may all these sacraments in which it is our privilege to participate, be the means of our puri fication; and grant that this, thy sacrifice, may not be to us a ground of accusation for our punishment, but a salutary intercession for our pardon: may it serve for the washing away of our guilt, for the strengthening of our frailty, and for a support against all the dangers of the world, and to all thy faithful people, whether living or dead, for the remission of all their sins; through Jesus Christ our Lord. *Amen.*

THE COMMUNION.

At the signal given by the little bell, when the Priest before receiving the Sacred Host, strikes his breast three times, do the same, and say each time,

LORD! I am not worthy that thou shouldst enter under my roof, but only speak the word, and my soul shall be healed.

Here you may make the Spiritual Communion (see page 114,) uniting yourself in desire with the communion of the Priest. After which recite the following prayer of the Church:

TO Almighty God, O dear departed Brethren. we now commend you. May the bright company of the Angels come to seek you; may the senate of the Apostles come to greet you, may the triumphant army of glorious Martyrs come to meet you; the glittering throng of Confessors encompass you with their lilies in their hands; the choir of Virgins receive you with songs of joy; and a happy rest embrace you on the bosoms of the Patriarchs. May Jesus Christ appear to you with a mild and cheerful smile, and give you a place in his presence for ever. May you be far removed from the horrible darkness, the hissing flames, the agonizing torments. May Christ, who was crucified for you, deliver you from your pains. May Christ, the Son of the living God place you in the ever green and pleasant pastures of Paradise, and may he, the true Shepherd, acknowledge you among his flock. May he absolve you from all your sins, and place you at his right hand in the inheritance of his elect. May you see your Redeemer face to face, and always in his presence, with the happy company of the Blessed, enjoy the sweetness of the vision of God for evermore. *Amen.*

THE LAST GOSPEL.

For the last Gospel, read what follows:

I KNOW that my Redeemer liveth, and in the last day I shall rise out of the earth: and I shall be clothed again with my skin, and in my flesh I shall see my God: whom I myself shall see, and my eyes shall behold, and not another. This my hope is laid up for me in my bosom. Job, xix. 25—I am the Resurrection and the

Life: he that believeth in me, although he be dead, shall live; and every one that liveth and believeth in me, shall not die for ever: S. John, xi. 25—And I heard a voice saying unto me: Write, blessed are the dead who die in the Lord; from henceforth now, saith the Spirit, that they may rest from their labors, for their works follow them. Apoc. xiv. 13.

R. Thanks be to God.

Finally recommend yourselves to the souls in Purgatory, and say:

BLESSED Souls, I have prayed for you: I now entreat you, who are so dear to God, and so secure of never losing him any more, to pray for me a miserable sinner, that am exposed to sin every day, liable to die every day, and in danger of being damned and of losing God for ever.

On hearing the Word of God.

"*He that is of God, heareth the words of God.*" St. John, viii. 47.

An important part of the Christian worship is listening to the word of God from the mouth of the Priest. Let no one think himself so wise and so learned that he can do without it. Preaching is the means appointed by God to speak to our heart. Therefore, he who will not hear the preachers of the Catholic Church, shuts his ears against the voice of God, and despises Jesus Christ, who says: "*He that heareth you, heareth me, and he that despiseth you, despiseth me.*"

Let no one say: I can read the word of God for myself in the Bible; of what use is preaching to me? What! do you dare to think that a human mind like yours, created, limited, and full of darkness, is able, of itself, to comprehend the mind of the eternal God? O! beware, that you do not substitute your own thought for that of God. No! dear Christian, the church of the living God alone, guided and enlightened as it is by the Holy Ghost, is able to know the mind of God with infallible certainty, and to interpret the Holy Scriptures without danger of error. She it is who announces to us the true doctrine of Jesus Christ, by her Bishops, and their fellow-laborers, the Priests, and they are the teachers to whom we must listen, unless we are willing through a spirit of pride to expose ourselves to the most dangerous errors.

But will you say: I have at home excellent explanations of the Gospels, and other good books of instruction; these will serve my purpose instead of preaching. To this objection of yours, Saint Thomas of Villanova has already answered. "Tell me not, I am learned, I have at home the works of Augustin, of Bernard, &c The letter is dead, the voice is living. The preacher is the living voice of God. He is 'the voice of one crying in the wilderness.' Jesus Christ said: 'The letter killeth, the spirit maketh alive.' The world, how was it converted? Through the divine word PREACHED by the Apostles."

Listen, then, to sermons with a pious and humble mind; judge not the Preacher; look not for beautiful words; do not apply the sermon to others, but to yourself alone; consider the word of the Priest as the voice of God, sounding in the ear of your heart, and calling you to penance, and often before and during the sermon repeat in your heart the words of holy Samuel: "*Speak, Lord! for thy servant heareth.*"

PRAYER BEFORE THE SERMON.

COME, Holy Ghost, fill the hearts of thy faithful, and kindle in them the fire of thy love: thou, who hast gathered the people of every tongue into the unity of the faith.

O God, who hast instructed the hearts of the faithful by the illumination of the Holy Ghost, grant us by the same spirit to understand what is right, and to rejoice always in his consolation, through Christ our Lord. *Amen.*

PRAYER AFTER THE SERMON.

O LORD Jesus Christ, I thank thee for having sown this day the seed of thy divine word in my soul. Never permit, O Lord, this good seed to be taken away from my heart, or consumed by the heat of impure and earthly desires, or choked up by the thorns of worldly care; but grant rather, that through thy blessing, thy word may bring forth fruit in me an hundred fold, to eternal life. *Amen.*

Devotions at Vespers.

Although there is no express commandment which makes it a mortal sin to be absent from Vespers, yet every good Catholic will make it his duty to attend when he can, and see that his family are present also. We are commanded to sanctify the Lord's day, and the other Holy days of obligation; but if a Catholic neglects the public service of the Church on Sunday afternoons, without any reasonable excuse, how can it be expected that he will apply himself to sanctify it in other ways?

Be present, therefore, always in the church at Vespers, and employ the moments you spend there in praying devoutly.

While the Priest and Choir are singing the Office, you can follow them by using the following translation; or, if you prefer, you may make use of some other prayers, according to your devotion.

PRAYER BEFORE THE OFFICE.

O LORD, open my lips to praise thy holy name: cleanse my heart also from all vain, perverse, and wandering thoughts; enlighten my mind and inflame my heart, so that I may recite this office worthily, attentively, and devoutly, and merit a gracious hearing in the presence of thy divine Majesty: through Christ our Lord. *Amen.*

THE VESPERS OF SUNDAY.

First recite an "*Our Father*," and a "*Hail Mary*," and then begin with the sign of the Cross, thus:

V. Deus in adjutorium meum intende.	V. ✠ Incline unto my aid, O God.
R. Domine, ad adjuvandum me festina.	R. O Lord, make haste to help me.
Gloria Patri, et Filio, * et Spiritui Sancto. Sicut erat in principio, et nunc, et semper, * et in sæcula sæculorum. Amen.	Glory be to the Father, and to the Son, and to the Holy Ghost, as it was in the beginning, is now, and ever shall be, world without end. *Amen.*

Before and after each Psalm is sung an Antiphon, which varies according to the Festivals.

Ant. Dixit Dominus.	*Antiphon.* The Lord said—

PSALM CIX.

(Dixit Dominus.)

A prophecy of the exaltation and everlasting Priesthood of Jesus Christ.

1. Dixit Dominus Domino meo, * Sede à dextris meis.	The Lord said to my Lord: Sit thou at my right hand, until I make thy enemies thy footstool.
2. Donec ponam inimicos tuos, * scabellum pedum tuorum.	
3. Virgam virtutis tuæ emittet Dominus ex Sion:	The Lord will send forth the sceptre of thy

* dominare in medio inimicorum tuorum.

4. Tecum principium in die virtutis tuæ, in splendoribus sanctorum: * ex utero ante luciferum genui te.

5. Juravit Dominus, et non pœnitebit eum: * Tu es sacerdos in æternum secundum ordinem Melchisedech.

6. Dominus à dextris tuis: * confregit in die iræ suæ reges.

7. Judicabit in nationibus, implebit ruinas: * conquassabit capita in terra multorum.

8. De torrente in via bibet: * propterea exaltabit caput.

Gloria Patri, &c.

Ant. Dixit Dominus Domino meo, Sede á dextris meis.

Ant. Fidelia.

power out of Sion: rule thou in the midst of thy enemies.

With thee is the principality in the day of thy strength, in the brightness of thy saints: from the womb before the day-star I begot thee.

The Lord hath sworn, and he will not repent: Thou art a priest forever according to the order of Melchisedech.

The Lord at thy right hand hath broken kings in the day of his wrath.

He shall judge among nations, he shall fill ruins, he shall crush the heads in the land of many.

He shall drink of the torrent in the way: therefore shall he lift up the head.

Glory be to the Father, &c.

Ant. The Lord said to my Lord, Sit thou at my right hand.

Ant. All his commandments—

PSALM CX.

(Confitebor tibi, Domine.)

The Prophet gives thanks to God, and praises him for all his graces and benefits to his Church.

---

1. Confitebor tibi, Domine, in toto corde meo: * in concilio justorum, et congregatione.	I will praise thee, O Lord, with my whole heart: in the assembly of the righteous, and in the congregation.
2. Magna opera Domini: * exquisita in omnes voluntates ejus.	Great are the works of the Lord: exquisite and agreeable to all his designs.
3. Confessio et magnificentia opus ejus: * et justitia ejus manet in sæculum sæculi.	His work is his praise and glory; and his justice remaineth forever.
4. Memoriam fecit mirabilium suorum, misericors et miserator Dominus: * escam dedit timentibus se.	The merciful and gracious Lord hath appointed a memorial of his wonderful works: he hath given food to them that fear him.
5. Memor erit in sæculum testamenti sui: * virtutem operum suorum annuntiabit populo suo.	He will be forever mindful of his covenant: the greatness of his works will he publish to his people.
6. Ut det illis hæreditatem Gentium: * opera manuum ejus, veritas et judicium.	To give them the inheritance of the Gentiles: the works of his hands are truth and justice.
7. Fidelia omnia mandata ejus, confirmata in	True and lasting are all his ordinances, confirmed

sæculum sæculi: * facta in veritate et æquitate.

forever and ever; made in truth and justice.

8. Redemptionem misit populo suo: * mandavit in æternum testamentum suum.

He hath sent redemption to his people: he hath appointed his covenant forever.

9. Sanctum et terribile nomen ejus: * initium sapientiæ timor Domini.

Holy and awful is his name: the fear of the Lord is the beginning of wisdom.

10. Intellectus bonus omnibus facientibus eum: * laudatio ejus manet in sæculum sæculi.

All understand it right, who practise it: his praise endureth forever and ever.

Gloria Patri, &c.

Glory be to the Father, &c.

Ant. Fidelia omnia mandata ejus; confirmata in sæculum sæculi.

Ant. All his commandments are faithful, confirmed forever and ever.

Ant. In mandatis.

Ant. He shall delight—

PSALM CXI.

(Beatus vir.)

This Psalm teaches us that the good will be surely happy, but the wicked shall perish forever.

---

1. Beatus vir qui timet Dominum: * in mandatis ejus volet nimis.

Blessed is the man that feareth the Lord: in his commandments he shall take great delight.

2. Potens in terra erit semen ejus: * generatio rectorum benedicetur.

Mighty on earth shall be his seed: the generation of the righteous shall be blessed.

3. Gloria et divitiæ in domo ejus: * et justitia

Glory and wealth shall be in his house: and his

ejus manet in sæculum sæculi.

4. Exortum est in tenebris lumen rectis: * misericors, et miserator et justus.

5 Jucundus homo qui miseretur et commodat, disponet sermones suos in judicio: * quia in æternum non commovebitur.

6. In memoria æterna erit justus: * ab auditione mala non timebit.

7. Paratum cor ejus sperare in Domino, confirmatum est cor ejus: * non commovebitur donec despiciat inimicos suos.

8. Dispersit, dedit pauperibus, justitia ejus manet in sæculum sæculi: * cornu ejus exaltabitur in gloria.

9. Peccator videbit et irascetur, dentibus suis fremet et tabescet: * desiderium peccatorum peribit.

Gloria Patri, &c.

Ant. In mandatis ejus cupit nimis.

Ant. Sit nomen Domini.

righteousness endureth forever and ever.

He is risen in darkness, a light to the upright: he is merciful and just, compassionate.

Acceptable is the man that showeth mercy and lendeth: he shall order his words with judgment, and he shall never give way.

The righteous man shall be in eternal remembrance: he shall not fear an evil report.

His heart is ready to hope in the Lord: his heart is strengthened: he shall not yield till he despise his enemies.

He hath distributed and given to the poor; his righteousness remaineth forever: his power shall be exalted in glory.

The sinner shall see it, and be enraged: he shall gnash his teeth and pine away: the desire of sinners shall perish.

Glory be to the Father, &c.

Ant. He shall delight exceedingly in his commandments.

Ant. Blessed be the name

PSALM CXII.

(Laudate, pueri, Dominum.)

The Prophet exhorts us to praise God, because although infinitely high himself, he does not forget the poor and the humble.

---

1. Laudate, pueri, Dominum: * laudate nomen Domini.

Praise the Lord, ye servants of the Lord: praise ye the name of the Lord.

2. Sit nomen Domini benedictum: * ex hoc nunc, et usque in sæculum.

Let the name of the Lord be blessed: now and for evermore:

3. A solis ortu usque ad occasum: * laudabile nomen Domini.

From the rising of the sun to the setting thereof: worthy of praise is the name of the Lord.

4. Excelsus super omnes gentes Dominus: * et super cœlos gloria ejus.

High is the Lord above all the nations: and above the heavens is his glory.

5. Quis sicut Dominus Deus noster, qui in altis habitat: * et humilia respicit in cœlo et in terra?

Who is like unto the Lord our God, who dwelleth on high: and beholdeth what is below in heaven and on earth?

6. Suscitans à terra inopem: * et de stercore erigens pauperem.

Who from the earth raiseth up the needy one: and from the dunghill lifteth up the poor one:

7. Ut collocet eum cum principibus: * cum principibus populi sui.

To place him with the princes: with the princes of his people.

8. Qui habitare facit sterilem in domo: * matrem filiorum lætantem.

Who maketh the barren woman to dwell in her house: the joyful mother of many children.

Gloria Patri, &c.

Glory be to the Father, &c.

Ant. Sit nomen Domini benedictum in sæcula.

Ant. Blessed be the name of the Lord for evermore.

Ant. Nos qui vivimus.

Ant. But we that live —

PSALM CXVI.

(Laudate Dominum.)

The Psalmist invites the whole world to join in praising God for his mercy and truth.

---

1. Laudate Dominum, omnes gentes: * laudate eum, omnes populi.

O praise the Lord, all ye nations; praise him, all ye people.

2. Quoniam confirmata est super nos misericordia ejus: * et veritas Domini manet in æternum.

For his mercy is confirmed upon us: and the truth of the Lord remaineth forever.

Gloria Patri, &c.

Glory be to the Father, &c.

Ant. Nos qui vivimus benedicimus Domino.

Ant. But we that live bless the Lord.

THE LITTLE CHAPTER, 2 COR. I.

Benedictus Deus, et Pater Domini nostri Jesu Christi, Pater misericordiarum, et Deus totius consolationis, qui consolatur nos in omni tribulatione nostra.

Blessed be the God an Father of our Lord Jesu Christ, the Father of mercies, and the God of all comfort, who comforteth us in all our tribulation.

R. Deo Gratias.

R. Thanks be to God.

Then follows the Hymn, which is not always the same. The one here given is usually sung on the Feasts of the Blessed Virgin.

HYMN.

(Ave Maris Stella.)

Ave Maris Stella Dei Mater Alma Atque semper Virgo Felix Cœli porta.	Gentle Star of ocean! Portal of the sky! Ever Virgin Mother Of the Lord Most High!
Sumens illud Ave Gabrielis ore, Funda nos in pace Mutans Evæ nomen.	Oh! by Gabriel's Ave, Utter'd long ago, Eva's name reversing, Stablish peace below.
Solve vincla reis Profer lumen cæcis Mala nostra pelle Bona cuncta posce.	Break the captive's fetters; Light on blindness pour; All our ills expelling, Every bliss implore.
Monstra te esse matrem Sumat per te preces Qui pro nobis natus Tulit esse tuus.	Show thyself a Mother; Offer him our sighs, Who for us incarnate Did not thee despise.
Virgo singularis, Inter omnes mitis Nos culpis solutos Mites fac et castos.	Virgin of all Virgins! To thy shelter take us; Gentlest of the gentle! Chaste and gentle make us.
Vitam præsta puram, Iter para tutum, Ut videntes Jesum Semper collætemur.	Still as on we journey, Help our weak endeavor; Till with thee and Jesus We rejoice forever.
Sit laus Deo Patri, Summo Christo decus,	Through the highest Heaven, To the Almighty Three,

Spiritui Sancto, Tribus honor unus. Amen.	Father, Son, and Spirit, One same glory be.
V. Dirigatur, Domine, oratio mea, R. Sicut incensum in conspectu tuo.	V. May my prayer, O Lord, be directed, R. As incense in thy sight.

Before and after the Magnificat is sung an Antiphon, which varies with the different Feasts and seasons of the year.

THE MAGNIFICAT,

or Canticle of the Blessed Virgin Mary.

1. MAGNIFICAT * anima mea Dominum. 2. Et exultavit spiritus meus: * in Deo salutari meo.	My soul doth magnify the Lord, and my spirit hath rejoiced in God my Saviour:
3. Quia respexit humilitatem ancillæ suæ: * ecce enim ex hoc, beatam me dicent omnes generationes.	Because he hath regarded the humility of his handmaid, for behold from henceforth all generations shall call me blessed.
4. Quia fecit mihi magna qui potens est: * et sanctum nomen ejus.	For he that is mighty hath done great things to me, and holy is his name.
5. Et misericordia ejus à progenie in progenies, * timentibus eum.	And his mercy is from generation to generation, to them that fear him.
6. Fecit potentiam in brachio suo: * dispersit superbos mente cordis sui.	He hath showed might in his arm: he hath scattered the proud in the conceit of their heart.
7. Deposuit potentes de sede: * et exaltavit humiles.	He hath put down the mighty from their seat, and hath exalted the humble.

8. Esurientes implevit bonis: * et divites dimisit inanes.

He hath filled the hungry with good things, and the rich he hath sent away empty.

9. Suscepit Israel puerum suum: * recordatus misericordiæ suæ.

He hath received Israel his servant, being mindful of his mercy.

10. Sicut locutus est ad patres nostros: * Abraham, et semini ejus in sæcula.

As he spoke to our fathers, to Abraham and to his seed forever.

Gloria Patri, &c.

Glory, &c.

PRAYER.

WE beseech thee, O Lord, let all thy Saints assist us wherever we may be: that while we venerate their virtues, we may also feel their protection: Grant to these times in which we live thy holy peace, and drive away all evil from thy Church: Direct our lives, our actions, and our wills, and those of all thy servants in the prosperous way of thy salvation: return an everlasting reward to all our benefactors; and to all the faithful departed grant eternal rest. Through Jesus Christ our Lord. Amen.

After the Prayer, which is different every Sunday, follow the versicles and responses.

V. Dominus vobiscum.

V. The Lord be with you.

R. Et cum spiritu tuo.

R. And with thy spirit.

V. Benedicamus Domino.

V. Let us bless the Lord.

R. Deo Gratias.

R. Thanks be to God.

V. Fidelium animæ per

V. May the souls of the

misericordiam Dei requiescant in pace.

R. Amen.

faithful, through the mercy of God, rest in peace.

R. Amen.

Then repeat, "*Our Father*," &c., and afterwards,

V. Dominus det nobis suam pacem.

R. Et vitam æternam. Amen.

V. May God grant us his peace.

R. And everlasting life. *Amen.*

Then follows the ANTHEM in honor of the Mother of God, which differs according to the season.

(*During Advent, and until the Purification.*)

ALMA REDEMPTORIS MATER.

Alma Redemptoris Mater, quæ pervia cœli
Porta manes, et stella maris, succurre cadenti
Surgere qui curat populo; tu quæ genuisti,
Natura mirante, tuum sanctum Génitorem,
Virgo priùs ac posteriùs; Gabrielis ab ore,
Sumens illud Ave, peccatorum miserere.

Mother of Jesus, heaven's open gate,
Star of the sea, uphold our fallen state.
O thou, whose sacred womb thy Maker bore,
Remaining ever virginal and pure,
From sinful lips receive that earnest Hail,
Which first from Gabriel, hallowed herald, fell.

V. Angelus Domini nuntiavit Mariæ.

R. Et concepit de Spiritu Sancto.

V. The Angel of the Lord declared unto Mary,

R. And she conceived by the Holy Ghost.

PRAYER.

GRATIAM tuam, quæsumus, Domine, mentibus nostris infunde: ut

POUR forth, we beseech thee, O Lord, thy grace into our hearts, that

qui angelo nuntiante Christi Filii tui incarnationem cognovimus, per passionem ejus et crucem ad resurrectionis gloriam perducamur. Per eundem Christum Dominum nostrum. Amen.	we, to whom the incarnation of Christ thy Son has been made known by the message of an angel, may, by his passion and cross, be brought to the glory of his resurrection, thro the same Christ our Lord Amen.

(*From the Purification until Easter.*)

AVE, REGINA CŒLORUM.

Ave, regina cœlorum,	Hail Mary, Queen of heaven above,
Ave, domina angelorum,	Whom radiant Angels own and love!
Salve radix, salve porta,	Hail fruitful root, hail portal bright,
Ex qua mundo lux est orta.	Whence streamed on earth celestial light.
Gaude virgo gloriosa,	Hail glorious Maid, with beauty blessed,
Super omnes speciosa;	Far lovelier than the loveliest,
Vale ô valde, decora,	O! crowned with grace and glory thus,
Et pro nobis Christum exora.	Pray, Mary, pray to Christ for us!
V. Dignare me, laudare te, Virgo sacrata.	V. O deign to let me praise thee, Sacred Virgin!
R. Da mihi virtutem contra hostes tuos.	*R. And give me power against thy enemies.*

PRAYER.

CONCEDE, misericors Deus, fragilitati nostræ præsidium: ut qui sanctæ Dei Genetricis memoriam agimus, intercessionis ejus auxilio, à nostris iniquitatibus resurgamus. Per eundem Christum Dominum nostrum. Amen.

GRANT us, O merciful God, a safeguard against all our weakness, that we, who celebrate the memory of the holy Mother of God, may, by the help of her intercession, rise again from our iniquities, through the same Christ our Lord. Amen.

(*From Easter until Trinity.*)

REGINA CŒLI.

Regina cœli lætare, Alleluia.
Quia quem meruisti portare, Alleluia.
Resurrexit sicut dixit, Alleluia.
Ora pro nobis Deum, Alleluia.

V. Gaude et lætare, Virgo Maria, Alleluia.
R. Quia surrexit Dominus vere. Alleluia.

Joy to thee, O Queen of heaven, Alleluia!
He whom thou wast meet to bear, Alleluia!
As he promised, hath arisen, Alleluia!
Pour for us to him thy prayer. Alleluia!

V. Rejoice and be glad, O Virgin Mary, Alleluia!
R. For the Lord is truly risen. Alleluia!

PRAYER.

DEUS, qui per resurrectionem Filii tui Domini nostri Jesu Christi mundum lætificare dignatus es; præsta quæsu-

O GOD, who, by the resurrection of thy Son, our Lord Jesus Christ, hast been pleased to fill the world with joy, grant, mus, ut per ejus genitricem virginem Mariam perpetuæ capiamus gaudia vitæ. Per eundem Christum Dominum nostrum. Amen.

we beseech thee, that by his Mother, the Virgin Mary, we may receive the joys of eternal life, through the same Christ our Lord. Amen.

(From Trinity Sunday until Advent.)

SALVE, REGINA.

Salve, Regina, mater misericordiæ!—vita, dulcedo, et spes nostra, salve!

Mother of mercy, hail! O gentle Queen.
Our life, our sweetness, and our hope, all hail!

Ad te clamamus exules Filii Hevæ.

Children of Eve,
To thee we cry from our sad banishment;

Ad te suspiramus gementes et flentes in hac lacrymarum valle.

To thee we send our sighs,
Weeping and mourning in this tearful vale.

Eia ergo, advocata nostra, illos tuos misericordes oculos ad nos converte.
Et Jesum, benedictum fructum ventris tui, nobis post hoc exilium ostende.

Come then, our Advocate,
O! turn on us those pitying eyes of thine:
And, our long exile past,
Show us at last
Jesus, of thy pure womb the fruit divine;

O clemens, O pia, O dulcis virgo Maria.

O Virgin Mary, Mother blest!
O sweetest, gentlest, holiest!

V. Ora pro nobis, sancta Dei genitrix.

V. Pray for us, O holy Mother of God!

R. Ut digni efficiamur promissionibus Christi.

R. That we may be made worthy of the promises of Christ.

PRAYER.

OMNIPOTENS sempiterne Deus, qui gloriosæ Virginis Matris Mariæ corpus et animam, ut dignum Filii tui habitaculum effici mereretur, Spiritu Sancto co-operante, præparasti: da, ut cujus commemoratione lætamur, ejus pia intercessione ab instantibus malis et a morte perpetua liberemur. Per eundem Christum Dominum nostrum. Amen.

ALMIGHTY and eternal God! who, by the co operation of the Holy Ghost, didst prepare the body and soul of the glorious Virgin Mother, Mary, that she might become a worthy habitation for thy Son, grant, that as with joy we celebrate her memory, so by her pious intercession we may be delivered from present evils, and from eternal death, through the same Christ our Lord. Amen.

V. Divinum auxilium maneat semper nobiscum.

R. Amen.

V. May the divine assistance remain always with us.

R. Amen.

CONCLUDING PRAYER.

TO the most Holy and undivided Trinity, to the crucified humanity of our Lord Jesus Christ, to the most blessed and glorious and ever-faithful virginity of the Virgin Mary, and to the assembly of all the Saints in heaven, may everlasting praise, honor, power, and glory be given, by every creature, and to us also the remission of all our sins, through never ending ages. Amen.

V. Blessed be the womb of the Virgin Mary, which bore the Son of the eternal Father!

R. And blessed be the breasts which nourished Christ our Lord.

"Our Father," *and* "Hail Mary."

BENEDICTION OF THE BLESSED SACRAMENT.

Ordinarily at the close of the Sunday Vespers, and sometimes on other occasions, is given the Benediction with the Blessed Sacrament. This is done in the following manner:

The Priest, or sometimes a Deacon assisting the priest goes up to the altar, and opening the tabernacle, takes out the MOST BLESSED SACRAMENT which is kept there, and leaves it thus on or above the altar, exposed in full view to the adoration of the faithful. The Priest then descends from the altar, and while he incenses the SACRED HOST, the Choir sing the following hymn, the people remaining all the while on their knees, in prayer and adoration.

HYMN.

(*O Salutaris Hostia.*)

O Salutaris Hostia,	O! Salutary Sacrifice!
Quæ cœli pandis ostium:	Whose death has opened Paradise:
Bella premunt hostilia:	By hostile war oppressed, afraid,
Da robur fer auxilium	To thee we look for strength and aid.

Uni trinoque Domino,	Now to the triune God in Heaven,
Sit sempiterna gloria:	Be everlasting glory given;
Qui vitam sine termino,	Where life eternal in his hand
Nobis donet in patria.	Invites us to our Father land.

Sometimes, also, other Anthems are here sung, or the Litany of the Blessed Virgin, during which time you can make use of that Litany, or of one of the Visits to the Blessed Sacrament. (See page 116.) Last of all is sung the following

HYMN.

(*Tantum ergo Sacramentum.*)

Tantum ergo sacramentum,	Down in adoration falling,
Veneremur cernui;	Lo! the Sacred Host we hail;
Et antiquum documentum,	Lo! o'er ancient forms departing,
Novo cedat ritui;	Newer rights of grace prevail;
Præstet fides supplementum,	Faith for all defects supplying,
Sensuum defectui.	Where the feeble senses fail.
Genitori, Genitoque,	To the everlasting Father,
Laus et jubilatio,	And the Son who reigns on high,
Salus, honor, virtus quoque,	With the Holy Ghost proceeding
Sit et benedictio:	Forth from each eternally,
Procedenti ab utroque,	Be salvation, honor, blessing,

Compar sit laudatio.
Amen.

V. Panem de cœlo præstitisti eis.
R. Omne delectamentum in se habentem.

Might, and endless majesty. *Amen.*

V. Thou hast given them bread from heaven.
R. Replenished with all sweetness and delight.

PRAYER.

DEUS qui nobis, sub sacramento mirabili, passionis tuæ memoriam reliquisti: tribue, quæsumus, ita nos corporis et sanguinis tui sacra mysteria venerari, ut redemptionis tui fructum in nobis jugiter sentiamus. Qui vivis et regnas in sæcula sæculorum. Amen.

O GOD, who has left us in this wonderful Sacrament a perpetual memorial of thy passion: grant us we beseech thee, so to reverence the sacred mysteries of thy Body and Blood, that we may continually find in our souls the fruit of thy Redemption: Thou who livest and reignest world without end. *Amen.*

After the Priest has sung this prayer, the white veil is laid over his shoulders, and he then mounts the steps of the altar, and taking in his hands the monstrance which contains the BLESSED SACRAMENT, gives the Benediction by making with it over the Congregation the sign of the cross. At this moment kneel more profoundly than before, to receive this divine blessing of your Saviour, and say:

O MY God, I am sorry—I am sorry for my sins: forgive me them, and give me my part in this heavenly blessing! I love thee, I will love thee always, and seek to please thee in every thought, in every word, and every action of my life. ✠ In the name of the Father, and of the Son, and of the Holy Ghost. *Amen.*

Confession.

EXERCISES OF DEVOTION,

PREPARATORY TO CONFESSION.

Call to mind that this confession may be the last of your life. Therefore, prepare yourself for it, as if you were lying sick upon your deathbed, and already at the borders of the grave. Ask God to give you the grace to make a good examination of conscience, and the light to see your sins clearly, and as they really are.

INVOCATION.

O GOD, the Father of light! Thou who enlightenest all men that come into this world, send into my poor soul a ray of the holy light of love and contrition, that I may know, detest, and confess the sins, which I have committed against thee. I desire to see my sins in all their enormity, and just as they are in thy sight: I wish to detest them for the love of thee, and to confess them with the same sincerity, as I should wish to do at the moment of my death. Jesus, my God and Saviour, I offer to thee the examination which I am going to make, and I look to thee with confidence for the grace to do it well. And do thou, O Mother of God, assist me, thou who art so full of compassion for sinners that strive truly to repent of their sins.

Help me, my holy Guardian Angel! help me to know all the offences which I have committed against my God. O! all ye Saints in heaven, pray for me that I may bring forth worthy fruits of penance. *Amen.*

*Now make your examination of conscience.**

Having finished this examination, make the three following short meditations, in order to excite in yourself a true contrition for your sins:

I. Consideration. *Of the enormity of sin.*

Consider, first, the enormity of a mortal sin. It is an insult to Almighty God, and a contempt of his holy law. Call to mind that you have sinned before Him who knows all things, and sees the most secret actions, and the silent thoughts of the heart; that you have given the death blow to your immortal soul; that you have drawn down upon yourself the anger and punishment of the living God, a God who in his just vengeance is awful and terrible; that he it is who cast forever into hell the holy angels when they first rebelled against him; that, alas! many of the damned who are now groaning in the eternal pains of hell, have not committed so great, and so many sins as you; and that while death is perhaps already very near, it is onl

---

* Persons whose consciences are tender, and who often receive the Sacraments, ought not to dwell too long upon this examination, but make it quietly, and without scruples. For such souls, it is sufficient to cast a careful glance upon those faults and imperfections into which they fall the oftenest, or they may use the form of Examination on p. 22.

On the contrary, those who have been a long while without confession, should give all that time to the examination of conscience, which so important an affair really demands, so that they may call to mind, as far as possible, the nature and number of their mortal sins. For this purpose, they make use of the form of Examination given in this Manual, page 317.

the infinite patience of this most merciful God that makes him wait until now for your conversion.

CONTRITE PRAYER.

O MY God! O infinite and holy God, what have I done? I confess that my sins are more in number than the hairs of my head, or the sands on the sea-shore. And yet only a single one of them all was enough for my ruin. Yes, one of these mortal sins was enough to rob me of heaven, enough to bring down thy anger upon my defenceless head. Hell opened under my feet when I committed the first, and yet others followed, until now, like a mountain they lie heavy upon my soul. Alas! why am I not penetrated with horror and fear at the remembrance of my guilt? Sinful soul, what hast thou gained by all these sins? Nothing, O my Lord, nothing but shame and sorrow, guilt and remorse. They have left me without joy in the past, or hope beyond the grave.

But no, my most merciful Lord, there is still hope for me: for I know that if I do penance thou wilt forgive me. I do repent of all my sins. I hate and detest them from the bottom of my heart. I am truly sorry for my mad and senseless conduct, and I am resolved to sin no more. From this moment I devote the rest of my days to penance and a holy life. Yes, holy and merciful God, hear my firm resolve: For give me this once, and rather will I lose, a thousand times over. all the world has of goods, pleasures, honors, health, even life itself, than ever separate from thy grace again!

II. CONSIDERATION. *Of the favors received from a God who has been offended by our sins.*

Hear, sinner, the voice of God thy Father and benefactor, who complains thus of the bitter return which thou hast made him for a thousand thousand benefits.

Tell me, ungrateful sinner, what could I do for thee that I have not done? I created thee out of nothing, and made thee in my own likeness, without having the least need of thee. I redeemed thee by the blood of my only Son. I made thee a Christian and a Catholic, while millions of men like thee were left in the darkness of infidelity and heresy. I have borne with thee patiently until this moment, in all thy sins and vices. I have given thee so many and so easy means to secure thy salvation. And on thy side what hast thou done? For all this, thou hast only returned ingratitude! I made all creatures for thy sake, and thou makest use of them only to offend me!—"*Hear! O ye heavens, and give ear, O earth! I have brought up children, and exalted them, but they have despised me.*" Isa. i. 2.

CONTRITE PRAYER.

O WHAT base ingratitude! No, there is not, there cannot be any thing like it under the sun. Yes, my most tender Father, and loving Benefactor! this is the way I have shown my gratitude to thee for having drawn me out of that nothing where I was, and where I should be still, except for thee. Alas! alas! so have I hitherto prized all those precious graces which thou hast showered upon my thankless head.

O, ungrateful sinner that I am! Who will give sighs enough to my heart, and tears to my eyes, that I may weep for the death of my soul, and do penance as I ought for this treachery to my God, of which I have been guilty? O, most merciful Lord, have mercy on me! I have a sincere desire, and make now the firm resolution to offend thee no more.

Alas! was it just, was it right, that after being brought into existence by God, and receiving innumerable benefits at his hand, I should so often and so deeply offend him as I have done? When this unseen and omnipotent hand formed me in my mother's womb, and gave me hands, feet, eyes, ears, and a heart, was it for me to use them in this way as so many instruments to insult and violate thy sublime majesty? Ah! unhappy eyes! O wicked hands! O faithless heart! you by your sins have been the cause of grief to a God of infinite goodness, the most loving and tender of Fathers.

III. CONSIDERATION. *Upon the love of Jesus Christ, who suffered for our sins.*

Look upon your loving Saviour on the cross of Calvary! His sacred hands and feet are pierced through and through with rude nails hammered deep into the wood: his kingly head is crowned with thorns: his sacred body is covered with marks of the cruel scourges; and his unspeakable agony appears in his dying eyes, and the convulsions of his suffering limbs. Who is it? and what is the cause of this bloody spectacle? Ah! sinner, it is your Saviour, and your sins have brought him to this sad extremity. Yes, for your sake he became man, for the pardon of your sins he suffered and died. Cruel Jews! cruel soldiers! but far more cruel sinners who, in our day, still crucify their Lord and mock at his pains; for the Apostle speaks of them when he says: "*They crucify again to themselves the Son of God, and make a mockery of him.*" Heb. vi. 6.

CONTRITE PRAYER.

ALAS! accursed sins! how could I treat the Son of God so cruelly? Miserable that I am, who will give rivers of tears to my eyes, that I may weep according to the multitude of my sins! Is this thy reward, my dearest Saviour, for that innocent blood which thou hast shed with so much love and sorrow for my sake? Could I make thee no better return than this?—by my guilty pleasures, my brutal passions, my cold contempt of thy holy laws, to cover again thy face with shame, and open thy bleeding wounds afresh?

O Lamb of God! sacrificed and lifeless on the cross, remember that I am a soul redeemed by thy precious blood: pardon me my sins, for I am sorry for them from the bottom of my heart. Yes! raise thy wounded hand to bless and pardon me. Receive the traitor that now casts himself in sorrow at thy feet. My sins fill me with terror, for I know that I deserve to be in hell this moment, but surely, since thou hast died for me, thou wilt not now refuse me mercy: Behold me here, O my God! what wilt thou have me do? shall I weep over my sins? Indeed, I am sorry for them, and detest them with my whole soul. Shall I forsake them? I do renounce them, now and forever. Shall I spend the remainder of my life in loving thee, and serving thee? This is my desire, and I am resolved to do so. Behold now I go to confess my sins! Great God! give me grace to confess them thoroughly, sincerely, and humbly, and from this moment, never, never offend thee any more. Holy Mary, mother of mercy! I recommend myself to thee, in this solemn hour. My Guardian Angel, and all my patron Saints, pray to the Lord my God for me.

For particular directions as to the manner of making your confessions, see INSTRUCTIONS OF THE SACRAMENT OF PENANCE, page 285.

A SHORTER EXERCISE.

(*For persons who confess frequently.*)

INVOCATION.

O HOLY God, who art always ready to receive sinners into thy favor, and to pardon them, look mercifully upon my poor soul, which after so many offences returns again to thee. in order to obtain pardon through thy Holy Sacrament. Grant me the necessary preparation for this: enlighten my understanding, that I may see all my sins; soften my heart, that I may be truly sorry for them; direct my words, that I may make a good confession, and thereby obtain forgiveness; and let not my self-love blind me in any way.

Holy Mary, Mother of mercy, and refuge of poor sinners, pray for me now, that I may make this confession well, and so obtain pardon, and the grace to amend my life.

CONTRITE PRAYER.

THOU seest at thy feet, O God of infinite Majesty, the traitor who has so often offended thee, but now humbly implores thee to pardon him. "*A contrite and humble heart, O God, thou wilt not despise.*" I thank thee that thou hast waited for me until this day, and hast not left me to die in my sins. I hope, through the merits of Jesus Christ, that having been patient with me hitherto, thou wilt pardon me now in this confession all the sins which I have committed. O my God, I repent of all my sins, and am deeply grieved for having committed them, because I have sinned against a merciful and loving Father, and at the risk of my eternal salvation. Yes! I am sorry for them all, and with my whole heart, but not so much because of the punishment which they deserve as because they have offended thee, O infinite Goodness!

O my supreme and only Good, I love thee, and because I love thee, I lament all the offences which I have been guilty of towards thee. I have neglected thee: I have not paid thee that honor which belongs to thee: I have despised thy favor and thy friendship, and I have deserved to lose thee forever. For Jesus' sake forgive me all my sins! With my whole heart I repent of them. I detest them. I repent not only of every mortal sin which I have ever committed, but also of my venial sins, because by them also I have offended thee. I resolve for the time to come with the help of thy grace, to offend thee no more. Yes! my God, I prefer to die rather than to fall into sin any more.

If you should confess some sin into which you are in especial danger of falling again, make a particular resolution not to commit that one any more. Promise to avoid those occasions which expose you to it, and ask your Father-Confessor to point out to you the surest means of amendment.

PRAYER AFTER CONFESSION

O JESUS, how worthy art thou of my love, and what thanks do I not owe! I hope that through the merits of thy blood, thou hast forgiven me my sins For this I thank thee with my whole heart, and I burn with the desire to praise thy mercy in heaven through all eternity. Until now, O my God, I have offended thee often, but for the time to come, I will never offend thee again. I am anxious to change my life. Thou dost merit all my love, and therefore I will love thee truly and dearly. I will never again be separated from thee. I have already promised thee rather to die than offend thee again. Once more I make this promise, and hope through thy mercy to keep it.

I promise also to shun the occasions of sin, and to take the following means to keep me from falling again (*here name the means*). But thou knowest my weakness, O my God. Give me thy grace, that I may remain true unto thee until my death, and teach me, in the hour of temptation, to have recourse to thee. Mary, help me! Thou art the Mother of perseverance, I place all my hopes in Thee.

Of Holy Communion.

INSTRUCTION.

(*Taken from the writings of St. Alphonsus Liguori.*)

OF all the holy Sacraments, the Sacrament of the Altar is the holiest, the most excellent, and the greatest. The other sacraments contain the graces and gifts of God, but the Sacrament of the Altar contains God himself. Hence the Angelic Doctor St. Thomas Aquinas says: "The other sacraments are established by Jesus Christ, in order to render men fit either for receiving or administering this most holy sacrament, which is the complement of spiritual life, since the whole perfection of our soul proceeds from this same sacrament. For, indeed, the whole perfection of man consists in his union with God; but there is no more powerful means of uniting us with God, than Holy Communion, through which the soul becomes one, as it were, with Jesus, as he himself declared when he said, '*He that eateth my flesh, and drinketh my blood, abideth in me, and I in him.*'" John vi. 57.

The principal effect of this most holy Sacrament is, to preserve in man the life of grace. For this reason it is called bread, because, just as common bread sustains the life of the body, so this heavenly bread preserves the life of the soul, which life is the grace of God. Therefore, according to the Council of Trent, "it is the most powerful remedy to free us from our daily faults, and to preserve us from mortal sin." (Trid. Sess. xiii. c. 2.)

First of all, the Holy Communion infuses into our

hearts the love of God. Jesus Christ has expressly declared that he came into the world for no other cause than to kindle in our hearts the fire of his divine love. "*I am come to cast fire on the earth, and what will I but that it be kindled?*" St. Luke xii. 49. What is there now on the earth that can better inflame the heart of man with divine love, than the Holy Sacrament of the Altar, where the divine Redeemer gives us himself entire? Therefore the holy Council of Trent teaches us that our Saviour in this Sacrament "has poured out all the treasures of his love for us." Sess. xiii. c. 2.

Men should desire nothing more or more ardently than to receive Jesus Christ, as often as possible, in the Holy Communion.

It is known that the first Christians, as St. Luke declares, went daily to the table of the Lord. "*They continued daily with one accord in the temple, and broke bread from house to house.*" Acts, ii. 46. By bread all orthodox interpreters of Scripture understand the Holy Communion. It is further known that the Holy Church in the Council of Trent expressed the wish that the faithful who were present at the sacrifice of the Mass, should receive communion every time not only spiritually, but actually. Sess. xxii. c. 6. It is also known that the greatest saints made use often of Holy Communion as the most effectual means of advancing in piety and virtue.

What shall we say, then, of those Christians who do not conform to the wishes of Jesus Christ and of the holy Catholic Church, and who will not imitate the example of all holy souls? Alas! I know that they excuse themselves with the wretched pretext: We are not worthy to go so often to the table of the Lord.

O my God! if worthiness were to be considered, who would be found truly worthy to receive communion? No one but Jesus Christ would be so, because God alone is worthy to receive God. But I assure you, my dear Christian, that the longer you are absent from communion, all the more unworthy will you be to receive it; the more rarely you go to the table of the Lord, so much the more numerous will be your faults, because you are thus deprived of the principal means of freeing yourself from sin, and amending your life, namely, the Holy Communion.

But perhaps you will answer: "I do not know whether I am in the grace of God, therefore I do not trust myself to receive communion." But tell me what do you then require, in order to know if you are in the grace of God or not? Do you expect that an angel of God will come to tell you? Should it not satisfy you, if your Father-Confessor allows you your communion? Be sure that if your confessor permit you to receive it, you may trust more to that than if all the angels gave you permission, for Jesus Christ has appointed, not the angels, but the priests, to be to you in the place of God.

"But what will people say," you answer, "when they see me going so often to communion? They will either look upon it as a profanation, and blame it, or ridicule me, and make a laughing-stock of me." To this I answer, make your communion as often as your Father-Confessor permits, and with the good intention of advancing in virtue, and let people say what they will. The celebrated John of Avila says, that those who blame others for frequently approaching Holy Communion, perform the office of the devil; and will you be so foolish as to care for them?

Hear, too, what St. Francis of Sales says: "If the children of the world ask you why you so often receive Holy Communion, answer them: Two classes of men should go to communion often; namely, the perfect and the imperfect: the perfect, that they may continue so, and the imperfect, that they may attain perfection

The strong, that they may not become weak, and the weak, that they may become strong. The sick, that they may recover health, and the healthy, that they may not become sick. As for yourself, go often to communion, as one imperfect, sick, and weak."

O my God! of what avail are all these miserable evasions and excuses? Speak the truth, say it outright, that you are not willing to go any oftener to Holy Communion, because then you must quit the vanities and sinful satisfactions of the world, and that you do not love this food of angels, because you still love creatures with inordinate affection; that you do not dare often to receive Jesus Christ, because you fear the reproof which your Saviour might give you, on account of your disorderly and sinful way of life, if you were to receive him often in the most holy Sacrament. But take it seriously into consideration, lest your sinful lukewarmness should be your ruin. Never fear that on your death-bed you will reproach yourself on account of these communions which you have received with contrition and devotion; but fear lest then—alas perhaps too late!—you may repent of having robbed yourself of so many graces, which you might have obtained through the frequent worthy reception of Holy Communion.

Go to communion then, often, my dear Christian, as often as your Father-Confessor will permit you to do so. At least, never omit to receive it on the principal Feast-days.

Live, nevertheless, in such a way that you might go to communion daily; for St Augustine teaches us that such is the desire of the Holy Catholic Church.

PREPARATION FOR COMMUNION.

To go to the table of our Lord, it is necessary: **1st, To be in a state of grace.** Woe to him who would venture to approach the most holy table of the Lord with a conscience stained with mortal sin. Such a bad Christian would be guilty, like the traitor Judas, of sacrilege; for of such an unfortunate one, it is written: "*And after the morsel* (the Holy Communion), *Satan entered into him.*"

Therefore, St. Paul in words of earnest warning says to us: "*But let a man prove himself, and so let him eat of that bread, and drink of the chalice; for he that eateth and drinketh unworthily, eateth and drinketh judgment to himself, not discerning the Body of the Lord.*" 1 Cor. xi. 28.

By this is meant that he who receives communion unwortnily, commits the greatest outrage against the Body and Blood of Jesus Christ, and, like the Jews who killed Jesus Christ, becomes also guilty of his murder.

2. One must live with his neighbors in peace and Christian unity. Communion means *union*, and is so called because it is the image of the perfect union and brotherly love of all the faithful in Christ. Jesus Christ teaches us that we must not bring our sacrifices to the altar, if we remember that our neighbor has any thing against us; with how much greater reason are we bound not to approach the table of the Lord, if we ourselves cherish in our heart a hatred against our neighbor! We must first be reconciled with our enemy.

3. On the evening before communion, you ought to prepare for it by devout prayer, and by reading some pious book, and withdraw, in reverence for the holy Sacrament, from all noisy and distracting amusements.

4. The Body of Christ must be received fasting, that is, we must neither eat nor drink any thing after midnight. But those who are dangerously sick, and receive this holy Sacrament as a viaticum, are dispensed from this.

5. Every one should approach the table of the Lord

with devotion, decently and modestly dressed, and without any vain ornaments, or display of fashion.

PRAYERS BEFORE COMMUNION.

ACT OF FAITH.

"*Behold he cometh, leaping over the mountains.*" Cant. ii. 18.

AH! my dearest Saviour, what wonderful and almost insurmountable difficulties thou hadst to break through, in order that thou mightest come and unite thyself to me in this holy Sacrament! Being God, it was necessary to become man; being infinite, to become an infant; being Lord of all, to become a slave; from the bosom of thy eternal Father, thou must pass into the womb of a virgin, from heaven into a stable, and from thy throne of glory to an infamous gibbet. And this morning again from thy heavenly home thou dost come to dwell in my heart.

"*Behold he standeth behind our wall, looking through the windows, looking through the lattices.*" (Cant. ii. 9.) O my soul, behold thy dear Jesus all burning with that same love which he bore thee, when he died for thee on the cross--behold him now under the sacramental species! Like an ardent lover he gazes upon thee from the consecrated Host, and desires to have thee answer to his love. From there, although himself unseen, he sees thee; closely he watches thee that goest this morning to feed on his sacred flesh, that he may discover what thy thoughts are, what thou lovest best, what thou desirest, what thou wouldst have from him, and what offering thou hast to present him in return.

Courage! O my soul, and prepare thyself to receive Jesus, first by faith, saying: Is it then true, O my Beloved Redeemer, that in a few moments thou wilt come into my heart? O! my God, hidden and unrecognized by the most of men, I believe that thou art really present in the most holy Sacrament of the Altar. I confess thee with my whole heart, and adore thee in this sacrament as my Lord and Saviour, and to confess this truth I would gladly give my life. Thou dost come to enrich me with thy graces, and to unite me wholly to thyself: how great then should be my confidence in a visit so loving as this!

ACT OF CONFIDENCE.

O MY heart, open wide to receive Him! Thy Jesus can enrich thee with all good, he loves thee so much; hope, then, for great favors from thy Saviour, who comes to thee so full of tenderness and love. Yes, dearest Jesus, thou art my hope. This is what I look for from thy love—that since thou givest thyself entirely to me this day, thou wilt enkindle in my heart a beautiful flame of pure love, and excite in me a sincere desire to please thee, that for the time to come my only wish may be to do what is pleasing to thee.

ACT OF LOVE.

O MY God, my God, thou alone art the true friend of my soul. Couldst thou do more to win my love than thou hast done for me? Thou hast not only been willing to die for me, O my Divine Saviour, but thou hast even been pleased to institute this holy sacrament, in order to give me thyself altogether, and thus unite thyself intimately with so mean and ungrateful a creature as I am. But this is not all—thou dost invite me thyself to receive thee, and this is thine ardent desire. O infinite, O incomprehensible love! A God desires to give himself wholly to me! O my soul, dost thou believe this? What art thou doing then? Hast thou nothing to say? O yes, my God! infinite God! worthy of all love, thou alone dost deserve the love of all thy creatures. I love thee with my whole heart. I love thee above all things; I love thee more than my life. O! why can I not see thee loved by all, cherished by all hearts as thou deservest? I love thee, O my God! and in the fervor of my love, I unite my poor heart with the hearts of all the seraphim, and with the heart of Mary, and wish that I might have the same love for thee which all the saints bear thee the same with which thy divine Mother is inflamed. I love only thee, for thou alone deservest all my love. O! blessed Mary, mother of holy love, help to love my God as thou desirest to see him loved.

ACT OF HUMILITY.

SO then, my soul, in a few moments thou art going to nourish thyself with the sacred flesh of Jesus Christ. Art thou then worthy to receive it? O my God, who am I, and who art thou? Indeed, I know well who thou art, thou that givest thyself to me; but thou, Lord, knowest thou who I am, I that am to receive thee?

Is it possible, O my Jesus, that thou who ar purity itself, art so desirous to come and dwel in my soul, which has so often been the dwellin of thine enemy, and loaded with so many sins I acknowledge, O Lord, all thy Majesty, and m own deep misery. I blush and am ashamed t appear before thee; I would in reverence wit draw from thee, but if I leave thee, my Lif whither shall I turn? Where should I seek hel what will become of me? No, no! I will no leave thee. I will rather draw nearer and nearer to thee every day. Thou lovest to have me receive thee for my food, and ever invitest me Well, then, I come, O my dearest Saviour! Yes ashamed and deeply humbled by my sins, but full of confidence in thy mercy and thy love to me, I come to receive thee into my heart this day.

ACT OF SORROW.

IT grieves me deeply, O God of my soul, that hitherto I have not loved thee, that instead of loving thee I have frequently even offended and displeased thy infinite goodness, in order to satisfy my wicked inclinations. I have abandoned thee, in contempt of thy grace and of thy friendship: in a word, I have lost thee, O my God, and that willfully. I am sorry for it; yes, Lord, my whole soul is full of grief. I hate and detest all the sins that I have committed, both mortal and venial; I detest them more than any other evil, because they have injured thee who art infinitely good. I hope that thou hast already forgiven me, but if it be not so, O forgive me before I receive thee; cleanse, O my God, with thy precious blood, this soul into which thou art coming soon to dwell.

ACT OF DESIRE.

HAVE courage, my soul. See! the happy moment has arrived, and thy Jesus is coming to dwell in thy heart. Behold the Lord of heaven and of earth, thy Saviour and thy God who is drawing nigh to thee, and who intends to visit thee. Prepare thyself to receive him lovingly, invite him with burning desires, and say to him: Come, O Jesus, come into this heart that longs for thee; but before thou givest thyself to me, I will first give myself to thee; see! I give up to thee this poor heart, receive it, and hasten to take possession of it.

Come, O my God, come promptly and without delay! My only and infinite good, my treasure, my life, my paradise, my love, my all! O that I could receive thee with that same love wherewith all the holiest and most ardent souls have received thee until now, and with which the most holy Virgin Mary received thee. I unite this communion of mine with theirs.

O most holy Virgin, Mary my Mother, see, I am going now to receive thy divine Son. I wish I might have thy heart in this moment, and that love with which thou didst make communion. Give thy Jesus this morning to me, as thou didst give him to the Shepherds, and to the three holy Kings. I desire to receive him from thy pure hands. Tell him that I am thy devoted servant, then he will love me more, and unite me more closely in this happy moment to himself.

When the Priest elevates the most Sacred Host, repeat with him three times the following words:

O LORD, I am not worthy that thou shouldst come under my roof, but say only the word, and my soul shall be healed.

Then with your eyes modestly cast down, but your head erect, open your mouth, and advance your tongue a little, and thus receive the Holy Sacrament. Be sure not to make any hasty movement with your mouth, but let the Priest himself lay it upon your tongue. Endeavor to swallow the holy Host by means of the moisture on your tongue, without touching it with your teeth, and least of all with your finger. If other communicants are still coming, and need to occupy your place, then, shortly after receiving, but not immediately, retire and make room for them; otherwise, especially when the Communion is given out of Mass, you may remain until the Priest gives his benediction.

THANKSGIVING AFTER COMMUNION.

There is no prayer more acceptable to God and more profitable to our own souls, than that which is offered in thanksgiving after holy Communion. Christ our Saviour remains present with us until the sacramental species are consumed. During these sacred moments, we may imagine that we hear from the mouth of Jesus Christ himself these words, which he spake formerly to his disciples: "*But me ye have not always with you.*" S. John, xii. 8.

It is not well immediately after Communion to begin reading in a book; it is far better to pass some few moments in a solitary and confidential conversation with Jesus Christ, thus kindly present in our heart, and to give silent encouragement to those emotions and desires which naturally arise. It will not do, however, to lose this precious time; and if the mind begins to wander, we must fix our attention immediately by means of the Prayer-Book.

O what treasures of grace can a pious soul obtain if she converses in spirit with her beloved Jesus at least a half-hour after holy Communion!

During the rest of the day the devout soul should often think of that great guest, whom she has received in her communion.

PRAYERS AFTER COMMUNION.

ACT OF FAITH.

BEHOLD! already my God is come to visit me, already my Saviour is come to dwell in my soul, already my Jesus is within me; he is come to be one with me, and to make me one with him, so that Jesus now belongs to me, and I belong to Jesus. Yes! Jesus is all mine, and I am all his. O infinite goodness! O infinite mercy! O infinite love! a God has united himself with me, a God who desires to be wholly mine! O my soul, now that thou art so closely united to Jesus, now that thou art one with him, what art thou doing? Hast thou nothing to say to him, wilt thou not speak to thy God who is present within thee? Awaken then thy faith anew, remember that the angels are around about thee adoring their God, who now dwells in thy heart. Adore thy Lord with them! Keep recollected, and banish every other thought call together all thy affections, and lay them before thy God, and say to him:

ACT OF WELCOME.

O MY Jesus! my love, my infinite Good, my all, I welcome thee; be always welcome to this home which I keep for thee in my poor heart. Ah! Lord. where art thou, whither hast thou come? Into my heart, worse than the stable where thou wast born; into my heart full of attachments, of self-love, and of disorderly appetites. How couldst thou choose such a dwelling as this? Well might I say to thee with St. Peter: *Depart from me, O Lord, for I am a sinner:* I am too unworthy to have a God of infinite goodness for my guest. Go rather repose in those pure souls, who serve thee with so much love. But no, my Redeemer, what do I say? Do not depart from me, for if thou leave me I am lost. I embrace thee, O my life, I attach myself inseparably to thee. I have been only too foolish in separating myself from thee for love of creatures; ungrateful wretch that I am, I have driven thee away from my heart. But now I will never separate myself from thee any more, I am resolved to live and die united to thee.

Most holy Virgin Mary, seraphs, souls who love God with a pure love, lend me your affections, that I may entertain my dear Lord as ought.

ACT OF THANKSGIVING.

I THANK thee, O my Lord and my God, for the grace which thou hast shown to me this morning by coming to dwell in my soul. Would that I could thank thee in a manner worthy of thee, and of the signal favor which I have received! But what do I say? what worthy thanks could I render thee, miserable creature that I am?

Father Segneri says that the most suitable affection for a soul after communion, is the wonder which gives rise to this thought: a God mine! a God mine! "*What shall I render to the Lord for all that he hath rendered to me?*" So said David: and I, what shall I render to thee, O my Jesus, to thee, who after so many favors, hast given me thyself this morning? Therefore, O my soul, bless thy God, and thank him with all thy power. And thou, Mary my mother, and you my patron Saints, my Guardian Angel, and all ye souls who burn with divine love, "*come and I will tell you what good things the Lord hath done to my soul.*" Come bless and thank my God for me, and admire the wondrous grace which I have received.

ACT OF SELF-OFFERING.

"*MY Beloved to me, and I to him.*" (Cant. i. 16.) If a king were to come and visit a poor shepherd in his hut, what could the shepherd offer him but his hut such as it is? Since then, O my divine King Jesus, thou art come to visit this poor house of my soul, I offer thee my house, and my whole self, with my liberty and my will. "*My Beloved to me, and I to him.*" Thou hast given thyself all to me, I give myself all to thee. No more, my Jesus, will I be my own; henceforth I wish to belong to thee, entirely to thee, and that all my senses may be so entirely thine, that they may serve only to please thee. And indeed, what greater pleasure can one have, said St. Peter of Alcantara, than to please thee, God most amiable, most loving and most grateful. I give up to thee all the powers of my soul, that they may be all and altogether thine. Let my memory serve only to recall thy benefits and thy love, my mind to think of thee alone, who thinkest always of my welfare, my heart to love only thee, my God, my all, and to will only that which thou willest.

To thee, then, O my dearest Saviour, I consecrate and immolate all I have, all I am, my senses, my thoughts, my affections, my desires, my tastes, my inclinations, my liberty—in a word, I give up my body and soul into thy hands. Receive, O infinite Majesty, this sacrifice made to thee here, by the most ungrateful sinner that ever existed on earth, who now, however, offers and gives himself all to thee. O Lord, do with me and dispose of me according to thy pleasure.

Come, O burning fire, O love divine, and consume in me all there is of me which is not pleasing to thy pure eyes, so that hereafter I may be all to thee, may live only to accomplish thy commandments and thy counsels, thy holy desires and thy good pleasure in all things. *Amen.*

O most holy Mary! do thou present with thine own hands, this my offering to the Most Holy Trinity; obtain for me the acceptance of it, and that I may have the grace to be faithful until death. *Amen, Amen, Amen.*

ACT OF PETITION.

O MY soul, what art thou doing now? Thou must not lose a moment of time, for this time is precious, for thou now canst very easily obtain all the graces thou wilt ask.

Seest thou not how lovingly the Eternal Father looks upon thee, now that he beholds in thy heart his beloved Son, the object of his most tender love? Banish then every other thought, awaken thy faith, open thy heart, and ask whatever thou wilt. Dost thou not hear how Jesus himself says to thee: "What wilt thou have me do for thee? Speak, beloved soul, what dost thou desire of me? I have come in order to make thee rich and happy; ask with confidence, and thou shalt receive every thing thou desirest."

Ah! my dearest Saviour, since thou art come to me to fill me with graces, and desirest me to ask them of thee, I ask for no earthly goods, nor riches, nor honors, nor pleasures. Give me, I beseech thee, a great sorrow for all the displeasure which thou hast received from me. Give me a great light to show me the vanity of the world.

and now much thou art worthy of being loved. Change my heart, detach it from all earthly affections, and give me a heart perfectly conformed to thy holy will, which seeks after thy good pleasure alone, and aspires to nothing else than to thy holy love.

I do not deserve all this, O my Jesus, but thou deservest it, thou who hast come to dwell in my soul. I ask it through thy merits, through the merits of thy holy Mother, and by the love thou bearest to thy eternal Father.

Here pause for a time, and ask of Jesus some special grace for yourself or your neighbor. Do not forget poor sinners, and the souls in purgatory

Eternal Father! Jesus Christ himself has said to us "Amen, amen, I say to you; if you ask the Father any thing in my name, he will give it you." John xvi. 23. For love of this thy divine Son, who now dwells in my heart, hear me, and grant me what I now ask.

Objects of my dearest love, Jesus and Mary! let me suffer for you, let me die for you, grant that I may belong wholly to you, and never to myself any more.

Praised and blessed forever be the most holy Sacrament of the Altar, and blessed be the holy and immaculate conception of the most holy Virgin Mary.

OF SPIRITUAL COMMUNION.

Spiritual Communion, which unhappily at the present day is so little practised by Christians, is so excellent a treasure of devotion, that, according to the opinion of many saints, it can produce in the soul, when made aright, something like the same grace as the actual reception of the most holy Sacrament of the Altar; that is to say, when we are prevented from receiving communion in reality.

In order to receive Holy Communion spiritually, nothing farther is necessary than to excite in the heart a very earnest desire to receive it in reality, if it were possible. St. Thomas Aquinas teaches that spiritual communion consists in an ardent desire to receive Jesus Christ in the most holy Sacrament, and in an intimate union of affection with him, as if one had actually received him.

The holy Council of Trent bestows especial praises upon this kind of communion, and encourages all the faithful to make it, particularly during holy Mass, when they do not receive the sacrament in reality.

According to this, God will bestow great graces upon those who are desirous to receive Jesus Christ their loving Redeemer, but frequently cannot; but who make at least the spiritual communion. This can be done very frequently, at any hour, any moment, and at all places. One can make it without being observed by any one, without being obliged to fast, and without the permission of a spiritual director.

This Spiritual Communion may be made in the following form:

ACT OF SPIRITUAL COMMUNION.

O MY Jesus, I believe that thou art truly present in this holy sacrament. I love thee above all things, and I desire thee with my whole soul, but since I cannot now receive thee sacramentally, come at least spiritually into my heart. I embrace thee as if thou wert already come, I unite myself wholly to thee. Never suffer me to be separated from thee!

It is necessary, however, to remark that any one who should know himself to be in mortal sin, would make this holy exercise in vain. Indeed, it would be no small offence for the sinner to embrace spiritually that sacred Host, which it would be an awful sacrilege to receive in reality. It is, nevertheless, always right for such persons to pray before the Holy Sacrament, and to lament that they are unworthy to receive it. They may, perhaps, obtain the grace of conversion by the following prayer:

ACT OF REGRET.

O HOLY Lord Jesus Christ, I believe that thou art truly present in this Holy Sacrament. Alas! for me, that I am in mortal sin, and dare not go forward to receive thee with the rest; O forgive me all my sins, and restore me to thy grace, that I may become worthy of this heavenly food Yes! my Saviour, yes! I am resolved. I will go and confess my sins, fully and sincerely, and then I will come to meet thee here at this holy table, never to separate from thee again.

PARTICULAR DEVOTIONS.

Devotion to the Blessed Sacrament.

(*From the Visits of St. Liguori.*)

Faith teaches, and we are bound to believe, that Jesus Christ is really present in the consecrated Host, under the appearance of bread. But we must know, also, that he remains on our altars, as on a throne of love and mercy, there to dispense his graces to us, and to show his love. He remains with us night and day, in this hidden manner, that Christians may visit him in the Church, and by their devotions, their thanksgivings and affections, gratefully acknowledge and honor the loving presence of Jesus Christ, dwelling in the Sacrament of the Altar. In the following visits you will find many examples of the tender affection with which souls inflamed with the love of God, desired to remain in the presence of the most Holy Sacrament. You will find that all the saints have been enamored of this sweet devotion. On this earth we cannot find a more brilliant jewel, or a more lovely treasure, than Jesus in the Sacrament. O how delightful it is to remain with faith, and with a tender devotion, at the foot of the altar, and to converse familiarly with Jesus Christ who dwells in our tabernacles, for the purpose of hearing the prayers of all who visit him! How delightful to implore his pardon for our offences, to lay before him all our wants, as one friend does to another in whom he places all his confidence, to ask his grace, his love, and his glory! But O what a Paradise to continue in acts of love to that Lord, who remains on the altar interceding before his Father in our behalf, and burning with love for us. Blessed Henry Suso used to say, that Jesus, on the altar, hears the prayers of the faithful more readily than he does in any other place. Make a trial of this devotion, and you will see the great fruit which you will gather from it. Be sure that of all the moments of your life, the time which you spend in devotion before this divine Sacrament will be that which shall give you the greatest support during life, and the greatest consolation at the hour of death, and for all eternity. And be persuaded that you will gain more in a quarter of an hour spent in prayer before the Holy Eucharist, than in all the other spiritual exercises of the day.

Do not then, O devout soul, refuse to begin this devotion. From this day forward, retire each day from the conversation of men, and remain for some time, for a half-hour, or at least a quarter, in some church, before Jesus Christ in the Holy Sacrament.

VISITS TO THE BL. SACRAMENT.

(*For every day in the week.*)

PRAYER BEFORE EACH VISIT.

O JESUS Christ, my Lord, who, for the love which thou bearest to men, dost dwell night and day in this Sacrament, full of goodness and love, waiting for, inviting and welcoming all those who come to visit thee, I believe thee here presen in the Sacrament of the Altar. From the dee abyss of my own nothingness, I adore thee an

I thank thee for all thy graces granted to me hitherto, and especially for having given thyself to me in this Sacrament, for having given me also thy holy Mother Mary, to be my advocate, and for having called me to visit thee in this church. I adore thy most loving heart this day and I adore it with this threefold intention: first, in thanksgiving for so great a gift; secondly, to make satisfaction for so many injuries which thou hast received from thy enemies in this Sacrament; and thirdly, by this visit I wish to adore thee in all those places throughout the world, where thou art least honored, and most neglected in this divine Sacrament. My Jesus, I love thee with my whole heart! I am sorry for having offended thy infinite goodness so often in time past. I am resolved, by the help of thy grace to offend thee no more for the future; and at this present moment, all miserable as I am, I consecrate myself entirely to thee. I give and abandon to thee my whole will, all my affections my desires, and all I have. Hereafter, do with me, and with mine, whatever thou wilt. My only desire and petition is, that I may have thy holy love, the grace of final perseverance, and may be able to fulfill in all things thy holy will. I recommend to thee the souls in purgatory, especially those who have been most devout to thee in this Holy Sacrament, and to the Blessed

Virgin Mary. I recommend to thee, moreover, all poor sinners. Finally, my dear Redeemer, I unite all my desires to the desires of thy own heart so full of love; and thus united, I offer them to thy eternal Father, and beseech him in thy name to receive them, and for thy love's sake to grant them.

FOR SUNDAY.

Behold the source of every good, Jesus in the Blessed Sacrament, who says to us: "*If any man thirst, let him come to me.*" S. Jo. vii. 37. O! how many graces have the saints always drawn at this fountain of the most Holy Sacrament, where Jesus dispenses to us all the merits of his passion, as the Prophet foretold: "*You shall draw waters with joy out of the Saviour's fountains.*" (Isai. xii. 3.) The Countess of Feria, that distinguished discipl of the Venerable Father Avila, who became a Nun of the order of St. Clare, and was named the Bride of the Blessed Sacrament, on account of her long and frequen devotions in presence of the most blessed Sacrament, was asked one day, what she was doing all those long hours she spent in the presence of her Lord? She replied: "I would remain there for all eternity. Have I not there the essence of God, who will be the aliment of the blessed in heaven? Good God! what is one doing before him? Ah! rather, what does one not do? One loves, one praises, one gives thanks, one prays. What does a beggar in presence of a rich man? What does a sick man in presence of his physician? What does a thirsty man before a fountain of pure water? What does a hungry man before a table well prepared?"

O MOST lovely, most sweet, and dearest Jesus! life, hope, treasure, and only love of my soul. O! how much has it not cost thee to remain with us in this Sacrament! It was necessary for thee to die in order to remain afterwards upon our altars; and how many injuries hast thou not been made to suffer, in consequence of this presence among us! But thy love, and thy desire to be loved by us, have surmounted all. Come, then, Lord, come and occupy my heart, and afterwards close the gate to it for ever, so that no creature may ever enter there again to take away a part of this love which belongs entirely to thee, and which I am unwilling to give to any other. Do thou alone, my dear Redeemer, reign over me! Do thou alone possess me entirely; and if at any time I should not obey thee perfectly, punish me severely, that for the future I may be more careful to please thee, according to thy desire. Let me no more desire nor seek for any other pleasure than to please thee, to visit thee often at thy altar, to converse with thee, and to receive thee in the holy communion. Let them look for other oods who will! For me, I love only, I desire nly the treasure of thy love. The only favor I sk at the foot of this altar is, that I may forget nyself altogether, only to remember thy goodess. Blessed Seraphs, I do not envy you your lory! but by the love which you bear to your od and mine, O teach me what I must do, to ove him and please him like you!

Short prayer to remember and repeat.--O ny Jesus, thee only I love, thee only will lease!

o conclude, make your spiritual Communion. (See, at the end of Devotions for Communion, page 114.)

FOR MONDAY.

Jesus addresses to every soul that visits him n the most Holy Sacrament, the same words ddressed to the sacred Spouse of the Canticles: *Arise, make haste! my love, my beautiful one, nd come.*" (Cant. ii.) Soul, who comest to visit e, arise! come out from all thy misery; I am ere to enrich thee with graces. Come near to ne: do not fear my majesty, which has humbled tself in this Sacrament, in order to take away ny fear, and to inspire thee with confidence Thou art my friend. Yes! no longer my enemy, but my beloved friend, since thou lovest me, and I love thee also. Thou art my beautiful one, for my grace has made thee beautiful. Come then, come and unite thyself to me, and with th greatest confidence ask what thou wilt. It is St Theresa who says that this great King of glory has put on the appearance of bread in the Holy Sacrament, and hidden his majesty from ou eyes, in order to encourage us to approach with more confidence to his divine heart.

Let us draw near, then, with great confidenc and love. Let us unite ourselves to him, and ask him for his holy grace.

WHAT joy ought mine to be, O eternal Wor made man, and become Sacrament for me knowing that I am in thy presence, that thou ar my God, that thou art infinite in majesty, infini in goodness, and that thou hast such a tender re gard for my soul? O! all ye souls who lo God, wherever you are, in heaven or on earth love him for me too! Mary, my Mother, hel me to love him! and thou, most loving Lor render thyself the object of all my affections make away with all my will: take possession me entirely. I consecrate to thee my who mind, so that I may think always of thy goo ness; I consecrate to thee my body also, so th it may assist me to please thee; I consecrate thee my soul, so that it may be always thin How I desire, O Beloved of my soul, that al men knew the tenderness of thy love to them They would then all live only to honor and pleas hee, as thou desirest, and deservest. As for me, t least, let me live always thus, charmed with ny infinite beauty! I desire to do all in my ower hereafter, to make myself agreeable in ny sight.

I resolve, moreover, to abandon any thing, no natter what it may be, so soon as I shall know hat such is thy desire, no matter what suffering t may cause me, if I were called even to lose ny life. Happy would I be to lose all and gain hee, O my God, my treasure, my love, my all!

Short prayer to remember and repeat.—Jesus, ny love, take me entirely, possess me entirely.

The Spiritual Communion, as before, page 114.

FOR TUESDAY.

"*In that day*," says the Prophet, "*there shall e a fountain open to the house of David, and to he inhabitants of Jerusalem, for the washing of e sinner.*" (Zach. xiii. 1.) Jesus in the Blessed acrament is this fountain foretold by the Prophet, hich is open to all, and where, as often as we ke, we can wash away from our souls all those ots with which they are contaminated by daily n. What better remedy can we find for any ault into which we have fallen, than to have mmediate recourse to the Blessed Sacrament? Yes, y Jesus, so will I always do, for well I know that the water of this salutary fountain, a the same time that it washes my soul, will giv me the light and strength to fall no more; an while it inflames me with thy love, will teach m to suffer adversity with joy. This is the reason I know it well, why thou dost wait for my visit here, and why thou payest the visits of thos that love thee with such abundant graces. Be i so then, O my Jesus! wash away all the fault which I have committed this day, and which am now sorry for, because they have displease thee. Give me the strength not to fall agai and give me also an ardent desire to love the more than I do. O! why can I not be near the always, like thy faithful servant Mary Diaz, wh lived in the time of St. Theresa, and who obtain of the Bishop of Avila the permission to dwell i the gallery of the church? There she remaine almost always in presence of the Blessed Sacra ment, which she called her neighbor never goin out from there except for confession or comm nion. The venerable brother Francis of the I fant Jesus, barefooted Carmelite, whenever h passed before a church where the Holy Sacr ment was kept, could not help entering to vis it, for he said it was not becoming for one t pass before the house of his friend without going in to greet him, and to say one word at least But he was not contented with a word, he alway emained in presence of his dearly beloved Lord as long as he was permitted.

MY only, my infinite good! I understand full well why thou hast been pleased to institute this Sacrament, and to remain thus upon his altar—it is to gain my love, and for the same reason thou hast given me a heart capable of loving much. Why, then, thankless sinner that I am, do I not love thee, or why do I love thee so little? No! it is not just to love feebly, goodness so worthy of love as thine. Thy love to me deserves a far greater return of love on my part. Thou art the infinite God, and I am only a miserable worm of the earth. It would be but little if I were to die, and to become annihilated for thee, since for me thou hast died, and for love of me thou dost sacrifice thyself daily upon the altar. Much thou deservest to be loved, and I desire to love thee much. Help me, my Jesus, help me to love thee, that thus I may do what is so pleasing in thy sight, and that thou demandest so earnestly of me.

Short prayer to remember and repeat.—My beloved is mine, and I am his.

The Spiritual Communion, page 114.

FOR WEDNESDAY.

St. Paul, praising the obedience of Jesus Christ, says that he was "*obedient unto death*" to his Eternal Father. (Phil. ii.) But in this Sacrament our divine Lord has carried his obedience farther still, for he is content to obey not only his Eternal Father, but even man himself, and not only until death, but even unto the end of the world. He has made himself obedient, one may say, until the consummation of ages. King of Heaven as he is, he comes down, nevertheless, out of obedience to man, and remains afterwards upon the altar, only, as it would seem, out of obedience to man. "*As for me,*" he says by his Prophet, "*I make no resistance.*" (Isai. l. 5.) There he remains without any movement of his own; he allows himself to be placed wherever they may choose to place him whether exposed to view in the ostensorium, or shut up in the ciborium; he lets himself be carried where they please to carry him, either through the street, or in the house; he allows himself to be given in communion to every one as they think fit to give him—to the just or the sinner. When he was living on the earth as St. Luke tells us, he was obedient to the Blessed Virgin Mary and to St. Joseph, but in this Sacrament he obeys as many creatures as there are priests on the earth—"*As for me, I make no resistance.*"

O LISTEN while I venture to address thee most loving heart of my Jesus! heart from hich so many sacraments have issued, and specially this Sacrament of Love! Would that could procure as much honor and glory for hee as thou dost promote the honor and glory f thy Eternal Father by means of the holy acrament in our churches! I know that on is altar thou dost love me with that same love hich moved thee to sacrifice thy divine life for e in a sea of sorrows on the cross. Enlighten, divine Heart! those who do not know thee, order that they may know thee. Deliver rough thy merits all who are in Purgatory, or t least comfort those suffering souls which thou st already chosen to be thy spouses for eterni-. I adore thee, I thank thee, and I love thee ith all the souls that love thee in this moment, hether on earth or in heaven. O! most pure nd holy Heart of Jesus, purify my heart from l attachment to creatures, and fill it with thy oly love. O! most tender Heart of Jesus, take ossession of my whole heart, in such a way that may be all thine own, and may always be ble to repeat with confidence, "*Who shall sepa-te me from the love of God which is in Jesus hrist?*" (Rom. viii.) O! most holy Heart, ngrave in my heart those bitter pains which hou didst suffer on the earth for so many years, and with such great love for me, so that, moved o compassion at the sight, I may always desire, or at least suffer with patience for thy sake, a the pains of this life. O! most humble Hea of Jesus, impart to me thy spirit of humilit O! most gentle Heart of Jesus, lend me som thing of thy gentleness. Take away from m heart all that does not please thee, convert it e tirely to thee, so that it may will nothing, wi nothing, except what thou wilt. In a word (dispose of me that I may live only to obey the to love thee, and to please thee. I acknowled that I am most deeply in thy debt; yes, tha am bound to thee by the heaviest obligatio and it would be still only a small return if could annihilate and sacrifice myself entirely f thee.

Short prayer to remember and repeat.—O Hea of Jesus, thou only shalt be master in my hear

Spiritual Communion, page 114.

FOR THURSDAY.

God having given us his own Son (so reasons Paul,) *how can we fear that he will ever refuse any thing?* (Rom. viii.) And this all the mo *since we know that the eternal Father has gi all things into his hands.* (St. John, xiii.) L us then always thank the goodness, the merc and the bounty of our most gracious God, wh has been pleased to enrich us with every goo and every grace, by giving us Jesus Christ in th

.crament of the Altar. (1 Cor. i.) Have I not ·od reason then to think, O Saviour of the ɔrld, O incarnate Word, that thou art mine, .d if I desire it, wholly mine? But can I say truly that I am wholly thine as thou wouldst .ve me? Ah! my Lord, grant that the worl' ay be no longer witness to this injustice an. gratitude which I show thee by not yielding yself up entirely to thee, according to thy de- ·e.

Ah! let it be so no more. Let the future be nething far different from the past. To-day th the most steadfast resolution, I consecrate ·self all to thee. I consecrate to thee my life, · will, my thoughts, my actions, and my suffer- ;s, while time lasts, and eternally. Behold! I ı all thine; like a victim devoted to thee, I de- :h myself from creatures, and offer myself all thee: consume me with the flames of thy di- ıe love. No! I am unwilling that creatures ›uld any longer have a place in my heart. The ɑy marks of love which thou hast given me, ən when I did not love thee,—these make me ›e with confidence that thou wilt accept me w that I do love thee, and give myself away to əe through love.

ᒣTERNAL Father! I offer thee to-day all l the virtues, the acts, and the affections of the eart of Jesus. Accept them on my behalf·

and through his merits which are all mine, sir he has given them to me, grant me those grac which Jesus asks for me. For all thy merci shown to me, I offer thee my thanks, in uni with those same merits. Through them als hope to satisfy for what is still due to thy just for my sins. Through them, finally, I hope every grace at thy hand, for pardon, for per verance, for paradise, and above all, for the g of thy pure love. I see clearly that in all I I only put obstacles in the way of this, but this evil apply a remedy also. I ask it of t in the name of Jesus Christ, who has promised *that thou wilt grant all we ask of thee in his na* (St. John, xiv.,) and therefore thou canst not fuse me. Lord! my only desire is to love th to give myself entirely to thee, and no longer remain so ungrateful as I have been hither Look upon me, and grant my prayer. Fr this very day may I be thoroughly converted thee, never to fall away from thy love ag My God, I love thee! Infinite Goodness, I l thee! I love thee, for thou art indeed my lo my paradise, my good, my life, my all.

Short prayer to remember and repeat.—M Jesus! my all! it is thy will to have me thir and my will is to have thee mine.

Spiritua Communion, page 114.

FOR FRIDAY.

"*Why hidest thou thy face?*" (Job, xiv.) Job
filled with alarm when he saw that God had
d his face fr m him ; but if Jesus Christ in the
sed Sacrament hides his majesty from our
es, we have no reason to be afraid, but to be
imated all the more with confidence and love.
is only to manifest his love more clearly, and
inspire us with greater confidence, says Nova-
io, that he hides himself under the semblance
bread and stations himself on the altar. For
io, indeed, would ever dare to approach with
nfidence, and make known all his desires and
ections, if this King of Heaven were to appear
the altar with full splendor and glory ?

H! my Jesus, what an invention of love is
this Blessed Sacrament! Thou hidest thy-
lf under the appearance of bread, in order to
in our love, and so that every one who seeks
thee, may find thee even here on earth. It is
without great reason that the Prophet calls
us to proclaim to the whole world the inven-
ns of that love which our God has for us. (Isa.
. 4.) O Heart of Jesus, full of love, and wor-
y to possess the hearts of all creatures! Heart
ways full of the flames of purest love! O burn-
g fire that thou art, consume me wholly, and
e me a new life of love and of grace! Unite

me to thyself in such a way that I may nev separate from thee again. Heart of Jesus! op refuge for souls, receive me, Heart of Jesus, afflicted on the cross for the sins of the wor give me a true sorrow for my sins. I know th in this divine sacrament thou preservest the sar sentiments of love which thou didst feel in dyi for me on Calvary, and therefore thou dost a dently wish me to be united to thee. Can I th any longer refuse to yield myself up entirely thy love, to thy desire? Ah! my beloved J sus, by thy own merits I entreat thee, wound m soul with thy love, and bind and unite me e tirely to thy heart. I resolve this day, with th assistance of thy grace, to do all in my power please thee, and for thy sake to trample und foot all human respect, every inclination or r pugnance, all pleasures and comforts, which ma be in any way hindrances to the perfect accor plishment of thy will. Grant, O Lord, that may keep this resolution, so that henceforth a my actions, and all my feelings and affectior may be in all things conformable to thy will. Love of God, banish from my heart all other lov O Mary, my hope, thou art all powerful wi God, obtain for me the grace to be until death t faithful servant of Jesus and of his pure lov Amen! amen! Behold my hope and my desir for time and for eternity.

Short prayer to remember and repeat.—"Who hall separate me from the charity of Christ?"

The Spiritual Communion, page 114.

FOR SATURDAY.

O how beautiful a sight it was to behold our ear Redeemer that day when, "*weary with his iourney*," but full of sweetness and love, he was eated by the fountain, waiting for the Samaritan voman, to convert and save her! "*Jesus there- ore sat thus on the well.*" (St. John, iv. 6.) Does t not seem that the same thing is repeated every ay, when descending from heaven upon our altars, ie remains there as if by the side of so many ountains of grace, waiting for souls, and inviting nem to keep him company for a little while at east, that he may draw them in this way to his perfect love? From each altar where Jesus lwells in the Blessed Sacrament, he seems to peak to us, and say: Christians, why do you fly rom my presence? Why will you not come, why will you not draw near to one who loves you so tenderly, and who humbles himself to re- nain in this place for your sake? What do you ear? I am not come to judge you, but I am hidden in this Sacrament of Love only to do good, and to save every one who will have re- course to me. "*I came not to judge the world, but to save the world.*" St. John, xii. 47.

Let us then be persuaded that as Jesus Christ in heaven "*is always living to make intercession for us*" (Heb. vii.), so in the Sacrament of the Altar he is fulfilling night and day the office of our advocate, offering himself as a victim to his eternal Father, to obtain for us mercy and graces without number. Hence, the devout à Kempis says that we ought to pray to Jesus in the Bless ed Sacrament as one speaks to a beloved friend: "*As lover speaks to one beloved, as friend to friend.*"

SO then, O my Lord and King, hidden in this Sacrament, since thou dost invite me to converse with thee, I will open my heart with confidence, and speak. O my Jesus, ardent lover of souls, I know too well the injustice and ingratitude of men towards thee. Thou lovest them, and they do not love thee: thou dost confer benefits on them, and they return thee insults: thou wouldst have them hear thy voice, and they will not listen: thou dost offer them graces, and they refuse them. Ah! my Jesus, I too have been once among the number of these ungrateful souls. O my God, it is only too true. But I desire to amend, and I wish to compensate for the injuries I have done thee, by doing all I can to please thee for the remainder of my life. Tell me, O Lord, what thou dost require of me. I will do it without the least reserve. Make known to me thy will by the way of holy obedience, and I hope to accomplish it. My God! I firmly promise never to leave undone any act which I know to be agreeable to thee, although the performance of it should cost me the loss of all things, of relations, friends, character, health, and even life itself. Let me lose all, if only I may do thy will! Happy loss, when all is sacrificed to content thy heart, O God of my soul! I love thee, O sovereign good, above all goods worthy of my love, and in loving thee I unite my feeble heart with the hearts of all the Seraphim. I unite it with the heart of Mary, and with the heart of Jesus. I love thee with my whole soul; I wish to love thee alone, now and forever.

Short prayer to remember and repeat.—My God! my God! I am thine, and thou art mine.

The Spiritual Communion, page 114.

The Way of the Cross.

It was a very frequent and most touching devotion of Christians in former times to make a pilgrimage to the Holy Land of Palestine, where our Blessed Redeemer lived and died, and there to visit every spot of ground which had been made sacred by his presence, and especially those which were known as the stations of his passion and death, and to honor these holy places by prayer and by penance. Afterwards, when the Holy Land had fallen into the hands of the infidel Saracens, and Christians could no longer make this pilgrimage with safety, this exercise of the Way of the Cross was invented as a substitute. Pictures representing the most moving and remarkable events of our Lord's passion, from the time of his sentence to his burial, are hung about the walls of the church, and by visiting these in succession, and praying before each one, we are able in some manner to imitate the devotion of Catholics of other days, although by a pilgrimage far less long and painful. The Way of the Cross, in its present form, was instituted in the middle of the fourteenth century, by the Franciscans. The Sovereign Pontiffs have attached to it many indulgences, which are too numerous to mention here. Any one who is in a state of grace may gain these indulgences by making the round of these fourteen stations, meditating before each one upon the mystery it represents. No form of prayer is required, nor is it necessary that these meditations should be long. (S. C Ind. 22 Sept., 1829 do. 7 April, 1831.)

The following beautiful method of performing this devotion is from the pen of St. Alphonsus.

PRAYER BEFORE THE HIGH ALTAR.

O JESUS Christ, my Lord, with what great love thou didst pass over this painful road, which led thee to death; and I—how often have I abandoned thee! But now, I love thee with my whole soul, and because I love thee, I am sincerely sorry for having offended thee. My Jesus, pardon me, and permit me to accompany thee in this journey. Thou art going to die for love of me, and it is my wish also, O my dearest Redeemer, to die for love of thee. O yes, my Jesus, in thy love I wish to live, in thy love I wish to die.

FIRST STATION.

Jesus is condemned to death.

℣. We adore Thee, O Christ, and praise Thee
℟. Because by thy holy Cross Thou hast redeemed the world.

Consider how Jesus, after having been scourged and crowned with thorns, was unjustly condemned by Pilate to die on the Cross. (*Pause awhile.*)

MY adorable Jesus, it was not Pilate; no, it was my sins that condemned thee to die. I beseech thee, by the merits of this sorrowful journey, to assist my soul in her journey towards eternity. I love Thee, my beloved Jesus; I love Thee more than myself; I repent with my whole heart of having offended Thee. Never permit me to separate myself from Thee again. Grant that I may love Thee always; and then do with me what Thou wilt.

Our Father. Hail Mary. Glory be, &c.

Jesus! for the love of me
You go to die on Calvary;
Let me, Jesus, follow too,
That I may suffer, Lord, with you.

SECOND STATION.

Jesus is made to bear his Cross.

V. We adore Thee, O Christ, and praise Thee.

R. Because by thy Holy Cross Thou hast redeemed the world.

Consider how Jesus, in making this journey with the cross on his shoulders, thought of us, and offered for us to his Father the death He was about to undergo. (*Pause awhile.*)

MY most beloved Jesus! I embrace all the tribulations Thou hast destined for me until death. I beseech Thee, by the merits of the pain Thou didst suffer in carrying Thy Cross, to give me the necessary help to carry mine with perfect patience and resignation. I love Thee, Jesus, my love, above all things; I repent with my whole heart of having offended Thee. Never permit me to separate myself from Thee again. Grant that I may love Thee always, and then do with me what Thou wilt.

Our Father. Hail Mary. Glory be, &c.

Jesus! for the love of me
You go to die on Calvary;
Let me, Jesus, follow too,
That I may suffer, Lord, with you.

THIRD STATION.

Jesus falls the first time under his Cross.

V. We adore Thee, O Christ, and praise Thee.

R. Because by thy Holy Cross Thou hast redeemed the world.

Consider this first fall of Jesus under His Cross. His flesh was torn by the scourges. His head crowned with thorns, and He had lost a great quantity of blood. He was so weakened He could scarcely walk, and yet he had to carry this great load upon his shoulders. The soldiers struck Him rudely, and thus He fell several times. (*Pause awhile.*)

MY Jesus, it is not the weight of the Cross, but of my sins, which has made Thee suffer so much pain. Ah, by the merits of this first fall, deliver me from the misfortune of falling into mortal sin. I love Thee, O my Jesus; I repent with my whole heart of having offended Thee. Never permit me to separate myself from Thee again. Grant that I may love Thee always; and then do with me what Thou wilt.

Our Father. Hail Mary. Glory be, &c.

Jesus! for the love of me
You go to die on Calvary;
Let me, Jesus, follow too,
That I may suffer, Lord, with you.

FOURTH STATION.

Jesus meets his afflicted Mother.

V. We adore Thee, O Christ, and praise Thee.

R. Because by thy holy Cross Thou hast redeemed the world.

Consider the meeting of the Son and the Mother, which took place on this journey. Their looks became like so many arrows to wound those hearts which loved each other so tenderly. (*Pause awhile.*)

MY sweet Jesus, by the sorrow Thou didst experience in this meeting, grant me the grace of a truly devoted love for Thy most holy Mother. And thou, my Queen, who wast overwhelmed with sorrow, obtain for me, by thy intercession, a continual and tender remembrance of the passion of thy Son. I love Thee, Jesus my love, above all things; I repent of ever having offended Thee. Never permit me to separate myself from Thee again. Grant that I may love Thee always; and then do with me what Thou wilt.

Our Father. Hail Mary. Glory be, &c.

Jesus! for the love of me
You go to die on Calvary;
Let me, Jesus, follow too,
That I may suffer, Lord, with you.

FIFTH STATION.

The Cyrenian helps Jesus to carry his Cross.

V. We adore Thee, O Christ, and praise Thee.

R. Because by thy holy Cross Thou hast redeemed the world.

Consider how the Jews, seeing that at each step Jesus was on the point of expiring, and fearing He would die on the way, when they wished him to die the ignominious death of the cross, constrained Simon the Cyrenian to carry the cross behind our Lord. (*Pause awhile.*)

MY most beloved Jesus, I will not refuse the cross as the Cyrenian did; I accept it; I embrace it. I accept in particular the death Thou hast destined for me, with all its pains; I unite it to Thy death, I offer it to Thee. Thou hast died for love of me; I will die for love of Thee. Help me by Thy grace. I love Thee, Jesus my love, above all things; I repent with my whole heart of having offended Thee. Never permit me to separate myself from Thee again. Grant that I may love Thee always; and then do with me what Thou wilt.

Our Father. Hail Mary. Glory be, &c.

Jesus! for the love of me
You go to die on Calvary;
Let me, Jesus, follow too,
That I may suffer, Lord, with you.

SIXTH STATION.

Veronica wipes the face of Jesus.

V. We adore Thee, O Christ, and praise Thee.

R. Because by thy holy Cross Thou hast re-eemed the world.

Consider how the holy woman named Veronica eing Jesus so ill used, and His face bathed i weat and blood, presented Him with a towel ith which He wiped His adorable face, leavin n it the impression of His holy countenance *Pause awhile.*)

MY most beloved Jesus, Thy face was beautifu before, but in this journey it has lost all it eauty, and wounds and blood have disfigured it las! my soul also was once beautiful, when i. ceived Thy grace in baptism; but I have dis-gured it since by my sins; Thou alone, my edeemer, canst restore it to its former beauty. o this by Thy passion, O Jesus. I repent with y whole heart of having offended Thee. Never ermit me to separate myself from Thee again. rant that I may love Thee always; and then d th me what Thou wilt.

Our Father. Hail Mary. Glory be, &c.

Jesus! for the love of me
You go to die on Calvary;
Let me, Jesus, follow too,
That I may suffer, Lord, with you.

SEVENTH STATION.

Jesus falls the second time.

V. We adore Thee, O Christ, and praise Thee
R. Because by thy holy Cross Thou hast re deemed the world.

Consider the second fall of Jesus under th Cross; a fall which renews the pain of all th wounds of His head and members. (*Pau awhile.*)

MY most sweet Jesus, how many times Th hast pardoned me, and how many tim have I fallen again, and begun again to offe Thee? O! by the merits of this second fa give me the necessary helps to persevere in T grace until death. Grant that in all temptati which assail me I may always commend myse to Thee. I love Thee, Jesus my love, above things; I repent with my whole heart of havi offended Thee. Never permit me to separ myself from Thee again. Grant that I may lo Thee always; and then do with me what T wilt.

Our Father. Hail Mary. Glory be, &c.

Jesus! for the love of me
You go to die on Calvary;
Let me, Jesus, follow too,
That I may suffer, Lord, with you.

EIGHTH STATION.

Jesus speaks to the Daughters of Jerusalem.

V. We adore Thee, O Christ, and praise Thee.
R. Because by thy holy Cross Thou hast re
eemed the world.

Consider how these women wept with com-
ıssion at seeing Jesus in such a pitiable state,
:eaming with blood, as He walked along. "*My*
ildren," said He, "*weep not for Me, but for your*
ildren." (*Pause awhile.*)

MY Jesus, laden with sorrows, I weep for the
offences I have committed against Thee, be-
ıse of the pains they have deserved, and still
re because of the displeasure they have caused
ee, who hast loved me so much. It is Thy
e more than the fear of hell, which causes me
weep for my sins. My Jesus, I love Thee
re than myself; I repent with my whole heart
having offended Thee. Never permit me to
parate myself from Thee again. Grant that I
love Thee always; and then do with me
at Thou wilt.

Our Father. Hail Mary. Glory be, &c.

Jesus! for the love of me
You go to die on Calvary;
Let me, Jesus, follow too,
That I may suffer, Lord, with you.

NINTH STATION.

Jesus falls the third time

℣. We adore Thee, O Christ, and praise The
℟. Because by thy holy Cross Thou hast r
'eemed the world.

Consider the third fall of Jesus Christ. I. weakness was extreme, and the cruelty of I' executioners excessive, who u ed to hasten I steps when He could scarcely move. (*Pa awhile.*)

AH, my outraged Jesus, by the merits of weakness Thou didst suffer in going to (vary. give me strength sufficient to conquer human respect, and all my wicked passions, wl have led me to despise Thy friendship. I l Thee, Jesus my love, above all things; I rep with my whole heart of having offended T) Never permit me to separate myself fro T again. Grant that I may love Thee always then do with me what Thou wilt.

Our Father. Hail Mary. Glory be, &c.

Jesus! for the love of me
You go to die on Calvary;
Let me, Jesus, follow too,
That I may suffer, Lord, with you.

TENTH STATION.

Jesus is stripped of his Garments.

V. We adore Thee, O Christ, and praise Thee.
R. Because by thy holy Cross Thou hast redeemed the world.

Consider the violence with which the execu-
ioners stripped Jesus. His inner garments ad-
ered to his torn flesh, and they dragged them off
o roughly, that the skin came with them. Com-
assionate your Saviour thus cruelly treated.
Pause awhile.)

MY innocent Jesus, by the merits of the torment Thou hast felt, help me to strip my-
lf of all affection to things of earth, in order
at I may place all my love in Thee, who art so
orthy of my love. I love Thee, O Jesus, above
l things; I repent with my whole heart of hav-
g offended Thee. Never permit me to separate
yself from Thee again. Grant that I may love
ee always; and then do with me what Thou
ilt.

Our Father. Hail Mary. Glory be, &c.

Jesus! for the love of me
You go to die on Calvary;
Let me, Jesus, follow too,
That I may suffer, Lord, with you.

ELEVENTH STATION.

Jesus is nailed to the Cross.

V. We adore Thee, O Christ, and praise Thee
R. Because by thy holy Cross Thou hast redeemed the world.

Consider how Jesus, after being thrown on the Cross, extended His hands, and offered to His eternal Father the sacrifice of His life for our salvation. These barbarians fastened Him with nails, and then, securing the Cross, allowed Him to die with anguish on this infamous gibbet (*Pause awhile.*)

MY Jesus, loaded with contempt, nail my heart to Thy feet, that it may ever remain there, to love Thee, and never quit Thee again I love Thee more than myself; I repent with my whole heart of having offended Thee. Never permit me to separate myself from Thee again Grant that I may love Thee always; and then do with me what Thou wilt.

Our Father. Hail Mary. Glory be, &c.

Jesus! for the love of me
You go to die on Calvary;
Let me, Jesus, follow too,
That I may suffer Lord, with you.

TWELFTH STATION.

Jesus dies on the Cross.

V. We adore Thee, O Christ, and praise Thee
R. Because by thy holy Cross Thou hast redeemed the world.

Consider how Jesus, after three hours' agony on the Cross, consumed with anguish, abandoned himself to the weight of His body, bowed His head, and died. (*Pause awhile.*)

O MY dying Jesus, I kiss devoutly the Cross on which Thou didst die for love of me. I have merited by my sins to die a miserable death, but Thy death is my hope. Ah! by the merits of thy death, give me grace to die embracing Thy feet, and burning with love to Thee. I commit my soul into Thy hands. I love Thee, O Jesus, above all things; I repent of ever having offended Thee. Permit not that I ever offend Thee again. Grant that I may love Thee always; and then do with me what Thou wilt.

Our Father. Hail Mary. Glory be, &c.

Jesus! for the love of me
You came to die on Calvary;
Let me, Jesus, follow too,
That I may suffer, Lord, with you.

THIRTEENTH STATION.

Jesus is taken down from the Cross.

V. We adore Thee, O Christ, and praise Thee.
R. Because by thy holy Cross Thou hast redeemed the world.

Consider how our Lord, having expired, two of his disciples, Joseph and Nicodemus, took Him down from the Cross, and placed Him in the arms of His afflicted Mother, who received Him with unutterable tenderness, and pressed Him to her bosom. (*Pause awhile.*)

O MOTHER of sorrow, for the love of thi Son, accept me for thy servant, and pray for me. And Thou, my Redeemer, since thou has died for me, permit me to love Thee: for I wish but Thee, and nothing more. I love Thee, my Jesus, above all things; I repent of ever having offended Thee. Never permit me to offend Thee again. Grant that I may love Thee always; and then do with me what Thou wilt.

Our Father. Hail Mary. Glory be, &c.

Jesus! for the love of me
You came to die on Calvary;
Let me, Jesus, follow too,
That I may suffer, Lord, with you.

FOURTEENTH STATION.

Jesus is placed in the Sepulchre.

V. We adore Thee, O Christ, and praise Thee.
℟. Because by thy holy Cross Thou hast redeemed the world.

Consider how the disciples carried the body of Jesus to bury it, accompanied by His holy Mother, who arranged it in the sepulchre with her own hands. They then closed the tomb, and all withdrew. (*Pause awhile.*)

AH, my buried Jesus, I kiss the stone that incloses Thee. But Thou didst rise again the third day. I beseech Thee by Thy resurrection, to make me rise glorious with Thee at the last day, to be always united with Thee in heaven, to praise Thee, and love Thee forever. O Jesus, I love Thee, and I repent of ever having offended Thee. Permit not that I ever offend Thee again. Grant that I may love Thee; and then do with me what Thou wilt.

Our Father. Hail Mary. Glory be, &c.

Jesus! for the love of me
You came to die on Calvary;
Let me, Jesus, follow too,
That I may suffer, Lord, with you.

Finally say, Our Father, Hail Mary, Glory be, &c., *five times, to gain other Indulgences.*

The Steps of our Saviour's Passion.

An excel.ent Devotion for Fridays, and for Lent, com posed by St. Augustin.]

I. O dearest Jesus, so sorrowfully praying to thy Father in the Garden, whilst trembling with agony, and covered with a sweat of blood; have mercy on us.

R. Have mercy on us, Lord, have mercy on us

II. O dearest Jesus, betrayed by a traitor's kiss into wicked hands, seized upon, and bound like a robber, and abandoned by thy disciples: have mercy on us.

R. Have mercy on us, Lord, have mercy on us

III. O dearest Jesus, by the unjust council of the Jews, found guilty of death, led to Pilate as malefactor, spurned and mocked by unjust Herod; have mercy on us.

R. Have mercy on us, Lord, have mercy on u.

IV. O dearest Jesus, stripped of all thy garments, and most cruelly scourged at the pillar; have mercy on us.

R. Have mercy on us, Lord, have mercy on us.

V. O dearest Jesus, crowned with thorns, buf

feted, smitten with a reed, blindfolded, covered with a purple garment, derided in every way, and saturated with contempt; have mercy on us.

R. Have mercy on us, Lord, have mercy on us.

VI. O dearest Jesus, less valued than the robber Barabbas, rejected by the Jews, and unjustly condemned to the death of the cross; have mercy on us.

R. Have mercy on us, Lord, have mercy on us.

VII. O dearest Jesus, laden with the cross of wood, and led to thy place of punishment like a lamb to slaughter; have mercy on us.

R. Have mercy on us, Lord, have mercy on us.

VIII. O dearest Jesus, ranked among thieves, blasphemed and derided, with gall and vinegar insulted in thy thirst, and from the sixth to the ninth hour left hanging on the cross in dreadful torment; have mercy on us.

R. Have mercy on us, Lord, have mercy on us.

IX. O dearest Jesus, extended lifeless on the gibbet of the cross, in presence of thy holy Mother pierced with a lance, and shedding blood and water in one mingled stream; have mercy on us.

R. Have mercy on us, Lord, have mercy on us.

X. O dearest Jesus, taken down from the cross, and by thy virgin Mother bathed with tears of most bitter sorrow; have mercy on us.

R. Have mercy on us, Lord, have mercy on us.

XI. O dearest Jesus, shrouded with stripes, marked with five wounds, embalmed with spices, and laid in the sepulchre; have mercy on us.

R. Have mercy on us, Lord, have mercy on us.

V. Surely he hath borne our infirmities,

R. And carried our sorrows.

PRAYER.

O GOD, who for the world's redemption wast pleased to be born, circumcised, rejected by the Jews, betrayed by the kiss of the traitor Judas, bound with chains, led like an innocent lamb to sacrifice, and shamefully presented before Annas, Caiphas, Pilate, and Herod, accused by false witnesses, beaten with whips and buffets, insulted, spit upon, crowned with thorns, smitten with a reed, blindfolded, stripped of thy garments, fastened with nails to the cross, and lifted up on high, reputed among thieves, made to drink of gall and vinegar, and wounded by a lance;—O! by these most sacred sufferings, which, unworthy as I am, I thus commemorate, and by thy holy cross and death, deliver me Lord, from the pains of hell, and deign to lead me where thou didst lead that thief who was crucified by thy side: thou, who with the Father and the Holy Ghost, livest and reignest world without end, Amen

The Steps of our Saviour's Childhood.

An excellent Devotion for Advent, and until Epiphany.

I. O dearest Infant Jesus, from the bosom of the Father descending for our salvation, conceived of the Holy Ghost, abhorring not the Virgin's womb, Word made flesh, receiving the form of a slave; have mercy on us.

R. Have mercy on us, Infant Jesus.

II. O dearest Infant Jesus, with thy Virgin Mother visiting Elizabeth, filling John the Baptist, thy Forerunner, with the Holy Ghost, and sanctifying him while yet in his Mother's womb; have mercy on us.

R. Have mercy on us, Infant Jesus.

III. O dearest Infant Jesus, nine months imprisoned in the womb, anxiously expected by the Virgin Mary and St. Joseph, and by God the Father offered for the world's salvation; have mercy on us.

R. Have mercy on us, Infant Jesus.

IV. O dearest Infant Jesus, born in Bethlehem of the Virgin Mary, wrapped in swaddling clothes, and laid in the manger, heralded by

Angels, and visited by Shepherds; have mercy on us.

R. Have mercy on us, Infant Jesus.

V. O dearest Infant Jesus, after eight days wounded in thy circumcision, called by the glorious name of Jesus, and thus foreshadowing both by name and blood a Saviour's office; have mercy on us.

R. Have mercy on us, Infant Jesus.

VI. O dearest Infant Jesus, revealed to the three Wise men by a star, adored by them on thy Mother's bosom, and presented with mystical gifts of gold, frankincense, and myrrh; have mercy on us.

R. Have mercy on us, Infant Jesus.

VII. O dearest Infant Jesus, presented in the temple by thy Virgin Mother, caressed in the arms of Simeon, and by Anna the prophetess made known to Israel; have mercy on us.

R. Have mercy on us, Infant Jesus.

VIII. O dearest Infant Jesus, sought for by wicked Herod to be put to death, carried by Saint Joseph with thy Mother into Egypt, rescued from the cruel slaughter, and glorified by the fame of the martyred Innocents; have mercy on us.

R. Have mercy on us, Infant Jesus.

IX. O dearest Infant Jesus, in Egypt remaining with most Holy Mary, and the Holy Patriarch Joseph, until the death of Herod; have mercy on us.

R. Have mercy on us, Infant Jesus.

X. O dearest Infant Jesus, returning back from Egypt to the land of Israel, wearied by many labors in the way, and into the city of Nazareth retiring to dwell; have mercy on us.

R. Have mercy on us, Infant Jesus.

XI. O dearest Infant Jesus, obediently remaining in the holy house of Nazareth, there dwelling piously with thy parents, and rapidly advancing in wisdom, age, and grace; have mercy on us.

R. Have mercy on us, Infant Jesus.

XII. O dearest Infant Jesus, led to Jerusalem at the age of twelve, there sought by thy Parents with great sorrow, but after three days found with joy among the Doctors; have mercy on us.

R. Have mercy on us, Infant Jesus.

V. The Word was made flesh. Alleluia.

R. And dwelt among us. Alleluia.

PRAYER.

ALMIGHTY and everlasting God, Lord of heaven and earth, who revealest thyself to the humble; grant, we beseech thee, that commemorating with due honor, and following with worthy imitation these most sacred mysteries of thy Son, the Infant Jesus, we may happily arrive at that heavenly kingdom which thou hast promised to thy little ones; through the same Jesus Christ our Lord. *Amen.*

Of Devotion to the Blessed Virgin Mary.

Every true and pious Catholic will preserve in his heart a tender devotion to the Blessed Virgin Mary, and this for many and most obvious reasons, among which are the following:

1. It is Mary who gave birth to Jesus Christ our Redeemer: she is, therefore, the true Mother of God. Think seriously for a moment, Christian, on these few words: Mary is the Mother of God. Could God bestow on her a nobler name, or a greater dignity? O, then, with what eyes will not one day Jesus look on those who would not honor his Blessed Mother, although he himself has honored her so much! Is there, indeed, a creature more beloved by God than Mary, and will you not love her whom God loves so much?

2. The holy Church of God itself teaches us devotion to Mary. How many churches and altars have been erected in her honor, how many feasts instituted for her glory, how many confraternities and even religious orders established under her name, how many treasures of grace and of indulgences have been attached by the Church to the practice of honoring Mary!

Has not God performed innumerable miracles through her intercession, as so many privileged places of devotion and of pilgrimage show us? Have not kings and princes placed their states under her protection? All who truly revere Jesus Christ raise their voices in honor of Mary. For how can he honor the Son, who despises the Mother?

3. Mary is our HOPE. The Holy Church names her ɔ, when she salutes her with these words: "Hail, our Iope!" God refuses her nothing that she asks, beıuse he is her Son. Neither will she refuse any thing) us, because she is our Mother. Jesus gave her to s for our Mother, with these words: "*Woman, behold hy Son!*" She is the tenderest, the most devoted, ıe most compassionate, and most loving of all mothers. re you a great sinner? Do not despair of salvation n that account; pray to Mary, the refuge of sinners, ıd you will not sink in the stormy waves of the sea ' life. Would you grow in virtue, ask of Mary, the ıeen of saints, and she will certainly obtain grace for ɔu. Are you troubled, call on Mary, the consoler of ıe unhappy, and you will certainly be comforted.

"Remember, O most compassionate Virgin," St. ugustine exclaims, "that it never was heard that ıy one had sought for refuge under thy protection, ithout obtaining relief!"

Cultivate carefully, then, in your heart, this devotion the blessed Mother of God, and be sure that Mary 'll obtain for you great graces in return for the little :ts of love and homage which you offer to her. In ırticular, do not neglect those devotions which are so ɔll approved, and so generally practised by devout ıtholics, such as the visits to the Blessed Virgin, the tany, and the Rosary.

VISITS TO THE BLESSED VIRGIN.

(*For every day in the week.*)

These visits usually follow immediately after those to the Blessed Sacrament (p. 116.) They are made by kneeling down before the altar of the Blessed Virgin in the church, or before any image of hers, in whatever place it may be, and making use devoutly of the following reflections and prayers. Those who cannot always have access to the church, will do well to keep a small image for this purpose, in some retired part of the house.

FOR SUNDAY.

A fertile source of grace which it is our great happiness to possess, is Mary our Mother, so rich in goods and graces, says St. Bernard, that there is not a man in the world who does not participate in them. We all receive of her fulness God himself has filled her with grace, as the Angel said to her, "Hail! full of grace!" It is not for herself alone, but for us also, adds St. Peter Chrysologus, that she received this great treasure of grace, so that afterwards she might communicate it to her devout followers in every age.

Prayer of St. Ephraim.

O QUEEN of the universe, and most bountiful sovereign! thou art the great advocate of sinners, the sure port of those who have suffered shipwreck the resource of the world, the ransom of captives, the solace of the weak, the comfort of the afflicted, the refuge and salvation of every creature. O! full of grace! enlighten my understanding, and loosen my tongue, that I may recount thy praises, and sing to thee that angelical salutation which thou dost so justly merit. Hail! thou who art the peace, the joy, the consolation of the whole world! Hail! Paradise of delight, the sure asylum of all who are in danger, the source of grace, the mediatrix between God and man!

Short prayer to remember and repeat.—Refuge of sinners, take pity on me.

[At the end of each visit, repeat the following prayer in order to obtain the powerful patronage of the Mother of God:]

MOST holy and immaculate Virgin, my Mother Mary, it is to thee, the Mother of my God, the Queen of the world, the advocate, the hope, and the refuge of sinners, that I have recourse to-day, I, who am the most miserable of all. I render thee my humble homage, O great Queen, and I thank thee for all the graces which thou hast bestowed upon me until now, particularly for having delivered me from hell, which I have so often deserved. I love thee, O most amiable Sovereign, and for the love I bear thee, I promise to serve thee always, and to do all in my power to make others love thee also. I place in thee, after God, all my hopes. I confide my salvation to thy care. Accept me for thy servant, and receive me under thy mantle, O Mother of mercy, and since thou art so powerful with God, deliver me from all temptations, or rather obtain for me the strength to triumph over them until death. Obtain for me, I beseech thee, a perfect love for Jesus Christ. To thee I look for grace to make a good death. O my Mother, by the love which thou bearest to God, I beseech thee to help me at all times, and particularly at the decisive moment of death. Do not leave me until thou seest me safe in heaven, occupied in blessing thee, and singing thy mercies throughout eternity. *Amen.*

FOR MONDAY.

" *Whoever is a little one, let him come to me.*" (Prov. ix.) Mary engages all those children who have need of a mother to come to her, as to the most tender of all mothers. The love of all the mothers in the world, says the pious Nieremberg, is no more than a shadow compared with that love which Mary bears to each one of us. My mother! mother of my soul thou who, after God, lovest me, and desirest my salvation more than all the world beside,—O my mother, show thyself to be indeed a mother.

Prayer of St. Bernard.

MOST sweet and amiable Mary, no one can pronounce thy name without feeling the greatest desire to love thee; and those who do love thee, cannot call thee to mind without being animated to love thee more. Pray for us to thy divine Son, that he may vouchsafe to strengthen our weakness: no one is better entitled to speak in our favor to thy God, and ours, than thyself, who art the nearest to him. Intercede, then, for us, O blessed Mother, because thy Son hears thee, and thou canst obtain whatever thou wilt ask.

Short prayer, &c.—O Mary, obtain for me the grace to have constant recourse to thee.

(Conclude as on page 161.)

FOR TUESDAY.

O sweetest, most compassionate, and most amiable Sovereign! with what tender confidence St. Bernard inspires me, when I have recourse to thee! Thou dost not examine, he says, the merits of each one that has recourse to thy goodness, but thou dost promise help to all who will pray to thee. Thou wilt hear me willingly, therefore, if I pray. Behold, then, my petition! Listen: I am a poor sinner, and deserve a thousand hells. I desire, however, to change my life; I wish to love that God whom I have so much offended. I consecrate myself to thy service, I give myself to thee, all miserable as I am. O then, save now a penitent who is thine, and no more his own. O my Queen, hast thou heard me? Indeed, I hope thou hast both heard and answered me.

Prayer of St. Germain.

MOST holy Virgin! who art the greatest consolation that I receive from God; thou who art the heavenly dew which assuages all my pains; thou who art the light of my soul when it is enveloped in darkness; thou who art my guide in unknown paths, the support of my weakness, my treasure in poverty, my remedy in sickness, my comfort in trouble, my refuge in misery, and the hope of my salvation: hear my supplications, have pity on me as become the Mother of so good a God, and obtain for me the favorable reception of all my petitions at the throne of mercy.

Short prayer, &c.—O merciful! O pious! sweet Virgin Mary!

(Conclude as on page 161.)

FOR WEDNESDAY.

St. Bernard says, that Mary is that celestial ark which will surely save us from the wreck of eternal damnation, if we only take refuge there in time. The ark which saved Noe from the universal deluge was the type of Mary; but, says Hesychius, Mary is an ark more vast, more powerful, and more charitable. The ark of Noe could only receive the few men and animals who were saved in it, but Mary receives and saves with certainty all those who take refuge under her mantle. How unhappy should we be if we had not Mary; but, O my Queen, how many men are lost! And why? Because they will not have recourse to thee. Who would ever be lost that had recourse to thee?

Prayer of St. Anselm.

HELP us, O queen of mercy, without regarding the multitude of our sins. Remember that our Creator took of thee a human body, not to condemn, but to save sinners. Hadst thou been chosen to be the Mother of God for thy own benefit alone, thou mightest then be said to have no particular interest in our salvation; but God clothed himself in thy flesh for the sake of all mankind. Help us, therefore, and protect us. Thou knowest the need which we have of thy assistance, and we earnestly recommend ourselves to thy prayers. Pray that we may not be eternally lost, but with thee may love and serve Jesus Christ forever.

Short prayer, &c.—O Mary, all my hopes are placed in thee.

(Conclude as on page 161.)

FOR THURSDAY.

What comfort I find in my troubles, how I am consoled in my sorrows, what strength I find in my temptations, when I think of thee, and call thee to my aid, O my sweet and holy mother Mary! O saints of Paradise, you had great reason to give to my Sovereign those beautiful names of "Harbor of the Afflicted," like St. Ephrem; "Remedy of our Misery," and "Consolation of the Unhappy," like St. Bonaventure; "End of our Tears," like St. Germain. Dear Mary, console me, then, for I see myself all covered with sins, and surrounded by enemies, without virtue, and grown cold in the love of God. Comfort me, comfort me! Bring me the consolation which springs from the beginning of a new life, a life truly pleasing to thy Son and to thee.

Prayer of St. John Damascenus.

HAIL, MARY! thou hope of Christians. Hear the petition of a sinner who wishes to love thee with the greatest tenderness, and to honor thee as thou deservest, and who reposes in thee, next after God, his hope of salvation. Indebted as I am to thee for the preservation of my life, entreat thee to restore me to the grace of thy divine Son. Thou art the surest pledge of my salvation: deliver me then, by thy prayers, from the heavy load of my sins. Disperse the darkness of my understanding; banish every inordinate affection from my heart; repress the temptations of my spiritual enemies, and so order my life, that, under thy protection, I may arrive at eternal repose in heaven.

Short prayer, &c.—Change me, Mary, my Mother; thou canst do it.

(Conclude as on page 161.)

FOR FRIDAY.

St. Bernard assures us that the charity of Mary towards us could not be more tender, nor more powerful than it is, for her heart is always full of compassion for us, and her good-will is accompanied with power to help us. So then, most pure and virgin Queen, thou art rich in power, and rich in compassion. Thou art both able and desirous to save us all. I will pray to thee to-day and always, in the words of the devout Blosius: O my Sovereign, protect me in my combats, fortify me in my weakness. O most holy Mary, in this great contest which I sustain against hell, aid me always: but if ever thou seest me wavering and ready to yield, O my Sovereign, stretch out thy hand to me without delay, and sustain me still more powerfully. ‹ God, what temptations still remain to be su mounted until death! Ah! Mary, my refug my strength, and my hope, never permit that should lose the grace of God, for I am resolvec in all my temptations, to have always immediat recourse to thee.

Prayer of St. Bernard.

REMEMBER, Mary, that it never was hear of, that a sinner had fled to thy protectioı and been abandoned by thee. O Mother of Go‹ thou prayest for all; pray, then, for me, who aı the greatest of sinners, and therefore have tḥ greatest need of thy intercession.

Short prayer, &c.—Help me, Mary! Mary help me!

(Conclude as on page 161.)

FOR SATURDAY.

The blessed Amadeus says that Mary, ouı most glorious Queen, remains continually in the presence of God, as our advocate, interposing ir our favor the assistance of her prayers, whicł are all-powerful before him. For, he continues she sees our miseries and our dangers, and ir her clemency, this amiable Sovereign has pity on us, and comes to our aid with a mother' love. O my advocate, and my most tende mother, it is then true that thou seest the miseries of my soul, the dangers by which I am surrounded, and that thou prayest for me. Pray, yea, pray on, and do not cease to pray, until thou see me safe in Paradise, there occupied in praising thee. The pious Blosius assures me that thou art, after Jesus, the sure salvation of those who are thy faithful servants. Ah! the grace which I ask of thee to-day is, that thou wilt grant to me the happiness to be thy faithful slave until death, in order that after death I may go to bless thee in heaven, certain there to be no more exposed to stray away from thy sacred feet, so long as God is God.

Prayer of St. Ildefonsus.

O MY Sovereign, and Mother of my God, thou art blessed amongst all women, pure amongst all virgins, and queen of all the heavenly host: all nations call thee blessed. Vouchsafe that I may publish as much as possible thy greatness, that I may love thee to the utmost of my power and that I may serve thee with all the capacity of my soul.

Short prayer, &c.—O that I may learn to praise thee, most sacred Virgin!

(Conclude as on pag

The Rosary of the Blessed Virgin

[*Otherwise called "the Beads."*]

The Rosary is one of the most beautiful, most profitable, and most popular of all devotions. It was revealed to St. Dominic by the divine Mother herself about the beginning of the thirteenth century, and has continued ever since to be so general a favorite with all classes of the faithful, that to neglect it may be attributed, in most cases, to a lack of piety, whilst to despise it is the sure indication of an uncatholic spirit.

The Rosary, when practised in the most perfect manner, consists of two distinct modes of prayer joined together in one exercise. It is a combination of mental prayer, or meditation, with vocal prayer. The meditation is made by the consideration of the most memorable and touching "mysteries" or events in the life, passion, and victory of Jesus Christ our Redeemer. The vocal prayer consists of the recitation on the beads, of the Lord's Prayer, the Hail Mary, and the Gloria Patri, or Doxology.

The Mysteries to be meditated are 15 in number, and divided into three parts, which are named the joyful, the 5 sorrowful, and the 5 glorious mysteries. The rosary-beads on which the vocal prayers are recited are also divided, in a corresponding manner, into 3 parts, and each part into 5 decades (or tens), each decade consisting of 1 bead for the Pater and 10 the Aves. The Gloria at the end of every decade

:ited on the same bead as the Pater which begins ; decade that follows.

The Chaplet, or, as it is sometimes called, "the sary of 5 decades," constitutes only a third part of e full rosary, and is the common form in which the ads are made and used at the present day, it not ing usual to recite more than one part at a time.

INDULGENCES.

The indulgences attached to the recitation of the sary are of two kinds, viz: the ordinary indul- nces, and those (so called) of St. Bridget. Among ese indulgences, the principal are the following:

1st. Those who are accustomed to recite weekly the aplet, or Rosary of 5 decades, blessed in the ordi- ry manner, gain an indulgence of 100 days each ae.

2d. If the Rosary has been blessed by a Priest au- orized to give the Bridgetine indulgences, one gains, every time he recites the 5 decades, an indulgence 100 days for each bead. The Rosaries blessed ring the mission receive these as well as the ordi- ry indulgences.

N. B.—Those who are not capable of meditating the ysteries, may gain the above indulgences by simply ying their beads with piety.

A METHOD OF SAYING THE ROSARY WITH THE MYSTERIES.

[*By St. Alphonsus Liguori.*]

Taking your beads in your right hand, by the medal o cross, bless yourself, and say, "*In the name of the Fa ther*," &c. Then recite, by way of introduction th *Creed*, 1 *Pater*, 3 *Aves*, and 1 *Gloria*; after which, yo go on with the meditation of the mysteries, and th recitation of the decades, as follows:

THE FIVE JOYFUL MYSTERIES.

I.

THE MESSAGE OF THE ANGEL.

In this mystery we contemplate how the bless ed Virgin Mary received from the Archange Gabriel the news that she should conceive an bring forth into the world our Lord Jesus Chris O, the tender pity of our God, who might hav saved us by sending an angel to redeem us, bu chose rather to come himself, and to die for ou salvation! But, alas! where is the gratitude o men, where is that return of love we owe to God so full of mercy? Holy Mother of God, full always of love to Jesus Christ, who becan thy Son that he might deliver us from hell, ob tain for us the grace to love him also with a our heart.

Then say on your beads, 1 *Pater*, 10 *Aves*, and 1 *Glori* in honor of the divine Mother, and to obtain this ho love of God.

II.

THE VISITATION.

In this mystery we contemplate how the essed Virgin Mary, having learned that St. izabeth, her cousin, was with child, set out nmediately to visit her, and remained with her ree months. The visit of Mary was the source grace to this whole family. Happy indeed is ery soul which Mary deigns to visit! Let us ay, then, to our dear Lady, that she will be eased to visit our souls, to sanctify and save em.

ay now to this intention, 1 *Pater,* 10 *Aves,* and 1 *Gloria,* on your beads.

III.

THE BIRTH OF OUR LORD.

In this mystery we contemplate how the Vir n Mary brought forth our Redeemer, at mid ght, in the stable of Bethlehem, between two mals of the stall. When the time of her de ry arrived, Mary was in the city of Bethle n, but being very poor, was unable to pro re any lodging, so that she was obliged to take elter in a cave, which was used as a stable for ttle, and there she gave birth to the Son of od, and laid him on a bed of straw in the man r. It pleased our Lord Jesus Christ to come into the world in the form of a babe, and in a manger, in order that sinners might have more confidence to approach him. Sinners then that we are, let us take courage, and beseech the blessed Virgin to obtain for us a true and unchanging confidence in the mercy of her Son our Redeemer.

1 *Pater,* 10 *Aves,* and 1 *Gloria,* on the beads.

IV.

THE PRESENTATION IN THE TEMPLE.

In this mystery we contemplate how, forty days after the birth of our Lord, the blessed Virgin, that she might fulfil the precept of the purification, offered her divine Son in the temple and placed him in the arms of the aged Simeon. Mary had no need to be purified, because she was always free from stain; but in order to obey the law, and through humility, she went to be purified, and to appear sullied, like other women. Since, then, Mary, who was so pure, was not ashamed to appear as if she needed to be purified, how shall we ever be ashamed to confess our sins? Let us pray to the blessed Virgin while we recite this next decade, that she will help us always to overcome every repugnance to confess our sins.

1 *Pater* 10 *Aves* and 1 *Gloria,* on the beads.

V.

THE FINDING IN THE TEMPLE.

In this mystery we contemplate how Mary ıaving lost her Son, sought for him during three lays, and found him again the third day, disputng in the midst of the doctors. The blessed Virgin and St. Joseph, having gone to Jerusalem o visit the temple, took with them the little hild Jesus, then only twelve years old. On ıeir return, they lost him. For three days, hen, they sought after him, with many sighs nd tears, and found him at last in the temple. Mary never lost the grace of her Son, but only 's presence, and nevertheless, she sought after im with tears. O, how much greater reason the nner has to search for Jesus Christ, and that ith many tears, when he has lost his grace! Whoever seeks for him in this way, will find ım surely. Let us pray, then, to the blessed irgin for so many poor sinners who have lost esus Christ, that she may obtain for them a true rrow for their sins.

cite 1 *Pater*, 10 *Aves*, and 1 *Gloria*, on the beads; and then conclude with the following prayer:

PRAYER.

O GOD! whose only begotten Son, by his life, death, and resurrection, has purchased for us the rewards of eternal life: grant, we beseec thee, that while we meditate upon these mysteric in the most holy Rosary of the Blessed Virgı Mary, we may imitate what they contain, an obtain what they promise: through the sam Christ our Lord. *Amen.*

THE FIVE SORROWFUL MYSTERIES

In the name of the Father, &c.
The Creed, 1 Pater, 3 Aves, 1 Gloria.

I.

THE AGONY IN THE GARDEN.

In the first sorrowful mystery, we contempla how Jesus Christ sweat drops of blood, wh praying in the Garden of Olives.

Our Lord was seized with such great sadne in the Garden of Olives that, as he said, it w enough to take away his life. "*My soul is s rowful even unto death.*" What was it, th afflicted Jesus Christ so much in the gard What was it made him sweat those drops blood? It was the sight of our sins that caus him this cruel agony. Let us unite our sorro with that of Jesus Christ. Let us beseech t' Blessed Virgin to obtain for us such a true a

sting sorrow for our sins, that we may never
iore give our Saviour any cause to weep for us.
hen say on your beads 1 *Pater*, 10 *Aves*, and 1 *Gloria.*

II.

THE SCOURGING AT THE PILLAR.

In the second sorrowful mystery, we contem late how Jesus was cruelly scourged in the house f Pilate, where, according to the revelation made c St. Bridget, he received more than 6,000 blows. 'his scourging was so cruel, that his sacred Body ecame like a leper's; that is to say, one continual 'ound from head to foot, according to the pro- hecy of Isaias, "*And we have thought him as it 'ere a leper.*" The doctors assure us that Jesus 'hrist was pleased to suffer this great punishment, specially to satisfy for the sins of men against hastity. Alas! alas! the impurities of sinners re the scourges which made our Saviour suffer)! let us pray to the Blessed Virgin to deliver s from this vice which makes hell so full, and to d us in the time of temptation.

Recite 1 *Pater*, 10 *Aves*, and 1 *Gloria*, on the beads.

III.

THE CROWNING WITH THORNS.

In the third sorrowful mystery, we contemplate ow Jesus Christ was crowned with thorns, and reated like a mock king. After having been scourged, he was made to sit upon a stone step; they put a reed in his hand to represent a sceptre, a rag upon his shoulders for a royal mantle, and on his head, in place of a crown, a wreath of thorns, which they struck with canes to make them penetrate. The soldiers then insulted him, saying, "*Hail! King of the Jews*," and buffeted him. Sinners do the same; for they confess, but scarcely risen from the feet of their confessor they go home from the church to give Jesus Christ new blows on the face. Let us beseech the Blessed Virgin to obtain for us that we may die sooner than ever offend our Lord any more.

1 *Pater*, 10 *Aves*, and 1 *Gloria*, on the beads.

IV.

THE CARRYING OF THE CROSS.

In the fourth sorrowful mystery we contemplate how Jesus Christ, having been condemned to death by Pilate, was made to bear the cross upon his shoulders. With great affection Jesus embraced this cross, to satisfy for our sins. It is therefore just that we, in our turn, to satisfy the offences which we have given him, should embrace the crosses which God sends us. Let us pray Mary to obtain for us a holy spirit of resignation, and patience under every trial.

1 *Pater*, 10 *Aves*, and 1 *Gloria*, on the beads.

V

THE CRUCIFIXION OF OUR LORD.

In the fifth sorrowful mystery, we contemplate w Jesus Christ, having come to the hill of Cal- ry, was stripped, and nailed to the cross, where died for love of us, in the presence of Mary s afflicted Mother. Consider what a bitter ath our Saviour suffered to purchase our love. et us keep by us always some beautiful image Jesus crucified, and, often looking at it, let us y to him · I love thee, my Jesus, because thou st died for me. Now, let us pray that afflicted other Mary to obtain for us the grace to think ten of the dying love of Jesus Christ for us.

Pater, 10 *Aves*, and 1 *Gloria*, on the beads; and then conclude with the same *Prayer* given at the end of the Joyful Mysteries, page 175.

THE FIVE GLORIOUS MYSTERIES.

In the name of the Father, &c.

The *Creed*, 1 *Pater*, 3 *Aves*, and 1 *Gloria*.

I.

THE RESURRECTION OF OUR LORD.

In the first glorious mystery, we contemplate w, the third day after his death, Jesus rose again triumphant and glorious to die no more Consider the glory of our Redeemer when h arose from the sepulchre, after having vanquishe Satan, and delivered the human race, which tha tyrant held in bondage. O! how great is th folly of the sinner, who, having been delivere once from the power of the devil, is willing t become his slave again for some wretched gair or for the passing pleasures of this world. Le us pray the Virgin Mary to unite us so closel by love to Jesus Christ, that we may never agai by a mortal sin become the slave of Lucifer.

Say on your beads for this intention, 1 *Pater,* 10 *Ave* and 1 *Gloria.*

II.

THE ASCENSION OF OUR LORD INTO HEAVEN.

In the second glorious mystery we contempla how Jesus Christ, forty days after his resurre tion, ascended into heaven in triumph, in t sight of his Mother, and of his disciples. Befo Jesus Christ died for us, Paradise was clos against us: but by his death, Jesus has oper it for all those who love him. Ah! what a p that after our Saviour has suffered so much obtain this Paradise, this happy kingdom for u so many foolish sinners should renounce it, ar give themselves up to hell, for a worthles pleasure, for a mere nothing. Let us besee our dear Lady to obtain for us the light to s clearly how miserable are the goods of this world, and how great the delight which God offers in the world to come, to those who love him.

1 *Pater*, 10 *Aves*, and 1 *Gloria*, on the beads.

III.

THE MISSION OF THE HOLY GHOST.

In the third glorious mystery, we contemplate how Jesus Christ, seated at the right hand of his Father, sent down the Holy Ghost to the chamber where the apostles, with the Virgin Mary, were assembled. Before receiving the Holy Ghost, the apostles were so feeble, so cold in the love of God, that at the time of Jesus' passion, one betrayed him, another denied him, and all abandoned him. But as soon as they had all received the Holy Ghost, they were so much inflamed with love, that they gave up their lives generously for Jesus Christ. St. Augustine says, "*He who loves does not labor.*" He who loves God feels no affliction under crosses, but rejoices rather. Let us ask of Mary to obtain for us from the Holy Ghost the gift of his divine love, for then all the crosses of this life will seem sweet to us.

1 *Pater*, 10 *Aves*, and 1 *Gloria*, on the beads.

IV.

THE ASSUMPTION OF OUR BLESSED LADY.

In the fourth glorious mystery, we contemplate

how Mary, twelve years after the resurrection of Jesus Christ, departed this life, and was carried up by angels to heaven. The death of Mary was full of peace and consolation, because her life had been all holy. Our death will not be like hers, for our sins will be then a subject of alarm. But if we abandon our sins, and consecrate ourselves to the service of Mary, then that good Mother will succor and comfort us in that last moment, as she has done already to so many of her faithful servants. Let us place ourselves, then, under her protection, with the firm purpose to amend our lives, and let us ask her now to assist us in the hour of our death.

1 *Pater*, 10 *Aves*, and 1 *Gloria*, on the beads

V

THE CORONATION OF OUR BLESSED LADY.

In the fifth glorious mystery, we contemplate how Mary was crowned by her divine Son, and we contemplate her glory among the saints. When Mary was crowned in heaven by the hand of God, she was appointed also to be our advocate: for this reason, St. Amadeus says, that she prays for us incessantly. It is true that Mary prays for all men, but she prays especially for those who have recourse confidently to her intercession. Let us love, then, to say over and over again with St. Philip Neri: Mary, Mother of God, pray to Jesus for us; and while we recite this last decade of the Rosary, let us repeat with fervor those words of the holy Church, *Holy Mary, Mother of God, pray for us!*

Recite 1 *Pater*, 10 *Aves*, and 1 *Gloria*, on the beads, and then conclude, as before, at the end of the Joyful Mysteries, page 175.

ANOTHER SHORT AND EASY METHOD OF SAYING THE BEADS WITH THE MYSTERIES.

Another very good method of reciting the Rosary with the Mysteries, is to express the mystery appropriate to each decade in the middle of each AVE, immediately after the name of JESUS.

The following is an example of this method: Begin as usual with the SIGN OF THE CROSS, and recite the CREED, the PATER, the three AVES, and the GLORIA, and then go on with the recitation of the decades, as follows:

When you make use of the FIVE JOYFUL MYSTERIES say the Aves of the first decade in this manner: "Hail Mary, full of grace, the Lord is with thee; blessed art thou amongst women, and blessed is the fruit of thy womb, Jesus, *whom thou didst conceive at the message of an angel:* Holy Mary, Mother of God, pray for us sinners, now, and at the hour of our death. Amen." In the second decade, instead of the words, "*whom thou didst conceive,*" &c., say, "*whom thou didst carry in thy womb on thy visit to Elizabeth.*" In the third decade, "*who was born of thee at Bethlehem.*" In the fourth, "*whom thou didst present in the temple.*" In the fifth, "*whom thou didst find in the temple.*" Having thus recited the five decades, end with the same prayer given in the other method. (See page 175.)

When you select for your devotion the SORROWFUL MYSTERIES, say in the middle of each Ave of the first decade, "*who sweat blood for us in the garden.*" In the second decade, "*who was scourged for us.*" In the third, "*who was crowned with thorns for us.*" In the fourth, "*who carried his cross for us.*" In the fifth, "*who was crucified for us.*"

For the GLORIOUS MYSTERIES, in the first decade say, "*who arose from the dead.*" In the second, "*who ascended into heaven.*" In the third, "*who sent the Holy Ghost.*" In the fourth, "*who took thee up into heaven.*" In the fifth, "*who crowned thee Queen of heaven.*"

This method is perhaps the best of all, especially for those who recite their Rosary often, and alone, because it requires no book, and helps to keep the mind constantly fixed on the mystery to be meditated.

The Litany of the Blessed Virgin.

(*Called also the Litany of Loretto.*)

KYRIE eleison.	LORD, have mercy upon us.
Christe eleison.	*Christ, have mercy upon us.*
Kyrie eleison.	Lord, have mercy upon us.
Christe audi nos.	Christ, hear us.
Christe exaudi nos.	*Christ, graciously hear us.*
Pater de cœlis Deus, *miserere nobis.*	God, the Father of heaven, *have mercy upon us.*
Fili Redemptor mundi Deus, *miserere nobis.*	God, the Son, Redeemer of the world, *have mercy upon us.*
Spiritus Sancte Deus, *miserere nobis.*	God, the Holy Ghost, *have mercy upon us.*
Sancta Trinitas, unus Deus, *miserere nobis.*	Holy Trinity, one God, *have mercy upon us.*
Sancta Maria, *ora pro nobis.*	Holy Mary, *pray for us.*
Sancta Dei Genitrix, Sancta Virgo Virginum, Mater Christi, Mater divinæ gratiæ, Mater purissima, Mater castissima, } *Ora pro nobis.*	Holy Mother of God, Holy Virgin of Virgins, Mother of Christ, Mother of divine grace, Mother most pure, Mother most chaste, } *Pray for us.*

Latin (*Ora pro nobis.*)	English (*Pray for us.*)
Mater inviolata,	Mother undefiled,
Mater intemerata,	Mother inviolate,
Mater amabilis,	Mother most amiable,
Mater admirabilis,	Mother most admirable,
Mater Creatoris,	Mother of our Creator,
Mater Salvatoris,	Mother of our Redeemer,
Virgo prudentissima,	Virgin most prudent,
Virgo veneranda,	Virgin most venerable,
Virgo prædicanda,	Virgin most renowned,
Virgo potens,	Virgin most powerful,
Virgo clemens,	Virgin most merciful,
Virgo fidelis,	Virgin most faithful,
Speculum justitiæ,	Mirror of justice,
Sedes sapientiæ,	Seat of wisdom,
Causa nostræ lætitiæ,	Cause of our joy,
Vas spirituale,	Spiritual vessel,
Vas honorabile,	Vessel of honor,
Vas insigne devotionis,	Vessel of singular devotion,
Rosa mystica,	Mystical rose,
Turris Davidica,	Tower of David,
Turris eburnea,	Tower of ivory,
Domus aurea,	House of gold,
Fœderis arca,	Ark of the covenant,
Janua cœli,	Gate of heaven,
Stella matutina,	Morning star,
Salus infirmorum,	Health of the weak,
Refugium peccatorum	Refuge of sinners,
Consolatrix afflictorum,	Comfortress of the afflicted,

Auxilium Christianorum,	*Ora pro nobis.*	Help of Christians,	*Pray for us.*
Regina Angelorum,		Queen of Angels,	
Regina Patriarcharum,		Queen of Patriarchs,	
Regina Prophetarum,		Queen of Prophets,	
Regina Apostolorum,		Queen of Apostles,	
Regina Martyrum,		Queen of Martyrs,	
Regina Confessorum,		Queen of Confessors,	
Regina Virginum,		Queen of Virgins,	
Regina Sanctorum omnium,		Queen of all saints,	
Regina sine labe originali concepta,		Queen conceived without the stain of original sin.	

Agnus Dei, qui tollis peccata mundi, *parce nobis Domine.*	Lamb of God, who takest away the sins of the world, *spare us, O Lord.*
Agnus Dei, qui tollis peccata mundi, *audi nos Domine.*	Lamb of God, who takest away the sins of the world, *hear us, O Lord.*
Agnus Dei, qui tollis peccata mundi, *miserere nobis.*	Lamb of God, who takest away the sins of the world, *have mercy upon us.*
V. Ora pro nobis Sancta Dei Genitrix.	V. Pray for us, O holy Mother of God.
R. *Ut digni efficiamur promissionibus Christi.*	R. *That we may be made worthy of the promises of Christ.*

Oremus.	*Let us pray.*
GRATIAM tuam, quæsumus Domine, mentibus nostris infunde; ut qui, angelo nuntiante, Christi Filii tui incarnationem cognovimus, per	POUR forth, we beseech thee, O Lord, thy divine grace into our hearts, that we to whom the incarnation of Christ thy Son was made known by

passionem ejus et crucem ad resurrectionis gloriam perducamur: Per eundem Christum Dominum nostrum. *Amen.*

the message of an angel, may by his passion and cross be brought to the glory of his resurrection; through the same Christ our Lord. *Amen.*

THE MEMORARE OF SAINT BERNARD.

REMEMBER, O most merciful Virgin Mary that it is unheard of, that any one flying to thee for protection, imploring thy help, or seeking thy intercession, was ever forsaken. Animated by this unerring confidence, I hasten to thee, Virgin of Virgins; I fly to thee, O sweet Mother; a wretched sinner, I prostrate myself groaning at thy feet; despise not my prayer, O Mother of the Divine Word, but graciously hear and grant the same. Amen.

THE SCAPULAR OF THE BLESSED VIRGIN MARY.

JUST as men love to have their servants wear their livery, so Mary loves to see her servants wear her Scapular, to show their tender devotion to her, and that they belong to her family. Heretics, according to their fashion, laugh at this devotion, but the Holy Church has approved it by bulls and indulgences. It is related that, about the year 1251, the Blessed Virgin appeared to St. Simon Stock, an English Carmelite and giving him this scapular, assured him that all who should die invested with it, would be saved from eternal fire. This vision is so well attested, that Pope Benedict XIV. does not hesitate to say, "We believe his vision to be true, and think it ought to be so con-idered by every one." No wonder, then, that this eautiful devotion has become so widely spread, and ontinues to flourish throughout the Catholic Church.

ADVANTAGES OF THE SCAPULAR.

The advantages and privileges of this devotion are ery great.

1. In the first place, it is not only the badge of our ove and veneration for the holy Mother of God, but a sweet pledge of her protection. It entitles us to the benefit of her promise above mentioned, so that, if we wear it faithfully, Mary will surely assist us to perse-vere in the grace of God, and give us her most special and powerful protection in the hour of death.

2. By wearing the scapular, we participate in all the good works of the Carmelite order, as is expressed in the formula of the reception, which says: "In virtue of the power intrusted to me, I receive and admit you to the full participation of all the prayers, penances, suffrages, alms, watchings, masses, offices, and other spiritual duties, which are performed day and night, in every part of the world, through the mercy of Jesus Christ, by all the Religious of the holy order of Mount Carmel."

3. By means of it we may gain many most valuable ndulgences, among which are the following:

INDULGENCES.

A plenary indulgence on the day of receiving it; nd another on the Feast of our Lady of Mount Car-nel, July 16, upon the usual conditions of confession and communion on those days, and praying for the ordinary intentions of the Church. A plenary indul-gence also at the article of death, provided we pro-nounce, at least with the heart, if we cannot with the mouth, the holy name of Jesus. There is also an indulgence of one hundred days for every time w lodge a poor person, or give him alms in his necessity or perform some other work of mercy, and one of forty days for those who recite every day 7 Paters and ' Aves in honor of the Blessed Virgin. All these indul gences are applicable to the souls in Purgatory.

SABBATINE INDULGENCE.

The holy Mother of God appearing once to Pop John XXII. in a vision, accorded a further and mos. precious privilege to those who wear the Scapular This is what goes usually by the name of the Sabba tine Indulgence, and mention is made of it in the Ro man Breviary. "It is not only in this life," so say. the Breviary, "that the blessed Virgin Mary show. herself favorable to her children of Mount Carmel; i is also in the life to come, for her power and her good ness extend everywhere. All those who, wearing th Scapular, are careful to recite the few prayers pre scribed, and preserve their chastity according to thei state of life, may piously hope that, should they hav to suffer the fire of Purgatory, Mary will come to con sole them in her maternal tenderness, and cause then very soon to enter their heavenly country. This happy release may be looked for on the Saturday next afte death.

THE DUTIES TO BE FULFILLED.

The only obligation, properly speaking, attached the Scapular, is to wear it constantly with devotion.

The obligations or duties (so called) are only im posed as necessary conditions to gain the Sabbatin indulgence, and these are—to recite daily the Littl Office of the Blessed Virgin Mary, or in place of it to abstain on Wednesdays and Fridays. Any one neglecting to fulfil these conditions commits no si thereby, nor does he forfeit the other privileges of th Scapular, or lose his title to the other indulgences.

REMARKS.

1 To be received, in the first place, into the confra·
'nity, and entitled to its privileges, it is necessary to
invested by a priest duly authorized.

2. When the first is worn out, or lost, or has been
d by, another may be taken and worn, which does
t need to be blessed again.

3. It is not enough to carry the Scapular in the
cket, around the waist, or on the arm. It must be
orn about the neck; but it makes no difference
hether over or under the dress.

"My brethren," said St. Simon Stock to all the chil-
en of Mount Carmel, "treasure up in your hearts,
d think often of the promises which the Mother of
od has made us. Labor continually to assure your
cation by your good works, and to confirm by your
nduct the choice which Mary has made of you to be
r children. Be watchful, and persevere in that
atitude you owe for so great a mercy of God in your
gard. Pray without ceasing, that the promise which
s been given me may be accomplished in you, to the
ry of the most Holy Trinity, of God the Father, of
sus Christ, his divine Son, and of the Holy Ghost,
d also of the most blessed Virgin Mary, whose
aises and happiness all nations are to celebrate, ac-
rding to the prophecy contained in the sacred Scrip-
es: '*Behold, henceforth all nations shall call me*
ed!' *Amen.*"

Devotion to the Saints.

THE Church militant on earth, and the Church ! umphant in heaven, is one and the same Church, a unites her children all in one blest family. The Sain who reign with Christ in glory are separated from o sight, but the communion remains unbroken, and t sweet intercourse of charity goes on. For ever secu from danger, and inundated with joy, they can recei nothing, it is true, from us but our tribute of vene tion and praise. But we, on the other hand, can hc great things from them, for they are able and willi to help us, and they know our wants.

They are able to help us. For if we value the praye of a good man on earth, although still encumbered li ourselves by faults and miseries, how much more av ing must be the intercession of these familiar frier and servants of God, who are so dear to him, and s him always face to face! If he has promised so mu even to our poor prayers, how shall he deny anythi to them!

They are willing to help us. For surely, the b of Paradise has not taken away, but rather increa beyond measure, the only charity and sympathy wh burned in their hearts when on earth.

They know our wants. They are not ignorant what takes place here below. "*There is joy in heav upon one sinner that doth penance.*" St. Luke, x 7-10 Either the swift angels bring the tidings, o they read it in the smile of God, whose face they alwa behold. And when the good Christian prays, do th not know this also? O yes! in that safe harbor whe ey rest, they look back and see us all floating on the a of life; they witness our struggles, our fears, our opes, and mingle their prayers with ours.

Let us therefore honor these holy Saints, and invoke em in all our necessities. This devotion is most ceptable to God, who is glorified in the glory of his ints. "*Mirabilis est Deus in Sanctis suis.*"

He is the fountain from which their glory springs d the infinite ocean to which it all returns.

THE LITANY OF THE SAINTS.

ord, have mercy on us.
hrist, have mercy on us.
ord, have mercy on us.
hrist, hear us.
hrist, graciously hear us.
od, the Father of heaven, *Have mercy on us.*
od the Son, Redeemer of the world, *Have mercy on us.*
od the Holy Ghost, *Have mercy on us.*
oly Trinity, one God, *Have mercy on us.*
oly Mary, *Pray for us.*
oly Mother of God,
oly Virgin of Virgins,
. Michael,
t. Gabriel,
t. Raphael,
ll ye holy Angels and Archangels,
ll ye holy orders of blessed spirits,

Pray for us.

St. John Baptist,
St. Joseph,
All ye holy Patriarchs and Prophets,
St. Peter,
St. Paul,
St. Andrew,
St. James,
St. John,
St. Thomas,
St. James,
St. Philip,
St. Bartholomew,
St. Matthew,
St. Simon,
St. Thaddeus,
St. Matthias,
St. Barnaby,
St. Luke,
St. Mark,
All ye holy Apostles and Evangelists,
All ye holy Disciples of our Lord,
All ye holy Innocents,
St. Stephen,
St. Laurence,
St. Vincent,
SS. Fabian and Sebastian,
SS. John and Paul,
SS. Cosmas and Damian,
SS. Gervasius and Protasius

ll ye holy Martyrs,
Sylvester,
Gregory,
Ambrose,
t. Augustin,
Jerome,
Martin,
t. Nicholas,
ll ye holy Bishops and Confessors,
ll ye holy Doctors,
t. Anthony,
Benedict,
Bernard,
Dominic,
t. Francis,
ll ye holy Priests and Levites,
ll ye holy Monks and Hermits,
Mary Magdalen,
Lucy,
Agnes,
Cecily,
Agatha,
Catharine,
Anastasia,
ll ye holy Virgins and Widows,

Pray for us.

ll ye men and women, saints of God, *make intercession for us.*

merciful unto us. *Spare us, O Lord.*

merciful unto us. *Graciously hear us, O Lord.*

From all evil,
From all sin,
From thy wrath,
From sudden and unprovided death,
From the deceits of the devil,
From anger, hatred, and all ill-will,
From the spirit of fornication,
From lightning and tempest,
From everlasting death,
Through the mystery of thy holy incarnation,
Through thy coming,
Through thy nativity,
Through thy baptism and holy fasting,
Through thy cross and passion,
Through thy death and burial,
Through thy holy resurrection,
Through thy admirable ascension,
Through the coming of the Holy Ghost the Comforter,
In the day of judgment,

We sinners, *do beseech thee to hear us.*

That thou spare us,
That thou pardon us,
That thou vouchsafe to bring us to true penance,
That thou vouchsafe to govern and preserve thy holy Church,
That thou vouchsafe to preserve our apos-

tolic Prelate, and all ecclesiastical Orders in holy religion,

hat thou vouchsafe to humble the enemies of the holy Church,

hat thou vouchsafe to give peace and true concord to Christian Kings and Princes,

hat thou vouchsafe to grant peace and unity to all Christian people,

hat thou vouchsafe to confirm and preserve us in thy holy service,

hat thou lift up our minds to heavenly desires,

hat thou render eternal good things to all our benefactors,

hat thou deliver our souls, and those of our brethren, kinsfolks, and benefactors, from eternal damnation,

hat thou vouchsafe to give and preserve the fruits of the earth,

hat thou vouchsafe to give eternal rest to all the faithful departed,

at thou vouchsafe graciously to hear us,

n of God,

We beseech thee to hear us.

mb of God, who takest away the sins of the world, *spare us, O Lord.*

amb of God, who takest away the sins of th world, *graciously hear us, O Lord.*

amb of God, who takest away the sins of the world, *have mercy on us.*

PRAYER.

O GOD, whose property is always to hav mercy, and to spare, receive our petition that we, and all thy servants who are bound b he chain of sins, may by the compassion of th goodness mercifully be absolved.

Hear, we beseech thee, O Lord, the prayers c the suppliant, and pardon the sins of them th confess to thee; that in thy bounty thou mayes both give us pardon and peace.

Out of thy clemency, O Lord, show thy u speakable mercy to us, that so thou mayest bot acquit us of our sins, and deliver us from th punishments we deserve for them.

O God, who by sin art offended, and by per ance pacified, mercifully regard the prayers o thy people making supplication to thee, and tur away the scourges of thy anger, which we deserv for our sins.

O Almighty and Eternal God, have mercy o thy servant N—, our chief Bishop, and dire him according to thy clemency, irto the way everlasting salvation; that by thy grace he m desire those things that are agreeable to thee, an perform them with all his strength.

O God, from whom are all holy desires, righ counsels, and just works, give to thy servan' that peace which the wcrld cannot give; th both our hearts may be disposed to keep thy commandments, and the fear of enemies being removed, the times by thy protection may be peaceable.

Inflame, O Lord, our reins and hearts with the fire of thy Holy Spirit, that we may serve thee with a chaste body, and please thee with a clear heart.

O God, the Creator and Redeemer of all the faithful, give to the souls of thy servants departed the remission of all their sins; that through pious supplications they may obtain the pardon which they have always desired.

Forerun, we beseech thee, O Lord, our actions by thy holy inspirations, and carry them on by thy gracious assistance: that every prayer and work of ours may begin always from thee, and by thee be happily ended.

O Almighty and Eternal God, who hast dominion over the living and the dead, and art merciful to all whom thou foreknowest shall be thine by faith and good works; we humbly beseech thee that they, for whom we have determined to offer up our prayers, whether this world still detains them in the flesh, or the world to come has already received them out of their bodies, may by the clemency of thy goodness, all thy saints interceding for them, obtain pardon and full remission of all their sins, through our

Lord Jesus Christ thy Son, who liveth and reigneth, &c. *Amen.*

V. O Lord, hear my prayer.

R. And let my cry come unto thee.

V. May the Almighty and most merciful Lord graciously hear us. *R. Amen.*

V. And may the souls of the faithful departed, through the mercy of God, rest in peace. *R. Amen.*

Devotion to St. Joseph.

"I do not remember," says St. Teresa, "ever to have asked any thing of St. Joseph, until this moment, which he did not obtain for me. One would be astonished, were I to tell of all the numberless graces which God has granted me by the intercession of this Saint, and of the perils, both of body and soul, from which he has delivered me. It seems to be the privilege of other saints to assist us in some particular necessities, but experience proves that this Saint assists us in all, as if by this the Lord would have us understand that as he was pleased to be subject to St. Joseph while on earth, so he is resolved to grant all his requests in heaven. This is what other persons have proved, to whom I had given counsel to recommend themselves to him. Such is the long experience I have of the great favors which he obtains from God, that I would gladly persuade the whole world to be devout to this Saint. I have never known any one that rendered some special homage to him, who has not made manifest progress in virtue. For several years I have been accustomed to ask some favor of him on the day of his festival, and always I perceive that I have been heard. If any one does not believe it, I beg of him for the love of God, to make the experiment. For my part, I do not know how any one can think of the Queen of Angels, and of the care which she took of Jesus in his childhood, without thanking St. Joseph for the succor he gave, during this time, to both mother and son." *Life of St. Teresa*, ch. vi.

DEVOUT PRAYERS IN HONOR OF ST. JOSEPH.

Choice of St. Joseph as patron.

O BLESSED Joseph, faithful guardian of my Redeemer Jesus Christ, protector of thy chaste spouse the virgin Mother of God, I choose thee this day to be my especial patron and advocate, and I firmly resolve to honor thee as such from this time forth and always. Therefore I humbly beseech thee to receive me for thy client, to instruct me in every doubt, to comfort me in every affliction, and finally to defend and protect me in the hour of death. *Amen.*

For his safe-conduct through life.

O BLESSED Joseph, father and guide of Jesus Christ in his childhood and youth, who didst lead him safely in his flight through the desert, and in all the ways of his earthly pilgrimage, be also my companion and guide in this pilgrimage of life, and never permit me to turn aside from the way of God's commandments; be my refuge in adversity, my support in temptation, my solace in affliction, until at length I arrive at the land of the living, where with thee, and Mary thy most holy Spouse, and all the Saints, I may rejoice forever in Jesus my Lord. *Amen.*

For grace to communicate devoutly.

O BLESSED Joseph, how sweet and wonderful a privilege was thine, not only to see, but to carry in thy arms, to kiss and to embrace with fatherly affection that only begotten Son of God, whom so many Kings and Prophets desired to see, but were not able. O that, inspired by thy example and aided by thy patronage, I may often, with like feelings of love and reverence, embrace my Lord and Redeemer in the Blessed Sacrament of the altar, so that when my life on earth is ended, I may merit to embrace him eternally in heaven. *Amen.*

For other particular graces.

O BLESSED Joseph, since Jesus while on earth was subject to thee, rendered prompt obedience to thy commands, and cherished thee with most especial love and honor, how shall he now refuse thee any thing in heaven, where all thy merits receive their full reward! Pray for me therefore, O holy Patriarch, and obtain for me these necessary graces: first of all, that I may have a sincere contrition for my sins, that I may ever hate and fear all that is evil, and fly from it with firmness and constancy, especially from my most besetting sins; secondly, that I may amend my life daily more and more, and constantly apply myself to the acquirement of virtue, especially those virtues which I need most; and lastly, that I may be kept safe amidst the various temptations and occasions by which my soul may be exposed to the peril of damnation. For these and all other needful graces, O holy Joseph, I commend myself to the goodness and mercy of my God, and to thy fatherly care and intercession. *Amen.*

For a happy death.

O BLESSED Joseph, who didst yield thy last breath in the fond embrace of Jesus and of Mary,—when the seal of death shall close my career of life, come, holy Father, with Jesus and Mary, to aid me, and obtain for me this only solace which I ask for in that hour, to die encircled by their holy arms. Into your sacred hands. living and dying, Jesus, Mary, Joseph, I commend my soul. *Amen.*

V. Pray for us, O most blessed Joseph.

R. That we may be made worthy of the promises of Christ.

PRAYER.

WE beseech thee, O Lord, that we may be assisted by the merits of the Spouse of th most Holy Mother; so that what we are unab to obtain for ourselves, may be granted us throug his intercession; Who livest and reignest worl without end. *Amen.*

Devotion to the Holy Angels.

"*Are they not all ministering spirits, sent to minister for them who shall receive the inheritance of salvation?*" Heb. i. 14.

"The Angels," says St. Augustine, "love us as their fellow-citizens, and hope to see us fill up what has been lost to their own number by the fall of the rebel angels. For this reason they are always present with us, and watch over us with the greatest care. At all times, and in every place, they are ready to help us, and to provide for our wants. They walk with us in all our ways; going out and coming in, they follow us still, anxiously considering whether we live piously and purely in the midst of a wicked world. They assist those who labor; they guard those who rest; they encourage those who fight; they crown those who conquer; they rejoice with the joyful, and sympathize with the suffering. When we do well, the angels are glad, but the devils are sad. When we sin, the devils rejoice, but the angels are cheated of their joy." (Solil. cap. 27.)

We ought, therefore, to honor these blessed spirits with very great reverence and affection, and to pray to them, especially our guardian angels, to whom God has given charge over us, to keep us in all our ways (Ps. xc.), and we may be sure that this devotion will be most pleasing to them, and most useful to ourselves.

THE ANGEL PSALTER.

(*Extracted from various Psalms.*)

O ye angels of the Lord, bless the Lord: praise him and exalt him above all forever.

Praise the Lord from the heavens: praise ye him in the high places. Praise him, all ye his angels; praise ye him, all his hosts.

Bless the Lord, all ye his angels, you that are mighty in strength, and execute his word, hearkening to the voice of his orders.

Bless the Lord, all ye his hosts; ye ministers of his that do his will.

Bless the Lord, O my soul, and never forget all he hath done for thee.

Who redeemeth thy life from destruction, who crowneth thee with mercy and compassion.

For he hath given his angels charge over thee to keep thee in all thy ways.

In their hands they shall bear thee up, lest thou dash thy foot against a stone.

Thou shalt walk upon the asp and the basilisk and thou shalt trample under foot the lion and the dragon.

The Angel of the Lord shall encamp round about them that fear him, and shall deliver them.

Glory be to the Father, &c.

V. I will sing praise to thee, O my God, in the sight of the Angels.

R. I will worship towards thy holy temple, and I will give glory to thy name.

PRAYER.

O GOD, who, in most admirable order, dost assign the various offices, both of angels and of men: grant, we beseech thee, that they who always minister before thy face in heaven, may also defend us in this our life on earth. Through Jesus Christ thy Son our Lord. *Amen.*

PRAYER TO ONE'S GUARDIAN ANGEL.

O BLESSED Angel, my guardian and defender, since by the kind providence of God I have been committed to thy care, I beseech thee to direct me always in the way of peace, safety, and salvation. Remain especially this day (or night) by my side, to defend me from all danger, and every evil temptation. Remember, O dearest guardian, how once the watchful love of God preserved thee with the good angels in grace and glory, while so many others were cast down from heaven for their pride. I beseech thee, therefore to watch over me in this my lifetime of trial, and bring me such efficacious aid from heaven, that in no danger I may ever fall and lose the grace of my God and Creator until I come to appear be fore his face in my heavenly home; there, wi thee and all the saints and angels, to praise ar adore him, through the endless ages of eternit *Amen.*

[There is an indulgence of 100 days attached to the fo lowing prayer, for each time of reciting it.

Angele Dei, Qui custos es mei, Me tibi commissum pietate superna, Hodie illumina, custodi, rege et guberna. *Amen*	O Angel of God, Who art my guard, Committed by heavenl care to thy ward, Rule, govern, enlighte: and keep me this day. *Amen.*

Devotion to the Holy Souls in Purgatory.

(*By St. Alphonsus Liguori.*)

THE practice of recommending to God the souls in Purgatory, that he may mitigate the great pain which they suffer, and that he may soon bring them to his glory, is most pleasing to the Lord, and most profitable to us. For these blessed souls are his eternal spouses, and most grateful are they to those who obtain their deliverance from prison, or even a mitigation of their torments. When, therefore, they arrive in heaven, they will be sure to remember all who have prayed for them. It is a pious belief that God manifests to them our prayers in their behalf, that they also may pray for us. It is true, these blessed souls are not in a state to pray for themselves, because they are, so to speak, criminals atoning for their faults. However, because they are very dear to God, they can pray for us, and obtain for us the divine graces. St. Katharine of Bologna, when she wished to obtain any grace, had recourse to the souls in Purgatory, and her prayers were heard immediately. She declared that, by praying to those holy souls, she obtained many favors, which she had sought through the intercession of the saints without obtaining. The graces which devout persons are said to have received through these holy souls, are innumerable.

But, if we wish for the aid of their prayers, it is just, it is even a duty to relieve them by our suffrages. I say, *it is even a duty;* for Christian charity commands us to relieve our neighbors who stand in need of our assistance. But who among all our neighbors have so great need of our help as these holy prisoners? They are continually in that fire which torments more severely than any earthly fire. They are deprived of the sight of God, a torment far more excruciating than all other pains. Let us reflect that among these suffering souls, are parents or brothers, or relations and friends, who look to us for succor. Let us remember, moreover, that, being in the condition of debtors for their sins, they cannot assist themselves. This thought should urge us forward to relieve them to the best of our ability. By assisting them we shall not only give great pleasure to God, but will acquire also great merit for ourselves. And in return for our suffrages, these blessed souls will not neglect to obtain for us many graces from God, but particularly the grace of eternal life. I hold for certain that a soul delivered from Purgatory by the suffrages of a Christian, when she enters Paradise, will not fail to say to God: "Lord, do not suffer to be lost that person who has liberated me from the prison of Purgatory, and has brought me to the enjoyment of thy glory sooner than I had deserved!"

St. Liguori then goes on to urge the faithful to do all in their power to relieve and liberate these blessed souls, by procuring masses to be said for them, by alms, and by their own fervent prayers.

PRAYERS FOR THE SUFFERING SOULS IN PURGATORY.

O dearest Jesus, by the bloody sweat which thou didst suffer in the Garden of Gethsemani have mercy on these blessed souls.

R. Have mercy on them, O Lord, have mercy on them.

O dearest Jesus, by the pains which thou didst suffer during thy most cruel scourging, have mercy on them.

R. Have mercy on them, &c.

O dearest Jesus, by the pains which thou didst suffer from thy most painful crown of thorns, have mercy on them.

R Have mercy on them, &c.

O dearest Jesus, by the pains which thou didst suffer in carrying thy cross to Calvary, have mercy on them.

R. Have mercy on them, &c.

O dearest Jesus, by the pains which thou didst suffer in thy most cruel crucifixion, have mercy on them.

R. Have mercy on them, &c.

O dearest Jesus, by the pains which thou didst suffer in thy most bitter agony on the cross, have mercy on them.

R. Have mercy on them, &c.

O dearest Jesus, by that intense pain which thou didst suffer in breathing forth thy blessed soul, have mercy on them.

R. Have mercy on them, &c.

Then recite the following Psalm:

DE PROFUNDIS.

Out of the depths I have cried to thee, O Lord: **Lord**, hear my voice.

Let thy ears be attentive to the voice of my supplication.

If thou, O Lord, wilt mark iniquities, Lord, who shall stand it?

For with thee there is merciful forgiveness; and by reason of thy law I have waited for thee, O Lord.

My soul hath relied on his word; my soul hath hoped in the Lord.

From the morning watch even until night, let Israel hope in the Lord.

Because with the Lord there is mercy, and with him plentiful redemption.

And he shall redeem Israel from all his iniquities.

V. Give them eternal rest, O Lord.

R. And let perpetual light shine on them.

V. May they rest in peace.

R. Amen.

PRAYER.

O GOD, the author of mercy and lover of the salvation of mankind, we address thy clemency in behalf of our brethren, relations, and benefactors who are departed this life, that by the intercession of blessed Mary ever Virgin, and of all the saints, thou wouldst receive them into the enjoyment of eternal happiness; through Christ our Lord. *Amen.*

Now recommend yourself to the souls in Purgatory, and say:

Blessed Souls! we have prayed for you. We entreat you, who are so dear to God, and so sure of never losing him, to pray for us miserabl sinners, who are in danger of being damned, an of losing God forever.

THE LITANY FOR A GOOD DEATH.

LORD, have mercy on us.
Christ, have mercy on us
Lord, have mercy on us.
Christ, hear us.
God the Father, who for our sake didst deliver up thy beloved Son to death, *have mercy on us.*
God the Son, who didst mercifully submit to the law of death, that we may thereby gain eternal life, *have mercy on us.*
Holy Ghost, great comforter of the dying Christian, *have mercy on us.*
O divine Jesus! when I shall be seized with my last illness, and warned to prepare for the approach of my Judge, *then, merciful Jesus, have mercy on me.*
When my eyes, darkened with the mist of death, shall fix their last dying looks on thy crucified image, *then, merciful Jesus, have mercy on me.*

When my pale and ghastly countenance shall fill others with compassion and terror,
When my ears, about to close forever to all human discourse, shall await the dreadful sound of thy irrevocable sentence,
When my feet, unable to move, shall remind me that my earthly course is drawing to an end,
When my imagination, disturbed with gloomy and frightful phantoms, shall fill my heart with deadly horror,
When my soul, terrified at the view of my sins, and agonized with fear of thy rigorous justice, shall struggle with the angel of darkness,
When my heart, weakened and overwhelmed with the pains of sickness, shall be seized with the last agonies of death, and violently assailed with the last efforts of Satan,
When my friends, assembled round me, shall compassionate my sufferings, and weep for my approaching dissolution,
When all my senses shall fail, and this world for ever vanish from my view,
When the symptoms of death shall appear, and the last tear shall trickle down my cheeks,
When, tortured by the pangs of death, and oppressed with lengthened agony,

Then, merciful Jesus, have mercy on me.

When the last heavy sighs of my heart shall press my soul to leave my body,
When my soul, fluttering at my lips, shall be on the point of beholding her Almighty Judge,
When my soul shall at length depart from this valley of tears, and leave my body pale, cold, and hideous,
When I shall stand all alone before my Judge, and behold at one glance all the sins of my life, and all thy claims, O my God, on my love,
When thou shalt pronounce that awful sentence, which no human power can revoke, and no human art elude,
Then, merciful Jesus, have mercy on me.

V. Through thy painful agony and precious death,
R. Deliver us, O Jesus.

PRAYER.

O GOD, who hast condemned us all to die, but concealed the moment and the hour of death; grant, that passing all the days of my life in justice and holiness, I may merit to breathe my last in the peace of a good conscience, and die in thy love: through Jesus Christ our Lord. *Amen.*

The Seven Penitential Psalms.

Ant. Remember not, O Lord, our offences, nor those of our parents, and take not revenge on our sins.

Psalm vi. *Domine, ne in furore.*

O Lord, rebuke me not in thy indignation, nor chastise me in thy wrath.

Have mercy on me, O Lord, for I am weak: heal me, O Lord, for my bones are troubled.

And my soul is troubled exceedingly: but thou, O Lord, how long?

Turn to me, O Lord, and deliver my soul; O save me for thy mercy's sake.

For there is no one in death that is mindful of thee, and who shall confess to thee in hell?

I have labored in my groanings; every night I will wash my bed, I will water my couch with my tears.

My eye is troubled through indignation; I have grown old among all my enemies.

Depart from me, all ye workers of iniquity, for the Lord hath heard the voice of my weeping.

The Lord hath heard my supplication: the Lord hath received my prayer.

Let my enemies be ashamed, and be very much troubled: let them be turned back and be ashamed very speedily. Glory be, &c.

PSALM XXXI. *Beati quorum.*

Blessed are they whose iniquities are forgiven. and whose sins are covered.

Blessed is the man to whom the Lord hath not imputed sin, and in whose spirit there is no guile.

Because I was silent my bones grew old; whilst I cried out all the day long.

For day and night thy hand was heavy upon me; I am turned in my anguish whilst the thorn is fastened.

I have acknowledged my sin to thee; and my injustice I have not concealed.

I said I will confess against myself in my injustice to the Lord, and thou hast forgiven the wickedness of my sin.

For this shall every one that is holy pray to thee, in a seasonable time.

And yet in a flood of many waters, they shall ot come nigh unto him.

Thou art my refuge from the trouble which hath encompassed me: my joy, deliver me from them that surround me.

I will give thee understanding, and I will instruct thee in this way in which thou shalt go I will fix my eyes upon thee.

Do not become like the horse and the mule, who have no understanding.

With bit and bridle bind fast their jaws, who come not near unto thee.

Many are the scourges of the sinner, but mercy shall encompass him that hopeth in th Lord.

Be glad in the Lord, and rejoice, ye just: and glory all ye right of heart. Glory be, &c.

PSALM XXXVII. *Domine, ne in furore.*

Rebuke me not, O Lord, in thy indignation, nor chastise me in thy wrath.

For thy arrows are fastened in me; and thy hand hath been strong upon me.

There is no health in my flesh, because of thy wrath; there is no peace for my bones, because of my sins.

For my iniquities are gone over my head; and as a heavy burden have become heavy upon me.

My sores are putrefied and corrupted, because of my foolishness.

I am become miserable, and am bowed down even to the end; I walked sorrowful all the day long.

For my loins are filled with illusions; and there is no health in my flesh.

I am afflicted and humbled exceedingly; I roared with the groaning of my heart.

Lord, all my desire is before thee: and my groaning is not hid from thee.

My heart is troubled, my strength hath left me, and the light of my eyes itself is not with me.

My friends and my neighbors have drawn near, and stood against me.

And they that were near me stood afar off; and they that sought my soul used violence.

And they that sought evils to me spoke vain things, and studied deceits all the day long.

But I, as a deaf man, heard not; and was as a dumb man not opening his mouth.

And I became as a man that heareth not; and that hath no reproofs in his mouth.

For in thee, O Lord, have I hoped; thou wilt hear me, O Lord my God.

For I said, lest at any time my enemies rejoice over me: and whilst my feet are moved, they speak great things against me.

For I am ready for scourges; and my sorrow is continually before me.

For I will declare my iniquity, and I will think for my sin.

But my enemies live and are stronger than I; and they that hate me wrongfully are multiplied.

They that render evil for good, have detracted me, because I followed goodness.

Forsake me not, O Lord my God; do not thou depart from me.

Attend unto my help, O Lord, the God of my salvation. Glory be, &c.

Psalm l. *Miserere.*

Have mercy on me, O God, according to thy great mercy.

And according to the multitude of thy tender mercies, blot out my iniquity.

Wash me yet more from my iniquity, and cleanse me from my sin.

For I know my iniquity, and my sin is always before me.

To thee only have I sinned, and have done evil before thee; that thou mayest be justified in thy words, and mayest overcome when thou art judged.

For behold I was conceived in iniquities, and in sins did my mother conceive me.

For behold thou hast loved truth; the uncertain and hidden things of thy wisdom thou hast made manifest to me.

Thou shalt sprinkle me with hyssop, and shall be cleansed; thou shalt wash me, and I shall be made whiter than snow.

To my hearing thou shalt give joy and gladness; and the bones that have been humbled shall rejoice.

Turn away thy face from my sins, and blot out all my iniquities.

Create a clean heart in me, O God; and renew a right spirit within my bowels.

Cast me not away from thy face; and take not thy Holy Spirit from me.

Restore unto me the joy of thy salvation, and strengthen me with a perfect spirit.

I will teach the unjust thy ways; and the wicked shall be converted to thee.

Deliver me from blood, O God, thou God of my salvation; and my tongue shall extol thy justice.

O Lord, thou wilt open my lips; and my mouth shall declare thy praise.

For if thou hadst desired sacrifice, I would indeed have given it; with burnt-offerings thou wilt not be delighted.

A sacrifice to God is an afflicted spirit; a contrite and humbled heart, O God, thou wilt not despise.

Deal favorably, O Lord, in thy good-will with Sion; that the walls of Jerusalem may be built up.

Then shalt thou accept the sacrifice of justice, oblations, and whole burnt-offerings; then shall they lay calves upon thy altar. Glory be, &c.

PSALM CI. *Domine, exaudi.*

Hear, O Lord, my prayer, and let my cry come unto thee.

Turn not away thy face from me: in the day when I am in trouble, incline thy ear to me.

In what day soever I shall call upon thee; hear me speedily.

For my days are vanished like smoke; and my bones are grown dry like fuel for the fire.

I am smitten as grass, and my heart is withered; because I forgot to eat my bread.

Through the voice of my groaning my bone hath cleaved to my flesh.

I am become like to a pelican of the wilderness; I am like a night-raven in the house.

I have watched, and am become as a sparrow, all alone on the house-top.

All the day long my enemies reproach me; and they that praised me did swear against me.

For I did eat ashes like bread; and mingled my drink with weeping.

Because of thy anger and indignation; for having lifted me up, thou hast thrown me down.

My days have declined like a shadow; and I am withered like grass.

But thou, O Lord, endurest forever; and thy memorial to all generations.

Thou shalt arise and have mercy on Sion; for it is time to have mercy on it, for the time is come.

For the stones thereof have pleased thy servants, and they shall have pity on the earth thereof.

And the gentiles shall fear thy name, O Lord; and all the kings of the earth thy glory.

For the Lord hath built up Sion; and he shall be seen in his glory.

He hath had regard to the prayer of the humble; and he hath not despised their petition.

Let these things be written unto another generation; and the people that shall be created shall praise the Lord.

Because he hath looked forth from his high sanctuary; from heaven the Lord hath looked upon the earth.

That he might hear the groans of them that are in fetters; that he might release the children of the slain.

That they may declare the name of the Lord in Sion; and his praise in Jerusalem.

When the people assembled together, and kings to serve the Lord.

He answered him in the way of his strength; declare unto me the fewness of my days.

Call me not away in the midst of my days: thy years are unto generation and generation.

In the beginning, O Lord, thou foundest the earth; and the heavens are the works of thy hands.

They shall perish, but thou remainest: and all them shall grow old like a garment.

And as a vesture thou shalt change them, and

they shall be changed; but thou art always the self-same, and thy years shall not fail.

The children of thy servants shall continue; and their seed shall be directed for ever.

Glory be to the Father, &c.

PSALM CXXIX. *De Profundis.*

Out of the depths I have cried to thee, O Lord; ord, hear my voice.

Let thy ears be attentive to the voice of my supplication.

If thou, O Lord, wilt mark iniquities, Lord, who shall stand it.

For with thee there is merciful forgiveness: and by reason of thy law I have waited for thee, O Lord.

My soul hath relied on his word; my soul hath hoped in the Lord.

From the morning watch even until night, let Israel hope in the Lord.

Because with the Lord there is mercy, and with him plentiful redemption.

And he shall redeem Israel from all his in aities.

Glory be, &c.

PSALM CXLII. *Domine, exaudi.*

Hear, O Lord, my prayer; give ear to m supplication in thy truth; hear me in thy justic

And enter not into judgment with thy servant; for in thy sight no man living shall be justified.

For the enemy hath persecuted my soul; he hath brought down my life to the earth.

He hath made me to dwell in darkness, as those that have been dead of old; and my spirit is in anguish within me: my heart within me is troubled.

I remembered the days of old, I meditated on all thy works: I mused upon the works of thy hands.

I stretched forth my hands to thee: my soul is as earth without water unto thee.

Hear me speedily, O Lord; my spirit hath fainted away.

Turn not away thy face from me, lest I be like unto them that go down into the pit.

Cause me to hear thy mercy in the morning; for in thee have I hoped.

Make the way known to me wherein I should walk; for I have lifted up my soul to thee.

Deliver me from my enemies, O Lord, to thee have I fled; teach me to do thy will, for thou art my God.

Thy good spirit shall lead me into the right land; for thy name's sake, O Lord, thou wilt quicken me in thy justice.

Thou wilt bring my soul out of troubles: and in thy mercy thou wilt destroy my enemies.

And thou wilt cut off all them that afflict my soul; for I am thy servant. Glory be to the Father, &c.

Ant. Remember not, O Lord, our offences, nor those of our parents; and take not revenge on our sins.

PRAYER.

HEAR, I beseech thee, O Lord, the prayers of thy supplicants, and pardon the sins of those who confess to thee; and in thy bounty, give me pardon and peace; through Jesus Christ our Lord. *Amen.*

On Mental Prayer or Meditation.

MEDITATION is morally necessary to salvation, be cause it is impossible to know the truths and the mysteries of our holy religion, except by the eyes of the soul, in other words, by frequent and serious reflection. He who neglects this, walks, as St. Augustine says, with his eyes shut, and in this way it will be impossible for him to discover the road which he ought to choose, and the means which he ought to employ in order to arrive at his destination, namely, at heaven.

But meditation is chiefly necessary to salvation, because he who is not in the habit of meditating, does not pray, and so is lost. He who does not meditate continually, cannot acquire any solid virtues, for no one will persevere in the practice of virtue unless he perseveres at the same time in prayer. For this reason it is that our Lord has said: "*We must always pray and never faint.*" He who does not meditate, will scarcely be able for any length of time to avoid mortal sin, for he will live in continual distraction, and will not be conscious of his own wants. He will make no account of the dangers which surround him, he will not exert himself to employ the means to escape from them, and finally, recognizing no longer how necessary prayer is to his salvation, he will abandon it, and so be lost.

The world is filled with sins, and hell with damned souls, because Christians no longer meditate upon eternal truths. "*With desolation is all the land made desolate, because there is none that considereth in the heart.*" (Jerm. xii.) But on the contrary, he who often thinks of death, judgment and eternity, will abandon sin; otherwise he must leave off meditating, for it is impossible that meditation and sin should be found in company. "*Remember thy last end, and thou shalt never sin.*" (Eccl. vii. 40.)

It is God that speaks to you in meditation, and God speaks to you much better than any preacher can. It is through meditation that the saints have been sanctified, for it is in meditation we learn to turn away our hearts from the goods of this world, and direct them towards God.

According to the counsel of the saints, we ought to choose for the principal subject of our meditations the eternal truths, and the great mysteries of our holy religion. We ought to meditate, therefore, upon sin, heaven, and hell, the incarnation of Jesus Christ, his passion, and his love for men, as displayed in a most especial manner, in his sacred Heart, that centre of his affections, and in the most holy Sacrament, the most precious pledge that he has left us of his love, remaining there with us, and giving himself to us altogether. We ought also to meditate often upon the powerful intercession of the most holy Virgin Mary, the dispenser of graces, and upon St. Joseph, the patron of the interior life, because all these considerations will increase our confidence, and prepare our hearts to receive those graces which Jesus Christ is willing to bestow upon us, through the merits of his passion, and by the intercession of Mary and of the Saints.

The Church is the most proper place for meditation but since one has not always either the time or the means to go there, it will do also to meditate in one's chamber at home, and even in the open air, or while one is occupied in some manual labor, which does no hinder the soul from raising itself upwards to God.

The early hours of the morning are the fittest fo meditation, for when one's morning prayers hav been well said, every thing goes on better throughout the whole day. If one has time, it is good also before lying down to sleep, to consecrate a half-hour to meditation, as in the morning: but if this is quite impossible, it is enough for beginners to meditate for one half-hour each day.

HOW TO MEDITATE.

Before meditation, place yourself devoutly upon your knees. If you are able to remain kneeling without injury to yonr health, it should be done; but if that is likely to prove injurious, you may stand or sit.

Then begin the preparation to your meditation, in which you must never forget to place yourself, first of all, in the presence of God. This may be done by repeating the following Acts: "O my God! I am firmly persuaded that thou art here present, and I adore thee from the bottom of my nothingness."

Then humble yourself before God, saying: "O my God, I deserve to be burning this moment in hell. I am sorry for all my sins. Pardon me in thine infinite mercy."

Lastly, pray God to enlighten you: "Eternal Father! for the love of Jesus and of Mary, enlighten me in this meditation, in order that I may profit by it."

It is well to add to these preparatory prayers, an *Ave* to the Blessed Virgin Mary, and a *Gloria* in honor of St. Joseph, of our patron Saint, and of our guardian Angel. These acts and prayers must be made with great attention, but without dwelling on them too long.

Before you enter upon the meditation itself, read with attention one of the points given in your book of Meditations. (See page 232.) If already in the commencement you feel touched by any truth, then read no farther. We must do, says St. Francis de Sales, as the bees do, for they stop on each flower, until they have sucked out all the honey. If, on the contrary, the first point of the Meditation proves to be a difficult one to make use of, go on at once to the second point.

It is necessary to remark, that although one makes use ordinarily of the understanding to consider the truths of faith, yet the essential point of meditation consists in the following things:

1. *To awaken the affections.*—We ought therefore to humble ourselves with heartfelt sincerity, to animate our faith and our hope, and above all to make acts of contrition, and of love to God, of conformity to his holy will, and to offer ourselves up entirely to him. We should repeat the same affections over and over again, especially those to which we feel the most inclined.

2. *We must make petitions.*—It is in meditation that God shows us our misery, and how much we need his grace to conquer our evil inclinations and our other enemies. For this reason the time of meditation is the fittest time for prayer. God ordinarily gives his grace, and especially the grace of perseverance, to those who pray. "*Ask, and you shall receive:*" therefore, says St. Teresa, if any one does not ask, he will not receive.

3. *We must make good resolutions.*—After having discovered by meditation what we have to do on our part, in order to live in conformity with the holy will of God, and having asked his assistance, it still remains for us to put in practice what we have thus seen to be necessary; otherwise our meditation will be fruitless. We must therefore make a serious resolve to avoid such or such a fault, to do this or that good work the very first occasion. It is necessary also, from time to time during the day, to recall the good resolution we have taken, for fear lest, when the occasion arrives, it should be already forgotten. After the good resolution comes the end of the meditation. Then we must thank God for the holy inspirations which he has given us, and beseech him, for the love of Jesus and of Mary, to help us to carry out in practice the good resolutions we have made. Also, before the meditation is over, we ought

to recommend to God the souls in Purgatory, the Holy Church, our friends and benefactors, and all poor sinners, saying for this purpose a *Pater* and an *Ave*, which are the most efficacious of all prayers, being the same which our Lord Jesus Christ and the Holy Church have taught us.

Having once, with the advice of your confessor fixed upon a certain time in the day for meditation be careful not to omit it on account of aridity or distractions, and do not be troubled or discouraged when you no longer feel the consolations of devotion. St. Francis of Sales says, that a great number of courtiers wait every day on the king, as a testimony of their respect, and are content if only he condescends to look at them. We, too, when we are in meditation, testify our reverence towards God, and give him proofs of our love. If he is willing then to converse with us, and console us, we must be grateful for so sweet a favor; but if he is not disposed to grant us this grace, we must be content to remain recollected in his presence, adoring him and making known our wants. For although God should not speak to your heart, dear Christian, in a sensible manner, be sure he will not fail to regard with a favorable eye these testimonies of your fidelity, he will reward your confidence, and answer your prayer.

The simplest method of meditating is the following: after having invoked the Holy Ghost, you read a few lines in a book of meditations, and then ask yourself the following questions:

1. What does the holy faith here say to me?
2. What must I do to put in practice its teaching in this matter?
3. What have I done hitherto?
4. What am I willing to do in future?

Then ask of God, through Mary, to give you his assistance, and renew over and over again the resolution you have made before the Cross of Jesus Christ.

MEDITATIONS

FOR EVERY DAY OF THE WEEK.

(From the writings of St. Alphonsus Liguori.)

MEDITATION FOR SUNDAY.

On the End of Man.

I. Consider, O my soul, that God has given thee existence, made thee after his own image, without any merit of thine, and adopted thee for his own child in holy Baptism. He has loved thee more than a father, and has created thee to love and serve him in this life, that thou mayest eternally enjoy him in paradise. Therefore, thou art not created and must not live to be happy here on earth, to enjoy riches and authority, or to eat, drink and sleep as do the animals, but only to love thy God and win thy eternal salvation.

And thy Lord has given thee created things for this use, to help thee to reach thy great end. O wretch that I am! I have thought of anything else rather than of my eternal end. *(For example; of this or that thing. Examine here to see what is your chief vice.)*

My Father! for the love of Jesus, grant that I may begin a new life, perfectly holy and conformable to thy divine will. *(Here endeavor to excite the deepest spirit of penance, and make the firmest resolution—especially, never more to think of this or that bad or vain object, but rather on something quite opposite.)*

II. Consider what stings of conscience it will give you at the moment of death, to remember that you have not thought of serving God. What sorrow, when at the end of your days you see that there is nothing left to you, at that hour, of all your possessions, honors splendor, and pleasures, but a handful of dust! What consternation, then, to see that you have lost the favor of God, and your immortal soul, for the sake of vain trifles and things that perish, when it is too late to remedy the evil, too late for you to try the better way. O what despair! O cruel torment! You will then see, but too late, how great is the value of time; you would willingly purchase it then with your blood, but alas! you will not be able. O bitter day for him who has not served and loved God! *(Awaken in your breast the sentiment of contrition, and make a firm resolution.)*

III. Consider how men neglect their salvation, that great end of man. They do not forget to amass riches, to eat, to prepare entertainments, and make all things comfortable about them:—but they think little of serving God. You never have thought of saving your soul, and you consider your everlasting end a thing of little consequence. And thus the greater part of Christians are hurrying, feasting, singing, dancing, and playing on their way to hell. O if they only knew the meaning of that word *Hell!* O man! what pains thou takest to be lost, and wilt thou do nothing to be saved?

When once the private secretary of a king was lying on his death-bed, he exclaimed: Miserable man that I am! I have used so much paper in writing letters for my prince, and have not employed a single leaf to help me examine my sins and prepare for a good confession.

But of what use to him then were those sighs and lamentations? They served at best only to increase his despair. But made wise at the cost of others, learn, Christian, to live mindful of your eternal salvation, if you would not fall into the same despair. And remember that every thing you do, say, or think, if it is not for God, is lost. *(Reflect again on your besetting sin.)* It is indeed time for you to change your life. What! will you wait for the moment of death to wake from your delusion—at the door of eternity, on the borders of the abyss? There is yet time, yet opportunity, to correct your error.

My God! spare me! I love thee above all things. I am sorry for having offended thee more than for every other evil. Mary, my hope! pray to Jesus for me. (*Excite your will to contrition, and make a firm resolution.*)

MEDITATION FOR MONDAY.

On the importance of securing our end.

I. Consider, O man! how much depends upon gaining your great end, that is, your salvation. Every thing is at stake; for if you reach it, then you are saved, then you will be forever blessed, and you will enjoy forever every possible good of soul and body; but, if you fail, you will lose soul and body, Paradise and God; you will be forever miserable; you will be lost eternally. Behold here the greatest of all affairs, the only important, the only necessary business—to serve God and save your soul. Then say no longer, O Christian; I will live now for my own pleasure, and after that I will give myself to God, and hope to be saved after all. O, how many has this false hope thrown into hell, who once spoke thus, and who now are lost, for whom there is now no deliverance! What man would ever wish to be damned? Yet he is accursed of God who sins in the hope of mercy. "*Cursed is the man who sins in hope.*" You say, I will commit this sin and afterwards confess it. Who knows if you will have time for that? Who can give you the assurance that you will not die immediately after you have committed this sin? Meanwhile you lose the favor of God; and what will become of you if you do not obtain it again? God is merciful to those who fear him, but not towards those who despise him. "*His mercy is to them that fear Him.*" (Luke, i. 50.) Do not say, it is all the same whether I have two sins to confess, or three: no; for God may pardon you two sins, but not perhaps the third. God suffers long, but he will not suffer always. "*He will punish them in the fulness of their sins.*" (Zech. vi. 14.) When the measure is full, God pardons no more, but punishes sinners suddenly with death, and casts them from him, so that they go on from one sin to another, until they fall into hell—a punishment far worse than death itself. O, my brethren, mark well what you now read: cease from sin and give yourself to God. Fear lest this should be the last warning which God will send you. You have gone on in your offences long enough. He has borne with you long enough. Tremble lest the first mortal sin you again commit after this, God will pardon you no more. Consider well; your soul is at stake; all eternity is at stake. How many have been moved by this great thought of eternity to leave the world and live in cloisters, deserts, and caves! O, unhappy sinner that I am! What have I gained by so many sins? (*Reflect on the frequent repetition of your besetting sin.*) A guilty conscience, a heavy heart, a burdened soul, hell deserved, and God lost! Ah, my God and Father, unite me to thee once more and forever in sacred charity. (*Excite the spirit of contrition in your heart, and make a firm resolution.*)

II. Consider how this, the only important concern, the most neglected of all. We think of every thing ıt our salvation. We have time for every thing but od. Exhort a man of the world to receive the Sacaments oftener, or to make a meditation of half an ıour, and he will answer you: I have children, I have property to take care of, I have business, I have so nuch to do. O my God! Have you not a soul too? Call upon all your possessions, and your children and relations, to help you at the hour of death, they will give you no relief, neither can they rescue you from hell, when you are damned. Flatter yourself not with the hope that you can reconcile God and the world, Paradise and sin. The affair of your salvation is not a thing which can be arranged easily; you must lay out efforts; you must do yourself violence if you would win the crown of eternal life. (*Think of that besetting sin which lies in your way.*) Ah! how many Christians who are now in hell, flattered themselves that at some future time they would serve God and save their souls. What folly to think always of what finishes so soon, and to think so little of that which will never end! O Christian! think of your true home, remember that you will soon quit this earth and enter into the dwelling of eternity. O horrible misfortune for you, should you be damned! Then, remember it well, that there is no more help for you. (*Arouse in yourself the spirit of contrition, and make a firm resolution.*)

III. Consider well, O Christian! and say to yourself: I have only one soul; if I lose that I lose all. I have only one immortal soul; if I gain the whole world and ruin that, what does it profit me? If I raise myself to high honor and distinction, and lose my soul, what does it profit me? If I succeed in becoming rich, and enlarge my house, and provide well for my children, and lose my soul, what will it profit me? How much have the splendors, amusements and vanities of life helped those who once lived in this world, and who have now become dust in the grave, and their sou' the prey of hell? Since this soul is mine, and since have only one, which if once lost is lost for ever, the ought I indeed most seriously to think of my salvation. Something of far greater than common importance depends on it; for eternal happiness or eternal misery is involved. O my God, deeply penetrated with shame, I see that I have hitherto lived like one blind, and that I have wandered far from thee. (*Think here once more of your besetting sin.*) I have not thought of saving my soul. Save me, O my Father! for Jesus Christ's sake. I am content to lose all things, if only I do not lose thee, O my God! Mary, my hope! O save me by thy intercession. (*Excite your heart to a deep contrition, and make a firm resolution.*)

MEDITATION FOR TUESDAY.

On mortal Sin.

I. Consider that God has created you in order that you may love him; but you have rebelled against him with the blackest ingratitude; you have treated him as an enemy; you have despised his grace and his friendship. You knew that by your sins you would displease him, and yet you have committed them. What does he, that man who commits sin? He turns his back on God; he loses respect for him; he lifts his hand, it may be said, to strike him; he grieves the heart of his God. Is. lxiii. 10. He who sins, says in fact to God: Withdraw from me, I will not obey thee, I will not serve thee, I will not acknowledge thee as my Lord, I will not have thee for my God; this pleasure, that worldly advantage, this gratification of my revenge must be my God. So do you speak in your heart, whenever you prefer a creature to your God. St. Mary Magdalen of Pazzi could not comprehend how a Christian, with his eyes open, could commit sin. And you who now are reading this, what do you say? How many mortal sins have you not already committed? (*Examine yourself.*) My God! pardon me, and have mercy on me. I have offended thy infinite goodness; I hate my sins, I love thee, and repent of having offended thee, O my God, thou who art so infinitely lovely! (*Arouse yourself to repentance, and make a firm resolution.*)

II. Consider that in the moment when you are committing sin, God says to you: "My son! I am thy God, who have created thee from nothing, who have redeemed thee with my blood. I forbid thee, under pain of my displeasure, to commit these sins." But when you sin, you answer your God and say: "O Lord! I will not obey thee, I will procure for myself this satisfaction · it is of no importance to me, whether it pleases thee or not." Alas! O my God, more than once have I done this! (*Examine yourself.*) How was it possible for thee to bear with me so long? O that I had died before offending thee! I will never displease thee more: I will love thee, O infinite goodness! give me only the grace of perseverance! give me thy holy love! (*Excite your heart to contrition, and make a firm resolution.*)

III. Consider that when the number of sins exceed a certain limit, God abandons the sinner. "*The Lord patiently expecteth, that when the day of judgment shall come, he may punish them in the fulness of their sins.*" 2 Mach. vi. 14. When, then, my brethren, you are tempted again to sin, never more say I will confess my sins afterwards. If God should let you die first, if he should entirely desert you, what would become of you for all eternity? Alas! how many in this way have been lost! They too hoped for pardon, but the hour of death came and they were lost. O tremble, for fear the same thing should befall you.

He deserves no mercy who takes advantage of the goodness of God to offend him. God has already pardoned you so many sins. You have reason enough to fear that God will not forgive the next mortal sin you commit. Thank him for having waited for you so kindly and so long, and make the firm resolution rather to suffer death than to commit sin again.

From this day forward always say: O my God! I have often offended thee! I will not employ the remnant of my life in displeasing thee more; no, thou dost not merit such treatment as this. I will employ it only in loving thee, and in sorrow for the sins I have committed against thee. I repent of them with my whole heart. My Jesus, I am anxious to love thee; wilt thou give me strength and help me? Amen. (*Excite in your soul a sorrow for sin and make a firm resolution.*)

MEDITATION FOR WEDNESDAY.

On Death.

I. Consider that this life must one day end. Already has the sentence gone forth: "Thou must die." Death is certain, but you know not when it will come. One little drop flowing through your heart; a vein bursting in your breast; a suffocating cold in the throat, a violent rush of blood, the bite of a poisonous reptile, a fever, a wound, a freshet, an earthquake, a flash of lightning, is enough to deprive you of life. Death will come to you when you least expect it. How many have laid down to sleep at night in health, and in the morning have been found dead! May not this happen as well to you? All those who have died so suddenly, little thought that they were to die in this way, and if they were then in the state of sin, where are they now? and where will they be through all eternity? Let it be as it may with them, this is certain, that a time will one day come, when for you, a night will close in, followed by no morning; or a day will begin for you that will be interrupted by no night. Jesus Christ said, I will come as a thief, unseen and in secret. Your merciful Saviour warns you in season, for he desires that you may be saved. Do what God desires of you, profit by the warning, prepare yourself to die well before death itself comes. "Be ready," for when there is no more time for preparation, it is necessary to be already prepared. (*Examine here your besetting sins.*) It is certain that you must die. The drama of this world must close for you, and you know not when. Who knows whether you will live a year, a month, or even till to-morrow? Jesus! enlighten me and pardon me. (*Arouse your soul to contrition, and make a firm resolution.*)

II. Consider how you will lie, at the hour of death,

stretched upon a bed, surrounded by your weeping friends, a priest by your side to assist your soul; a crucifix at your head, the lighted taper at your feet; in fine, already just at the entrance of eternity. Dreadful pains afflict your distracted head, it grows dark around you, your tongue is parched, your breath is short, your breast is burdened, your blood chilled, your flesh shrunken, your heart rent with anguish, all you have is gliding from you, and, poor and naked, you will be thrown into a grave to rot. There worms and insects will gnaw your flesh, and nothing of you will be left but the crumbling bones and a little dust. Open some grave and look! what has become of that rich, that avaricious man, that vain and worldly woman?

Thus ends life. At the hour of death you will find yourself surrounded by evil spirits, who will bring up before you all the sins you have committed from your childhood. Now the devil conceals and excuses your sins, that he may lead you into sin; he says to you, This vanity, this pleasure, this dangerous company, this inclination is no great sin; you have no bad intention in this acquaintance; but at the hour of death he will show you all the enormity of your sins. (*Examine yourself thoroughly as to your besetting sin.*) By the light of that eternity into which you are just entering, you will then see what an evil it was to have offended an infinite God. Now, while there is yet time, while you can do it, remedy the evil, for then it will be too late. (*Awaken your contrition, and make a firm resolution.*)

III. Consider that death is a moment upon which a whole eternity depends. Behold! here lies a man just dying, and therefore near to both eternities, near an eternity of happiness, or an eternity of misery. See, his fate for eternity depends upon his last breath, after which his soul will be forever happy or forever lost.

O, the end of life! the last breath! that last moment, on which an eternity depends—an eternity of glory or of pain—of happiness or of misery; of joy, or of despair; an eternity of every good, or an eternity of every evil; an eternity in heaven, or an eternity in hell! For, if in that last moment you are saved, you will have nothing more to suffer, you will be forever happy and blessed; but if you die in sin, and are damned, you will be wretched, and in despair, so long as God is God. In death, you will see what mean those words, heaven, hell, sin, an offended God, contempt of the divine Law, sins hidden in confession, goods of others not restored. "O, miserable being that I am," the dying man will exclaim, "I must now, in a few moments, appear in the presence of God! Who knows what judgment will meet me there? Whither am I going, to heaven or to hell? Shall I rejoice forever with the angels, or shall I burn eternally with the damned? Shall I be a child of God, or a slave of the devil? Alas! soon, too soon, I shall know, and where I find myself the first moment, there shall I remain through eternity. Ah! what will become of me in a few hours, in a few moments? What will become of me when I can no longer repair that scandal? when I cannot restore those ill-gotten goods? when I cannot pardon my enemies from my heart? when I cannot any longer make good that confession?" (*Examine yourself as to your principal sin.*) Then will you curse a thousand times that day in which you sinned; you will curse that pleasure, that revenge which you have taken, but too late, and without avail, because you will do it then only from the fear of punishment, and not from love to God! Ah! Lord, behold—now, at this very moment, I turn to thee; I will not wait for death; now, and always, I will love thee; I embrace thee, and in my embrace will I die! My mother, Mary, let me die under thy protecting mantle; help me in my death! Amen. (*Awaken your contrition, and make a firm resolution.*)

MEDITATION FOR THURSDAY.

On the Judgment.

I. Consider how the soul, as soon as it has left the body, will be immediately taken before the tribunal of God, to be judged. Your Judge is Almighty God, offended and enraged with you. Your accusers are the devils, your enemies. You are to be judged for your sins. The judgment is one which cannot be recalled; the punishment is hell. There, you have no companions, no parents, no friends; you will be alone there, you and your God. Then you will feel all the enormity of your sins, and you will no longer be able to excuse them as you have before. All the sins you have committed, in thought, word, or deed, will be examined; all the sins of indulgence, of omission, and of commission. (*Here examine into the vast number of your sins.*) Every thing will be weighed in the great balance of divine justice, and if in any one point you are found guilty, you will be eternally lost. My Jesus, thou who wilt be my judge, pardon me before thou judgest me. (*Excite a tender sorrow for your sins, and make a firm resolution.*)

II. Consider how the divine justice will judge all people in the valley of Jehoshaphat, when, at the end of the world, their bodies will arise, that, together with the soul, they may receive reward or punishment according to their works. Remember that if condemned you will again receive your body, which will serve for the eternal prison of your soul. Then will the soul curse the body, and the body the soul, so that body and soul, which are now united in the search of forbidden pleasures, will be again united to torment each other after death. If, on the other hand, you are saved, then will your body arise in perfect beauty, radiant and incapable of suffering, so that both soul and body will be worthy of eternal life. Thus will this life, l ke the acting of a drama, end. All the delight, as well as the pomp of this world, will end. All is over then. Nothing remains but two eternities, the one of glory and the other of punishment; one of bliss, the other of misery; one of joy, and the other of suffering; the just in heaven, the sinners in hell. (*Examine how you stand, and especially with regard to your besetting sin.*) Poor, then, will be that man who has loved the world, and who, for the miserable joys of this world, has lost every thing—every thing, soul, body, heaven, and God. (*Awaken your contrition, and make a firm resolution.*)

III. Consider the eternal sentence. Jesus Christ the judge will turn towards the reprobates and say. It is all over with you; now, ungrateful souls, all is over! My hour is now come; the hour of truth and justice, the hour of wrath and vengeance. *Depart from me, ye cursed, into everlasting fire.* Matt. xxv. Away, ye sinners. You have loved cursing, and now let it come upon you. Accursed be ye all, now and throughout all eternity! Depart from my presence; go, deprived of all you possessed, laden with torments, go into eternal fire! (*In view of this judgment, examine yourself on your besetting sin.*)

Then will Jesus turn to the elect, and say: Come, blessed children of my Father, come receive the kingdom which is prepared for you; come, no more to bear the cross with me, but with me to wear the crown. Come and be heirs of my kingdom, companions of my glory, come to praise my mercy through all eternity; come from exile to your home, come from misery to joy, come from weeping to rejoicing, come from suffering to eternal rest! "*Come, ye blessed of my Father, possess the kingdom prepared for you.*" O my Jesus!

I also hope to be among these blessed ones. I love thee above all things. O give me thy blessing now! And do thou, my mother Mary, bless me also. (*Make a fervent act of contrition, with a firm resolution to prepare during life for judgment.*)

MEDITATION FOR FRIDAY.

On Hell.

I. Contemplate for a moment that frightful prison of hell, filled with fire, where the damned suffer eternally. Into this fire they are, so to speak, plunged and buried. Under them a sea of fire, over them a sea of fire, around on all sides fire—fire in the eyes, fire in the mouth, fire penetrating every where. There each and every sense has a torment of its own. The eyes are tormented by darkness and smoke, and, at the same time, by the sight of the devils and the rest of the damned. Day and night, the ears hear nothing else but howling, and weeping, and cursing. The sense of smell is sickened by the insupportable stench of so many putrid and infected bodies. The taste is tormented by a burning thirst, and a cruel hunger, while never a drop of water can be had or the least refreshment. And thus these miserable captives, suffering every want, devoured by fire, tormented by every pain, weep, groan, howl, and despair, whilst they cannot find, and for all eternity never will find, rest or consolation. O Hell! Hell! is it necessary that men should wait until they are swallowed by thy flames, to believe in thee? You, who even now are reading on this page, what do you say? (*Pause here awhile, and with this terrible truth in view, think on your besetting sin.*) If you had to die this moment, where would you go? What! you cannot bear even a spark of fire on your hand; and do you think to be able to live in an ocean of fire, where, abandoned by every creature, desolate and desperate you will have to pass a never-ending eternity? (*Encourage in your heart the deepest sentiments of contrition, and make a firm resolution.*)

II. Consider well those pains which afflict the faculties of the soul in hell. The memory will be everlastingly tormented by the stings of conscience. This is that worm which will forever gnaw in the conscience of the damned, to remind him how foolishly he consented to his own ruin for the sake of a few poisoned pleasures. O God! how will each moment of sinful pleasure appear to him then, after a hundred, after a thousand years spent in hell! That gnawing worm will recall to his mind the time which God gave him for conversion, all the opportunities and means he had to secure the salvation of his soul, the good example of his friends, all the holy resolutions made, alas! but broken. (*Examine yourself well on these points, and place before your eyes your predominant sin.*) And then he will see that there is no longer any way of escaping from his eternal ruin. O God! O God! what a double hell will this be! The will, too, is doomed to be always thwarted; it will never have that which it desires, and will ever have that which it desires not, that is to say, every possible suffering. The understanding will see clearly what great rewards it has lost; namely, heaven and God! O God! my God! pardon me for the love of Jesus. (*Excite your heart to contrition, and make a firm resolution.*)

III. Sinner, you who are now so indifferent whether or not you lose heaven and God, you will know how great has been your blindness, when you shall see the triumph and joy of the blessed in heaven; and you yourself driven like an unclean creature from that blessed home, cast out from the presence of God, and the company of Mary, of the angels and the saints of God. Then in a frenzy of despair you will exclaim: O Heaven, O place of joy! O God! O infinite good, thou art not for me, thou wilt never more be mine! Alas!

poor sinner, do penance rather now! amend your life at once. (*Examine your conscience again, and place before you your besetting sin.*) O yes, wait not till time with you shall be no longer!—give yourself wholly to God. Begin to love him truly. Pray to Jesus, pray to Mary, that they may have mercy on you. (*Make a fervent act of contrition and a strong resolution.*)

MEDITATION FOR SATURDAY.

On the eternity of punishment.

1. Consider that Hell has no end. There, all kinds of suffering are found, and for all eternity. Hundreds and thousands of years will pass in these torments, and yet hell will be always as if just beginning. Hundreds of thousands, hundreds of millions of years and of centuries will pass away, and Hell will be still at its commencement. If at this very hour an angel should carry the tidings to one of the damned, that God had consented to free him from hell—and when? hear! when so many millions of centuries shall have passed away as there are drops of water in the ocean, leaves on the trees, sands in the sea, and on the earth—you would shudder at this, but still it is true that such tidings would give greater joy to that soul, than you would feel if you were told that you had become the king of a great kingdom. Yes, certainly! for that poor damned sinner would say: It is true that many, many centuries will first pass by, but at length a day will come, in which my sufferings will end! Alas! all these centuries will pass away, but Hell will ever be beginning anew; all these centuries may be multiplied like the sands, the rain-drops and the leaves, but Hell is still beginning anew. Every lost soul would gladly, if he might, enter into this agreement with God: Lord if it please thee, increase my pain! O Lord! prolong my pains as long as it may please thee, I am satisfied

if it will only one day end, I am content. But no, this end will never come—never! But perhaps this poor lost sinner will delude and flatter himself, and say inwardly: Perhaps God will one day have mercy on me and deliver me from Hell—No! the condemned soul will always have before his eyes the sentence of his eternal condemnation, and his language will be this: Alas! it is sure, too sure! all these torments which now suffer, this fire, this sorrow, this cry of despair will never end! never, never, O never! no, it will last forever, forever. O eternity, O Hell! how is it possible that men believe in you, and yet continue to live in sin! (*Look steadily here upon your besetting sin, and with eternity in view, excite your soul to contrition, and make a firm resolution.*)

II. My Christian friend, think well of this, and consider that hell is waiting for you also, if you sin. Even now its horrid flames are burning under your feet, and O, at this moment, even while you are reading these words, how many souls are falling into it! Remember that when you have once entered there, you can never leave it. And if you have deserved Hell, thank God that he has not yet cast you into it, and hasten, hasten, as soon as possible, to remedy the evil. Mourn for your sins, and use all the means that are in your power for your salvation. Go frequently to confession, read daily some spiritual book, say the Rosary every day in honor of the Mother of God, that you may obtain great devotion to her, fast if possible every Saturday in honor of Mary, resist temptations, and often call upon Jesus and Mary when you are tempted. Avoid the occasions of sin, and if God should call you to leave the world, then do it, yes, do it! Ah! every thing that we can do to avoid an eternity of suffering is little, is nothing. "No certainty can be too great, where we are in peril for eternity," so says St. Bernard. In order to place yourself in safety for eternity, no foresight is too far-reaching. See how many hermits, that they might avoid Hell, have gone into caves and deserts, and there lived! And what are you doing for your soul? what are you doing, you that have so often deserved Hell? what are you doing? (*Think of your besetting sin.*) See to it, that you are not lost. Give yourself once for all to God, and say to him, O Lord! behold me ready to do every thing thou requirest of me. O Mary, help me. (*Endeavor to arouse your will to the deepest contrition, and make a firm resolution.*)

PLAIN INSTRUCTIONS

PLAIN INSTRUCTIONS

The Little Catechism;

OR,

QUESTIONS AND ANSWERS ON THOSE TRUTHS WHICH ARE THE MOST NECESSARY FOR A CHRISTIAN TO KNOW.

AN ADMONITION TO PARENTS.

As soon as children begin to talk, their parents, or those who supply to them the place of parents, should teach them to pronounce with reverence the holy names of Jesus and Mary. They should teach them to know their Father in heaven, who is so full of love, and so worthy of being loved; to know also his only begotten Son, and the Holy Ghost; and speak to them often also of Mary, the divine Mother. Then they should be taught to bless themselves with the sign of the Cross, and to pray before the Crucifix, and finally to repeat the Lord's Prayer, the Hail Mary, and the Creed, slowly and with devotion.

PRELIMINARY QUESTIONS.

OF THE CATHOLIC FAITH.

Question. What is the faith of a true Catholic Christian?

Answer. The faith of a true Catholic is, a firm belief, without doubting, of all that God has revealed and teaches through the Holy Catholic Church.

Q. Is it not enough for each one to read the Holy

Scriptures, and to believe only what he can find in them?

A. No: for two reasons. First, because the Word of God is not contained in the Bible alone, but also in the tradition of the Church; and secondly, because the Church is the only authorized teacher and interpreter of the word of God.

Q. Why must we believe without doubting?

A. Because the Catholic Faith has been revealed by God, who cannot be deceived, and is incapable of deceiving us, and who has promised that his Holy Church shall never err.

Q. Is it necessary for every one to know all the truths which God has revealed to his Church?

A. No. For many persons this would be impossible. Some of these truths, however, are necessary for all to know; as to the rest, it is sufficient to confide in the doctrine of the Church, and to believe that whatever she believes and teaches is true.

PART FIRST.

THINGS WHICH EVERY CATHOLIC MUST KNOW, AS NECESSARY MEANS OF SALVATION.

Q. Are there any doctrines which every one is bound to know, under pain of mortal sin?

A. Yes; it is absolutely necessary for all to know in substance the following: viz., the existence of one God, the mystery of the Holy Trinity, the Redemption of mankind by the incarnation and death of Jesus Christ, and the Future State of reward or punishment. Those who are ignorant of these things cannot receive the sacraments.

1. Of God.

Q. What is God?

A. God is the supreme, and infinitely perfect Being.

Q. How is God supreme?

A. God is supreme, for that he alone is the Lord and Ruler of the world. All things were made by him, and are subject to his power.

Q. How is God infinitely perfect?

A. God is infinitely perfect, because he possesses in himself every kind of goodness in an infinite degree.

Q. Is God eternal?

A. God is eternal; for he always was, is, and will be.

Q. Does God ever change?

A. No; God is unchangeable; he is forever the same.

Q. Is God good?

A. God is infinitely good. All that is good comes from him.

Q. Is there any thing which God does not know?

A. God knows every thing, even the most secret things, and the very thoughts of our hearts.

Q. Is there any thing which God cannot do?

A. No, God is almighty. He created heaven and earth, the angels and men, and every creature that exists, and made them out of nothing.

Q. Is there any place where God is not?

A. No; God is everywhere.

Q. Can God lie?

A. No, God is infinitely true and faithful. All that he says is true, and all that he promises he will do.

Q. Is God holy?

A. God is infinitely holy. He loves every thing that is good, and hates every thing that is wicked.

Q. Is God just?

A. God is infinitely just. He always rewards what is good, and punishes what is wicked.

Q. Is God merciful?

A. God is infinitely merciful. He is always ready to forgive the penitent sinner.

Q. Has God a body?

A. No: God has no body. He is a pure Spirit.

Q. Is there more than one God?

A. No: there is only one God.

2. Of the Holy Trinity.

Q. Is God only one person?

A. There are three persons in God, but only one essence.

Q. How do we call these three divine Persons

A. They are named: 1. The Father; 2. The Son; 3. The Holy Ghost. The Father is of himself; the Son is begotten of the Father; the Holy Ghost is not begotten, but proceeds equally from the Father and the Son. And all three are alike uncreated and eternal.

Q. You say there is only one God in three Persons: what must we understand by this?

A. We must understand that although, in some manner, we can distinguish in our thoughts and in our prayers between the Father, and the Son, and the Holy Ghost, yet it is necessary to believe that these three are only one and the same divine Being, having only one mind, and one will. This is a great mystery, but God has not yet revealed himself to us more clearly than this.

Q. How do we confess the Holy Trinity?

A. We confess our belief in the Holy Trinity every time we bless ourselves with the sign of the cross, by touching our forehead, our breast, and our shoulders, and saying: "*In the name of the Father,* ✠ *and of the Son,* ✠ *and of the Holy Ghost.* ✠ *Amen.*

3. Of the Redemption of Mankind.

Q. Have men always remained obedient to God?

A. No: the very first of all, Adam and Eve, disobeyed God by eating of the forbidden fruit in Paradise, and thereby sinned.

Q. Did this sin injure the first man only?

A. This original sin not only injured our first parents, but it has also descended from them to all their children.

Q. Have then all men been cast away forever from God, like the rebellious angels ?

A. No : for God, in his great mercy, has given us a Redeemer, who is Jesus Christ.

Q. Why do we call Jesus Christ our Redeemer ?

A. Because he has redeemed us from the slavery of the devil, by dying for us.

4. The Incarnation and Death of Jesus Christ.

Q. Is not Jesus Christ God ?

A. Yes : he is the second Person of the Holy Trinity ; that is to say, God the Son, begotten of the Father from all eternity.

Q. Since Jesus Christ is God, how could he die for us ?

A. He became incarnate for that purpose.

Q. What is meant by the incarnation of Jesus Christ ?

A. It means that the eternal Son of God came down from heaven to earth, and took to himself a human body and soul ; in other words, he became a Man like ourselves, in order that he might thus be able to die for us.

Q. How did he accomplish this wonderful work of the incarnation ?

A. He was conceived by the power of the Holy Ghost, in the womb of a virgin, and born of her into the world.

Q. Who was this wonderful woman ?

A. It was the Blessed Virgin Mary. And for this reason she is rightly called the Mother of God.

Q. How did Jesus Christ die for us ?

A. He was accused falsely by the Jews, and condemned to death by Pontius Pilate. He then allowed himself to be nailed to the cross, on Mount Calvary, near the city of Jerusalem, where he died in great agony.

Q. What became of the body of our Blessed Lord after his death ?

A. It was laid in a sepulchre or tomb near by.

Q. And what became of his soul?

A. His soul descended into Hell; that is to say into Limbo, where the souls of the Patriarchs an other holy men of old were waiting for the Redemp tion.

Q. Did the soul of our Lord remain long in Limbo?

A. No. After three days his soul came back to b united once more to his body, and Jesus Christ raise himself again to life by his own power, and came ou from the tomb.

Q. Did our Lord then appear again in this world

A. Yes; but only for a little while. Forty days a ter his Resurrection, he ascended into heaven from th Mount of Olives, in presence of his disciples.

5. Future Rewards and Punishments.

Q. Will our Lord Jesus Christ ever come again?

A. Yes. He will come again at the last day, accon panied by the holy angels, to judge the whole worl that he may reward the good and punish the wicke This is called the General Judgment.

Q. Will the bodies of the dead be present also a this judgment?

A. Yes; body and soul will be judged together: fo the bodies of the dead will arise on that day from the graves to be united once more to their souls, neve again to be separated.

Q. Will there be no other judgment before the ge eral judgment at the end of the world?

A. Yes, certainly; the soul of each man will b judged at the moment of his death. This is called th Particular Judgment.

Q. After this particular judgment what will happe

A. The soul will then go either to Purgatory, or Paradise, or to Hell.

Q. What is Purgatory?

A. Purgatory is a place where some souls suffer

awhile, on account of those sins which they have not expiated during this life.

Q. What souls are they which go to Purgatory?

A. The souls of those who die in the grace of God, but are nevertheless still soiled by venial sins, or who have not done during their life sufficient penance for their sins.

Q. How may these poor souls in Purgatory be aided by us?

A. They may be aided, 1. By Prayer. 2. By the Holy Sacrifice of the Mass. 3. By other good works done for their sake. 4. By indulgences.

Q. What is Hell?

A. Hell is a place of eternal torment, where the damned are punished forever. Those who die in mortal sin go there.

Q. What is Heaven?

A. Heaven is the blessed abode of the Saints, where the faithful servants of God are rewarded, and enjoy his presence forever. Those go to heaven who die in the grace of God.

Q. Will all those be saved who have believed and professed the true Faith?

A. No: Faith is necessary to salvation, but of itself alone it is not sufficient.

Q. Upon what other principle, then, will men be rewarded or punished at the day of judgment?

A. They will be judged according to their works; that is to say, according to the sins they shall have committed, or the good works they may have done.

6. Of Sin.

Q. What is sin?

A. Sin is a wilful transgression of the law of God.

Q. How many kinds of sin are there?

A. There two kinds of sin; namely, 1. Original sin. . Actual sin.

Q. What is original sin?

A. Original sin is that sin which Adam committed in Paradise, and which we have inherited from him, being all born in sin.

Q. How is original sin remitted?

A. Original sin is remitted in holy Baptism.

Q. What is actual sin?

A. Actual sin is any sin which we commit ourselves in other words, it is the wilful violation of the law of God, after one has come to the age of reason. It is committed by thoughts, words, or actions, or by the omission of what we ought to do.

Q. What is mortal sin?

A. Mortal sin is a grievous offence against God which kills the soul.

Q. How does mortal sin kill the soul?

A. Mortal sin kills the soul, by separating it from God, and subjecting it to the punishment of hell.

Q. What is venial sin?

A. Venial sin is a less grievous transgression of th divine law. It offends God and stains the soul, bu does not ruin it.

7. Of Good Works.

Q. Is it true that good works are necessary to salvation?

A. Yes; good works are certainly necessary to salvation, for "*faith without works is dead.*" St. James ii. 20.

Q. What is meant by good works?

A. A good work is any right action, done in a stat of grace, and with some holy motive.

Q. Can a man, by any strength of his own, perform such good works, so as to merit eternal life?

A. No: those truly good works which possess me before God, and deserve salvation, can only be do. with the help of God's grace.

PART SECOND.

THINGS WHICH EVERY CATHOLIC IS BOUND TO KNOW BY COMMAND OF GOD OR OF THE CHURCH.

Q. What other things is every Catholic bound to know, besides what we have already mentioned?

A. Every Catholic is also bound to know, 1. The three most ordinary Christian prayers; viz., the Lord' Prayer, the Hail Mary, and the Apostles' Creed: and also, at least in substance, 2. The Commandments of God; 3. The Precepts of the Church; 4. The Sacraments, and especially those three which are necessary to every one; namely, Baptism, Penance, and the Holy Eucharist.

Q. Is it a mortal sin for a Christian to be ignorant of these things?

A. Yes, if it be through his own wilfulness or neglect.

I. THE ORDINARY CHRISTIAN PRAYERS.

Q. Is it necessary to pray?

A. Yes; it is very necessary to our salvation.

Q. Why is it so necessary?

A. Because it has been commanded by Jesus Christ.

Q. Is it necessary for any other reason?

A. It is necessary also, for the reason that every man needs the grace of God to avoid sin and practice virtue, and this grace is not obtained without prayer.

Q. What prayer contains every thing for which we ought to pray?

A. Every thing we need to pray for is included in the Lord's Prayer. It is called the Lord's Prayer, because it was made for us by Jesus Christ himself.

Q. Repeat the Lord's Prayer.

A. "Our Father," &c. (*See page* 17.)

Q. What prayer after this one is the most remarkable?

A. The Hail Mary.

Q. Why is the Hail Mary so remarkable?

A. Because it is a very holy and efficacious prayer, inspired by the Holy Ghost, and adopted by the Holy Church.

Q. Repeat the Hail Mary.

A. "Hail Mary, full of grace," &c. (*See page* 17.)

Q. Is it also necessary to know the Apostles' Creed?

A. Yes; the Holy Church would have every Catholic learn it by heart, and repeat it often.

Q. Why is it called the Apostles' Creed?

A. Because it is believed to have been composed by the Apostles themselves.

Q. Repeat the Apostles' Creed?

A. "I believe," &c. (*See page* 17.)

II. The Commandments of God.

Q. Why are the Ten Commandments called the commandments of God?

A. Because they were given to us by God himself on Mount Sinai.

Q. Which are these Ten Commandments?

A. They are contained, in substance, in the following verses, which may easily be committed to memory

1. One God alone, for evermore
   By faith, and hope, and love, adore.
2. Thou shalt not take his name in vain.
3. The Lord's day thou shalt not profane.
4. Honor thy father, and thy mother.
5. Thou shalt not hurt nor hate thy brother.
6. Thou shalt do no adultery.
7. Thou shalt not steal.
8. Thou shalt not lie.
9. Thou shalt have no impure desire.
10. Nor to thy neighbor's goods aspire.

Q. What do the first three commandments of God contain?

A. The first three commandments contain our duties towards God.

Q. What do the seven other commandments contain?

A. The seven other commandments contain our duties towards our neighbor.

Q. What does the First Commandment require?

A. The First Commandment requires us to believe in the one only true God, to hope in him, to love him and adore him.

Q. What does the first commandment forbid?

A. It forbids Idolatry, Infidelity, Heresy, Superstition, Witchcraft, Fortune-telling, and every kind of False worship.

Q. Is it right to venerate the Angels and Saints?

A. It is right; because we pay them no divine honor, but only honor them and implore their intercession with God, as being the friends of God.

Q. Is it permitted to venerate holy images?

A. The veneration of holy images is permitted, because this veneration is not paid to the image itself, but to that which it represents.

Q. Is it permitted to venerate holy relics?

A. The veneration of the relics of the Saints, or the remains of the bodies of the Saints, is also permitted, because this honor is referred to God, who is glorified in his Saints.

Q. Is it a sin to join in the worship of heretics, or schismatics, or to be present at their meetings or preachings?

A. Yes, it is a sin to countenance their doctrines, or their worship in any way.

Q. What does the Second Commandment forbid?

A. It forbids all blasphemy, and profanation of the holy Name of God; all perjury, and rash or foolish swearing; and all cursing.

Q. What does this commandment require?

A. It requires us to honor the name of God, to speak

with reverence of holy things, and to keep our lawful oaths and vows.

Q. What does the Third Commandment require?

A. It requires us to attend divine service on Sundays and Holydays, and to spend those days in devotion and good works.

Q. What does it forbid?

A. It forbids all servile labor done on those days without strong reasons of necessity, charity, or devotion.

Q. What does the Fourth Commandment require?

A. It requires that we should love, honor, obey, and help our parents; that parents should provide for the wants of their children, instruct, govern, and watch over them; that husband and wife should live together in all duty and affection; and that we should obey all our superiors, both spiritual and temporal, and respect their authority.

Q. What does this commandment forbid?

A. It forbids all disobedience, hatred, contempt, mocking, cursing, or abuse of parents and superiors.

Q. What does the Fifth Commandment forbid?

A. It forbids every outward act of violence against our neighbor; such as murder, striking, &c., and all injurious and insulting words. It forbids, also, all inward hatred, anger, and enmity.

Q. What else does this commandment forbid?

A. It forbids suicide, or self-murder, and the exposure of one's life and health without necessity or duty; also, to destroy or impair one's reason by drunkenness.

Q. What does the Fifth Commandment require?

A. It requires us to love our neighbor, and even our enemies; to live in peace and union with all, and to show a good example to those around us.

Q. What does the Sixth Commandment forbid?

A. It forbids adultery, and every such like act of impurity; all immodest looks, kisses, touches, and embraces, and all such light conduct, conversation, and familiarity as lead to sin.

Q. What does this commandment require?

A. It requires us to be pure and chaste in all our words and actions; to govern and restrain all our sensual appetites, and also to avoid the occasions of sin.

Q. What does the Seventh Commandment forbid?

A. It forbids all robbery, stealing, cheating, extortion, violation of a lawful contract, and every species of injustice.

Q. What does this commandment require?

A. It requires us to render to every one his due; and if we have done any wrong to our neighbor, to repair it.

Q. What does the Eighth Commandment forbid?

A. It forbids all false witness, lying, slander, detraction, unjust suspicion, and tale-bearing.

Q. What does this commandment require?

A. It requires us to be truthful and sincere; to defend the good name of our neighbor, and if we have said any thing to his injury, to repair it.

Q. What does the Ninth Commandment forbid?

A. It forbids us to desire any thing which the Sixth Commandment forbids us to do; also, to entertain any such dangerous thought, or take pleasure in it.

Q. What does this commandment require?

A. It requires us to cherish a strict purity in the heart, and to resist every unholy inclination from the beginning.

Q. What does the Tenth Commandment forbid?

A. It forbids us to entertain the thought of committing any theft, fraud, or injustice, or even to look upon the goods of our neighbor with a covetous eye.

Q. What does this commandment require?

A. It requires us to guard against the spirit of avarice, or the inordinate love of riches.

Q. What else do we learn from these last two commandments?

A. They teach us that God searches into our very hearts, and that he will judge our most secret thoughts and desires.

III. The Commandments of the Church.

Q. Are there no other commandments binding upon Christians?

A. Yes; besides the ten commandments of God, he Christian is bound to obey the commandments of the Church.

Q. Why is he bound to this?

A. The Christian is bound to keep the commandments of the Church, because the Church has received from God the power to make laws; and because, being our Spiritual Mother, we are bound as children to obey her.

Q. How many commandments of the Church are there?

A. We count commonly six. They are the following:

1. You must hear Mass every Sunday and Holiday.
2. You must fast and abstain, on the appointed days.
3. You must confess at least once a year.
4. You must receive the Blessed Sacrament once a year, during Easter-time.
5. You must not marry against the laws of the Church.
6. You must contribute to the support of the Church.

These precepts are expressed in the following verses:

1. Sundays and Holy Days observe
As feasts of obligation;
Attend at holy Mass, and keep
From servile occupation.

2. Lent, Ember-days, and vigils fast,
With one meal and collation.

3. On Friday, meat thou must not eat,
For sake of Christ's dear passion.

4. Once in the year at least, confess
With due examination.
At Easter-time receive thy Lord
With thanks and adoration.

5. In Lent or Advent marry not
With pomp and ostentation;
Wed before witnesses, and seek
The Church's approbation.

6. The worship of the Church maintain
With generous contribution.

Q. Are we bound to keep these laws of the Church as faithfully as the commandments of God?

A. We are; for our Lord spoke to the Church when he said: "*He that heareth you heareth me: and he that despiseth you, despiseth me.*" (St. Luke, x. 16.)

IV. Of Grace, and the Sacraments.

Q. Is man able to keep the commandments without the grace of God?

A. No; without God's grace, no man is able to keep the commandments, or to obtain salvation. "*Without me, you can do nothing,*" says our Lord Jesus Christ (St. John, xv. 5); and St. Paul: "*Our sufficiency is from God,*" (2 Cor. iii. 5.)

Q. What do we mean by Grace?

A. Grace is an inward and supernatural gift of God, by which either he pardons and admits sinners to his friendship, or enables the just to avoid sin, to do good, to advance in holiness, and to attain to eternal salvation.

Q. What are the principal channels by which the grace of God flows down to Christians?

A. The principal channels of grace are the seven Sacraments.

Q. What is a Sacrament?

A. A Sacrament *is a visible sign of an invisible grace, instituted by Jesus Christ himself for our sanc tification.* There is always an outward sign or ceremony which we can see; as, for example, the water in baptism. But there is also an inward grace which we cannot see; as in baptism the remission of sins is a grace which cannot be seen.

Q. How many sacraments are there, and what are they called?

A. There are seven Sacraments, namely: 1. Baptism. 2. Confirmation. 3. The Holy Eucharist. 4. Penance. 5. Extreme Unction. 6. Holy Orders. 7 Matrimony.

Q. Ought we to esteem the Holy Sacraments very highly?

A. Indeed, we ought to hold them in the highest veneration, because they were instituted by Jesus Christ himself, and because they are the fountains from which he supplies us with saving and sanctifying graces.

Of Baptism.

Q. What is Baptism?

A. Baptism *is the Sacrament of Regeneration, in which man is born again to eternal life. by the washing of water and the Word of God?*

Q. What are the effects of Baptism?

A. The principal effects of Baptism are, 1st, The pardon of sin, whether original or actual; 2d, The infusion of sanctifying graces into the soul; and 3d, The indelible impress of the Christian character.

Q. Is Baptism necessary to our salvation?

A. Yes; it is necessary, and for all men.

Q. Why is Baptism so necessary for all?

A. Because all men were born under the curse of sin; and because our Lord has said that "*unless a man be born again of water and the Holy Ghost, he cannot enter into the kingdom of God.*" (St. John iii. 5.)

Q. Who are authorized to baptize?

A. The Priests of the Church; but, in case of necessity, any one can baptize.

Q. How is this to be done?

A. Water is poured upon the head of the person to be baptized, while these words are pronounced: "*I baptize thee in the name of the Father, and of the Son, and of the Holy Ghost. Amen.*" The water must be common and natural water, and must be poured on by the same person who repeats the words; and care must be taken to repeat the words exactly and to pronounce them at the same time that the water is poured on.

Of Confirmation.

Q. What is the Sacrament of Confirmation?

A. Confirmation *is a Sacrament by which the Christian already baptized is fortified by the grace of the Holy Ghost to confess his faith firmly, and to regulate his life according to it.*

Q. How and by whom is confirmation administered?

A. It is administered by the Bishop, who lays his hand upon the candidate, at the same time anointing his forehead with the holy chrism, and pronouncing the sacramental words.

Q. What condition is necessary in order to receive this sacrament worthily?

A. It is above all necessary to be in a state of grace.

Of the Holy Eucharist.

Q. What is the Holy Eucharist?

A. The Holy Eucharist is the most holy of all the Sacraments: *it is the true body and blood of our Lord Jesus Christ under the appearances of bread and wine.*

Q. Are the soul and divinity of our Lord also present in this sacrament?

A. Yes; the whole person of Jesus Christ is there, living and entire.

Q. Is it right to adore the Blessed Eucharist?

A. Yes; we may and ought to adore it.

Q. How and when are the bread and wine changed into the Body and Blood of Jesus Christ?

A. This change is wrought by virtue of the words of consecration pronounced by the Priest during the Holy Mass.

Q. What is the Holy Mass?

A. Holy Mass is the unbloody sacrifice of the new covenant, the perpetual memorial of the bloody sacrifice of Jesus Christ upon the cross.

Q. Does Jesus Christ really die again in the sacrifice of the Mass?

A. No; his death and passion on the cross are only represented there, and a sacred remembrance made of it.

Q. Is Jesus Christ then not really present in the Mass?

A. Yes; he is truly present, and really offers himself to his Almighty Father for our sins, upon the altar.

Q. What is the Holy Communion?

A. The Holy Communion is that sacred feast, where the faithful receive the Body and Blood of Jesus Christ in the Eucharist, as their spiritual food.

Q. Is it necessary to receive sometimes the Holy Communion?

A. Yes; because Jesus Christ instituted this sacrament for the nourishing of our souls, and he himself has said: "*Except ye eat my flesh and drink my blood, ye have no life in you.*" (St. John, vi.)

Q. May every Christian, without condition, receive the Holy Communion?

A. No; to receive worthily we must be in the grac of God.

Q. What preparation then must the sinner make to entitle him to Communion?

A. He must do penance sincerely, and receive the absolution of his sins from the hand of a Priest.

Q. Is any preparation necessary for the body also?

A. Yes; it is necessary to be fasting from mid night.

Of Penance.

Q. What is the sacrament of Penance?

A. Penance is *a sacrament in which sins committed after Baptism, are remitted by the absolution of a Priest.*

Q. From whence have the Priests received this power?

A. This power was given to his Priests by Jesus Christ, when he said: "*Whose sins ye shall forgive, they are forgiven them, and whose sins you shall retain, they are retained.*" (St. John, xx. 23.)

Q. What conditions are necessary on the part of the penitent.

A. It is necessary that he should confess his sins, with true contrition, and make satisfaction for the past.

Q. What is Confession?

A. Confession is a faithful declaration of one's sins to a Priest.

Q. What is a sacrilegious confession?

A. A sacrilegious confession is when, in confessing, one wilfully hides some mortal sin; also when confession is made, without contrition, and the purpose of amendment.

Q. What is the value of such a confession?

A. It is good for nothing, and must be all made over again.

Q. What is the guilt of a sacrilegious confession?

A. It is a very grievous mortal sin, for it is a lie

to the Holy Ghost, and the profanation of a sacrament.

Q. What preparation is necessary in order to make a good confession?

A. It is necessary to pray to God for light and assistance, and to make a careful examinatian of conscience.

Q. How must the examination of consience be made?

A. It must be made with regard to all sinful thoughts, words, and actions; and also upon the number of our sins, and those circumstances which multiply the sin, and change the nature of it.

Q. What is Contrition?

A. Contrition is a hearty sorrow for sin, with the firm purpose of amendment.

Q. What kind of contrition is necessary?

A. Contrition must be supernatural, that is to say, proceeding from some holy motive of faith. These motives are contained in the usual act of contrition.

Q. Repeat this Act of Contrition.

A. "*O my God I am heartily sorry for all my sins, because by them I have lost heaven, and deserved the fire of hell, but more than all because I have offended thee, O my God, who art infinitely good, and worthy of all my love; but now I am firmly resolved, by the help of thy grace, never to sin against thee any more, and to avoid all the occasion of sin.*"

Q. What is meant by an occasion of sin?

A. An occasion of sin is any person, place, action, occupation, or amusement, which leads to the commission of sin.

Q. What is satisfaction?

A. Satisfaction is a temporal punishment accepted or self-imposed for sin. It consists in prayer, fasting alms-giving, and other works of penance. In th sacrament of Penance, it is the penalty imposed by th Priest upon the penitent who confesses.

Q. What is indulgence?

A. Indulgence is the remission, in whole or in part of those temporal punishments which, after the pardon of sins, we have still to suffer in this life, or in the other.

Q. What is necessary to gain an indulgence?

A. To gain an indulgence it is necessary, 1. To be in the state of grace; 2. To fulfil exactly the conditions prescribed.

Of Extreme Unction.

Q. What is Extreme unction?

A. Extreme Unction is *a sacrament in which by the unction of the blessed oil, and the prayers of the Priest, the sick who are in danger of death receive the grace of God to the benefit of the soul, and sometimes of their bodily health.*

Q. Why ought the sick not to neglect this sacrament?

A. The sick ought never to neglect it, on account of the many graces which they may obtain by receiving it.

Q. What are the effects of Holy Unction?

A. It confers, 1. The increase of sanctifying grace. 2. The remission of venial sins, and even of those mortal sins which the sinner cannot confess, or from which without his own fault he has never been absolved. 3. Deliverance from the debt of satisfaction still due to his sins. 4. Strength against temptations, and comfort in his dying hour. 5. Often also the restoration of health.

Of Holy Orders.

Q. What is the sacrament of Order?

A. It is *a sacrament by which spiritual power and grace are given to a Minister of the Church rightly ordained.*

Q. What power do the Priests of the Church receive through this sacrament?

A. The Priest receives at his ordination:

1. The power to change the bread and wine into the true Body aud Blood of our Saviour Jesus Christ.

2. The power to forgive sins.

Of Matrimony.

Q. What is the Sacrament of Matrimony?

A. Matrimony *is a sacrament by which man and woman are united in Christian marriage, and receive grace to fulfil the duties of that state.*

Q. Can husband and wife ever be divorced so that either may marry again?

A. No; nothing but death can break the bond of Christian marriage.

Q. What are those degrees of relationship within which it is unlawful to marry?

A. A marriage is not only unlawful, but also null and void:

1. When contracted with the third cousin, or any nearer relation by blood.

2. When contracted with a third cousin, or any nearer relation, of one's former wife or husband.

3. A Godfather or Godmother cannot marry with their Godchild, or with the father or mother of their Godchild; nor can a baptized person marry with the one who baptized him. And the same is true of sponsors in Confirmation, and the person confirmed.

Creed of Pope Pius IV.

I, N. N., with a firm faith believe and profess a[ll] and every one of those things which are contained [in] that creed which the holy Roman Church maketh u[se] of. To wit: I believe in one God, the Father A[l]mighty, Maker of heaven and earth, of all things vis ɔ̈e and invisible: and in one Lord Jesus Christ, the ɔnly-begotten Son of God, born of the Father before ıll ages; God of God; Light of light; true God of the ;rue God; begotten, not made, consubstantial with ;he Father, by whom all things were made. Who 'or us men, and for our salvation, came down from ıeaven, and was incarnate by the Holy Ghost of the Virgin Mary, and was made man. He was crucified ılso for us under Pontius Pilate, suffered, and was ɔuried. And the third day he arose again according ;o the Scriptures: he ascended into heaven, sitteth ıt the right hand of the Father, and shall come again vith glory to judge the living and the dead; oı vhose kingdom there shall be no end. I believe in .he Holy Ghost, the Lord and the life-giver, who ›roceedeth from the Father and the Son: who, to- ;ether with the Father and the Son, is adored and ;lorified; who spake by the prophets. And in one ıoly, Catholic, and Apostolic Church. I confess one ›aptism for the remission of sins; and I look for the 'esurrection of the dead, and the life of the world o come. Amen.

I most steadfastly admit and embrace the apos- olical and ecclesiastical Traditions, and all other ob- ervances and constitutions of the same Church.

I also admit the holy Scriptures, according to that ense which our holy mother the Church hath held ınd doth hold, to whom it belongeth to judge of he true sense and interpretation of the Scriptures; ıeither will I ever take and interpret them other- vise than according to the unanimous consent of he Fathers.

I also profess that there are truly and properly 'even Sacraments of the new law, instituted by esus Christ our Lord, and necessary for the salva- on of mankind, though not all for every one: to ' it, Baptism, Confirmation, the Eucharist, Penance, ; xtreme Unction, O der, and Matrimony: and that they confer grace: and that of these, Baptism, Confirmation, and Order cannot be repeated without sacrilege. I also receive and admit the received and approved ceremonies of the Catholic Church used in the solemn administration of the aforesaid sacraments.

I embrace and receive all and every one of the things which have been defined and declared in the holy Council of Trent concerning original sin and justification.

I profess, likewise, that in the Mass there is offered to God a true, proper, and propitiatory sacrifice for the living and the dead. And that in the most holy sacrament of the Eucharist there is truly really and substantially the Body and Blood, together with the soul and divinity, of our Lord Jesus Christ and that there is made a conversion of the whole substance of the bread into the Body, and of the whole substance of the wine into the Blood; which Conversion the Catholic Church calleth Transubstancation. I also confess that under either kind alone tihrist is received whole and entire, and a true sacrament.

I constantly hold that there is a Purgatory, and that the souls therein detained are helped by the suffrages of the faithful.

Likewise, that the Saints reigning together with Christ are to be honored and invocated, and that they offer prayers to God for us, and that their relics are to be had in veneration.

I most firmly assert that the Images of Christ, of the Mother of God ever Virgin, and also of other Saints, ought to be had and retained, and that due honor and veneration are to be given them.

I also affirm that the power of Indulgences was left by Christ in the Church, and that the use of them is most wholesome to Christian people.

I acknowledge the Holy, Catholic, Apostolic, R

man Church for the mother and mistress of all Churches; and I promise true obedience to the Bishop of Rome, successor of St. Peter, Prince of the Apostles, and Vicar of Jesus Christ.

I likewise undoubtingly receive and profess all other things delivered, defined, and declared by the sacred canons and General Councils, and particularly by the holy Council of Trent. And I condemn, reject, and anathematize all things contrary thereto, and all heresies which the Church hath condemned, rejected, and anathematized.

I, N. N., do at this present freely profess and sincerely hold this true Catholic faith, out of which no one can be saved: and I promise most constantly to retain and confess the same entire and inviolate, by God's assistance, to the end of my life.

Card for the Christian Instruction of Those who cannot Read.

☞ Whoever receives one of these cards from a Catholic who cannot read, will teach him by word of mouth, what follows:

First: The Our Father, Hail Mary, and Apostles' Creed.

Second: How to answer the following questions according to the form printed in the card.

1st. *Q.* How many Gods are there?

A. There is but one God.

2d. *Q.* How many persons in God?

A. Three: The Father, the Son, and the Holy Ghost.

3d. *Q.* Who is Jesus Christ?

A. God the Son, True God and True Man.

4th. *Q.* What did he do for man?

A. He died on the Cross for the sins of the world.

5th. *Q.* Where will the good go after death?

A. To Heaven, for all eternity.

6th. *Q.* Where will the wicked go?

A. To Hell, for all eternity.

7th. *Q.* What is the name of the True Church?

A. The Holy Catholic Church.

8th. *Q.* How can you obtain the pardon of you sins after baptism?

A. By a good confession.

9th. *Q.* When you make a good confession, wha does the Priest do for you?

A. He gives me absolution, or the pardon of my sins.

10th. *Q.* What is the Blessed Sacrament?

A. The Body and Blood of Jesus Christ under the appearances of Bread and Wine.

Of the Holy Sacrament of Penance.

"*If we confess our sins, he (God) is faithful and just to forgive us our sins, and to cleanse us from all iniquity.*" 1 John, i. 9.

GOD, who knows the weakness of human nature, is full of compassion, and always ready to receive again into his grace the sinner who sincerely desires to return to him. For this reason, in his infinite mercy, he has instituted the Sacrament of Penance, as a means of pardon and reconciliation for those who have lost the first innocence of their baptism. The original sin, in which all men are born, is washed away in the Sacrament of Baptism; but if, after baptism, the Christian falls again into mortal sin, the only means to escape from eternal death is penance.

The principal things to be considered in every Sacrament are the following: 1. The outward and visible sign or ceremony. 2. The invisible grace. 3. The Minister, or dispenser of the Sacrament; and 4. Its institution by Jesus Christ.

1. The outward visible sign of the unseen and inward grace given in the Sacrament of Penance, is the form of absolution pronounced by the Priest over the penitent, in these words: "*I absolve thee from thy sins, in the name of the Father, and of the Son, and of the Holy Ghost;*" and also the exterior signs manifested by the penitent, of an inward sorrow for his sins.

2. The invisible grace of this Sacrament of Penance is the pardon of sins.

3. The Ministers of this Sacrament are the Priests alone.

The institution of this great Sacrament by our Lord Jesus Christ is clearly seen in the Gospel. He, himself, in the most solemn manner, and with his own breath, gave the power to pardon sins to the Apostles, and after them to their successors, the Bishops and Priests of the Church, when he said: "*Receive ye the Holy Ghost. Whose sins you shall forgive, they are forgiven them; and whose sins you shall retain, they are retained.*" St. John, xx. 22.

Our Blessed Lord declares by these words, that he communicates by the Holy Ghost to the Apostles, and their lawful successors in the apostolical ministry, the power to exercise jurisdiction over the sins of men; that those whom they absolve, shall be absolved by him also, while those to whom they refuse pardon, shall remain unforgiven by himself.

The forgiving or retaining of sins is not, by any means, committed to the mere arbitrary will or caprice of the Priest. He is bound to know the condition of the sinner, that he may pronounce upon him a just judgment; but how could he come to any just decision, if he did not first know what the sinner had been guilty of?

The sinner, too, by these words of Christ is strictly bound to make known his sins to the Priest, that is, to confess, and leave himself to be judged by him according to his priestly power. Confession is therefore one of the most important and essential parts of the holy Sacrament of Penance.

THE EFFECTS OF THIS SACRAMENT.

The effects and advantages of this holy sacrament are almost beyond number. We can say with the Roman Catechism, that almost all the piety, holiness, and fear of God, which, through the divine mercy, are to be found in Christendom. are owing to sacramental possession.

Its principal effects are

1. The forgiveness of sins. When the penitent has with a sincere and contrite heart confessed his sins, and the priest with uplifted hand has repeated over him the words, "I absolve thee from thy sins," at that very moment all the guilt of the sinner is pardoned for all eternity. What a consolation in the hour of death and in the day of judgment for the sinner who can look back upon a sincere confession!

2. It restores to the sinner sanctifying grace, the friendship of God, and a right to heaven. How unhappy do we consider the man who has lost the favor of some great patron, or who is suffering from the loss of fortune, or who has some powerful person for his enemy! But far more unhappy is he who has lost God and Heaven.

3. This sacrament obtains the remission of eternal punishment, as St. Paul declares: "*There is, therefore, now no condemnation to them that are in Christ Jesus.*" The pains of Hell are not for those who through the mercy of God are restored to his grace in the sacrament of Penance.

4. It obtains that the merits of all the good works which we had done before, when we were in the state of grace, are restored to us again. O what a treasure of grace is the recovery of all our good works! What exertions will not a man make to recover again the temporal goods which he has lost? What then shall we consider too difficult for us, provided we can obtain the goods of eternal life?

5. It gives us a certain strength and divine power to preserve us from falling again into sin, and to make us persevere in virtue. O how many sinners have found in this sacrament the most sure defence against their passions, and the best remedy to heal their spiritual wounds!

6. It restores to the sinner his lost peace of soul and a quiet conscience. The Holy Spirit has declared

that "*there is no peace for the wicked*," and that their life is full of pain and sorrow. How many have experienced in their own case, that whereas they lived before confession as in a hell, full of distress and anxiety, no sooner did they receive absolution than they felt so great a consolation that they believed themselves in paradise.

7. In fine, the whole human family is deeply indebted to this holy sacrament, for it is the preserver of good order, peace, and justice. How many sins of injustice and impurity, how many quarrels have been hindered, or terminated by it! If it often happens that society is desolated with great crimes, it is commonly because holy confession has been despised or carelessly made. Which are those in every congregation who give the greatest cause of grief to a zealous Pastor? generally those who seldom or never go to confession. These so-called Christians, who hardly go once a year to confession, and then with a heart as cold as ice, are usually wicked and God-forsaken. Dominico Soto, confessor to the Emperor Charles V., and one whose testimony cannot be called in question, relates, that the city of Nuremberg having gone over to the side of the heretics, afterwards sent an ambassador to the Emperor, to implore him that he would, by an imperial mandate, once more establish confession among them, because, as they said, experience showed clearly that since confession had been given up among them, monstrous crimes had been committed, of such a horrible kind as had never been known there before.

In order to receive this holy sacrament rightly, the following conditions are required:

1. Examination of conscience.
2. Contrition and the purpose of amendment.
3. Confession.
4. The absolution of the Priest.
5. Satisfaction.

I. EXAMINATION OF CONSCIENCE.

THE chief hindrance to true conversion is, that we do not know ourselves. We try to deceive ourselves by imagining that this and that is no sin. Many Christians live in a criminal ignorance of the commands of God and the duties of their station,—live, as it were, sunk in low desires and lusts, in a disgusting indifference and carelessness for every thing spiritual and divine, so that they lose all knowledge of God and of themselves. They may not, it is true, be murderers or thieves; they may even have some natural virtues (as the heathen have also), and may call themselves honest and respectable people. but for all that they are any thing but good Christians, or agreeable to God. When such persons make their confession, it may happen that they do not find themselves guilty of any sin. Is it because they are so innocent and good? Alas! no,—all they need to lose this easy conscience is a true knowledge of themselves, a knowledge which they have not, because they never make a thorough examination of their conscience. And who are they, for the most part, these Christians, so righteous in their own eyes? Mostly those who go to confession only once in the year, or perhaps have not made their confession for many years, and have hitherto lived in complete forgetfulness of their duties. These are the Christians who comfort themselves and lead others astray by saying: "O such and such a thing is no sin." "I don't see any harm in that." If, however, they were willing to be honest and would examine themselves faithfully, they would find themselves like a sepulchre, full of corruption. It must never be forgotten, however, that the knowledge of one's self is a gift of God. St. Augustine prayed earnestly for it thus: "O Lord! grant that I may know Thee and myself also" Would you, dear Christian, from this time know yourself thoroughly, look to the Holy Ghost for light and help, and remember always to begin your self-examination by prayer.

HOW MUCH TIME OUGHT ONE TO EMPLOY IN THE EXAMINATION OF CONSCIENCE?

1. You must give as much time and attention to this as you are accustomed to give to any other very important business. What would a man do if he were involved in a lawsuit, the failure of which would cause him the loss of all his property? Would he not search with the greatest care for every thing that could be of some service to him in his suit? And you, sinner, have you not, by falling into mortal sin, lost your title to Heaven and deserved Hell? This very confession which you are about to make, and the examination of conscience before it, will perhaps decide for Heaven or Hell, for who knows if it is not the last one of your life?

2. The time required for your examination of conscience cannot be exactly determined. One who confesses often, and has a very tender or timid conscience, may easily tranquillize himself, for he is not likely to overlook any mortal sin. As to venial sins, he must not trouble himself too much, for, strictly speaking, he is not bound to confess them.

3. On the other hand, a man who has hitherto lived sunk in sin, who has hardly confessed once in a year, who at almost every occasion has broken the law of God, must not be satisfied with a passing glance at his conscience. He must commence this important business of self-examination some days before confession. During this time he should remain entirely recollected, and call to mind and seriously consider every place where he has been, the persons with whom he has kept company, the business which he carried on, &c.; otherwise he would only be able to confess a confused multitude of sins, without regard to number, kind, or circumstance.

4. Many examine themselves too superficially; and this is the reason why they find so few sins to accuse themselves of in the confessional. How many business men and trades-people, if they went to the bottom of their conscience, would find many lies of no small consequence, much fraud and usury, many unlawful and unjust contracts! But if they were to look carefully into their consciences, then the ill-gotten property belonging to others must be restored, with some damage, of course, to their own substance, and for this reason they are afraid to look into their own hearts. The shameless lovers of pleasure will not examine into their vices, because they do not wish to change their lives, and take great pains to convince themselves that what they are doing is no sin.

If you would not, my dear Christian, abuse this holy sacrament, but rightly make use of it for your own salvation, enter upon your examination of conscience as if Jesus Christ were judging you at the day of general judgment. Imagine yourself to be in the presence of your Saviour, really before you and sitting as your judge, and judge yourself in such a way that you may not be more severely judged some other day. "He who judges himself will not be judged."

II. OF CONTRITION AND THE PURPOSE OF AMENDMENT.

Contrition is *a hearty sorrow for sin, with the firm purpose to sin no more.* This true sorrow for sin, being the most important point in a good preparation for confession, requires to be carefully considered and understood.

1. Contrition is an essential condition of penance, so that the Priest can never absolve a sinner who gives no sign of true repentance. The absolution which a sinner receives who is not sincerely contrite,

is worthless and sacrilegious. A confessor would commit a great sin against the holy sacrament of Penance, if he did not in every proper way assure himself of the contrition of the sinner. They are foolish and unjust, therefore, who complain, when a wise confessor, and one who fears God, refuses them absolution, because he can find in them no sign of true contrition.

St. Gregory says: "He who is not truly converted receives no benefit, even if he does confess his sins." Christians without number make fruitless confessions, because they are not truly penitent. It is this want of contrition that makes the office of a Priest so difficult; for it is not their duty merely to hear confessions and give absolution, but to do so according to the will of God. O God! what anxiety and distress do confessors suffer on account of so many sinners, who with hearts all cold and indifferent, enter the holy confessional, to run over their sins in a careless manner, as they would any other indifferent affair, and whose whole conduct gives reason to suspect that they feel no sorrow for their sins.

2. True contrition, however be it well understood, is a supernatural virtue, and must be grounded upon supernatural motives. In other words, it must spring from motives of faith, awakened in the heart by the consideration of the eternal truths of religion. To be sorry for our sins because they have brought us into shame, poverty, sickness, or any mere worldly misfortune, is no true contrition, and will not procure the pardon of our sins. Some persons, when they go to confession, appear more anxious to tell of their vexations and miseries than to accuse themselves of their sins. They do not desire so much to be pardoned, as to be comforted in their misfortunes. On the contrary, true contrition is a sorrow which comes from higher and holier motives. It is our Faith that weeps for the misfortunes of the soul, and the injury done to God. If the unhappy sinner sincerely desires the pardon of

his sins, his contrition must be of this kind, for God will accept no other.

3. The best and purest motive for contrition is the divine love, which makes us grieve for our sins, and detest them because of their ingratitude, and the injury done to a good and holy God. When this is the predominant motive, contrition is called perfect, and is so excellent a disposition, that, according to the Council of Trent, the soul may be reconciled by it to God, even before confession and the priestly absolution, provided there is also an earnest desire for these. Imperfect contrition (or attrition) is where the sinner is excited to sorrow, and to the purpose of amendment, by the consideration of the turpitude of his sins, or from the fear of hell, or because he has forfeited his right to heaven. These motives, although less perfect than that first mentioned, are nevertheless good, for they are true impulses of the Holy Ghost, and dispose one to receive the grace of pardon through the sacrament of penance.

We must not, however, fall into the error of those who think that a *feeble* contrition is all they need, provided they confess their sins. True contrition, although it may be imperfect in its kind, is never feeble. It is true that the sincere penitent is often unconscious of any strong feeling of sorrow; for contrition does not properly consist in any feeling at all, but rather in the supernatural hatred and abhorrence of sin. Strictly speaking, however, a genuine contrition can never be feeble; otherwise it would not be sufficient to produce that firm and efficacious purpose of amendment, which is its natural and necessary fruit. It is therefore neither right nor safe to set narrow bounds to ourselves in this respect, but we should try to animate our souls more and more to a genuine, earnest, efficacious, and tender contrition. Our forgiveness becomes then easier and surer, and our reformation more complete and lasting.

4. The firm purpose of Amendment is the inseparable companion of true contrition, and therefore a necessary condition to the forgiveness of sin. God requires of the sinner a new spirit, and a new life "*When the wicked turneth himself away from his wickedness, which he hath wrought, and doeth judgment and justice, he shall save his soul alive.*" (Ezech. xviii. 27.) It is impossible for God to pardon the sinner who still retains the will to offend him. He must be resolved to offend God no more, and this resolution must be no mere promise of the lips, or momentary emotion, but a sincere, firm, and efficacious determination.

Can the purpose of Amendment be called sincere in that man, who says to God, that he repents with his whole heart of having offended him, but who falls immediately into the same sins, after receiving absolution? or that man who runs again into the same occasions of sin; who does not avoid the persons who led him into sin before; who frequents the same places of temptation; who will not repair the injury he has done; who will not consent to be reconciled with his enemy? in fine, who does not even make an honest, practical beginning of a good life, nor take the necessary means of perseverance? Who can doubt that the confession of such a man is a mere mockery of penance? Who can believe that his absolution was of any value?

5. What must you do, then, my dear Christian, in order to excite in yourself this salutary sorrow for your sins, and this firm purpose of amendment?

In the first place, it is necessary to place before your mind, and to meditate seriously upon those supernatural truths of our holy religion, which, as we have already seen, furnish the only true motives of a genuine contrition, and of an effectual and lasting conversion.

"*Remember thy last end,*" says the Prophet, "*and thou shalt never sin.*" (Ezech. vii. 20.) You will find the principal motives of this kind in the little Act of Contrition, (page 270,) which every one ought to learn by heart and repeat very often. You will find them also at much greater length in the Devout Exercises, preparatory to Confession.

But above all, it is necessary to pray. Yes, poor sinner, pray earnestly to God for a true contrition pray for a firm and lasting resolution to sin no more for these holy dispositions of heart are gifts of God which a man cannot have of himself, but must seek fo through prayer.

REMARK.—1. It is necessary for you to know, my dear Christian, that contrition for your sins must always go before absolution, and therefore, as soon as you have examined, and remembered your sins, you ought to repent of them immediately, with the intention to receive the holy sacrament of penance. For if you should not have in your heart this sincere sorrow for your sins until after absolution, then both your confession and your absolution will be good for nothing. 2. Do not be too anxious, lest your sins should not be forgiven by God, because you do not *feel* any contrition. As the good tree is known by its fruit, so will your true contrition be known by your improvement. Therefore, it may be said for your consolation, that you may confidently hope your repentance is tru when you have actually changed your life, and abandoned your sins.

III. OF CONFESSION.

CONFESSION, the third essential part of the holy sacrament of penance, is *the accusation of all the sins one has committed, made to a Priest duly authorized to receive it, in order to obtain from him the absolution or pardon of them.* In order to make this duty of confession more easy, attend to the following rules: 1. Imagine Jesus Christ himself before you, in the person of your confessor.

2. Choose for your ordinary confessor a priest who has a great deal of mildness, a prudent zeal, and a true charity for sinners. Yet you must not think that, because you have done this, you cannot sometimes make your confession to some other confessor.

3. Do not look on confession as a torture of the conscience, as infidels, heretics, and scoffers represent it, but the humble self-accusation of a child, who knows the kind compassion of his father, finds new consolation with every word, and is sure that his father will not be angry, but forgive him gladly.

4. Never let a long time pass without holy confession, for by this means you will find it easier, and certainly will derive more profit from it.

5. If you have had the misfortune to fall into any mortal sin, give yourself no rest until you have confessed it.

In order to secure yourself against the danger of hiding some sin through false shame, call to mind:

1. That by concealing your sins, you become guilty of another sin.

2. If you conceal it from your confessor, you cannot hide it from God.

3. Through such concealment you will only increase the trouble of your conscience, and sooner or later you must confess the hidden sin, or else die with it, and be eternally lost.

4. Sin deserves shame; and therefore it is only another mark of your impenitence, if you are unwilling to submit yourself to this mortification.

5. Such concealment exposes you to the danger of being put to shame in the presence of all creatures, at the day of judgment, and of burning for ever in hell fire. Ah! if a lost soul could come from hell, and find a Priest, would he be ashamed to confess?

6. Tell me, would you not show to the physician of your body your most secret wounds, if you hoped to be healed? Much more should you discover the sick

ness of your soul to your spiritual physician, if you would not die eternally.

7. Your confessor will be so much the more pleased, the more he sees in you the grace of conversion by the sincerity of your heart, for he knows only too well what human weakness and misery is, and therefore will have compassion for you, and is bound under the heaviest penalties, both of temporal and eternal punishment, to keep forever the strictest silence.

WHAT IS IT NECESSARY TO CONFESS?

1. *Every mortal sin must be confessed.* If knowingly you conceal a mortal sin in confession, you will not only obtain no pardon of your other sins, but you are guilty besides of sacrilege. If you have to confess the sins of many years, do not be distressed if you cannot remember all of them. A sincere intention to confess them all, with a careful examination of your conscience, is enough; all that you are really unable to do yourself, is supplied by this holy sacrament itself.

As for those smaller sins which are called venial, you are not bound to confess them, yet it is prudent and useful to do so, especially when you cannot well decide with certainty, between what is venial and what is mortal sin.

If you have a doubt whether you have committed a mortal sin, or whether you have already confessed it, the best way is to lay this doubt, together with the sin, before the priest.

2. *You must confess those circumstances which change the nature of the sin, or increase the number.* For example: If the person with whom you committed the sin of impurity was a married person, you must mention this fact, because it shows that you are also guilty of adultery. It is also a much more guilty thing to utter a calumny in presence of a large company than before a few persons; before neighbors of the

one you slander, than before strangers; or to steal a large sum of money, rather than a small one; or if you take a small sum very often, rather than once or twice only.

3. *You must confess the number of your mortal sins, as near as you can remember* If you cannot remember the exact number, then say: It was about so many times, or so many times, more or less.

If you have to make confession for many years back, and cannot exactly remember how often you have committed a sin, you should at least say how long the habit continued, about how often in a day, in a week, or a month, you fell into that sin; and if the habit was interrupted for a while, say how long.

REMARK.—Omit all other relations and circumstances which do not belong to confession. Never name the guilty persons connected with you; but, where it is necessary in order to show the nature of the sin, state simply the condition of the person, or your relationship with him, as far as may be, in general words, that the confessor, if possible, may not know who the other guilty person is. For example: "I have been guilty of the sin of impurity with a person related to me in the first, or in the second degree, or with a married person or with one consecrated by vow to God." That is enough; mention no names.

THE MANNER OF MAKING CONFESSION.

1. When you go to the confessional, do not press before others. While you are waiting for your turn do not distract yourself by looking around and talking but with a sorrowful, although trustful heart, pray to God for the forgiveness of your sins. If you have long to wait, you may read any thing in your prayer-book which relates to holy confession, or say the Rosary, or meditate upon some spiritual subject.

2. Do not place yourself so near the confessional a

o hear the confessions of those who are there before ·ou. If ever you should by any accident hear any sin confessed, you are bound to keep it secret under pain of sin. Any one who listens from curiosity is also guilty of sin.

3. When you are about to kneel down before your confessor, arouse yourself once more to a true contrition and sorrow for your sins, and imagine Jesus Christ actually before you in the person of the priest. Be very careful during confession to observe the greatest possible modesty in your words and manner. Do not speak too loud, so that persons around may hear, and not so low, that even your confessor cannot understand you. If you do not understand him well yourself, do not let him go on speaking to no purpose, but tell him so at once.

4. To begin your confession, make the sign of the cross, and say: "*Bless me, Father, for I have sinned.*" Then repeat the Confiteor, thus: "*I confess to Almighty God, to the Blessed Mary, ever Virgin,*" &c. (*See page* 32.) Then, first of all, tell your Confessor how long it is since you made your last confession—whether that confession was a good one—whether you received the absolution of your sins from the priest—and if you have performed your penance imposed upon you.

5. If at your last confession, or any former ones, you have concealed a mortal sin, you must now mention it, and explain whether it happened intentionally through false shame, or bad will, or only through forgetfulness. If in former confessions you have intentionally kept back your sins, you must make these confessions again, and tell also how many confessions and communions you have made since the first one in which you concealed your sin.

6. If at your last confession you did not receive absolution, you must not fail to mention it, and give the reason why it was refused you.

7. Likewise, if you did not perform the penance imposed upon you, did not make restitution of what belonged to another, did not make reparation for the injury you had done to another's reputation, were not reconciled to your enemy, or have not been careful to shun the occasions of sin, you must mention it.

8. These matters being explained as far as it is necessary, go on now to make your confession humbly penitently, clearly, and in few words, without covering up your sins, and without false excuses.

9. If at any time your confessor postpones giving you absolution, submit with docility to his decision consider in a spirit of justice and humility that he is bound to act according to his conscience and his priestly duty, and do not hasten to another confessor in the hopes of finding him more easy, and receiving a more speedy absolution.

10. If you have already made a good general confession, and, through the grace of God, from that time forward, have been kept from great sins, or if you have the pious custom of going to confession often, and cannot call to mind any great sin since your last confession then it is well to include in your present confession some sin already confessed of your former life, selecting for that purpose one for which you have a great contrition: say, for example, "I also wish to include in this confession a sin which I have formerly committed—of hatred—or impurity—or dishonesty," (as the case may be.) In this case, as it is something already confessed, you need not explain any further.

11. Conclude your confession in the following words: "*For these, and all my other sins which I may have forgotten, I am heartily sorry, and I humbly ask pardon of God, penance and absolution of you, my ghostly father.*" Listen now humbly to what ever your confessor may have to say:—pay attention to the penance which he imposes upon you for your sins, that you may not forget it; and when you p

ceive that he is about to give you his absolution, begin immediately the Act of Contrition.

"*O my God, I am heartily sorry for all my sins, because by them I have lost heaven, and deserved the fire of hell, but more than all because I have offended thee, O my God, who art infinitely good, and worthy of all my love; but now I am firmly resolved, by the help of thy grace, never to sin against thee any more, and to avoid all the occasions of sin.*"

12. Be sure never to speak with others unnecessarily of your confessions, even if it were only to tell them what good instruction your confessor has given you; for what the confessor has said to you is for you alone, and might be easily misunderstood and abused by others.

IV. OF ABSOLUTION.

ABSOLUTION *is the sentence pronounced by the priest in the place of God, forgiving the sinner who has confessed his sins.* He does what Jesus Christ would do if he were upon the earth. For the priest is sent by Jesus Christ the Son of God, with the same power to remit sins with which he himself was sent by his heavenly Father.

But the priests have not unlimited power to give absolution in the holy sacrament of penance to whom they will. For they must be governed in this matter by the laws of God and the holy Church. If a priest gives absolution to a sinner who does not sincerely wish to amend, and who has not the good dispositions of a true penitent, then God does not sanction the absolution.

Why do some Christians urge the priest so much to give them absolution? Why do they trouble him so much for what can only turn to their own sorrow? And why do they treat him with rudeness and insolence when he refuses them absolution, and try to injure him in the good opinion of others? Such calumniators only publish their own shame wherever they go, but the priest cannot, in order to please them, violate the laws of God and of the holy Church. Should he consent to damn himself eternally, and his penitent with him? Of what use can absolution be, if it is disavowed by God? Such an absolution could only bring to a man a vain and deceitful peace, which is more to be feared than the greatest anxiety!

WHAT PERSONS ARE UNFIT TO RECEIVE SACRAMENTAL ABSOLUTION?

1. Those who have relapsed into the habit of any mortal sin, after repeated promises to amend; for example, of drunkenness, impurity, blasphemy, violation of the fasts of the Church or of the Lord's day, &c. Absolution is a grace purchased at the cost of the blood of Christ, too dear a grace to be wasted upon triflers. Promises will not answer any longer. The sinner must now give proof of his sincerity by actually abandoning his sins, and after that he may hope for absolution. Can a person be trusted at confession who produces no other sign of true penance than a fine promise, such as he made often before and never kept? Indeed, he must show more than ordinary signs of contrition before the Priest can receive his promises again.

2. Those who will not avoid the proximate occasion of sin: for example, such as live in a criminal and dangerous connection with persons of another sex or of their own; or who allow others to be in such sinful occasions, when they can prevent it, and are in duty bound to do so; or those who, after repeated admonitions, read bad and corrupting books, or newspapers, or sell, or give them to others to read for love of money or false friendship; and again, those who will not refrain from visiting and encouraging secret societies forbidden by the Church, or meetings where religion and morality are spoken against. Those wo-

men also, who, in spite of every admonition, are the occasions to others of sin by their indecent and immodest dress; also all grocers, or tavern-keepers, or heads of families who permit gatherings at their houses during the time of divine service, and to the neglect of the same, or entertain disorderly company at late and scandalous hours.

3. Those who will not repair the injury they have done to their neighbor, either in body or soul, property, or good name; and also those who will not pay their debts when they are able to do so.

4. Those who will not be reconciled to their enemies, and those who will neither salute or speak to persons against whom they have an ill will.

5. Those, finally, who are not sufficiently instructed in the Faith, and especially in those articles necessary to salvation.

All these persons who have been mentioned above are unfit for absolution, so long as they remain in the same bad state.

V. OF SATISFACTION, OR WORKS OF PENANCE.

By Satisfaction, we mean *that reparation which the sinner is bound to make for his offences committed against God, and for the wrong he has done to his neighbor.*

We are under the strictest obligations to satisfy an offended God, and although the guilt and eternal punishment of sin is remitted by absolution, yet there is still remaining a temporal satisfaction to be made, either in this or in the other life.

Formerly, the Canons, or rules of penance in the Church, were very severe, although certainly very just, for the Church, tender mother that she is, would never inflict a heavier penance than God requires. In those days, the guilty sinner under penance in the Church was obliged to appear in public, with the garments of a penitent, fast on bread and water at least three times a week, and was not allowed to receive holy communion. Whoever, for example, had taken a false oath, must fast on bread and water forty days. Any one who performed servile labor on a Sunday or Holyday, must do penance three days on bread and water. Whoever engaged in talking during divine service, was required to fast ten days on bread and water. If a woman, in order to conceal her sin, destroyed her child, she was obliged to do penance for her sins on bread and water for ten years. A year of fasting was required of a young man for impurity committed with a maid; three years for adultery, and even sometimes fifteen. If any one cursed his parents, he was obliged to fast on bread and water forty days; and if he struck them, seven years.

When the zeal and faith of Christians had declined, the Church, that good and tender mother, condescending to their weakness, and anxious not to expose so great a number of her children to give themselves up to entire corruption, relaxed in a great measure from this former rigor, and the penances imposed at the present time are extremely mild. The Holy Church, however, expects of sinners, that they will voluntarily perform other good works of penance. She encourages them also to gain indulgences for the sins which they have committed, that they may have less to suffer in Purgatory.

Nevertheless, according to the holy Council of Trent, confessors are bound to "enjoin salutary and suitable penances, according to the magnitude of the sin, and the circumstances of the penitent, for fear that, by treating sinners with too great indulgence, and imposing on them slight penances for great sins, they may be held accountable for the sins of others." (Session, xiv.)

If, however, the slight penance that your Father-confessor gives you appears too great, remember that

God is just, that you will suffer far greater pains in another life, and that, with a different and easier penance, you would soon fall back into your former sin.

The works of satisfaction are: prayer, fasting, and almsgiving; for in these works are included all that is contrary to the corrupt nature of man. We can also make satisfaction to God by means of those sufferings which he himself sends, if we bear them patiently; for example, sickness, poverty, misfortunes, persecutions, &c.

The penitent is bound to accept the penance which his confessor gives him. But if he thinks it too difficult for him, either on account of weak health or poverty, or from want of time, or any other cause, he must say so to his confessor, and ask to have it changed. Although one has not received absolution, he ought, for all that, faithfully to perform the penance required of him, otherwise he would show that he has no serious desire to amend.

If, however, the penitent has received absolution, and accepted the penance imposed, but through his own fault neglects to perform his penance, or any considerable part of it, he commits a new sin, because nothing less than a very strong reason, as, for example, an attack of sickness, could absolve him from it; for the penance, being an integral part of the sacrament, it follows that it is one of the most necessary and important duties of a true penitent to perform it faithfully. For the same reason, the penance must be performed entirely at the time appointed, and devoutly.

HOW OFTEN OUGHT ONE TO GO TO CONFESSION?

That divine precept which makes confession necessary, obliges us especially:

1. *When we have committed a mortal sin*, and then as soon as possible. For reason itself teaches us to escape at once from a situation so dangerous as that into which we are brought by mortal sin How shock-

it is, then, for a Christian, who finds himself in a state of damnation, to remain unconcerned in that condition! Certainly those commit another great sin, who allow months and years to pass by without confessing the mortal sins which lie upon their souls.

2. *When we are at the point of death.* The Church directs the physician to admonish the sick who are dangerously ill, before any thing else to make thei. confession. Parents, guardians, friends, and attendants upon the sick, have also to fear a dreadful account before God, if they provide too late for the confession of the sick, or through their fault, allow them to die without confession.

3. *At least once in the year.* By the precept of the Church, all the faithful are required to confess their sins once every year

Although the above obligations are the only ones which are strictly binding, yet, of course, it is highly useful and advisable to confess much oftener, because it greatly promotes purity of heart, strengthens the weakness of our corrupt nature, makes us more humble, and increases in us the fear and dread of sin.

Besides this, you ought to confess often, that you may the oftener receive communion. For it is the desire of the Church, guided always by the Holy Ghost, that during Mass the faithful should, as much as possible, take part in the holy Sacrifice, not only spiritually, but also really by communicating, as we see in the decrees of the Council of Trent. (Sess. 22, Cap. 6.) The Roman Catechism, too, which explains this desire of the Council, admonishes all the clergy to exhort the faithful to receive communion oftener, and even daily, for as the body for its support needs daily food, so does the soul need spiritual nourishishment for its support.

If it is not possible to receive communion daily, it is at least possible to receive it more frequently than most Christians do.

General Confession.

For many Christians, if they are really desirous of a sincere and thorough conversion, it is necessary to make a general confession; and to others, it is highly important, in order to lay the foundation of a pious Christian life.

A general confession is one in which the penitent reviews the confessions of his past life; accusing himself sincerely, and with a contrite heart, of all the sins which he has committed, either from his youth up, or since his first mortal sin, or since the time when first he made a bad confession, or one which he has good reason to fear was bad.

St. Francis de Sales, that great saint, and most amiable Master in the spiritual life, says, "that for the greatest part of men, a general confession is necessary to secure the soul's salvation." "A general confession," says the saint, "gives us a more complete knowledge of ourselves; it fills us with a salutary shame at the sight of our sins; it relieves the mind of much anxiety, and gives the conscience true peace; it excites in us good resolutions; it shows us how wonderful is the mercy of God, which has waited for us with such great patience; it enables our confessor to give us more suitable directions; it opens the heart, so that in future we are able to make our confessions with more confidence."

The great advantage of a general confession is best seen at the hour of death. Who would not wish, when at the point of appearing before the tribunal of God—at that dreadful moment which is to decide his fate for all eternity—who would not wish then, that he had faithfully and penitently made a general confession of his whole life? What a consolation for a dying Christian, if, before sickness attacked him, he had thus already put in order all these pressing affairs of his soul? How can any one allow himself to approach that last moment, remaining still careless for the salvation of his soul? How awful for him, then, first, to open his eyes upon his whole past life, at the moment when he is about to close them forever! Our Saviour says: "*Watch ye and be ready, for the Lord of that servant shall come in a day that he hopeth not, and in an hour that he knoweth not.*" (St. Mat. xxiv.; St. Luke, xii.)

A man of high rank came one day to a missionary, and begged him to hear his general confession. The Priest asked him why he wished to make it then. "Ah, reverend sir," answered the gentleman, "am I not to die? After such a sinful life, I cannot die in peace, unless I make a general confession; and if I do not make it now, I foresee that at the hour of death I shall not be able to do it as I ought. My wife, my children, the terror of that last moment, my sufferings, will all deprive me of the necessary recollection of mind, and I shall not have that tranquillity so necessary to such an important duty. It, then, would be a great folly for me to delay this until the last moment of my life." This pious gentleman had well considered the words of our Saviour, in the gospel: "*Blessed are those servants whom the Lord, when he cometh, shall find watching.*" (St. Luke, xii. 37.)

If, then, dear Christian, you see that it would be useful for you to make a general confession, do not delay it too long, but set about it with promptitude and courage. But if this general confession is not only useful, but even necessary, allow yourself no rest until it is done. When you lie down on your bed to-night, remember that this night may be your last, and say to yourself: What should I wish I had done, if I were lying on my death-bed? Be not deceived by the devil, who will strive to quiet you with the vain delusion that you have not time, or that it is too difficult. He will bring up before you various obstacles, and a thousand occupations; to-day this, to-morrow that, and this he will continue until you have neither time nor opportunity left, and at length even have lost the grace to do what was so needful for your eternal salvation. Be on your guard against the deceptions of this lying spirit.

FOR WHOM IS GENERAL CONFESSION NECESSARY?

It is necessary to all those whose former confessions were bad.

When the confessor asks the penitent if there is nothing in his former confessions to cause him distress and anxiety, he answers commonly without reflection, and says: "I always confessed what I remembered." But if the confessor were to question him with regard to any particular sin, especially the sin of impurity, which makes many so dumb in the confessional, he would find in many cases that a general confession is necessary. Reflect, then, carefully, upon what follows:

1. Whoever, through shame or bad will, has concealed any mortal sin whatever, or has not been willing to confess some essential circumstance; or who, through a reckless indifference, or a guilty blindness of conscience, has not confessed some mortal sin, because he did not like to consider it as such, to him a general confession is necessary from the time when these bad confessions began, and this under the penalty of eternal damnation.

2. A general confession is necessay also for those who have always made their confessions carelessly,

and without a sufficient examination of conscience, and are almost sure in this way to have overlooked many a mortal sin.

3. For those also who have indeed confessed, and received absolution, but who are quite ignorant of the principal mysteries of faith; and those who, through their own fault, know little or nothing of the commandments of God, and of the Church, the nature of the holy Sacraments which they have received, and the necessary duties of their station.

4. For those also who have confessed merely through human respect or custom, without any true contrition for their sins, and without any intention not to commit them again. Still more it is necessary for those who have purposely selected for their confessor a Priest who could not understand them well, or one who always gave easy absolutions, without proving and questioning them, and even without seriously admonishing them, when they were engaged in sinful habits, or living in the occasions of sin.

5. For those also who have continued to live in the proximate occasions, or in the habits of mortal sin, the same after confession as before.

6. For those also who were bound to make restitution either of the property or of the good name of their neighbor, but who had no sincere intention when they confessed, to repair the injury done, promising, perhaps, but never willing to do so.

7. It is necessary also for those who have continued to live at enmity with their neighbors, without becoming reconciled to them, or even wishing to be reconciled.

All these have been unworthy of absolution; and if they received it, it was always good for nothing in the sight of God, and therefore they all need to make their confessions over again.

'OR WHOM IS A GENERAL CONFESSION VERY USEFUL?

1. For some, it is the beginning of a new and holy ife. Experience teaches that many Christians, after ι good general confession, fall no more back into their 'ormer sins. Therefore, St. Ignatius Loyola recom nends it to all those who are truly and earnestl lesirous of a thorough conversion to God.

2. For all who are thinking of a change of state, or who are about to enter on an important office, or commence a dangerous journey.

3. When death is drawing near, this is the best preparation for a happy eternity, and the most cer-ain means to obtain peace of conscience. Many aints, as for example, St. Elzear, and St. Margaret, nade a general confession before their last hour with he greatest contrition of heart.

OBSERVATION.—A general confession would be hurtful to those souls naturally timid and uneasy, vho wish to make one on account of false scruples of conscience. Such persons should rather content hemselves with frequent acts of contrition. Their only security is to be found in implicit obedience to heir confessor.

EXAMINATION OF CONSCIENCE FOR A GENERAL CONFESSION.

PREVIOUS QUESTIONS.

I. How long ago did you make your last confes-ion? Did you then receive absolution? Did you erform your penance?

II. Was that confession a good one or a bad one?*

---

* N. B.—Some persons who have made sacrilegious confessions, ink all can be made right again by making a general confession, ithout giving the true reason why they wish to do so. This is a 'stake. It is not only necessary to make all these confessions

Did you wilfully conceal any mortal sins? or, did you confess without true sorrow for them, having no sincere intention to amend your life? or, to perform your penance?

Did you go after this bad confession to communion? How many such sacrilegious confessions and communions have you made?

III. Have you been guilty of sacrilege, by violating any other sacraments? By receiving Baptism unworthily, or by receiving Confirmation, Marriage, or Extreme Unction in mortal sin?

ON THE FIRST COMMANDMENT.

"*I am the Lord thy God. Thou shalt not have strange gods before me,*" &c.

To fulfil this commandment, it is necessary to serve God by faith, by hope, by love, and by the proper acts of outward religious worship. Examine yourself, therefore, as follows:

I. Have you ever denied the Catholic Faith? Have you openly rejected any doctrine of the Catholic Church? Have you spoken against any such doctrine? Have you disbelieved or indulged doubts against any article of faith? Have you suggested or encouraged such doubts in others? How often?

Have you sometimes betrayed the Catholic faith by saying that all religions are good, or that a man may be saved in one as well as another? How many times?

Have you read Protestant Bibles, tracts, or other books on matters of religion, circulated by heretics? Have you kept them in your house, or sold them, or given them to others to read? How many times

over again, but they are bound to acknowledge that they have confessed and communed sacrilegiously, and how often; and to state also what other sacraments they have received in this state of sin.

Have you joined in the worship of heretics, either public or private? Have you gone to their churches? Have you listened to their preaching? How often?

Have you exposed your faith to danger by evil associations? Have you united yourself to the Free-Masons, or Odd-Fellows, or any similar society forbidden by the Church?

Have you by your own fault remained in ignorance of the doctrines and duties of your religion?

II. Have you lived in total neglect of prayer? Have you remained a long while, even a whole month, without prayer, or any act of love or gratitude to God?

III. Have you been guilty of great irreverence in the Church, by immodest actions or conversation,—by an indecent way of dressing, or by some gross misconduct in gazing about and laughing? How often?

Have you consulted fortune-tellers? Have you made use of card-cutting, tossing-cups, or any such superstitious practices, to find out things, or recover things lost? How many times? Have you been guilty of witchcraft, or made use of any spells, or charms, or other like inventions of the devil? How often?

Have you consulted dream-books, books of astrology, &c.? Have you kept them in your house, or given them to others to read? How often?

ON THE SECOND COMMANDMENT.

"*Thou shalt not take the name of the Lord thy God in vain.*"

This commandment is broken by blasphemy, by wicked oaths, by cursing, and by the violation of vows. Examine your conscience thus:

I. Have you been guilty of blasphemy, by angry,

injurious, or insulting words, spoken against God himself, against his power, his justice, his goodness or other perfections?

Have you pronounced any sacred name of God, or of the Saints, in a blasphemous or irreverent manner?

Have you spoken in a blasphemous manner of sacred things; for example, of the Holy Sacraments, the Crucifix, the cross, or sacred relics? How many times?

Have you abused the words of Holy Scripture, by any indecent, or grossly irreverent application? How often?

II. Have you ever sworn falsely, by any holy name or sacred thing? How many times? Have you done this to the prejudice of your neighbor?

Have you taken rash oaths? How often? Have you used foolish and thoughtless oaths? How many times? If it was a habit, how often in the day, the week, or the month, and for how long?

Have you violated any oath lawfully made, by not fulfilling your engagement? How many times? Have you persuaded others to swear falsely, or urged them to an unnecessary oath?

III. Have you cursed yourself or your neighbor? Was it from your heart? Had you the habit of cursing, and how long? How often in the day, the week or the month?

IV. Have you made any rash vows? Have you broken any lawful vow? Have you changed it without lawful permission? Have you put off the fulfilling of it?

Have you broken a marriage promise without good cause?

ON THE THIRD COMMANDMENT.

"*Remember that thou keep holy the Sabbath day.*"

The manner of keeping Sundays and other feasts of obligation is regulated by the Church. These Holy Days are profaned by servile labor. They are sanctified by hearing Mass, and by other exercises of piety. Under this commandment, also, it is customary to class all the Laws of the Church. Examine yourself, then, on these Laws, as follows:

I. Have you done servile work on Sundays, or Holy Days of obligation, without necessity, or lawful permission? How often? Have you caused others to do the same?

Have you spent Sunday, or Holy Days, in taverns, or elsewhere among ungodly companions? in dances, gambling, in drinking to excess, in criminal walks or visits, or scandalous parties of pleasure?

Have you omitted to hear Mass on these days by your own fault? How often?

Have you come too late to Mass, or gone away before it was over? Have you occupied yourself during Mass with other matters, such as talking, gazing about, or reading? How often?

Have you been habitually absent from the sermons and instructions given in the church?

II. Have you disregarded the fast days, by eating meat, or taking more than one meal, and the collation allowed in the evening? How often? Have you caused others to commit the same sin? How many times?

III. Have you broken the abstinence on Fridays, and other days when meat is not allowed? How many times? Have you been the cause of others doing the same? Have you given scandal so?

IV Have you sometimes allowed more than a year

to pass without confession? or, at least, without a good one?

Have you sometimes neglected to receive your Easter Communion? Or to receive it worthily? How often?*

V. Have you been married clandestinely, without the presence of a Priest and witnesses? Was it even before a heretic preacher?

Have you married within the forbidden degrees, and without dispensation? or with an unbaptized person? or with some other impediment which would make the marriage invalid?

Have you married in Advent time, or Lent, with pomp, show, or festivity? Have you indulged in balls, parties, and such-like amusements in Lent or Advent? How many times?

ON THE FOURTH COMMANDMENT.

"*Honor thy father and thy mother.*"

In this commandment are included all our duties to our parents and superiors. Examine yourself upon these duties, thus:

I. Have you been a very ungrateful child? Did you despise your parents? or even hate them? Did you wish for their death? or that some other misfortune might befall them? How often?

Have you given them injurious and insulting language? or mocked and ridiculed them? How often? Have you cursed them? How many times? Have you threatened them, or even lifted up your hand to strike them? How often?

Have you made them unhappy by your misconduct?

---

* N. B.—A sacrilegious confession, or communion, can never fulfil the Law of the Church. The obligation still remains, until they are made over again in a worthy manner. Persons who were unable to commune in the Easter-time, are also bound to do it afterwards. Those who are sick at this time must take care to have the Holy Communion brought to them.

Have you disobeyed them in any grievous matter? and how often? Have you promised or even contracted marriage without their knowledge?

Have you neglected them? Have you refused to aid them in their necessities? Have you been ashamed of them on account of their poverty?

Have you faithfully accomplished their last will? Have you been careful to pray for them?

II. Have you been disrespectful and disobedient to your spiritual superiors, the Bishops and Priests of the Church? Have you treated them in a haughty and insulting manner? Have you taken part with the disaffected and seditious?

Have you neglected to contribute, according to your means, to the support of your Pastors and the maintenance of your religion?

III. Have you put yourself in opposition to the awful authorities of the country? Have you taken part in any mob, or other combination to commit violence? Have you joined with any seditious party or faction to resist the laws, or to disturb the public peace?

ON THE FIFTH COMMANDMENT.

"Thou shalt not kill."

By this commandment are forbidden, not only murder and other acts of violence, but all hatred in the heart, and all violent and injurious language; also scandal, whether in words or actions, and all unfeeling conduct to the poor and afflicted.

I. Have you been guilty of the death of any one? by your own act, by participation, by instigation, by counsel, by consent? Have you attempted or intended to take the life of another? Have you engaged in serious fights, or injured others by wounds, blows, or other ill-treatment? How often?

Have you endeavored to take your own life? Have

you injured your health by excess in eating or drinking? Have you been drunk? How many times? If it was a habit, how often in the week, the month, or the year? Have you been the cause of drunkenness in others? How, and how often?

Have you done any thing to hinder the generation of children; or to destroy the fruit of the womb? By your own act? By your advice? By your consent? How many times?

II. Have you desired the death of others; or wished them some great misfortune! How many times? Have you had the intention to injure or ill-treat persons, if you could?

Have you been at enmity with your neighbors? or refused to speak to or salute them? How often? Are you now reconciled with all?

Have you engaged, through passion or revenge, in vexatious lawsuits; or maliciously defended yourself against the just claims of others?

Have you excited others to anger or revenge?

III. Have you done harm to the soul of any one by giving scandal? Do you remember any whose innocence has suffered by your wicked words or bad example?

Have you drawn the young and innocent into sin Have you taught them some vicious habit? Have you spoken to them of wicked or dangerous things, which they should not know? Have you thrown temptation in the way of the weak? Have you dissuaded, or discouraged those who were willing to repent and to reform? How often?

IV. Have you neglected to give alms in proportion to your ability? Have you remained insensible to the wants of the poor, even in time of general sickness famine, and distress? Have you refused your contribution to works of true Christian Charity? Have you refused your aid to the sick, the suffering, and the dying

ON THE SIXTH AND NINTH COMMANDMENTS.

"*Thou shalt not commit adultery. Thou shalt not covet thy neighbor's wife.*"

By these two commandments are forbidden all kinds of impurity. It must be borne in mind that every sin of this nature, whether in action, word, or even only in thought, when quite wilful and deliberate, is a mortal sin, and necessary to be confessed. On these commandments examine your thoughts, words, and actions, as follows:

I. Have you dwelt wilfully, and with complaisance, upon impure thoughts or imaginations? Have you, in fact, consented to them in your mind? How often?

II. Have you made use of impure language or allusions; or listened to it willingly and with complaisance? Was it sometimes before persons of another sex? Have you sung immodest songs, or listened to them? How often? Have you boasted of your former sins?

III. Have you been guilty of improper and dangerous freedoms with any of the other sex? How far have you carried this sinful conduct? Was the companion of your guilt a single person? How often? A married person? How often? A relation? How often Was there any thing else in the quality of the person, which made your sin more grievous? (*Whenever second person is concerned, the same distinctions must be made, whether the impurity be one of thought, word, or action.*)

Have you entertained a criminal or dangerous intimacy? Have you written improper letters, or received them? How often? Have you gazed immodestly upon yourself or others; upon pictures or statues, or any object which could excite evil desires? How often? Have you indulged in habits of secret sin? How long. How often?

Have you by the freedom of your manners, or your immodest dress, been the cause of temptation to others? Was this also your intention?

Have you read impure books, or newspapers? How often? Have you lent them to others? Have you exposed yourself voluntarily to the occasions of sin, by means of dances, shows, theatres, &c.; by intemperance, by reading romances and plays, by walking out at night, by frequenting society, or by remaining alone with persons of a different sex?

Have you been guilty of seduction; or even of violence? How often? Did you accomplish your evil designs by means of a false promise of marriage? Have you refused to repair the injury you have done?

Have you taken part in the sins of others by favoring their bad designs? How, and how often?

Have your sins against these two commandments been sometimes of an unnatural kind? How often?

ON THE SEVENTH AND TENTH COMMANDMENTS.

"*Thou shalt not steal. Thou shalt not covet thy neighbor's goods.*"

By these two commandments are forbidden injustice and covetousness of every kind. Examine yourself thus:

I. Have you stolen money or other property? What was it? Have you it still in your possession? What was its value? How much at a time? How often? (*It is necessary thoughout this whole examination, not only to number your sins, but also to estimate, as near as possible, the value of what you took, or the amount of damage caused by your injustice, that it may appear whether your sins were mortal, and what restitution you have to make.*)

Have you stolen any thing consecrated to God, or from a holy place? (This is sacrilege.)

Have you charged exorbitant prices? Have you made out false bills? Have you cheated in the weight, measure, quantity, or quality of your goods, under the excuse that others do the same? Have you otherwise cheated in buying or selling?

Have you cheated at cards or other games? Or on a still grander scale, by means of deceitful speculations, associations, or other enterprises, entered into in bad faith, and to the injury of the simple and unwary? Have you defrauded your creditors? Have you received exorbitant interest for your money? Have you been guilty of forgery? Have you passed counterfeit money or broken bills?

II. Having found things of some value, have you kept them, without taking the necessary pains to find the owner? Being trusted with money, have you kept back a part for yourself? Have you failed to return things borrowed?

Have you bought or received things which you knew or believed to be stolen? Have you taken charge of them, or allowed them to be kept in your house?

Have you neglected to pay your debts? Have you contracted debt without any reasonable hope of paying?

III. Have you been the cause of ruin or damage to the property of another? Have you been grossly careless or neglectful of what was intrusted to your care! Have you received pay for work or service which you had not done, or which was ill done?

Have you carried on an unjust lawsuit, or advised others to do so? Have you sought to gain your cause by bribery, threats, or other corrupt means?

Have you, in your dealings, taken advantage of the simple, the young and inexperienced? Have you made hard bargains with the poor, or those in embarrassment and distress? Have you delayed to pay them? Have you kept back their wages from your domestics and laborers, or paid them less than their just due?

Have you been guilty of fraud or embezzlement in any public office or private trust?

Have you injured any one in your profession, or employment, by negligence or a culpable ignorance?

IV. Have you taken part in the theft, fraud, or injustice of others? Have you concealed, when it was your duty to inform?

V. Have you attempted, intended, or desired to rob, or steal, or defraud, or commit any kind of injustice? How often?

REMARKS.—Do not forget to examine whether you have repaired all the injustice you have done, for your sins will not be pardoned while you refuse or neglect to make restitution. If the thing unjustly acquired is gone, return the value in some other way. If you cannot restore the whole, restore what you can, and do not delay. In fine, if it is impossible to make any restitution for the time being, it is necessary, at least, to have the sincere and firm resolution to do it as soon as you shall be able.

ON THE EIGHTH COMMANDMENT.

"*Thou shalt not bear false witness against thy neighbor.*"

By this commandment are forbidden all false witness, lying, and detraction. Examine your conscience thus:

I. Have you given false testimony before any tribunal or magistrate? Have you, by persuasion or advice, in any way procured false testimony, and how?

Have you signed any false papers or documents? Have you falsified letters or other writings? Wha injury have you done by these sins? How often?

II. Have you been guilty of lying, through malice, or for some bad purpose? Have you put in circulation, or repeated again, any scandalous report which you knew to be false, or did not believe to be true? How, and how often.

III. Have you been guilty of detraction in any serious matter, by making known the secret faults or defects of your neighbor? How often? Have you done any thing else to blacken his character, or injure his interests?

Have you caused mischief or ill-feeling between others by tale-bearing? How often?

Have you been careful to repair the mischief you have done, by contradicting your false reports, and doing what else you could to restore the wounded credit, honor, and reputation of your neighbor?

ON THE DUTIES OF YOUR STATE.

Now examine yourself on your obligations in particular, as a parent, a husband or wife, a master or servant, a magistrate, and on your conduct in the pursuit of your profession:

I. *If a Parent.* Have you always taken proper care of the life and health of your children? Have you not exposed them to great danger even before birth? or afterwards taken them to your own bed with danger of their being suffocated?

Have you taken care to provide for their wants, food, clothing, &c.? Have you done your best to procure them a good education, according to their condition?

Have you not manifested an unjust preference for one to the prejudice of another? Have you been neglectful, unkind, or even cruel to your step-children, or others under your protection?

Have you unreasonably forced your children into some profession, or state of life, for which they felt no vocation? Have you hindered them from pursuing their vocation, when called to a religious life? Have you, without sufficient cause, opposed their inclinations with regard to marriage?

Have you neglected the care of their salvation?

Have you endeavored in their tender years, to inspire them with the love of God, and the fear of sin? Have you neglected to teach them to pray?

Have you exposed their salvation to danger, by delaying their baptism? Have you neglected to have them prepared, and brought forward at the proper age to confession, confirmation and first communion?

Have you neglected to get them well instructed in their own religion? Have you sent them to heretic or godless schools, to the danger of their faith? Did you always take them to church on Sundays and Holy Days? Have you put them out to some service or situation where they could not practice their religion, or where their faith or their virtue was in danger?

Have you exposed their innocence to danger, by letting them sleep together without distinction, or by taking them to your own bed, or keeping them in the same room, when already old enough to be scandalized? How often?

Have you watched them carefully to see where they spent their time, in what company, &c.; or have you let them wander where they would? Have you left them to the care of loose or irreligious servants, or whose morals were doubtful?

Have you allowed them free intercourse with the other sex; to receive visits alone, and at improper hours; or to be out late at night? Have you permitted them to read romances, or other pernicious books?

Have you neglected to punish them for their own good? Have you allowed them to curse and swear, &c., in your presence without chastisement? Have you, in fine, by your indifference or foolish fondness, left them without restraint.

Have you on the contrary, treated them with violence and brutality in your anger? In what way? Have you cursed them? How often? Have you exasperated or scandalized them by your violent language, abusive names, &c.?

Have you otherwise given them scandal and bad example, by your neglect of your religion, and your sinful life?

II. *If you are married.* Did you enter into marriage through base and unchristian motives? Have you not by your light conduct given cause of jealousy and distress to your companion?

Have you been careful to observe, even in marriage, the laws of modesty? Have you profaned the holy state of matrimony by misuse? Have you done any thing to hinder its lawful end? How often?

Have you lived with your wife (or husband) in peace and union? Have you not sinned and given scandal by your disagreement and angry disputes? How long have you lived in this way?

Have you abandoned your wife (or husband) without just cause and lawful permission? Have you lived separate, or remained a long while absent?

As a Husband. Have you treated your wife in a gross, tyrannical, and cruel manner? Have you beat her in your anger or drunkenness, or injured her by any other outrage? How many times? Have you made her unhappy by your neglect, coldness, and unfeeling conduct, or by spending your leisure time away from home?

Have you treated her with attention and forbearance in the time of her pregnancy? Have you corrupted her mind by your immodesty and wicked conversation? Have you not tempted her or forced her to offend God? How often? Have you neglected to provide for her maintenance, and that of your children? Have you squandered her earnings and your own on your sinful pleasures?

As a Wife. Have you, without the knowledge of your husband, made useless and extravagant expenses, or dissipated a part of his property in favor of your own relations? How much? Have you not made difficulty in his family by your selfish jealousy and unfriendly conduct towards his relations?

Have you been respectful and obedient to him in every thing reasonable? Have you not made his home disagreeable, and his life unhappy, by your ill-temper and scolding tongue? Have you refused him his marriage rights? How often? Have you not persuaded him to offend God against the dictates of nature and of conscience? How often?

Have you done your part for the support of the family? Have you been idle and neglectful of your household duties?

III. *If you are Master, Mistress, or Employer.* Have you treated your servants in a harsh, tyrannical, and unfeeling manner? Have you not overburdened them with work? Have you obliged them to do unnecessary work on Sundays and other Holy Days? How often? Have you hindered them from hearing Mass on those days? How often?

Have you always given them proper and sufficient food and clothing? Have you treated them charitably in their sickness and distress? Have you dismissed them unjustly before the time agreed upon, or suddenly, by caprice, and with cruel haste?

Have you refused to your servants or laborers their just due, or wronged them by delaying to pay? Have you taken advantage of their poverty and want to engage them upon hard and unequal terms? How much have you wronged them, and how often?

Having slaves, have you cruelly parted parents from children, husband from wife, or allowed those to marry again who were still bound by a former marriage?

Have you been careful of the salvation of those depending upon you? Have you instructed them in the faith? Have you encouraged and exhorted them to frequent the church and the sacraments, and religious instructions?

Have you watched over their morals? Have you, on the contrary, retained them in your service, notwithstanding their corrupt and scandalous conduct, and perhaps with danger to yourself or your family? Have you permitted them to keep improper company and late hours, to frequent dangerous places and amusements?

Have you taken advantage of their condition to corrupt them, by your authority, your flattery, or your bribes? How, and how often? Have you allowed in your house persons of loose character, or dangerous gatherings, or tolerated in it any scandal of which you were aware? What, and how often?

IV. *If you are a Servant, Clerk, or Apprentice.* Have you served your employers diligently and faithfully? Have they suffered no harm by your fault? Have you wasted their substance? Have you given away their property to your own relations and friends? Have you stolen from them? Have you kept a part of what they trusted to you to make purchases for them? Have you kept or taken their property under pretence that your wages were too low? How much? How often?

Have you concealed from your employers the thefts or misconduct of your fellow-servants in matters belonging to your charge?

Have you revealed the faults of your superiors without necessity, and to their prejudice? Have you sown discord in their families, and how? Have you been the cause of other servants being sent away by your false or malicious complaints?

Have you engaged yourself in some service where your faith or your morals were in danger, or where you would not be allowed to fulfil the obligations of your religion? Have you allowed yourself to be enticed to the churches of heretics, to join in their family prayers, or to read their religious books? How many times?

Have you suffered yourself to be employed in some wicked service, or assisted your superiors in their criminal designs? What, and how often?

V. *If you are a Magistrate or public officer.* Have you been faithful and exact in the discharge of the duties of your office? Have you, through weakness, the fear of man, the desire of popularity, or anxiety for office and emolument, betrayed the public interest, or sacrificed the rights of particular persons, or suffered crime and disorder to go unchecked and unpunished? In what way, and how often?

Have you, directly or indirectly, received bribes; or allowed yourself to be influenced in the administration of justice, or your official conduct, by promises or presents? How and how often?

Have you been guilty of embezzlement of the public funds? Have you made use of them for your own interest? Have you enriched yourself or your friends by means of unequal contracts, at the expense of the public? In what way? How much?

Have you abused your official power by oppression and cruelty, or applied it to purposes of revenge? Have you unjustly favored your friends? Have you shielded or aided the wicked? Have you neglected the cause of the poor, the innocent, the helpless, and the oppressed? Have you given scandal by open neglect and disregard of the Catholic religion and your Christian duties?

VI. *If you are a Lawyer, Notary, or Clerk.* Have you advocated claims which you knew to be unjust, or sustained an unjust defence? How often? Did you thereby obtain an unjust decision? Have you undertaken a prosecution against an innocent person, or urged it on after having discovered his innocence? Have you defended the cause of the guilty by means of fraud, bribes, or dishonest means?

Have you injured the just cause of your client by your treachery, gross ignorance, want of study, or neglect? How often? Have you given treacherous, doubtful, or ill-considered advice? Have you unjustly flattered the hopes of your clients, or otherwise excited useless litigation?

Have you been guilty of fraud, bribery, or other injustice in your business? Have you procured false testimony, or encouraged to commit perjury? Have you by any artifice, obtained attestations to false affidavits and other documents, or sworn to them yourself? Have you been guilty of fraud in the drawing up of deeds, wills, contracts, and other instruments? Have you made them contrary to the intention of either party, or introduced ambiguous expressions? Have you falsified any document, or destroyed it, or substituted another in place of the true one? How often have you done any of these things?

Have you made out unjust bills of costs, demanding unlawful or exorbitant fees, or charging for services never rendered? How often?

What injury, and how much, have you caused to any one by any of the above sins? Have you ever repaired it, or made restitution?

VII. *If you are a Physician or Surgeon.* Have you undertaken the care of persons seriously sick, without sufficient science or experience? Have you treated serious or extraordinary cases with neglect, or applied insignificant remedies? How often, and with what result?

Being ignorant of the nature of the complaint, have you rashly hazarded dangerous remedies, and even with the peril of serious injury or death? Have you made merciless experiments upon the sick, especially those in the hospital, and the poor? How often, and with what result?

Have you failed to consult where you ought; or, in consulting, made choice of those not recommended by their skill? Have you made needless expense by calling in others, or followed their counsel against your own conscience? Have you kept patients lingering in sickness for sake of gain, or multiplied useless visits to their expense? Have you prescribed needless medicines for your own profit, or that of the apothecary? How much injury or injustice have you thus done? How often?

Have you undertaken surgical operations beyond your science or skill? Have you conducted them recklessly, with unnecessary hazard of life or loss of limb? How often? Have you intentionally taken the life of a child in the womb, or at its birth? Have you been guilty of procuring abortion, by your own act or advice, or by furnishing the means? How often?

Have you failed to warn those in danger of death, that they might receive the sacraments? Have you allowed infants to die without baptism, by your wilfulness or neglect? How often?

VIII. *If you keep a Hotel or Bar.* Have you not charged more to your guests than was just? Have you not adulterated your liquors? To what amount? How often?

Have you not given drink to drunkards, or to those already drunk, or allowed them in your house to drink to excess? How often? Have you not served those whom you knew to be ruining their family by their dissipation?

Have you kept your house open during divine service, or made it a place of dissipation on Sundays?

Have you allowed gambling in your establishment, or tolerated blasphemy, obscenity, and other wicked discourse? Have you permitted loose women to lodge in it, or frequent it? Has it not been a place of scandalous interviews, or other shameful immorality?

Have you allowed in it immoral shows or concerts, drunken festivity and dangerous dances? How often? Is not your business an occasion of sin to your neighbor, of harm to your children, and a hindrance to your own salvation?

Instruction on Matrimony.

"*This is a great Sacrament, but I speak in Christ and in the Church.*" (Ephes. v. 32.)

THE marriage state is no invention of man, nor of recent origin. It was instituted by God himself, and existed at the beginning of the world, in the innocent groves of Paradise. It was there our first parents, Adam and Eve, joined hands before the face of their Creator, and received the nuptial benediction from his own mouth. The account given of this first marriage in the book of Genesis is full of deep interest, and of a holy beauty, and should inspire all, especially married persons, with a deep feeling of gratitude, and also with a high and holy veneration for a state so divinely and so solemnly instituted.

THE SANCTITY OF MARRIAGE.

If marriage, according to its primitive institution, was already an honorable and holy state, how much more is it so under the Christian dispensation, now that Jesus Christ has elevated it to the rank and dignity of a sacrament! Among heretics marriage is, for the most part, regarded as a mere contract between a man and woman to cohabit together under the sanction of the law. "*The state of marriage,*" says Calvin, in Book IV. of his Institutes, "*is no otherwise good and holy than that of the farmer, the mason, the shoemaker, and the barber, which states are not sacraments.*" According to the Catholic doctrine, on the contrary, it is a true sacrament, and this is even an article of faith.

That marriage has always been regarded in the Church as a sacred engagement, raised high above the common actions of life, and the civil order of things, and solemnized by religious ceremonies, is seen clearly enough in the writings of the early Fathers, whose doctrine should be received by every reasonable man as the belief of Christians in primitive times. Tertullian, who lived in the second century, says, writing to his wife: "*How can we express the happiness of the marriage union contracted under the auspices of the Church, consecrated by the oblation of the Holy Sacrifice, and sealed by the benediction which the angels have witnessed, and which the Eternal Father has ratified?*" (Lib. II.) St. Cyril, Patriarch of of Alexandria, in the beginning of the fifth century, thus speaks of marriage: "*Jesus Christ himself assisted at the wedding to which he was invited, in order to sanctify the conjugal union: for it was fitting that he who was to regenerate the nature of man, should not only impart his benediction to those already born, but should prepare graces for those who were afterwards to be born, and consecrate the source of their origin.*" (Comment. in Joan. ch. xxii.) Beautifully clear are the words of the great St. Augustine: "*In the marriage of Christians, the sanctity of the marriage is more to be esteemed than the fruitfulness which is its consequence. Among all nations the advantage of the nuptial bond is to propagate the human race, and to unite the married pair by the fidelity they owe to each other. But with the people of God, a more precious good, and a stricter bond of union result from the sanctity of the sacrament. A wife, even when divorced from her husband, cannot without sacrilege contract another engagement during his life.*" (De vinculo Mat. xxiv.)

The Apostle Paul himself speaks of the marriage of Christians in the same exalted language. He expressly names it a sacrament, and compares it to the holy an wonderful union of Christ with his Church. "*This is a great sacrament: but I speak in Christ and in the Church.*" "*So ought men to love their wives as their own bodies. For no man ever hated his own flesh, but nourisheth and cherisheth it, as also Christ doth the Church.*" (Ephes. v. 28.)

Since marriage is a sacrament, it ought to have, like all the other sacraments, an inward and sanctifying grace for those who receive it; and so it has. When Christians marry in a state of mortal sin, then indeed they receive no grace. They join hands to commit a sacrilege, and receive a malediction with it. But in those who receive it in the love of God, this sacrament increases the sanctifying grace which they have already, and imparts a special grace to sanctify and bless their union, that they may dwell together in peace and charity, bear with each other, aid each other, preserve mutual fidelity, and bring up their children in the fear of God.

THE ENDS OF MARRIAGE.

If Christian marriage is a bond so holy, so holy in its divine Founder, so holy in its character of a sacrament, so holy in the grace it imparts, ought it not to be sanctified also by the holy aims, the pure motives of those who engage in it? Christians ought to unite with the same intentions which Almighty God had, when he instituted marriage. 1. That they may be mutual helps to each other: "*It is not good,*" said God, "*for man to be alone: let us make a help like unto himself.*" 2. To raise up children for the church and for heaven; holy children, who may inherit not so much the temporal riches as the faith of their parents, whom they may bring up in the fear of God, and in the practice of virtue and piety. 3. That they may find a safeguard and a remedy against temptation. Hence, although St. Paul declares, "*for the unmarried and widows, it is good if they continue even as I,*" yet he adds immediately, "*but if they do not contain, let them marry, for it is better to marry than to be burnt.*" A life of entire chastity is beyond all doubt a higher and more perfect state than that of marriage, but then it is a particular gift of God, which all do not receive. If a person, still free to choose, finds that he has not received this gift, let him recognize his own weakness, and have recourse to marriage.

To marry for this last-mentioned reason is justifiable, and often necessary; but it is not intended to sanction the wicked conduct of those persons who embrace this holy state only to gratify their passions, without any thought for the good of their souls. Marriages which begin in brutality, are almost sure to be continued in infidelity, and often end in shame and sorrow. A fearful example of the judgment of God is related in holy Scripture. We read there that the seven first husbands of Sara were strangled by a devil the very night of their marriage. This, as the angel Raphael explained to Tobias, was because they married this holy young woman out of mere sensuality. "*Over such,*" said the angel, "*the devil hath power. But thou, when thou shalt take her, go into the chamber, and for three days give thyself to nothing else but to prayers with her, and when the third night is passed, thou shalt take the virgin with the fear of the Lord, moved rather for the love of children than for lust, that in the seed of Abraham thou mayest obtain a blessing in children.*" (Tob. vi.)

MARRIAGE VOCATION.

The fact that matrimony is a state of great responsibility, and one which lasts for life, is enough to show that one ought not to embrace it lightly, nor without much thought and reflection. But besides this, its very sanctity shows it to be a divine vocation, and therefore Christians should never act in such a matter without consulting God. They ought always to ask counsel of virtuous friends, and wise guides, in order to know the divine will, and pray fervently like the Psalmist; "*O Lord, make known to me the way in which I am to walk!*"

They should seek to ascertain, in the first place, whether they are not perhaps called to a more perfect state; for it must not be forgotten, that there is a state still higher and holier, and that all are not called to marriage, either by nature or by the will of God.

If, however, it should appear that one has no call to a single life, either in the priesthood or in the cloister, or otherwise, it is still equally necessary to appeal to heaven for direction in the choice of a companion. There can be no doubt that when God calls persons to the married life, he marks out for each one a particular partner, in accordance with his own wise and holy will. So God formed Eve for our first father Adam, Rebecca was prepared for Isaac, and Sara was reserved for Tobias. In the Book of Proverbs we read: "*Houses and riches are given by parents, but a prudent wife is properly from the Lord.*" Trust not, young Christian, to your imagination, and the first impulse of your heart, for it is easy to be deceived. Remember, moreover, that your whole future happiness will depend upon the wisdom of your choice! A helpless, giddy, dressy, rambling girl, will make a vicious wife and mother: idle and dissipated young men grow easily into drunken and brutal husbands. The principal reason why so many marriages are unhappy, and disgraced by the most shameful scandals, is, because in these matters persons are guided more by passion and interest, than by virtue and religion. Money is preferred to good morals, showy accomplishments to industry, beauty to modesty and purity; who can wonder if shame and misery are the results? In this matter, therefore, dear young Christians, pray earnestly to God for direction, and ask good counsel of those whom he has given you for your spiritual guides.

Children are bound also to consult their parents, and ask their consent. "Christian modesty cannot suffer," says St. Ambrose, "that children marry without advice. Let them submit to the judgment of their parents." There is, besides, a great power in a father's and mother's blessing, and it is no small loss to lose it. If, however, parents, through avarice, or caprice, or other like motive, should refuse consent to the reason ble desires of their children, in such extreme cases, after consulting disinterested, enlightened, and virtuous guides, and receiving the approbation of the Church, the marriage may take place.

On the other hand, in giving their children in marriage, the great solicitude of parents ought to be, to select a person full of piety and virtue. The fear of God is the only foundation of peace and prosperity in a family. Every day we see crushed the proud schemes of some worldly-minded parent, whilst the words of the royal prophet are verified: "*Unless the Lord build the house, they labor in vain that build it.*" (Ps. cxxvi.)

IMPEDIMENTS OF MARRIAGE.

The Holy Church has, from the earliest ages, annexed certain conditions to the matrimonial contract, which are called impediments. These are of two kinds. 1. The Annulling Impediments, or those which make it impossible to contract any real marriage at all; and, 2. The Prohibitory Impediments, which do not take away the power to contract a valid marriage, but only make it unlawful and sinful.

I. THE ANNULLING IMPEDIMENTS.—A marriage contracted, notwithstanding an impediment of this kind, is null and void from the beginning, that is to say, no marriage at all in the sight of God. No law of the land can make such an alliance good. Both parties to it live together in crime, and under the anger of God, if they are aware of the impediment; and if they did not know of it in the beginning, they are bound to separate immediately when they discover it. Sometimes, indeed, the impediment may be dispensed with by the Church, but in that case they are bound to abstain from all use of marriage until the dispensation is obtained, and a valid marriage contracted. The principal impediments of this kind are the following.

1. *Consanguinity* is that impediment which exists between blood-relations to the fourth degree inclusively. In other words, marriage is forbidden between third cousins, or any nearer degree of kindred. And this impediment exists when the relationship arises from an illegitimate birth.

2. *Affinity* is relationship by marriage. It is forbidden to marry the third cousin, or any nearer blood relation of one's former husband or wife. The same is true of a person, and the blood-relations of any one with whom he has had unlawful connection; but in this case, the impediment extends only to the second degree (first cousin). Spiritual affinity is a species of relationship contracted by means of the sacraments of baptism and confirmation. For this reason, parents cannot marry with the sponsors of their child, or with any person who baptized it; nor can sponsors marry with their God-children. So, if one baptizes the child of another, even although it were a case of necessity, he cannot afterwards marry either with the child or its parent.

3. *Public decency* is an impediment which forbids one to marry with a parent, a child, with a brother or sister of the person to whom one has been validly engaged by a promise of marriage. Also, if one has contracted an invalid marriage, or a valid marriage which, however, was never consummated, it is forbidden, in such case, to marry with the blood-relations of the other party, as far as the fourth degree; that is to say, with a third cousin, or any thing nearer.

4. *Crime* is sometimes an impediment. Persons who are guilty of homicide, and adultery, with an en-

gagement to marry, are rendered incapable of contracting marriage together.

5. *Difference of religion* is an impediment which makes a marriage null and void between a baptized person and one who was never baptized.

6. *Vows.*—All persons who have made solemn vows of chastity, by entering into some religious order, are incapable of contracting marriage; and so are all orders of the clergy, beginning with sub-deacons and upwards.

7. *Clandestine marriages*, that is, those which are contracted without the presence of the parish priest, and of two witnesses, are made null and void by the Council of Trent. In the United States, however, where the decree of the Council has not yet been published,* these marriages, although sinful, are valid. It is a most wicked and detestable thing, that Catholics should ever so far forget all dictates of faith and piety, as to be coupled like heathen before a civil magistrate, and even sometimes before a heretic preacher, in contempt of the Church of God, and of the sancity of this Sacrament. In case of necessity, as when those who desire to marry live very far from any Church or Priest, they may lawfully apply to a Magistrate for that purpose, and it is better to do so, in order that their marriage may be more public, and be recorded, but it is never lawful to have recourse to an heretical minister. Such a marriage is indeed binding, but it binds like a curse.

Besides the sin, there are other evils which result from these clandestine unions. Commonly, no safe record is kept of the date, and of the names of the parties, and when proof of the marriage is required, sufficient proof is not to be found. Thus, wives or husbands may be deserted with impunity, title to property cannot be proved, children are often unable to show their legitimacy. How many young and thoughtless

* The Council has been published in St. Louis, New Orleans, and Detroit. In these dioceses, therefore, clandestine marriages are invalid.

persons engage themselves rashly and suddenly in a state of misery, from which death only can release them! But, worst of all, invalid marriages are often contracted in this way, with the most disastrous consequences. Unhappy females are ensnared by men already married, into secret or hasty unions, which, if not soon ended in shame, are continued in more lasting sorrow, and more horrible guilt. Those who violate the salutary laws of the Church will find, sooner or later, that "*the way of transgressors is hard.*"

8. *The bond of a previous marriage* is an impediment which death alone can remove. The Catholic Church holds that, by the institution and ordinance of Almighty God, marriage is indissoluble. No power on earth, no prince, no judge, no legislature, can break the bond which unites husband and wife. For certain just causes, especially for adultery, they may live separately, but they are still married, and cannot marry again. If, after such a separation, or after a divorce granted by the law of the land, either party should marry another person, it would be no true marriage before God, but an adultery. Jesus Christ has said it: "*Whosoever shall put away his wife, except it be for fornication, and shall marry another, committeth adultery.*" It is therefore permitted in such a case to separate, but the marriage bond is not broken, the parties remain still husband and wife; for our Lord goes on to say: "*he that shall marry her that is put away, committeth adultery.*" (St. Matt. xix.) If the first bond were really dissolved by such a separation, it might be forbidden, indeed, to the guilty party to contract a new one, but our Lord would never call the second marriage an adultery. Therefore, the words, "except it be for fornication," have reference to the lawfulness of putting away the guilty woman at all, but give no permission to the innocent party to marry again. "*What God hath joined together, let no man put asunder,*" says our Lord, in the same chapter, con-

demning beforehand the iniquity of those divorces which are obtained in Protestant Legislatures, or Courts of Law.

Let it be remembered, then, that no divorce, no guilt, no desertion, however wanton and unfeeling, no years of absence, can ever break the marriage bond. Nothing but a *certain knowledge* of the death of one party, can make it lawful for the other to marry. Although it might cause public scandal, although the honor of whole families may be at stake, although children would be exposed to shame and destitution by a separation, the guilty parties to these false second marriages must separate under pain of hell-fire.

In cases where a second contract has been made whilst both parties knew of the former one, and only doubted, but were not sure of the death of the first husband or wife, they have no right to live together under favor of this doubt, because they married in bad faith. If, however, one of them was ignorant of the previous marriage, or had been made to believe that the former wife or husband was surely dead, the party thus contracting in good faith retains a right under the second marriage, and is not bound to abandon it until something certain can be known in the matter; but the guilty one who contracted in bad faith has acquired no such right, and lives in adultery to the peril of his soul.

How horrible then the guilt of those, who enter knowingly into these sacrilegious unions! How foolish also are those who marry secretly or hastily with strangers, of whose character and former life they know little or nothing, without consent of parents and friends without any publication of the bans, sometimes without the presence of Priest or witnesses, and thus expose themselves to the danger of being betrayed into an unholy union, which they cannot break from without shame, nor hold to without adultery!

II. The Prohibitory Impediments.—A prohibitory

impediment is one which renders a marriage unlawful, but leaves it valid and binding. If persons marry, notwithstanding such an impediment, they commit a grievous sin, but cannot afterwards separate. There are three impediments of this kind, viz., a simple vow to preserve chastity, to enter into the priesthood, or into a religious order; a previous promise of marriage and a prohibition of the Church.

By the laws of the Church it is forbidden:

1. To solemnize marriage, in other words, to marry with any outward pomp or festivity, during the time of Advent or Lent; that is to say, from the first Sunday of Advent until Epiphany, and from the beginning of Lent to Low Sunday.

2. Mixed marriages are forbidden, viz., the union of a Catholic with heretics, and persons excommunicated by the Church. This prohibition is founded on reasons of the highest importance. In the first place, there is always something repugnant and unnatural in these unions. "*Bear not the yoke with unbelievers,*" says the Apostle Paul to the Corinthians. "*What fellowship hath light with darkness? or what part hath the faithful with the unbeliever?* Such marriages are moreover unfavorable to domestic peace. "*How,*" asks St. Ambrose, "*can there be a sincere union of the affections when persons are divided on religion?*" (Lib. II. de Abra.) But the worst feature in this sort of marriage is, that they are dangerous to the faith of the Catholic party, and of the children. Either domestic attachment, or fear, or ridicule, soon weakens the faith and dampens the fervor of the Catholic husband, or wife, whilst the children easily follow in practice the example of the parent whose religion affords the greatest liberty of indulgence.

When some grave reason exists, and the danger of perversion is removed, a dispensation may be obtained which will make such a marriage lawful. No valid dispensation can be given, however, unless upon the following conditions: 1st, It must be mutually agreed upon that the Catholic husband, or wife, shall enjoy a perfect liberty in the exercise of the Catholic religion; and 2dly, that all the children shall be educated in the Catholic faith. 3dly, Besides this, the Catholic party must promise to seek the conversion of the other, by prayer, good example, and other prudent means. When a dispensation has been obtained upon these conditions, the marriage may take place without sin: but still it must not be supposed that such unnatural unions are approved of by the Church. She only permits them reluctantly and mournfully. She forbids them to be celebrated within church-walls, or to receive the solemn benediction of the Priest.

PREPARATION FOR MARRIAGE.

1. *Publication of the Bans.*—In order to place a check upon clandestine marriages; to discover any impediments which might exist; to prevent deception and surprise; to afford parents and others interested an opportunity to interpose, and in order to procure the prayers of the faithful, that God may give light, grace, and prosperity to the contracting parties, the Council of Trent has decreed, "that the promises of marriage be published on three Sundays, or festival days, in succession, at the public offices of the Church, by the parish Priest of the parties." (Sess. xxiv.) There can be no doubt that if any one knows of an impediment in the way of the proposed marriage, he is bound to reveal it. A great amount of sin and misery may thus be prevented.

2. An innocent life is the best preparation for marriage; gay flowers and beautiful garments are poor substitutes. A heart defiled is a sad recommendation for the nuptial blessing, and a fraud on the mar

riage contract. Even between the parties themselves, the most perfect modesty and prudent reserve should be maintained. When Rebecca first beheld Isaac, her affianced husband, coming to meet her, *she took her cloak and covered herself.* (Gen. xxiv.) Beautiful example of a precaution inspired by true modesty. Parents who love their children truly, and in the fear of God, will never allow them to associate freely together, out of their own presence, and least of all, when they are already promised to each other. All secret interviews, lonely walks, and every familiarity contrary to Christian decorum, ought to be prohibited. How many young persons, by the neglect of such precautions, are already before marriage stained with sin, and disgraced in each other's eyes!

3. Never let it be forgotten that marriage is a sacrament, and must be received in a state of grace. For this reason, to avoid committing a sacrilege, and also to deserve more fully the blessing of God upon their union, the parties affianced ought to purify their hearts by a good confession, and on the very morning of their marriage receive the holy Communion. It is sometimes advisable to make even a general confession, or at least a review of several years, either to remedy the errors of a past sensual life, or in order to enter with more thorough and perfect dispositions of heart into a state so new and responsible. Dear young Catholics, do not imitate the blind children of this world, who pass the few days previous to this solemn step in making ready for an extravagant display of finery,—whilst a guilty conscience and unholy imaginations prepare them for the celebration of a sacrilege. Admire rather the holy example of young Tobias and his bride. They gave three entire days to prayer, that they might obtain the blessing of heaven on their marriage "*For we are the children of the Saints,*" said

they, "*and we must not be joined together like the heathen that know not God.*" Matrimony in our days is a more holy thing than then, and Christians have now better means to prepare for it, by confession and the Eucharist. Do not forget then to sanctify the morning of your marriage by receiving devoutly the Holy Communion.

THE MARRIAGE CEREMONY.

The Church desires that marriage should be celebrated in the morning, and in the church, because it is a sacrament, and in order to inspire the parties who wed, and all the witnesses, with religious sentiments worthy of so solemn an act. There at the foot of the altar they feel the sacred character of their union, and all evil thoughts are banished. There also they are aided by the prayers of their friends. Of course, it is not becoming to appear in the church with a show of worldly pomp and finery, and least of all immodestly dressed. Whatever innocent display and festivity the customs of society require, may take place afterwards at home, in the afternoon or evening.

In the morning of the day appointed, the Bridegroom and Bride, accompanied by their friends and relations, appear at the altar before the Priest, who is habited in a surplice and white stole, and assisted by a clerk who carries the book, and a vessel of holy water. The Priest first demands of each one as follows: "*N—, wilt thou take N— here present for thy lawful wife (or husband), according to the rite of our Holy Mother the Church?*" To this each one in turn replies, "*I will.*" Then ordering them to join their right hands, over which he throws one end of his stole, the Priest says: "*I join you together in matrimony. In the name of the Father, and of the Son, and of the Holy Ghost. Amen.*" He then sprinkles holy water upon them both. The next ceremony is to bless the nuptial ring, which he does in these words. "*Bless thou, O Lord, this ring which we bless in thy name, that she who wears it may preserve entire fidelity to her husband, may continue in peace and in obedience to thy holy will, and live always in the exercise of mutual charity: through Christ our Lord Amen.*" Then, having sprinkled the ring with holy water in the form of a cross, he gives it to the Bridegroom, who places it on the ring-finger of the Bride, while the Priest says: "*In the name of the Father, and of the Son, and of the Holy Ghost. Amen.*" Other ceremonies are sometimes observed, which are not in all places the same. Finally, having prayed for the happiness of this new union, he proceeds to the celebration of the marriage mass.

It must not be forgotten that the Holy Church has a particular mass for marriages, with an Epistle and Gospel of its own, and the most beautiful and appropriate prayers. What also makes this mass remarkable is, the solemn blessing of the marriage from the altar. After the "Pater Noster," the Priest, standing on the Epistle side, turns towards the married couple kneeling before him, and pronounces over them the benediction of the Church in the following words:

THE NUPTIAL BLESSING.

"O God, by whom woman is joined to man, and "this union, instituted in the beginning, is still accompanied by a blessing which has never been recalled, either by the punishment of original sin, or "by the judgment of the deluge, look kindly down "upon this thy handmaid, who being now to be "joined in wedlock, earnestly desires thy support "and protection. May she abide in the bond of love "and peace: may she marry in Christ faithful and "chaste: may she ever imitate the holy women of "old, be, like Rachel, beloved by her husband, dis-"creet like Rebecca, and like Sara grow old in "fidelity: may the author of sin have never any "share in her actions. May she remain attached to "the faith and the commandments: and firm in this "one union, shun every unlawful familiarity. May "she be fortified by a life of regularity and self-con-"trol: may she be modest and grave, bashful and "retiring, and well instructed in heavenly doctrine. "May she be fruitful in offspring; be approved, and "innocent; and may she at last arrive safely at the "rest of the Saints in the kingdom of heaven. May "they both see their children's children to the third "and fourth generation and live to a happy old age: "Through Jesus Christ our Lord. Amen."

Just before the last gospel, the Priest turns once more and blesses them, thus:

"MAY the God of Abraham, the God of Isaac, and "the God of Jacob be with you, and may He fulfil "His blessing in you; that you may see your chil-"dren's children to the third and fourth generation, "and afterwards enjoy eternal life, by the help of "our Lord Jesus Christ: who with the Father and "the Holy Ghost liveth and reigneth forever and "ever. Amen."

How beautiful a sight, when Christians marry thus! first purified by a good sincere confession; then joining innocent hands under the priestly stole, nd before the altar; then during Mass recommending themselves to God's protection by their prayers, and the devout reception of the Holy Communion; and lastly, kneeling to receive the pledge of that protection in the solemn Benediction of the Church. Is not this better than to marry in the house, amidst confusion, dissipation, profane jests, and laughter? Say rather, dear Catholic Christians, like Tobias and Sara: "*We are children of the Saints, and must not be joined together like the heathen, who know not God.*"

On the Duties of Particular States of Life

I. DUTIES OF MARRIED PERSONS.

"*Let every one of you in particular, love his wife as himself, and let the wife fear her husband.*" (Ephes. v. 33.)

HOW HUSBANDS AND WIVES SHOULD LIVE TOGETHER.

SINCE every man is placed in the world for this only end, that he may know God, love him, and serve him, and so work out his salvation, marriage is to Christians a means to serve God together,—to glorify him by their works,—and aid each other in the way to heaven. Husbands and wives ought therefore to encourage each other constantly, by word and example, to a holy life, by keeping the commandments of God, by their faith, their piety, and the practice of every virtue. This, however, they cannot do, unless they are also careful to fulfil those duties which they owe to each other.

1. The first duty of married persons to each other is that of mutual fidelity. The marriage bond is one of God's own making, and so close is this sacred union, that in Holy Scripture, husband and wife are said to have but one body: "*They shall be two in one flesh.*" (Gen. ii. 24.) How wicked then, and how abominable is that sin which violates a union, so intimate and holy! Sometimes females become less scrupulous after marriage than before, because they think they can sin with more impunity. But the eye of God is ever open, and he will punish them then more than ever, because their sin is greater, on

account of the greater wrong done, and the violation of a holy sacrament. "*What God hath joined together*," said our Lord Jesus Christ, in words of solemn warning, "*let no man put asunder.*" (S. Matt. xix. 6.) Woe! then, to the shameless woman, who defiles in her own person the marriage sacrament, and tramples on her most sacred vows! God will revenge both himself and her husband, and visit her sin upon her guilty head. Woe! to the guilty man who despises the warning of Jesus Christ, parting what He has joined together, and planting a poisoned dagger in his neighbor's bosom! "*Marriage is honorable in all, and the bed undefiled, but fornicators and adulterers* GOD *will judge.*" (Heb. xiii. 4.)

In this matter, dear Christians, do not trust even to your good intentions, but fly from danger at its first approach, and pray that you may not fall into temptation. And you especially, Christian wife, if you would be secure in that fidelity which you have plighted at the altar, treasure up these few words of advice: Shun carefully all books contrary to good morals. Do not allow yourself to indulge an excessive love of society; above all, never listen to strange and flattering tongues. And finally, put away all fondness for dress and vanity; and still more, shun all those fashions which are contrary to Christian modesty. A little spark can kindle a great fire; and again, none are so safe as those who fear to fall.

2. Let the husband consider his wife as his assistant, and not his servant. He is indeed the head of the woman, but as the head never plots mischief against the other members of the body, so must the husband never injure his wife, still less strike her, or in any way ill-treat her. "*Husband and wife are one body; no one ever hates his own flesh.*" (Ephes. v.)

The husband, too, in the marriage relation, repre

sents the person of Christ; and Jesus Christ compares himself to a lamb. The husband, then, must be kind to his wife; he must love her as Christ has loved his bride, the Church. And we know that Jesus Christ has undergone for his Church the hardest toils, the bitterest sorrows, yes, death itself, the most ignominious death—of the Cross.

3. On the other hand, the wife must be obedient to her husband in every thing which is right. "*Let women be subject to their husbands as to the Lord, for the husband is the head of the wife, as Christ is the head of the Church. Therefore, as the Church is subject to Christ, so also let the wives be to their husbands in all things.*" (Ephes. v. 22.) Remark this well, Christian wives, you must be subject to your husbands in all things; of course sin excepted.

Who does not know how many crosses and afflictions, yes, even bloody and most dreadful persecutions the Holy Church has suffered and still suffers, for her divine Bridegroom, Jesus Christ. Just so must the wife endure until death with Christian patience, all the contradictions of this life for her husband.

4. Both husbands and wives must love each other in sincerity, and think and speak well of one another. They should not be too curious to spy out each other's actions, but interpret all things favorably. They must not easily let suspicions enter their hearts; above all, let them avoid every tale-bearer and whisperer as a venomous snake, and allow such no entrance into their house. Ridicule and abusive language should never be heard between husband and wife; every thing should be done in Christian kindness and mildness, for one who is passionate cannot be agreeable to God, even if he should work miracles.

The husband will correct a scolding wife by kind words better than by blows and curses. The wife will subdue a violent husband by silence and patience, better than by contradiction and sharp answers.

When you see that by arguments you only make the matter worse, then wait awhile until the other party becomes quiet. A kind Christian admonition will not spoil by keeping.

And since God's blessing, and the precious inheritance of Jesus Christ depend on peace and unity, one ought to yield and submit to the other for the sake of peace. Bear patiently, then, each other's faults an infirmities; continue in the marriage bond, with Christian courage until death, and in the time of trial, say to yourself: God sees the disorderly life of my husband (or of my wife), and yet he is patient. Am I more than God? God has suffered me, sinner that I am, to remain in the world so many years; then I too will bear patiently the faults of my husband (or of my wife). Jesus Christ has saved the world by patience, and I must be saved by patience also.

5. If God does not give you children, or takes them early out of the world, you must not give up to immoderate grief, but resign yourself with courage to the will of God. What God does is well done. "O, Lord, thy will be done!" It is better to have no children, than (perhaps) wicked ones, who would grow up to be no consolation, but a sorrow to their parent.

6. According to the precept of the Apostle, it is necessary to be obedient to each other in the fulfilment of the marriage debt. To do otherwise would be to violate a duty, and to commit a sin. "*Defraud not one another, except perhaps by consent, for a time, that you may give yourselves to prayer, and return together again, lest Satan tempt you.*" (1 Cor. vii. 5.) But this must be understood always within the bounds of reason and religion. Christians are not permitted to abuse their liberty by giving each other scandal, and least of all by scandalizing their children. They must make use of marriage in all modesty and forbearance, and only according to the institution of God.

to them, especially, if they seek to hinder the sa

cred end for which marriage was principally instituted: namely, the propagation of children! For this crime, as we read in Holy Scripture, God punished one of the sons of the Patriarch Juda, with sudden death. Observe always then, you who are married, the warning of the Apostle Paul, and "*let marriage be honorable in all things, and the marriage bed undefiled.*"

7. Finally, dear Christians, keep with mutual fidelity until death, those promises you made so solemnly before God, on the day of your union. As Jesus Christ has only one spouse, the Holy Catholic Church, and the Church has only one Lord, which is Jesus Christ, so, dear children of Christ and of the Church, love each other always, chastely, but truly, constantly, tenderly, with patience and mutual forbearance. Aid each other in all the labors of life, cheer each other in its trials and sorrows, support each other in temptation by prayer and kindly counsel, that when hereafter you meet at the judgment, you may give joyful testimony for each other there, and receive your eternal reward together.

II. DUTIES OF PARENTS AND HEADS OF FAMILIES.

"*If any man have not care of his own, and especially of those of his house, he hath denied the faith, and is worse than an infidel.*" (1 Tim. v. 8.)

HOW THE FATHER OF A FAMILY OUGHT TO DO GOOD IN HIS OWN HOUSEHOLD.

The Father of a family ought to question his children out of the Catechism. (*See page 259 of this book.*) He should not fail to send those under his care to Holy Mass, and to receive Christian instruction on all Sundays and Holy Days. But if it is necessary to leave some one at home to take care of the house, let him not forget to take that one with him to church and instruction at another time. There should be no buying and selling during the time of divine service, that no one may be detained from worshipping God and hearing his holy word. If, in this way, the father of a family seeks first the kingdom of God, all the concerns of his household will be blessed by God. (Matth. vi. 33.) Let this be remembered well by all innkeepers, butchers, mechanics, grocers, trades-people, and those engaged in factories, and on public works, but especially by all in authority over others, because they particularly, in the day of judgment, will be called to a strict account by the just Judge of all. Let them be sure that all gains made during the time of divine service at the cost of immortal souls, will bring them nothing but misfortune and sorrow.

It is an excellent custom in many Christian families to have the Epistle and Gospel read by one of the children before dinner on Sundays and Holy Days.

A Christian Father ought often to question his children about the preaching and instructions which they have heard, and make them repeat to him what they can remember. It is the custom in truly Christian families to read aloud some pious Catholic book on Sundays and Holy Days, in the afternoon, or evening, and also to sing together devout hymns and canticles, or engage in pious conversation. How sweetly in this way the holy hours are spent, and how such a life brings down the blessing of God upon the household: for has not God himself promised: "*In every place where the memory of my name shall be, I will come to thee, and will bless thee.*" (Exod. xx. 24.)

The good Father of a family will do well to see that all the members of his household learn the beautiful practices and prayers recommended in the beginning of this book, for their morning and evening devotions; and also the method there given "to pass the day in a holy manner," (*page* 20.) For those who cannot read easily, or are too young to learn any longer prayers, he may teach them the following:

1. As soon as they awake, let them bless themselves with the sign of the cross, saying: "Jesus, Mary, Joseph, I give you my heart and my soul." (The same when they lie down to sleep.)

2. After they are dressed, let them kneel devoutly with their hands joined, and pray thus: "O my God, I believe that thou art here present, I adore thee and love thee with my whole heart: I thank thee for all thy goodness to me, and especially for having preserved me during this night. I offer thee all the thoughts, words, and actions of this day. May thy holy Angels lead me and keep me from sin." (In the evening they may say; "I thank thee for all thy goodness to me, "and especially for having preserved me during this "day. I offer thee my sleep, and every breath I draw "this night. May thy holy Angels watch over me "until morning.")

3. Then let them repeat the Creed, the Lord's Prayer, and the Hail Mary. Afterwards, three Hail Marys more in honor of the purity of the Blessed Virgin, and finally this prayer: "O Virgin Mary, my mother and "my hope, I place myself under thy mantle, and there "I wish to live and to die. Preserve me from sin, and "give me thy holy Benediction." (The same in the vening.)

The Christian Father should cultivate in his household a constant veneration for the holy Cross. For this purpose, he ought often to show one to his little children, that they may kiss the feet of Christ on the cross. He should try to engage his whole family in the beautiful devotion of the "Way of the Cross," so rich in holy indulgences. But if there are no stations of the cross erected in the church, or in the place where he lives, there is to be found at least in every town, in every church, and in every Christian house, a crucifix. He should therefore endeavor to inspire in his family the holy practice of contemplating the cross, especially after having committed any fault, and in the time of affliction, when their own cross is too heavy, so that they may become consoled and strengthened through Jesus crucified. What a beautiful example it would be, if the master of the family would in this give encouragement to the others by his own practice, and pray every day before the crucifix. It is a most excellent and edifying devotion to repeat very devoutly five Our Fathers, and five Hail Marys, in honor of the five holy Wounds of Jesus Christ.

HOW THE CHRISTIAN FATHER OF A FAMILY SHOULD BANISH EVIL FROM HIS HOUSE.

A Christian Head of a family must himself set a good example to his household. If you have yourself some bad habit, for example, that of swearing, how can you correct your own family, when they see in you the same fault which you would cure in them? If, then, you have contracted any such evil habit, inflict upon yourself for such offence some slight penance; for example, some prayer, until you have quite shaken this habit off.

Happy is the father of a family who persuades his household to go, at least once in a month, to confession and communion, and particularly on all great Festivals and Holy Days, because this is the most powerful means to banish all vice and immorality from the house.

He must see to it, moreover, that all say their morning prayers, and if work is very pressing, let them say a short one rather than none. The evening prayers should be said by the whole family together, and at the same time let all examine their consciences, to see how they have passed the day. No one should go to rest without true contrition and sorrow for his sins. Prayers, too, should be said in common, before and after meals. It is a beautiful Christian custom, and one which brings down the blessing of God, to say every evening, or at least every Saturday, and the eve of the feasts of the Mother of God, the Litany of Loretto, and the Holy Rosary, and to sing some pious hymn.

The Christian father should often admonish his household in a fatherly way, reminding them how, sooner or later, we must all die, and that no one knows when, or where, or how. He should warn them, furthermore, that the present moment is the only safe time we have to secure our eternal salvation, and how quickly the hours pass away, and that we must give a strict account of every ill-spent moment, yes, and of every idle word. (O, what shall we say, then, of curses and immodest words?) He should often place before their eyes the wickedness of sin; how dreadful it is, above all things; that it is a thousand times better to die than to offend the most holy God even by one venial sin; how we ought always to keep a guard on our eyes, our ears, and our tongues, that we may not fall into sin, and how gloriously those will be crowned in heaven who manfully and promptly resist all evil temptations.

He must not permit any of his family to wander away from home when they like, or to run about idly in the streets, particularly in the evenings. He should make it a point to know all those who visit his house, or with whom his children keep company, and what they occupy themselves about. He must provide, as far as possible, that at night they do not sleep together, two or more in one bed. This must always be forbidden to children, after they have reached the age of eight or ten years.

In no truly Christian house should dancing be tolerated, or any amusement of immoral tendency. The daughters should never be allowed to attend a party, or other place of amusement, without their mother, or some safe and experienced person, and whenever permitted to go out for their enjoyment, be careful that they come home early, and never leave them to be accompanied home at night by any man. And, Christian fathers, you should never permit your children to be present at balls, the theatre, or at immoral shows of any description.

The father of a family should carefully banish from his house all heretical books and tracts, and even those bibles which are published and circulated by heretics; so also all novels, romances, and love stories, and every indecent picture or statue. He should admonish his family against all superstitious practices, and suffer nothing of the kind under his roof. In like manner, he ought not knowingly to tolerate in his house any sin, such as profanity, slander, immodest language, &c. He ought to keep an eye upon all that goes on, or if he cannot himself oversee every thing, he should, at least, have some person on whom he can depend to do so for him. Let him be kind and affectionate to all in his family, without leaving any sin to go unreproved. Such fathers only will be able to stand without fear before the tribunal of God. He must not allow any ill-will to exist between the members of his household, but try to promote among them all a spirit of kind attention and of tender affection to each other.

The Christian father will not allow his children, of either sex, to grow up in idleness, remembering that idleness is the parent of every vice. If his means will not allow him to keep them occupied in their studies at school, he will occupy them at home, or put them out to labor, or to learn some useful trade. Do not, however, give way like so many parents in this country to a foolish pride, and endeavor to bring up your children in a style above their condition. If you are poor, be content with those schools where your children can learn to read and to write, &c., and do not allow them to waste their time with music, embroidery, drawing, and such like showy accomplishments, which will only make them proud, and teach them to despise their own parents, and to scorn all honest labor. If you bring up your children in this way, be sure your boys will become idle and wicked; your girls, on the other hand, will learn all the fashionable vices of the rich; they will be too proud to marry with any honest man of their own condition, and perhaps sooner or later become the victims of some well-dressed, flattering villain. "*God rejecteth the proud, but giveth his grace to the humble.*"

When Christian parents wish to give their sons and daughters in marriage, they should think more of the Christian virtue and sincere faith of the bride and bridegroom than of their riches. They should never permit the betrothed persons to live in the same house before marriage, or even to be much together without the presence of their parents. A great deal of sin is prevented where parents are wise enough to take these precautions.

HOW THE CHRISTIAN FATHER OF A FAMILY OUGHT TO ACT TOWARDS HIS SERVANTS.

He must by no means allow them to run out freely at night, and he ought not to receive persons of different sexes into his service without great precaution, or permit them to be much together. Let him close the house in the evening and keep the keys himself. He ought promptly to dismiss those servants who are likely to lead their fellow-servants or the children of his family into sin. Masters and mistresses should make it their business to inquire frequently whether at night all their servants, their apprentices, as well as all their children are at home. Let them rather be too strict than too easy in this respect, and never allow any night-walking, for in such matters indulgence is a fatal sword, which gives death to immortal souls. O how many children will curse their parents eternally in hell, how many servants their masters and mistresses, because of their indulgence to them in this respect!

Let the father of a family treat all those of his household with charity, and be like a true father to them all, and not like a tyrant. He must not keep them so hard at work as to prevent them from saying their prayers morning and evening, and from hearing the Word of God on Sundays and Holy Days. In sickness, too, he must be to them like a father. Let him give them always at the time agreed upon their fair and full wages, sufficient nourishment, and every thing else which they need. Be too liberal in these matters rather than too close, and you will always have faithful servants.

Finally, the Christian father of a family should try to establish and maintain in his household a truly religious and Catholic spirit. Let him teach all the members of his family to honor Jesus Christ their Lord in the Clergy of his Church, to receive all salutary admonitions from the directors of their souls with willing obedience, and always to love like a dear mother that one holy Catholic and only true Church, which alone is able to save us; and lastly, like good children, to cherish a tender confidence in Mary, the blessed mother of our Lord Jesus Christ, whom he charged in the very hour of his agony, to be a mother to us also.

IOW THE CHRISTIAN FATHER OF A FAMILY OUGHT TO CONDUCT HIMSELF TOWARDS HIS NEIGHBORS.

He ought not to meddle without good reason in the affairs of others. Let him show a compassionate heart towards his destitute neighbors, and do to others as he would have them do to him and to his family. He must not allow his wife or children to draw him into foolish disputes and jealousy with his neighbors; on the contrary, let him always try to preserve peace and yield to others as much as possible. He should always be ready to be reconciled with his adversary, and be willing to give up something if need be, in order to shun, as much as possible, all disputes, or lawsuits.

HOW THE CHRISTIAN FATHER OF A FAMILY SHOULD FULFIL THE DUTIES WHICH HE OWES TO HIMSELF.

Put a close restraint upon all your disorderly inclinations and passions. Do not obstinately hold fast to your own will, and your own ideas. In all doubtful and important matters take counsel of some man of piety and experience. Do not indulge in play or drink; avoid the tavern as much as possible, or else you will bring disgrace upon your head, and sorrow to your fireside. Those friends are not worth having whose hearts need liquor to make them warm. Be industrious and persevering in your business. Having first well reflected upon what you are about to do, begin promptly, and persevere with manly courage. Do not be afraid of hard labor; think how some you love look to you for their bread, and this thought will put strength in your arms. Finally, good Christian father, love prayer; yes, pray earnestly and constantly, out of love to God, for your own salvation, and that of your dear family, and heaven's best blessing shall be with you.

HOW THE GOOD CHRISTIAN MOTHER OUGHT TO FULFIL HER DUTIES TO HER CHILDREN.

1. Christian mother, it belongs to you to provide both for the temporal and eternal welfare of your little children. You must cherish with great care the precious fruit which you bear about in your womb, in order that it may come safely to the grace of holy baptism. Therefore, during the time of your pregnancy, be careful not to lift any heavy burden, or make any sudden effort; neither eat nor drink any thing that can injure you; guard yourself also against every violent emo-

tion, such as anger, grief, &c., and remember that you are charged with the safe keeping of an immortal being, whom God has created for eternal happiness. Do not take your little babes into bed with you during your sleep. How many mothers have mourned for their whole lifetime, because in this way they have caused the death of their children. Do not allow them, when more advanced, to sleep with their parents in the same bed, and if possible, not in the same room, for fear of giving scandal to their innocent minds. This thing becomes more horrible as they increase in years. When your children are already seven or eight years old, separate them in the night from each other, for in this way you will remove from them the occasion of committing many sins. Go often secretly to observe what your children are doing in the chambers, stables, and other by-places, for by such watchfulness you can prevent a great deal of mischief.

2. As soon as you have given birth to a child, give thanks to God; offer it to him, and promise him that you will bring it up in a Christian manner for his service.

When you lay your child down in the cradle, or take it up again, sign it with the holy sign of the cross, and sprinkle it with holy water. As soon as the child begins to speak, do you begin also to teach it to pray. Teach it how to make the sign of the cross, and to say, "Our Father," and the "Hail Mary." Teach it that there is only one God in three persons; that the Son of God became man for us, and has redeemed us by his death; that God is a just judge, who rewards the good, and punishes the wicked. As a Christian mother, see that your children say their prayers when they get up, and when they go to bed, and before and after meals. Take them early to church, and do not allow them to be guilty of any irreverence there. Often say to them what the holy Queen Blanche said to her little son, St. Louis: "My child, I would rather see you die, than to see you offend God by one sin."

3. Are your children bad, disobedient, and obstinate Do not, on that account, swear at them, and abuse them, for in this way you will only teach them to curse, and to be passionate also; but admonish them seriously, and if they do not amend, use the rod, not while you are in anger, but when your mind has become quiet and calm again. "He that spareth the rod, hateth his son:" so God himself teaches us in Holy Scripture. If you bring up your children in the fear of God, and in good habits, they will grow up for your own great consolation, for the glory of God, and the joy of the holy angels.

4. As to the education of your older children, you must contribute all in your power, and conscientiously endeavor to co-operate with your husband in this respect. When they are put to school, be careful to see that they go constantly, and always in good time. Do not lend yourself to those false excuses by which they seek to avoid study. Do not easily believe those reports which they sometimes bring home against their teachers, accusing them of partiality, injustice, or cruelty. It is a great folly for parents to be angry, when their children have been chastised at school for their idleness or misbehavior. On the contrary, you should not defend them, nor listen to their complaints, but be thankful to the teacher for his kindness and attention. Even when one of them should be moderately beaten by a neighbor, on account of some mischief, or impudence, do not make it a cause of quarrel. You will do much better in most cases, by taking part against your child, and applying your own hand to the same spot, while it is still red. On the other hand, it is not often prudent to beat the children of others, because most parents are too foolish to take this in good part.

Do not allow your daughters any intimacy with persons of the other sex; do not permit them to run about in the evening, or at night, or to be walking in lonely places; never leave them alone with any man, no matter who it may be; and try in every way to guard them from all occasions of sin. Do not bring up your daughters to be proud and vain. Clothe them neatly and suitably to their circumstances, but never allow them to dress gaudily, and still less to go about with neck and shoulders bare, for in this way you will be guilty of corrupting your own children, and teaching them to ruin the souls of others. Never permit your daughter to enter into a promise of marriage with any man without your knowledge. But even when she is engaged by a promise to some one with your own approval and consent, never let them be long together alone, either at home, or abroad, and least of all, at night.

Your duties towards your servant girls are, in this respect, the same as towards your daughters. Keep a very watchful eye over them, and never allow them any thing that may be to their soul's hurt.

Dear Christians! fathers and mothers, parents and guardians, masters and mistresses! consider well this earnest warning, which we give you: As many subjects as God has committed to your keeping in this world, so many souls you will one day have to give account for to him; for what St. Paul tells us of the clergy in his epistle to the Hebrews (xiii. 17), is true also of you: "*They watch as being to render an account of your souls.*" Remember, moreover, that these souls are purchased by the precious blood of Jesus Christ. Can there well be a greater responsibility than to have an account to give for the abuse of the precious blood of Jesus Christ?

III. DUTIES OF CHILDREN TO THEIR PARENTS.

"*Honor thy father and thy mother, that thou mayest be long-lived upon the land which the Lord thy God will give thee.*" (Exod. xx. 12.)

1. Children are bound to cherish a filial reverence

for their parents, and to manifest it at all times. No condition in life, no age whatever, can excuse you from this duty. Always make use of kind and respectful words to your parents, even if they treat you unjustly. Never return them rough, insolent, and surly answers; never give them nicknames. Be careful how you despise them, or feel ashamed of them, on account of their simplicity, poverty, or humble condition. Was the Son of God ever ashamed of his poor mother and his poor foster-father? Why, then, should you be ashamed of your poor parents, or despise them?

2. You owe your parents the most exact obedience in all things that are not sinful, and contrary to the will of God. Obey them most particularly in all they command you for your soul's salvation, and when they forbid you any thing that would be hurtful to your soul. Do you not know, my dear children, what a severe account those parents have to give to God, who do not bring up their children well? Why should you, then, take it ill if your parents do their duty as their conscience dictates, and try to keep you in the way of virtue? Would you wish that, for your satisfaction, they should lose their souls eternally, and burn forever in hell?

3. You owe to your parents the most tender love. Next to God, your parents are your greatest benefactors. How much trouble, sickness, and sorrow has your mother endured for you, even before she brought you into the world! How many years did she carry you in her arms, feed you with her milk, cherish and care for you with a mother's love! How much toil and care have you not cost your father, that he might feed, clothe, and educate you! See how God himself appeals to you in the Holy Scripture: "*With thy whole heart honor thy father, and forget not the groanings of thy mother: Remember that thou hadst not been born but through them, and*

make a return to them as they have done for thee. (Eccli. vii. 29.)

My dear son! my daughter! remember that you will bring down the curse of God upon yourself and your children, if you use your parents unkindly, if you despise them, or (which God forbid!) if you strike or push them, or if you do not take pity on them in their necessities. Call to mind the examples of the Saints; place before your eyes young Tobias, or Joseph in Egypt, and other Saints; as examples of filial love, and consider that it was on account of the love of these pious children for their parents, that God blessed them so abundantly, even on earth, and made them eternally happy in heaven.

4. Commonly speaking, you should not make choice of any state of life without the knowledge and approbation of your parents, especially when there is question of marriage. It requires very strong reasons indeed to excuse you for doing otherwise. Aid your parents as much as you can in their household duties; try to make their burdens lighter; sympathize with them in all their cares; do not abandon them in their old age; and when they become feeble and suffering, do not withhold from them that assistance which they have a right to expect from you, but contribute, with generous gratitude, all you can for their support and comfort, and God will bless you for it.

Attend upon them in sickness, nurse them with the greatest possible affection, call in a physician when they need one, and do not fail to have the holy Sacrament administered to them in good season.

After their death, see to it that they are decently buried, according to their condition, and take care that their poor souls shall not want for prayers, masses, and alms. Fulfil scrupulously their last will; pray for them; visit sometimes their graves.

in order to pray for them there, and try, by your own good Christian life, to honor your dear parents, even after they are dead.

IV OF THE DUTIES OF SERVANTS.

1. Hear what holy lessons God gives to servants, by the mouth of his Apostles. "*Servants, be obedient to your masters, with fear and trembling, in the simplicity of your heart, serving with a good will as to the Lord, knowing that whatsoever good thing any man shall do, the same shall he receive from the Lord.*" (Ephes. vi. 5–8.)

Therefore, Christian servant, although you should plainly perceive that your master and your mistress, or any other superior is wicked, still do every thing they command you, only do not imitate them in their sins. "*Servants, be subject to your masters with all fear,—not only to the good and gentle, but also to the froward.*" (1 Pet. ii. 18.)

If, however, they solicit you to commit sin, or order you to do any thing wrong, do not obey them, but resist all evil; for the favor of man continues from morning until evening, but the favor of God eternally. "*Fear not those that kill the body, but rather fear him that can destroy both soul and body in hell.*" (Matth. x. 28.) Quit, rather, as soon as possible, such a dangerous service, and say to yourself: What profit shall I have if I gain the whole world and lose my immortal soul?

2. Never forget that all men, as being the children of Adam and Eve, are born to labor. Be willing, therefore, to employ yourself about any kind of labor. He who works industriously has not much time to sin: on the contrary, he gains great merit, when often during his work he says to himself: "I will perform this labor for the love of God." He

who works with a good intention, prays continually. It is a beautiful and commendable custom to sweeten one's labor by pious songs, but for God's sake never sing immodest ones! Never take part in slander and idle talk, and let no false witness ever proceed out of your mouth.

For God's sake, be careful never to lend your example, your assistance, or your counsel to any one especially to a child of the family, or to a fellow servant, in any wicked act, whether of impurity or theft, or any other sin; otherwise you will be judged by the living God as a destroyer of souls. Keep yourself from all these sins, and to that end shun all the occasions of evil, and every dangerous party. Keep from intemperance, and from drinking companions; it will make you miserable for time and for eternity.

Especially keep the Sundays holy, and the Holy Days. Often make to yourself this serious reflection: Of what advantage is it to a poor servant or laborer to earn a little money every week, and that with difficulty too; and then afterwards, and above all, on Sundays and Holy Days, by licentious and impure conversation, by gaming and drinking, dancing and other wanton and wicked conduct, to lose what is more precious to him than all things else, the friendship of Jesus Christ, the hope of heaven, and the blessing of his God!

V. ON THE CONDUCT OF UNMARRIED PERSONS OF BOTH SEXES.

"*Remember thy Creator in the days of thy youth, before the time of affliction come.*" (Eccles. xii. 1.)

ADVICE TO YOUNG CATHOLIC MEN.

1. The young Catholic Christian should firmly maintain the holy faith of his baptism. He should

never be ashamed of it, but confess it openly and manfully before the whole world. Would it not be a thing to blush for, if, while Catholics are proud of their faith in other countries, where many of them are rich, noble, and powerful, they should, on the contrary, be ashamed of their religion here, because the high places of wealth, power, and fashion are occupied by heretics? The young Catholic should be above such mean and cowardly motives. Let him remember that his is the only true and divine faith; that the Catholic Church alone has survived the changes and revolutions of 1800 years; that millions of martyrs have bled for it, and millions more have confessed it before persecutors, before ever the world had heard or dreamed of Protestants. He should look with charity and pity upon all the perishing and deluded multitude of heretics and infidels around him, but never give in to their false principles, never deny his faith, nor hide it, nor darken it, nor blush for it. "*He that shall deny me before men,*" said our Lord Jesus Christ, "*I will also deny him before my Father who is in heaven.*" (St. Matt. x. 33.) From the same principle of faith, never allow yourself to be drawn into any dangerous order forbidden by the Holy Church, like that of the Free Masons, or Odd-Fellows. Join no secret societies, not even those which profess to be Catholic, or to be instituted for the reform of morals. To the Church alone, God has committed the task of reforming and saving the world.

2. The young Catholic Christian should practise faithfully the duties of his religion. You will not be saved only because you are a Catholic, but when you are a true and pious one. Let not weak and silly minds persuade you that it is an unmanly thing to engage in exercises of piety. Were not Josue, and David, and the brave Machabees, manly men? Listen to the following history of that great and virtu-

ous hero, Simon, Count of Montfort, who lived in the twelfth century, and was equally distinguished for his piety and his bravery. One morning while the Catholic army were encamped before the city of Toulouse, which they were besieging, Simon was devoutly occupied in prayer at the time of the Holy Mass. The intelligence was there brought to him that the enemy were approaching. Simon, however, did not move. Just as the Priest was about to consecrate, the word came again: "The battle is beginning, come immediately." "Let me alone," said Simon, "I will not go until I see my Saviour." He waited a moment longer until the consecration was ended, adored the sacred body of his Lord, and then went out to lead his army to a glorious victory. Do not say, then, young Christians, that piety is only a virtue of weak-minded men, as if heaven were made for the foolish and timid, and hell only for the brave and manly. Follow the example of all truly good and faithful Catholics. Be constant like them to your religious duties, such as daily prayer, confession, and the holy Communion, and never leave your place vacant on Sundays and Holy Days. Be not corrupted by the love of money, or of pleasure, but remember what Jesus Christ said: "*What doth it profit a man, if he gain the whole world, and suffer the loss of his own soul?*" (Matt. xvi. 26.)

3. Be always industrious. Man is born to labor; without this there can be no true piety nor virtue. Remember that excellent maxim, that idleness is the father of many vices. For this reason, no one looks for piety, honesty, or purity on the street corners, or under an idle hat. "*If any man will not work,*" says the Apostle Paul, "*neither let him eat. We charge them that are such, and beseech them by the Lord Jesus Christ, that working they would eat their own bread.*" (2 Thes. ii. 10.)

4. Be sober and temperate in all things. "*No*

drunkards shall possess the kingdom of God." (1 Cor vi. 10.) O how many young men of most excellent and amiable qualities, have been ruined by this vice, both for this world and for eternity! And yet, many of them had good intentions enough in some sort, they did not wish to be intemperate, or to die a drunkard's death. If then, my dear young friends, you would be safe, never frequent the taverns, or those places where intemperate men are accustomed to assemble, nor keep intoxicating liquors in your house, nor associate with wild, dissipated, and drinking young men. "*He that loveth danger*," says the Prophet, "*shall perish in it.*" (Eccli. iii. 27.)

5. Finally, young Christian, nothing can injure or dishonor you more than the sin of impurity. According to the maxims of the world, this sin ought not to be regarded as such, or, at least, as one of little consequence, a pardonable weakness. The religion of Jesus Christ, however, teaches a different lesson. It tells us that impurity is a dreadful sin, a dishonor to God our Sovereign Lord, an injury to Jesus Christ, who redeemed us, and a profanation of the Holy Ghost, who sanctifies us. The impure man dishonors God his sovereign Lord, for he makes of the object of his guilty passion an idol which he adores, sacrificing to it his peace, his health, his honor, his fortune, the grace of God, and his soul's life. God is no more the sovereign of his heart, but a creature of clay, to whom he offers up all his thoughts and desires. Is not this a great crime? Is it not a detestable ingratitude towards God?

The impure man dishonors Jesus Christ our Prince and Redeemer. "*Know you not that your bodies are the members of Christ? Shall I then take the members of Christ, and make them the members of a harlot? God forbid.*" So wrote the great Apostle of the Gentiles. (1 Cor. vi. 15.) Are we not made by baptism children of God, brethren of Jesus Christ, coheirs with him of the kingdom of his heavenly Father, and members even of his own body? How horribly, then, does the impure sinner treat the members of Jesus Christ?

Finally, the sin of impurity dishonors the Holy Ghost. "*Know you not,*" says the Apostle, "*that your members are the temple of the Holy Ghost, who is in you?*" (1 Cor. vi. 19.) But the Christian who commits a sin of impurity, chases away the Holy Ghost from his heart, and makes room in it for the impure spirit.

But would you, young Christian man, see still more clearly the greatness of this sin, call to mind the awful punishments by which God has chastised it. Open the books of Holy Scripture, and you will see there how God sent a universal deluge upon the earth, and how all men, with the exception of the one family of Noah, were swallowed up by the waters, and you will see there that impurity was the dreadful sin which made God so angry against the world, and for which he punished it so severely. You will see there, too, how some time after this terrible event, all the houses and inhabitants of Sodom and Gomorrah, and of three other cities, were burned to ashes by a shower of brimstone and fire. But what sin had the inhabitants of Sodom and Gomorrah committed, that they drew down vengeance from heaven in so terrible a manner? It was the sin of impurity. Afterwards, twenty-four thousand Israelites were slain in the wilderness, by the command of God, because they had sinned with the daughters of the Madianites. On account of their unnatural sins, Her and Onan, the sons of Juda, were struck dead, and the seven husbands of Sara were strangled in the night by the devil, in punishment of their wicked desires. Can any one look upon this sin as a trifle, or an excusable weakness, when it is punished so severely by an infinitely holy and just Judge?

But all these punishments, terrible as they may appear, cannot be compared with those which God has reserved for the impure, in the life to come. "*The Lord shall judge his people. It is a fearful thing to fall into the hands of the living God.*" (Heb. x. 30.) For this reason, in earlier times, the Church inflicted a severe penance of seven years upon the sin of impurity; and, if it was also adultery, fifteen years.

This sin is moreover beyond all others dangerous, for the reason that every thing which is done contrary to purity, if it is done deliberately, becomes at once a mortal sin.

When, for example, you are guilty of a slight falsehood, or are a little angry, &c., it is not at once a mortal sin; but as soon as you consent to impurity, if it be only in thought, it is already a great sin. Therefore, embraces, and such like indecent familiarities, cannot easily take place between persons of different sexes without mortal sin.

Therefore, dear Christian youth, avoid with horror this detestable vice, which dishonors and destroys both soul and body, and has contributed more to fill hell, than any other. Avoid all those dangerous places and amusements which lead to it, such as the theatre, the circus, dancing, reading novels, &c. Avoid as much as possible the society of females, especially those who are loose and familiar in their manners. Do not take part in immodest conversation, nor allow your ears to be defiled with it. Even when you are alone, think how God sees and judges all things. And finally, dear young Christians, pray. O! never forget to pray, especially in the moment of temptation. In this wicked and lost world, you must never cease to pray, if you would escape from the general ruin.

ADVICE TO YOUNG CATHOLIC WOMEN.

Innocence, young Christian maidens, is the most precious treasure you have on earth, and you ought to prefer death to losing it. In order, therefore, that you may not lose it, fly from every danger even the most remote, which could rob you of it. In every danger which you cannot avoid, fight like Christian heroines for the preservation of your purity; employ every possible means to guard it unstained, not only before man, but also in the eyes of God, and of your own conscience. "*Blessed are the clean of heart*," says our Saviour Jesus Christ, "*for they shall see God*." Pay attention, now, while I show you the principal dangers which threaten your innocence.

The most dangerous enemies to holy purity, and those which you ought to shun the most carefully, are:

1. Vain-glory, or an excessive desire to please the world.

Let it be your first endeavor to please God. When you are pleasing to God, you are pleasing to the Angels in heaven, and to all good Christians. Try, then, like noble-hearted Virgins, to be beautiful, not in the eyes of men, but in the eye of God.

2. Vanity in dress. "*The adorning of women*," writes the holy Apostle Peter, "*ought not to be the outward plaiting of the hair, or the wearing of gold, or the putting on of apparel, but the hidden man of the heart in the incorruptibility of a quiet and a meek spirit, which is rich in the sight of God*." (1 Pet. iii. 3.) The young woman who is truly pious will not try to draw upon herself the eyes of others by the color and gayety of her dress; she does not seek t obtain for herself praise and consideration by th display of vain ornaments and new fashions. "*Favor is deceitful and beauty is vain; the woman that feareth the Lord, she shall be praised*." (Prov. xxxi. 30.

If hitherto, young Christian woman, you hav given way to this foolish vanity, allow yourself to be admonished, and amend. Hear what happy effects have followed even in a heathen country, from the modesty of women in their apparel:

In Cortona, a city of Italy, in the year 529 before

the birth of Christ, the corruption of morals had become so great, that the whole city was threatened with ruin. Pythagoras, a wise philosopher of that day, represented to the inhabitants their danger in so forcible a manner, that they determined to amend. The women took the first steps. On a certain day they all, with one consent laying aside their jewels, and their garments embroidered with gold, hastened to the temple, and there solemnly promised to dress more modestly for the future, and to seek their true ornaments in simplicity and virtue. From that moment frugality and the love of order were restored in their families, a foundation was soon laid for the better education of the young, and the state was saved. See what female virtue can accomplish, and how important is modesty in dress to the maintenance of good morals.

3. Imprudence in looks, gestures, and words.

Keep, young maidens, to the example which St. Ambrose places before you of the blessed Virgin. He says: "She had nothing bold in her eyes, nothing free in her words, nothing unbecoming in her actions."

Let your eyes be modest. There is great meaning in that prayer of David: "*Turn away my eyes that they may not behold vanity.*" (Ps. cxviii. 37.) The young St. Aloysius, was for years in attendance on the queen of Spain, and did not know her face Speak little, and let that little be modest. "*In the multitude of words,*" said Solomon, "*there shall not want sin.*"

4. Bad company.

"*Evil communications corrupt good manners, and he that toucheth pitch shall be defiled with it.*" (Eccles. xiii. 1.) Dances, balls, and plays are dangerous and ruinous for a young woman. In the voluptuous dance innocence dies, and on the way home it will be buried. The first step on the dancing floor is, for the greatest part, the first step towards seduction. Young Christian women, never go out alone in the evening, shun all those parties, meetings, and entertainments where modesty must blush, and where there is improper conduct going on.

5. Familiarity with persons of the other sex.

In this way a spark is soon thrown into the heart, there it becomes fire, and fire burns and consumes. Never give up to a feeling of attachment for any man, for passion is blind and blinding. Your safety is in flight. Never remain alone with any man unless it be absolutely necessary. Do not trust to your own virtue, for: "*He that loveth danger shall perish in it.*" (Eccles. iii. 27.)

Receive no gift from any man. Do not sell your innocence for gold, for a gay dress, a pretty ring, &c. Remember that God is richest of all, and will give you something more beautiful in heaven. In the moment of dangerous solicitation, do not trifle with the danger by useless remonstrance, but fly at once, and if detained by force, cry aloud for help. This will cover you with honor, and your enemy with shame. Be willing to suffer death rather than consent to sin for one moment. And if your tempter threatens you that he will take your life or his own, fear not, and tell him boldly that you will not be lost for his sake. You have the right even to take his life, if you can, rather than to submit to his wicked will.

If in your father's house you are in danger from any person who lives there, tell your parents of it, that he may be sent away at once.

If you are out at service and any one lays a snare for your innocence, make complaint immediately to your master or mistress, and if they do not assist you, leave their service. It is better for you to suffer every kind of mockery, poverty, and persecution, than to fall into the hands of the living God as a guilty sinner.

At night lock the door of your chamber, do not listen to any tempting voice at the window, but say in your heart: O Jesus, stay here with me! For thee I wish to live and die! If you have in the same room a female companion who keeps improper company you should admonish her, and if that does no good, make it known to your master and mistress, that you may not yourself be corrupted by her. Think of the consequences of an impure life, and how bitter is that repentance which comes too late. A licentious youth brings a sad old age.

6. Improper reading.

For God's sake, never read any of those novels, romances, and other such dangerous books, which are now, unhappily, so very common. Alas! they have ruined too many souls already. Dear young Christians! make the firm resolution this very moment, that you will never read them any more. In fine, try in all respects to live in such a manner that when you stand before the sacred altar, on the day of your marriage, you may have a pure heart and a pure hand to give away; or if you remain single, that you may take the treasure of your innocence with you to the grave, and in heaven be numbered forever with that lovely band of Virgins, whose glorious privilege it is "*to follow the Lamb whithersoever He goeth.*" (Apoc. xiv. 1–6.)

ON DRUNKENNESS.

A LARGE portion of the sins and miseries prevailing in the world around us, are caused by the vice of drunkenness. What is the greatest evil with which in most parishes the pastor has to contend? It is drunkenness. What does the missionary find to be usually the most common and the most ruinous vice in the congregation where he gives a mission? It is drunkenness. What destroys, in a great measure the fruits of a good mission? It is drunkenness. What causes the relapse, and the final damnation of a great multitude after they have once made a good confession? It is drunkenness. What is the greatest scandal and reproach on the Catholic religion? The drunkenness which is frightfully prevalent among the bad and unworthy members of the holy Church of God.

Drunkenness is a most degrading and wicked sin The drunkard deprives himself of the use of his reason, and turns himself into a brute, in order to gratify a base, sensual passion. What can be more degrading to a reasonable man made in the image of God, and bearing the character of baptism, than to go staggering about, or to lie down helpless and stupid under the influence of liquor? One cannot deface the image of God in such a shocking way without grievously dishonoring and offending God.

Drunkenness is a mortal sin; it kills the soul, and deserves the everlasting fire of hell. "Be not deceived. Neither fornicators, nor *drunkards* shall possess the kingdom of God." (1 *Cor.* vi. 10.) Every person who gets drunk commits a mortal sin, by defacing the image of God, even though he gives no scandal, hurts no one, neglects no part of his work, and does not injure his health or property. Those who do not get stupidly drunk, but who drink so much, that they make themselves unfit for business, waste their money, injure their health, give scandal to others, or neglect and illtreat their families, are also guilty of mortal sin. All excess in drinking, however slight, is at least a venial sin, and if habitual, most dangerous, because it increases the appetite for liquor, and leads almost certainly to drunkenness

Drunkenness is the prolific mother of a multitude of miseries. It makes a man or woman weak and sickly, low-spirited, peevish and passionate. It bring on deadly diseases. and excruciating pains, and a pre mature death, amid the horrors of delirium tremens. It brings poverty, rags, starvation, and quarrelling into the family. The drunkard makes himself wretched in this life, and he makes his wife and children wretched also.

Drunkenness is also the parent of other sins. It leads directly to impurity. It is the cause of cursing, blasphemy, robbery, and murder. It leads to th neglect of religious duties, to sacrilege—often to des pair and to final impenitence. One who indulges in this sin, makes it very difficult to himself to repent afterwards in a solid and lasting way. He may confess and promise amendment, but the appetite for liquor is so strong, and the misery caused by the want of the habitual excitement is so great, that after a few feeble efforts, the unhappy man gives way to temptation, and goes back to his bottle. The end of all these miseries and sins is a bad death, and the eternal damnation of the wretched drunkard.

In the torments of the horrid prison of hell, he must be punished for his drunken revels, his blasphemies, his brutal treatment of wife and children, and his violation of all the promises and vows of repentance and amendment that he has made. Multitudes are now in hell who have been damned chiefly on account of drunkenness. And multitudes now living are preparing themselves for hell by drunkenness, when by overcoming this one vice, they might so easily be saved.

Dear Christian reader, are you terrified at this awful picture? Then if you are yet free from the chains of this vile and criminal habit, or if you have but just begun to give yourself to it, pause where you are, and save yourself in time from the temporal and eternal miseries of intemperance. It is easier for you to avoid falling into this vice than to get out of it after you have contracted it. Look around you on the sad and disgusting examples of drunkenness and take warning in time. How is it that the young man becomes a drunkard? Is it all at once, or by degrees? It is by degrees, and step by step. One man carries his bottle with him to his work, and visits it now and then during the day. His visits become more and more frequent, until at last he is a slave to his bottle, loses his work in consequence, becomes discouraged, drinks deeper to drown his grief and becomes a drunkard.

Another indulges at home in an occasional bout of drinking on holidays, or other times of leisure, and these become more frequent, until he, too, is a frequent drunkard.

A poor woman begins to take a drop when she is tired with working, to give herself a false strength. and she takes more and more until she has gone over the precipice. Another begins by taking an occasional glass of punch with her friends; another, by being a little delicate and requiring gin and brandy as a medicine; another, by flying to drink, out of spite at her husband's cruelty, or to drown her grief and troubles.

But most fall by social drinking. It is by resorting to bars and liquor stores, by lounging around where drinking is going on, by treating and being treated, by the occasional glass with a companion in the grog-shop, by staying out on Saturday nights to have a jovial time, that most begin, and go on, and end in the destructive and abominable school of drunkenness. Shun, then, these traps and temptations, and be cautious about the very approach of evil if you wish to keep sober and temperate.

But if you are so unhappy as to be already in the habit of excessive drinking and wish to get out of it, what must you do?

In the first place, cost what it will, you must give up drink. This is the only sure remedy. It may be hard and painful, but it is easier to do it than to suffer the miseries of drunkenness, and the pains of hell. You have sinned, and you must do penance for your sins by suffering. The longer you abstain from drink, the easier it will be, and the peace of conscience you will enjoy will give you strength to make the sacrifice of your unhealthy craving after liquor. You must go to the sacraments and pray regularly and frequently to obtain the grace of God.

And you must be careful not to relapse when th time of your penance is over. This, in a word, is what you must do. But go to a good and faithful priest, cast yourself at his feet, and beg him to tell you what to do, and he will tell you more fully and more efficaciously what you must do; obey his directions, follow his advice, fulfill his penance and return to him frequently, and he will rescue your soul from the slough of vice and misery. There are some who do this, who reform thoroughly, and who persevere; therefore do not be disheartened because so many relapse, but take courage by the example of those who persevere and resolve to become one of that happy number. If you do this, what a change for the better will take place in a short time in yourself and in your family. Your soul will be cleansed from the guilt of sin in the saving waters of penance, and refreshed and strengthened with the grace of the Holy Eucharist. Your body will be purified and renovated by abstinence. You will become once more decent and respectable in your dress and appearance. The money which you used to waste on liquors and gambling will go to furnish your family with suitable clothing, and your house with comforts. Your wife and children will smile and look happy again, and peace and harmony will reign in your household. When you accompany your wife and children to Mass on Sunday, all will be edified with the picture of a true Christian family; you will bless God for the change, and if you persevere you will bless Him on your deathbed and throughout eternity.

A Little Manual for the Sick and Dying.

"*Watch ye, therefore, because you know not at what hour your Lord will come.*" (Matt. xxiv. 42.)

I. INSTRUCTION FOR THE SICK.

1. WHEN you are sick, my dear Christian, let it be your first care to lift up your mind to God, who sends you this sickness as a trial. Say in your heart, with the patient Job: "*The hand of the Lord hath touched me.*" (xix. 21.) Receive this sickness from God, your heavenly Father, as a special favor, as Jesus Christ received the bitter cup of suffering from the hand of his heavenly Father. Say, with your divine Saviour: Not mine, O heavenly Father, but thy will be done! In this way, unite your will with the divine will, and pray to God for the grace of patience in your suffering.

2. Be as careful to provide for your soul's salvation, as if you were sure this sickness would be your last. Seek to reconcile yourself to God in good time, by a sincere and contrite confession, and if your Father-confessor approves it, by a general confession. Do not put off this confession from one day to another, until your sickness is at such a height as to make confession very difficult, or wholly impossible. Receive the holy Communion as the best medicine for your soul and body, and as a support upon your way to eternity. Welcome your Saviour with interior love, as the best friend and helper of your soul. When you receive extreme unction, do not be terrified, as if you must, therefore, instantly die; but let it rather be to you a consolation to receive this holy sacrament, which puri

fies the soul from sin, strengthens it for the last conflict with temptations, and is able even to procure for you health of body, when the good of the soul requires it. The Council of Trent, itself, assures us (Sess 22, Cap. 2), that health of body is sometimes obtained through this holy sacrament, when that health is profitable to the soul's salvation. It would be a great imprudence if you should delay to receive in season a sacrament so important and advantageous for body and soul.

3. When you have set in order the affairs of your conscience, then arrange your temporal affairs. Make your will with all the formalities which the law requires, or, in some other way, bring all your affairs into order, by a clear, plain and careful arrangement. Do not postpone this business so long, that at the very end of your life, when you should have no care but for your soul, the precious moments will be occupied with temporal affairs. Remember death may come suddenly, and that you will have to answer before the judgment of Jesus Christ, if through your carelessness any one has to suffer injustice. How many disorders, enmities, and lawsuits, have arisen from this neglect of the sick to make their last testament. If you have property belonging to another, restore it; if you have debts, pay them. Woe be to you, if your soul should remain burdened with any ill-gotten possessions, or if you enter into eternity with the conciousness that you have neglected to discharge your honest debts! Do not forget, also, in your last will, to provide for your own soul, by pious legacies, and benevolent bequests, for your children and other heirs will perhaps have little care for your soul's repose, when they have entered upon the enjoyment of your goods.

4. Do not neglect to make use of a physician, and of his remedies; this is the will of God, who, for your sake has given to medicine its power. But place your whole confidence in God, for he it is who must en-

lighten the physician, and give efficacy to his remedies If these remedies do not benefit you, do not murmur, nor complain about the physician and his practice. Do not make the task of your attendants, already difficult enough, more difficult by your impatience, but submit yourself entirely to the will of God, without whose permission not a hair of your head can fall.

5. Do not spend the time of your sickness in unprofitable conversation, or in excessive care of your bodily health, but remember that on the good use you make of this time of suffering, your eternal salvation is perhaps depending. At certain times of the day you can repeat certain prayers and devotional exercises, such as the Rosary, or the Penitential Psalms, or a Litany. Read also some spiritual book, or have one read to you, especially one that treats of the sufferings of Jesus Christ, or you may cheer your heart with pious and holy conversation. If you cannot exert yourself to pray and read much, elevate your mind to God by holy sighs and pious aspirations. Take the crucifix in your hand, press it often to your heart and to your lips, and say to yourself: "O my Jesus! I unite my sufferings with thy sufferings! I will bear them willingly in expiation of my sins."

Place opposite to your bed an image of the most blessed Virgin, and put great confidence in her. Turn to her as a beloved mother who will not leave you in the time of trouble. Honor also the angels and saints of God, especially those for whom you feel a peculiar devotion.

If your sickness is of long continuance, ask your Father-confessor to visit you sometimes, and administer from time to time the holy Communion for the comfort and support of your soul.

6. Besides the sufferings of Christ, which ought to be the principal subject of your meditations, meditate in your sickness also on the sufferings of the Saints and their patience. With what patience did not holy

Job suffer, striking image as he was of the Man of Sorrows! How resigned was the aged Tobias in his blindness! and St. Francis Xavier, who cried out in his sufferings: "Still more, O my Lord!" and St. Teresa, who was accustomed to say: "Either let me suffer or let me die!" The holy Virgin Ludwina suffered for eight and thirty years so distressing an illness, that her whose body was like one sore, and yet she preserved throughout the greatest patience and calm ness of soul. You will find in the lives of the Saints examples like these without number.

II. INSTRUCTION FOR THE DYING.

1. When your sickness increasing warns you that death is drawing near, do not be discouraged and desponding, but resign yourself to quit this world, which was never yours as a permanent abode, and enter your heavenly home. "*It is appointed for men once to die.*" (Hebr. ix. 27.) We are as strangers here, and it must not give us pain to go to our Father in heaven and our divine Saviour. By death you will be freed from all your misery, and from the risk of sinning any more. Death is the entrance to heaven. Death is the best satisfaction for your sins, if you receive it with submission to the will of God. Death makes you more like your divine Saviour; for Jesus died also, and he died for you.

2. If you have still any thing upon your conscience that troubles or oppresses you, do not conceal it, but send for your Confessor, and discover to him your whole heart in a penitent confession, that afterwards no distressing thoughts may disturb your peace of conscience.

3. If you have an enemy, seek to be reconciled to him; banish every unkind thought from your heart. Were not the last words of your divine Saviour a

prayer for his enemies? If you have a wife and children, and it is a burden on your heart to leave them, cheer yourself with the thought, that God will take care of them, and that you can pray for them still before His throne, and better than here on earth.

4. When you have set in order the affairs of your conscience and your temporal concerns, do not torment yourself too much with the thought how it will be with you after death, and whether you will be saved. Commit yourself wholly to the infinite and tender mercy of God, and ask for nothing else but that God may be glorified in you, and that his holy will may be fulfilled. This is the best way to die piously and to secure your eternal salvation; for it is impossible for a soul to be lost that submits itself entirely to God. Say often with your suffering and deserted Saviour on the cross: "*Father! into thy hands I commend my spirit.*"

5. Resist with courage and firmness all the assaults and temptations of hell. If a temptation arises concerning your faith, do not examine it, enter into no controversy with the enemy of your soul, but say: I believe what the Catholic Church believes, and in this faith will I die! If you are assailed by discouraging thoughts which tempt you to distrust in the goodness of god, either because of the number of your sins, or because you have so little time to do penance; or that it seems to you too difficult a thing to gain heaven because the way is narrow and the gate is strait, the number of the elect small and your good works very few; or that the coldness of your heart and your ingratitude to God make you unworthy of pardon, chase away promptly all these useless and discouraging fears. Think rather of the unbounded love and mercy of God and the infinite merits of Jesus Christ; surrender yourself with the greatest peace and serenity of mind to the divine will, and say in your heart: Father in heaven! into thy hands I wholly commit myself; my life, my death, my soul, my salvation, my temporal and

my eternal life! Do with me what thou wilt; living and dying I am thine!

6. Occupy yourself chiefly with acts of faith, hope, and charity; of contrition for the sins of your whole life, and of resignation to the will of God. I do not say this only by way of good advice. It is a duty to make these acts often during life, and there is a special obligation to make them at the approach of death. If it is not too fatiguing, get some one to read to you the history of the passion of Jesus Christ, or some other pious subject. Take often the crucifix in your hand and kiss it with fervor, and take care to have attached to it the plenary indulgence for the hour of death. Turn your eyes often to the image of the blessed Virgin Mary, and commend yourself to her powerful protection. Let the names of Jesus and Mary be always upon your lips until the last moment, and in that solemn moment also, let the blessed candle be burning by your side, or if possible take it even in your own hand, as a testimony that you have kept until the end the holy faith of your baptism.

III. INSTRUCTION FOR THOSE WHO ATTEND ON THE SICK AND DYING.

1. Of all the works of Christian charity to our neighbor, none is so meritorious and so pleasing to God as when we assist him in his sickness, and try to procure for him a happy death. Many a soul has been saved by this office of Christian love, which would otherwise have been eternally lost. Jesus Christ promises the kingdom of heaven to those who visit and assist his sick brethren. At the day of general judgment, he will say to them: "*Come, ye blessed of my Father, possess the kingdom prepared for you from the foundation of the world; for I was sick and you visited me.*' (St. Matt. xxv.)

St. Philip Neri calls the sick-chamber the spiritual gold-mine, where we can find infinite treasures of merit for heaven. For this reason, the family of the sick person, and the neighbors too, should always be very ready to give their help, not only to take care of him, and to watch with him, but also to console him, and if need be to counsel him for the good of his soul. "*Be not slow to visit the sick, for by these things thou shalt be confirmed in love.*" (Eccli. vii. 39.)

2. Let no unprofitable, foolish, and worldly conversation take place by the bedside of the dying. For they have need to be instructed, strengthened, and consoled for their journey into eternity. Therefore, all those visitors should be excluded who only come out of curiosity, and all those who by their noise and idle chattering, disturb and distract the mind of the sick person. Let only those persons be present whose attentions are necessary, and from time to time let them suggest to the dying person some pious reflection, some short prayer, or holy aspiration. Other friends who happen to be present should repeat the Litany, and other prayers for the agonizing, or the Rosary, in a room adjoining, or at a little distance away from the dying person.

3. All those should be carefully excluded from the sick-chamber whose presence might be an occasion of new temptations to the dying, or is calculated to disturb his peace of mind, as, for instance, those persons with whom in his lifetime he has lived in unlawful, or at least suspicious intercourse, and those who have been the cause of any considerable misfortune to him, or done him great injuries; and also those relations to whom he is the most strongly attached, especially when they are too little discreet, because by their immoderate grief they may disturb his peace of mind.

4. Ask the dying man if he has still any thing remaining upon his conscience, and if he says yes, let the priest be sent for without delay, who may satisfy

his conscience. When he enters upon his last agony, the bystanders ought to recite the prayers for the agonizing, which are at the end of this little manual (*see page* 431), and, if convenient, let the priest be called again.

5. It is necessary to make use of those prayers and pious exercises which are adapted to the condition of the sick. It is particularly important to persuade him to make acts of faith, hope, charity, contrition, of resignation to the will of God, and of desire for Heaven. The prayers and reading must not be in too loud a voice, or it will distress the sick person. Do not read too rapidly, or too much at once, but slowly, and now and then pause awhile, that he may have time to consider what he has heard. Remind him that it is enough if he follows with his heart what you read to him, and that it is not necessary for him to pray with his lips.

6. Those who are occupied in the sick-room have the opportunity to recall to his mind many pious thoughts; as, for instance, when they are arranging the bed, they can say to him: "You have a soft bed to rest on; but our Saviour had nowhere to lay his head." When he takes food or drink, or any other refreshment, they may say to him; "O, how good is our dear God, who refreshes us with food and drink; Jesus, the Son of God, for love of us, had no other refreshment than gall and vinegar." When the sick man turns from one side to the other, and can find no rest, say to him: "In God alone is true rest and refreshment to be found. In this world we can never find rest, until we submit ourselves to the most holy will of God." In this way, the sick man may be kep always united with God, and resigned to his will.

7. Encourage the dying person to look often upon the Crucifix, and kiss it. Let an image, too, of the blessed Virgin Mary be placed before his eyes, that he may have recourse to her. See that all things of a worldly character be taken out of the room, such as

firearms, profane pictures, and gay articles of dress, that his thoughts may not be attracted by them. Let the blessed candle be ready; often sprinkle his room and his bed with holy water, and when he comes to his last agony, whisper distinctly and slowly in his ear the last "Sighs of the Dying" (*see page* 392), bu especially repeat to him over and over again, the most holy names of Jesus and Mary.

IV. A FEW REMEDIES AGAINST THE VARIOUS TEMPTATIONS OF THE DYING.

The most holy names of Jesus and Mary are, beyond all doubt, their most powerful weapons against temptations of every kind; and then, also, the holy sign of the Cross. It is, nevertheless, very useful to know some special remedies against each kind of temptation.

1. *Temptations against Faith.*—If you would triumph in faith, and banish all doubts, you must not indulge in any subtle investigations, or in any discussions concerning your faith; but firmly declare, with the heart and the lips: "I believe what the holy Roman Catholic Church believes!" Thank God that he has called you to this true faith, and say: "I will live and die as a child of the Catholic Church!" Then, in order to turn your mind away from the temptation, occupy yourself with other pious acts, such as the acts of Hope and Charity. Do not enter into any arguments with the temptation, even if bright light and clear reasons should present themselves; for Satan often disguises himself like an angel of light. Think of the declaration of Jesus Christ: "*Blessed are they that have not seen, and have believed.*" (St. John, xx. 29.)

2. *Temptations against Hope.*—This temptation is one of the strongest and most dangerous. The sick man is often tormented by the number of his past sins, and with groundless fears that his confessions were

bad and insufficient; he is too much terrified by the thought of judgment, and of hell, although he has done his best to prepare against both. In order to triumph over this temptation, you must often think of the unbounded and infinite compassion of God. For St. Paul 2 Cor. i. 3) calls God "*the Father of mercies.*" God desires our salvation more than we do ourselves. He seeks for us as a good shepherd looks for his lost sheep he loves us more than a tender mother her beloved babe. "*As I live,*" saith the Lord God, "*I desire not the death of the wicked, but that the wicked turn from his way and live. If the wicked do penance, I will not remember all his iniquities which he hath done.*" (Ezech. xxxiii. 11. xviii. 21.) Only one sincere sigh of contrition from the heart of the sinner can obtain pardon for the greatest crimes, if the sinner has the serious will to amend, and to confess his sins as well as he is able. The publican mentioned in the Holy Gospel had scarcely spoken from a contrite heart these words, "Lord, be merciful to me, a sinner," than he was justified before God. The prodigal son had no sooner fallen at the feet of his father, than he embraced him, and forgave him his sins. And thus our heavenly Father deals with us when we return truly penitent to him.

One of the strongest motives of confidence in the mercy of God is the passion of Jesus Christ. He who has a good will need not be afraid of eternal condemnation, since Jesus has given himself up to the death of the cross to save us from eternal death. Our hope is still further strengthened by the promise of Jesus Christ, that he will give us every thing we ask of him. "*Amen, amen! I say to you,*" said he, "*if you ask the Father any thing in my name, he will give it you.*" (St. John, xiv. 23.) This promise embraces sinners, as well as others; for Jesus says, in another place, "*Every one that asketh, receiveth.*" (St. Matt. vii. 8.) Whoever prays sincerely for his soul's salvation, will certainly receive from God those graces and means which are necessary for his soul's salvation. "*The Lord is good to the soul that seeketh him.*" (Lam. iii. 25.) "*O, how good and sweet is thy Spirit, O Lord, in all things!*" (Wisd. xii. 1.)

Another most powerful motive to trust in the mercy of God is the intercession of Mary the divine Mother, and that of the saints and angels, whose prayers are so efficacious on our behalf. The holy Church calls Mary the refuge of sinners, our life and our Hope. Mary receives all who apply to her, even the most wicked and forsaken; no one ever had recourse to her without being heard. The other saints of God pray too before the throne of God for our salvation, and fly to our help in our last conflict. Invoke in a particular manner, the good St. Joseph, patron of a happy death, the holy archangel Michael, your guardian angel, and those saints whom you have honored most in time of health.

3. *Temptations to impatience.* When you are tempted to repine on account of the long continuance of your sickness, the greatness of your sufferings, &c., you should consider what the martyrs suffered for Jesus Christ, how they were burned, flayed alive, and crucified. Especially reflect on what the innocent Lamb of God has suffered for the love of us. Remember too that by your impatience you do not diminish your pains, and that if you are impatient under your sufferings, you will have to suffer both in this life and the next. But when you suffer with patience, you not only make your present pains lighter, but you diminish the pains which await you in purgatory, and acquire also much greater merit for heaven. "*Your sorrow shall be turned into joy,*" said Jesus to his Apostles. (St. John, xvi.) Remember that the cross is the sign of our predestination. God purifies his friends in this life by sufferings and crosses. Think only, with what sufferings and tedious maladies God has afflicted the saints. St. Clara

passed eight-and-twenty years in suffering. St. Lidwina was sick for thirty-eight years, and was afflicted with indescribable pains. Courage! my dear Christian, and exclaim with the holy Apostle Paul, "*The sufferings of this present time are not worthy to be compared with the glory to come, that shall be revealed in us.*" (Rom. viii. 18.) Finally, pray often to God for patience; for after all, it is a grace from God. Submit to the will of God, even when it seems to you that your physician does not treat you skilfully, or that your attendants do not serve you faithfully. Receive this too in the spirit of penance, for so you will make yourself very dear to God.

4. "*Death comes too early.*" This is a temptation which presents itself sometimes to the minds of the sick, when death comes to call them in the bloom of their youth, or the vigor of their years. Let such reflect that the present life is full of dangers, troubles, and anxieties; that new occasions of sin are ever waiting for us, and that the longer we live the greater is the danger of being eternally lost. This is the reason why the Saints desired death so earnestly. St. Teresa rejoiced whenever she heard the clock strike, because, she said, another hour of danger has gone by in which I might have lost my God. How often, while still in the flower of life, the holy Martyrs have gone lightly and joyfully to meet a cruel death! Hear what the Holy Spirit says: "*Blessed are the dead who die in the Lord, for they rest from their labors.*" (Apoc. xiv. 13.) We are here as pilgrims in a vale of tears, and have no permanent dwelling. Thank God that he did not let you die in mortal sin, and that he has given you the opportunity to confess your sins and to receive the last sacraments. You would wish, perhaps, to live longer, in order to do more penance? O be assured there is no penance more pleasing to God than when

you accept of death from his hand with a heart full of penitence and resignation.

5. *Family affections.* Some sick persons are troubled before death, because they must leave husband, wife, children, or relations. They should remember that God is the best of Fathers, and is best able to provide for those who are left behind. Think rather of saving your soul, for when you are in heaven you can do far more for those dear friends you leave behind, by one prayer before the throne of God, than if you remained with them. There in heaven you will find better friends than here on earth: there you will find Jesus, your divine Saviour, Mary, your tender mother, and all the blessed angels and saints of God. Are those you leave behind poor? God, who feeds the birds of the air, will he not provide for them what they need?

6. *Temptations of hatred and enmity.* If any one is assailed by these temptations, let him remember the commandment of Jesus Christ: "*Love your enemies!*" and that he has no hope of pardon from God who does not pardon his enemy. "*Forgive and you shall be forgiven.*" (St. Luke, vi. 37.) Has your enemy injured you, then remember how often you have offended God. Contemplate the example of the saints. St. James before his death embraced his accusers, St. Stephen prayed for his murderers, and St. Ambrose nourished for a long time the traitor who had betrayed him. Call to mind, especially, the example of Jesu Christ, who, while hanging on the cross, prayed earnestly to his heavenly Father for his persecutors and calumniators.

V. VARIOUS MOTIVES AND ACTS PROPER TO SUGGEST TO THE SICK AND DYING.

1. Motives and Acts of Confidence.

Jesus Christ has suffered death for us, that he might

obtain the pardon of our sins. "*He that spared not even his own Son, but delivered him up for us all, how hath he not also, with him, given us all things.*" (Rom. viii. 32.)

The Lord is my light and my salvation; whom shall I fear? (Ps. 26.)

Into thy hands I commend my spirit; thou hast redeemed me, O Lord God of truth.

We beseech thee, therefore, help thy servants, whom thou hast redeemed with thy most precious blood.

In thee, O Lord, have I hoped; let me never be confounded.

O, good Jesus! hide me in thy wounds. Thy wounds are my merits. (St. Bernard.)

O, my Jesus! thou wilt not refuse me pardon, for thou hast not refused me thy life and thy blood!

Passion of Jesus! thou art my hope. Merits of Jesus! ye are my hope. Wounds of Jesus! ye are my hope. Death of Jesus! thou art my hope.

O my Mother, Mary! pity me, and save me. Yes, thou wilt save me, for art thou not our hope?

Holy Mary, Mother of God! pray for me, a sinner. Under thy mantle we take refuge, holy Mother of God

2. Motives and Acts of Contrition.

St. Augustine says that each man is bound to deplore his sins until the last breath of life.

Enter not into judgment with thy servant, O Lord. (Ps. 142.) O Jesus, my judge, spare me before thou comest to judge me!

A contrite and humble heart, O God, thou wilt not despise. My God, would that I had never offended thee!

Father! I am not worthy to be called thy son. I have abandoned thee; I have despised thy grace; I have lost thee wilfully. With my whole heart I repent. O my God, for the love of Jesus Christ and his precious blood, spare me!

O cursed sins, which have robbed me of my God! I detest them; I abhor them.

O my God! what evil hast thou done to me, that I should so offend thee? For the love of Jesus Christ thy son, have mercy on me.

Never again, O Lord, so long as I live, will I offend thee; whether my life be short or long, I am determined to love thee hereafter.

In satisfaction for all my offences against thee, offer thee my death, and all the pains which until death I have still to suffer.

O Lord, it is just that thou shouldst punish me, but only in this life, I beseech thee, not in the other.

O Mary! obtain for me a true sorrow for my sins, and the pardon of them, and then the grace of perseverance.

3. Motives and Acts of Love to God.

O my God, thou art infinitely good, and I love thee above all things. I love thee more than myself. I love thee with my whole heart. My God! I am not worthy to say I love thee, because I have so much offended thee; but, for the love of Jesus, make me worthy.

O would that the whole world might love thee!

O sweet Jesus, I desire to suffer and die for thee, who hast deigned to suffer and die for me.

O Lord, chastise me as thou wilt, only let me not cease to love thee! O my God, save me; my salvation is to love thee.

I desire Paradise, that there, my dearest Lord, for all eternity, I may love thee with all my strength.

O my God, cast me not into hell, as I deserve! There I should only be able to hate thee, but I cannot bear to think of hating thee. What evil hast thou done to me, O Lord, that I should hate thee? O, no: only make me love thee, and then do with me what thou wilt.

I wish to suffer according to thy will: I wish to die that I may do thy will.

Bind me to thee, O my Jesus, and never permit me to be separated from thee.

O my God, grant that before I die, I may be all thine own!

When will the time come, that I shall be able to say, My God, I cannot lose thee any more?

O my God, I wish to love thee as much as thou deservest.

O Mary! draw me entirely to God!

O my Mother, I love thee dearly, and I wish to come to heaven, that I may love thee there forever.

4. Motives and Acts of Conformity to the Will of God.

All our happiness and our life consists in this, that we should be conformed to the will of God, according to those words of the Psalmist: "*Life is in his will.*" (Ps. 29.) God indeed wills the things which are for our best good. When our Lord appeared to St. Gertrude, offering her the choice of life and death, she answered: "*O Lord, what thou wilt, I will also.*" And in the same way, when Jesus offered once to St. Catharine of Sienna two crowns, one of jewels and one of thorns, she answered: "*I choose the one which pleases thee.*" Well, then, my dear Christian, what do you say? If God calls thee to another life, are you content? You are? Say then always:

O Lord, here I am; do with me what thou wilt. Thy will be always done. Thy will is my will. Let me suffer what thou wilt! Let me die when thou wilt.

Into thy hands I commend my soul and body, my life and death.

I will bless the Lord at all times. Comfort me, or afflict me, Lord, still I love thee; always will I love thee.

O my God, I unite my death with the death of Jesus, and so offer it to thee.

O will of God, thou art my love. O good pleasure of my God, as a holocaust I offer myself up entirely to thee.

5. Acts of Desire for Paradise.

The present life is a prison of pains, in which we cannot see God. For this reason David says well. "*Bring my soul out of prison that I may praise thy name.*" (Ps. 141.) And St. Augustin exclaims: "*Now, Lord, let me die, that I may see thee!*" St. Jerome calls death his sister, saying: "*Open to me, O my sister.*" And he spoke well, for is it not death that opens for us the gates of Paradise? Hear, also, how sweetly the Apostle persuades us to turn our desires upwards to heaven: "*Eye hath not seen, nor ear heard, neither hath it entered into the heart of man, what things God hath prepared for them that love him.*" (1 Cor. ii. 9.)

When shall I come and appear before the face of God? (Ps. 41.) When will the time come, O my God, that I shall behold thy infinite beauty, and see thee face to face?

In heaven, I shall love thee always: thou wilt love me always; yes, there we shall love each other for all eternity. O my God, my love, my all!

O my Jesus, when shall I kiss those sacred wounds, which bled for me?

O Mary! when shall I see myself at the feet of that Mother, who has loved me and assisted me so much? Come then.

" Come then, our advocate,
O, turn on us those pitying eyes of thine;
And, our long exile past,
Show us at last
Jesus, of thy pure womb the fruit divine;

O Virgin Mary, Mother blest!
O sweetest, gentlest, holiest!"

4. AFFECTIONS WHICH MAY BE SUGGESTED TO THE SICK, WHEN KISSING THE CRUCIFIX.

Kiss, my dear brother (*or* sister), those feet which came to seek thee out, when thou wast a lost sheep—those feet which have walked on many a weary journey for poor sinners.

O dearest Redeemer! I embrace thy feet like Mary Magdalen. O, like her, let me hear thee say that I am pardoned!

O my God, spare me for the love of Jesus Christ! O, teach me how to die well!

Eternal Father, thou hast given up thy dear Son for me, so I give myself away to thee.

Willingly will I die for thee, O my Jesus, for thou didst die for me.

Saviour! thou didst seek for me when I was a wanderer; wilt thou abandon me now, when I seek for thee?

O dearest Jesus! never let me be separated from thee.

Who shall separate me from the love of Christ? (Rom. 8.)

O Lord Jesus, by that bitter agony of thy most holy soul, when it left thy blessed body, have mercy on my sinful soul when it shall quit this body of mine.

O my Jesus, thou hast died for love of me; so will I die for love of thee.

DAILY PRAYERS FOR THE SICK.

MORNING PRAYER.

ALMIGHTY and eternal God! I thank the with my whole heart that thou hast preserved me during this night. I recommend myself again to-day to thy fatherly protection; I submit myself entirely to thy divine will, whether I am to live or die.

I offer to thee all the weakness, pain, and suffering that I am to endure this day. For love of thee, O my God, I will suffer all things. I unite my sufferings with the sufferings and death of Jesus Christ.

Whenever this day I sigh, or move my eyes, or speak, or draw breath, or eat, or drink, may every action serve, O my dearest Lord, to adore thee; to praise thee; to bless thee; to express my love to thee. O merciful God, whenever overpowered by weakness, or my great sufferings, I cannot think of offering every thing to thee; accept my good will and this present intention which I make in place of the deed.

Continue, O Almighty God, my life this day, and may thy holy name be praised. But if it should please thee to take me to-day away from this world, may thy holy will be done.

O Mary! health of the sick, next to God my only refuge, I implore thee to be my intercessor with thy dear Son, that through thy all-powerful prayers I may obtain health of body, or a happy death. Protect me from the enemy of my salvation; give me the grace, as a true child of thy love, to behold thee in heaven. O dearest Mother! I commend to thee the care of my body and of my soul, under thy protection. O powerful Virgin, and tender Mother, I confidently hope to obtain salvation.

O my holy guardian Angel, I thank thee for having so carefully watched over me this night. I pray thee and all the other holy angels to watch over me this day and to the end of my life.

And you also, blessed saints of God, especially you, my Patron Saint! help me by your intercession this day, and leave me not, if that moment should arrive on which my eternity is depending. Pray to the divine Judge for me, that I may be a child of election. *Amen.*

EVENING PRAYER.

O MOST Holy Trinity, God the Father, Son, and Holy Ghost, may endless thanks be given thee for all the blessings and the sufferings which thou hast sent upon me this day. If I have not borne these my sufferings with the patience I ought, I humbly implore thy pardon.

I commit myself to thy divine protection this night. I am sincerely sorry for my sins, because I have offended Thee, my highest good, whom I love above all things. O that I had never offended thee! I seriously intend to amend my life.

I offer to thee, O heavenly Father, for my sins, the infinite merit of thy divine Son Jesus Christ. Let not the value of his sufferings and death be lost to me!

Jesus! for thee I sleep; Jesus! for thee I wake; Jesus! for thee I live; Jesus! for thee I die; Jesus! living or dying, I am thine! *Amen.*

PIOUS ASPIRATIONS FOR THE SICK.

[The sick cannot ordinarily make long prayers, but they can send up their sighs to God, and God receives those sighs as prayers.]

Behold, O my God, in what misery I lie upon my bed, and how much I am suffering for thy sake.

My body is full of pain and my soul full of sorrow, but my spirit is prepared to suffer according to thy divine pleasure.

I offer to thee, O Jesus, my sorrows, in honor of the sorrows which thou hast suffered for me upon the cross.

I hide all my sufferings in thy five holy wounds, and unite them to thy bitter sufferings.

As thou, O Jesus! didst offer up all thy sorrows and pains to thy heavenly Father, so also I offer up all my sufferings to my heavenly Father.

As thou, O Jesus! didst bear all thy sufferings with the greatest patience, I will also bear my sickness with the greatest patience.

Most blessed Virgin and Mother of God, Mary! allay my sufferings this night. Be my protectress in the hour of trial, be my comforter, be my powerful intercessor with Jesus Christ, thy divine Son.

Holy Guardian Angels, and all ye Saints of God, protect me this night, and preserve me from all evil.

Merciful God! have compassion on the poor souls in purgatory. Give them eternal rest, and let eternal light shine upon them. O Lord, may they rest in peace! Amen.

As thou, O Jesus! didst give thanks to thy heavenly Father for the sufferings inflicted upon thee, I too would give thanks to my heavenly Father for the sickness sent upon me.

As thou, O Jesus! didst accept thy sufferings as an atonement for the sins of the whole world, so will I accept my sufferings for my numberless sins.

O heavenly Father, may my sufferings be accepted by thee, and serve for thy greater glory.

O Jesus Christ, unite my sufferings with thy cruel sufferings, and present them thus to thy heavenly Father, that they may be acceptable in his sight.

O Holy Ghost, grant me thy divine grace, that I may bear this sickness with patience.

O Mother of God, thou who hadst so great compassion for thy crucified Son, have compassion upon me also, thy poor child.

O my holy guardian Angel, watch over me by day and by night, and leave me not in my necessities.

O ye Saints of God, especially you my holy Patron Saint! pray for me, that the good God may be merciful and gracious unto me.

THE SACRAMENTS OF THE SICK.

When the Priest has been called to give communion to a sick person, or to administer the last sacraments to the dying, care must be taken to have every thing rightly prepared in the sick chamber. In the first place, see that the room be clean, and that every thing offensive be taken out of the way; and let not any clothing be lying scattered about, but neatly folded up, or put away. The sick person should be decently covered, and the bedclothes arranged in good order. Prepare, also, in the same room, a table neatly covered with a white linen cloth, in order to receive upon it the Holy Eucharist. On the table should be placed two candles and a crucifix, and a glass of pure water from the spring or well, and if there is any holy water in the house, place it near by, or at the door of the chamber. A clean white napkin should also be furnished, to serve as a communion-cloth for the sick.

When the Priest arrives, if you perceive that he has with him the Blessed Sacrament, kneel down, and do not begin immediately to talk in a noisy and familiar manner, but let one show the way to the sick-room, while the rest follow their Lord in silence and adoration. If however, it is necessary to say any thing, speak in a low and reverential manner. After the communion, do not remain to distract the sick person by your conversation, or by walking about the room, but leave him alone to make his thanksgiving in quiet. Sometimes, however, especially when he is very feeble, or unable to read, it is better for some one to be with him, both before and after communion, and read for him slowly and distinctly the necessary prayers.

PRAYERS

BEFORE RECEIVING THE HOLY VIATICUM, OR LAST COMMUNION.

O INFINITELY merciful Jesus! a great journey is before me, from this world to eternity. May thy most holy will be done, my heart is ready. Yes, let me depart from this world, for so it pleases thee.

But what can I do without thee, thou who art the Way, the Truth, and the Life! Without thee I should perish of hunger and thirst on the way.

Come then, O merciful Jesus, before I die. Come, and delay not; strengthen me through the most Holy Sacrament of the Altar; strengthen me with thy most holy flesh and blood, that by the power of this strong bread of angels, I may attain to the view of thy divine countenance.

As the hart panteth after the fresh fountains of water, so my soul longs for thee, O my God, thou living fountain of all good. O, when shall I come and appear before thy face? When shall my feet stand in thy delightful tabernacles, in the house of my Lord?

Why art thou sorrowful, O my soul, and why art thou disquieted? Hope in God. See! thy Beloved comes. He will come; he will strength en thee; he will take thee from the desert of this life to himself in thy heavenly home.

Ah, come then, my Saviour! come, beloved Jesus, come, and tarry not too long! I desire to enjoy thee as the true paschal Lamb, before I depart and die.

Come, O sweetest Jesus, come and enter my heart, unite thyself to me, remain with me, until I have overcome every thing, and have conquered death.

Come, O Jesus, come meet me in this supper, and lead me to the heavenly banquet in thy Father's house? Prepare for me a dwelling there, as thou hast promised, that I may be forever with thee, and rejoice with thee forever! *Amen.*

PRAYERS AFTER THE HOLY VIATICUM.

Remain for some time silent, in quiet and sweet union with your beloved Saviour. Excite in your heart a lively faith in his personal presence. Breathe forth many sighs of gratitude and love to him for all the temporal and spiritual blessings that he has bestowed on you during your whole life, but especially that he has so often fed you with his holy body, and has even granted you this last favor, to be your food and support on the way to eternity.

O MY dearest Jesus! I now am in possession of every thing to complete happily my pilgrimage here on earth, for I possess thee, who art the Way, the Truth, and the Life

Thou art the Way, and wilt guide me safely to my heavenly home. Thou art the Truth, and the wilt illuminate the darkness and the shadows of death. Thou art the Life, and art leading me to life eternal. For though I should walk in the midst of the shadow of death, I fear no evils, for thou art with me, my helper and my protector!

O, crucified Jesus! Thou who didst institute this Holy Sacrament for the memorial of thy bitter passion, may the merit of thy passion, not be lost on me. Thou who forgivest sins, purify me from every stain of sin, that I may appear entirely pure before thee.

Living Bread of heaven! support my weakness by thy grace, that I may not yield in the last struggle; that my faith may not waver, my hope sink, and my love grow cold. O, my most gracious Saviour! let this holy Viaticum be to me a pledge of my eternal salvation.

Now, O Lord! let me, thy servant, depart in peace, for mine eyes have seen thee, the Saviour of the world, and my heart hath received thee. Bless me, O Jesus! I will not let thee go, until thou hast given me thy holy blessing for my journey to eternity.

O Jesus! thou art my life, and death is my gain.

O Jesus, my Love. my God, my Desire, my all.

PRAYER OF ST IGNATIUS AFTER COMMUNION.

SOUL of Christ, sanctify me!
Body of Christ, save me!
Blood of Christ, inebriate me!
Water flowing from the side of Christ, cleanse me!
Passion of Christ, strengthen me!
O, good Jesus, hear me!
In thy holy wounds conceal me!
And let me not be separated from thee!
From the wicked enemy defend me!
In the hour of my death, call me!
And bid me, Lord, to come to thee!
That with thy Saints and Angels I may praise thee.
Throughout the ages of eternity! *Amen.*

PRAYERS BEFORE EXTREME UNCTION.

MOST merciful Lord, and loving Saviour, Jesus Christ, what a consoling promise thou hast attached to the reception of this sacrament: "*Is any one sick among you, let him bring in the Priests of the Church, and let them pray over him, ancinting him with oil, in the name of the Lord, and the prayer of faith shall save the sick man; and the Lord will lift him up, and if h be in sin, his sins shall be forgiven him*" (St. James, v.)

By thy infinite goodness, O Jesus, through which thou hast established this Holy Sacrament, I beseech thee to purify me from my sins, defend me from the enemy, strengthen me in temptation, and give me a happy end; or, if i be profitable for my soul's salvation, restore me to my former health. This I ask, through thy infinite merits, who, with God the Father, and the Holy Ghost, livest and reignest one only God forever! *Amen.*

During the anointing of each of the five senses of your body, pray in the silence of your heart, that God would pardon the sins which you have committed with each, and offer up for your sins those sufferings which Christ endured in this same sense for your sins.

PRAYER AFTER EXTREME UNCTION.

MOST merciful Jesus, I have now received this sacred Unction, which thou didst institute for the consolation and benefit of the sick. I thank thee for this powerful remedy of my soul and my body. Enable me to enjoy the full benefits of this Holy Sacrament, upon which I place my hope and confidence. *Amen.*

THE LAST SIGHS OF THE DYING.

I die in the Holy Roman Catholic Faith!

I believe all the Holy Church believes!

O my God, I believe in thee!

O my God, I hope in thee!

O my God, I love thee above all things!

O God, make haste to help me!

My God, my hope, my all!

O Jesus! into thy hands I commend my spirit.

O Jesus! be my Saviour and my deliverer!

Jesus! I wish to die that I may expiate my sins.

Jesus! I wish to die because thou hast died for me.

Jesus! I wish to die, that I may see thee and love thee eternally.

O Lord Jesus, in thee have I trusted, let me never be confounded!

O Mary! show thyself a mother to me.

O Mary! pray for me now, in the hour of my death!

O clement, O pious, O sweet Virgin Mary!

Jesus! Mary! Joseph! be always in my heart!

Jesus! Mary! Joseph! be always in my thoughts.

Jesus! Mary! Joseph! be always on my tongue.

Jesus! Mary! Joseph! my last thought, my last sigh.

Jesus! Mary! Joseph! I live for you.

Jesus! Mary! Joseph! I die for you
Jesus! I believe in thee. Jesus! I hope in thee.
Jesus! I love thee above all things!
Jesus! be merciful to me a poor sinner!
Jesus! into thy hands I commend my spirit!
Jesus! Jesus! Jesus!
Jesus! Mary! Joseph!

THE RECOMMENDATION OF A DEPARTING SOUL.

(From the Roman Breviary.)

LORD, have mercy on him (or her.)
Christ, have mercy upon him.
Lord, have mercy on him.

Pray for him (or her.)

Holy Mary,
All ye holy Angels and Archangels
Holy Abel,
All ye Choirs of the Just,
Holy Abraham,
St. John Baptist,
St. Joseph,
All ye holy Patriarchs and Prophets,
St. Peter,
St. Paul,
St. Andrew,
St. John,
All ye holy Apostles and Evangelists,
All ye holy Disciples of our Lord,

St. Stephen,
St. Lawrence,
All ye holy Martyrs,
All ye holy Innocents,
St. Sylvester,
St. Gregory,
St. Augustine,
All ye holy Bishops and Confessors,
St. Benedict,
St. Francis,
All ye holy Monks and Hermits,
St. Mary Magdalen,
St. Lucy,
All ye holy Virgins and Widows,
All ye Men and Women, Saints of God,
} *Pray for him (or her.)*

Be merciful unto him,
Be merciful unto him,
Be merciful unto him,
} *Spare him (or her), O Lord.*

From thy wrath,
From the danger of eternal death,
From an evil death,
From the pains of hell,
From all evil,
From the power of the devil,
By thy Nativity,
By thy Cross and Passion,
By thy Death and Burial,
By thy glorious Resurrection,
By thy wonderful Ascension,
} *Deliver him (or her), O Lord.*

By the grace of the Holy Ghost the Comforter, *deliver him (or her), O Lord.*

In the Day of Judgment, *deliver him (or her), O Lord.*

We sinners, *beseech thee hear us.*

That thou spare him, *we beseech thee hear us.*

Lord, have mercy on him.

Christ, have mercy on him.

Lord, have mercy on him.

PRAYER.

GO forth, O Christian soul, from this world in the name of God the Father Almighty, who created thee; in the name of Jesus Christ, the Son of the living God, who suffered for thee; in the name of the Holy Ghost, who has sanctified thee; in the name of the Angels and Archangels; in the name of the heavenly Thrones and Dominations; in the name of the Principalities and Powers; in the name of the Cherubim and Seraphim; in the name of the Patriarchs and Prophets; in the name of the holy Apostles and Evangelists; in the name of the holy Martyrs and Confessors; in the name of the holy Monks and Hermits; in the name of the holy Virgins and all the Saints of God; let thy place be this day in peace and thy abode in the holy Sion. Through the same Jesus Christ our Lord. *R. Amen.*

O MOST merciful and good God! Thou who, by the multitude of thy mercies, dost blot out the sins of the penitent, and dost remit the punishment of their past sins; graciously look upon this thy servant (thy handmaid), and hear his (her) supplication, since he (she) with his (her) whole heart confesses and begs thy forgiveness of his (her) sins. Renew in him (her), O most merciful Father, every thing that has been deformed through human frailty, or through the cunning of the devil, and receive this member, redeemed by the blood of thy Son, to the unity of the body of the Church. Have compassion, O Lord, upon his (her) sighs, have compassion on his (her) tears, and admit him (her) because he (she) has no hope but in thy mercy, to the grace of reconciliation to thee. *R. Amen.*

I COMMEND thee, dear brother (dear sister), to Almighty God, and commit thee to the hands of thy Creator, that then when thou, by death, hast paid the debt of nature, thou mayest return to thy Maker, who formed thee from the clay of the earth. When thy soul leaves the body, may the bright host of angels come to meet thee; the company of the Apostles who are to judge the world, receive thee; the triumphant army of Martyrs meet thee; the multitude of Confessors surround thee, with their lilies in their hands; the choir of joyful Virgins welcome thee;

and may the Patriarchs with loving embrace receive thee into their rest. May Jesus appear to thee with a mild and radiant face, and may he give thee a place among those who are ever near him. Mayest thou never know the dreadful darkness, the crackling flames, and the torments of the damned. May the devil, with his evil spirits depart from thee, trembling and flying into the horrid confusion of eternal night, when he sees thee accompanied by the angels. Let God arise and his enemies be put to flight, and all who hate him flee before his presence! Let them be driven away as smoke; as wax melts before the fire, so may sinners disappear before his countenance. But may the just rejoice and be glad in the presence of God. Let all the hosts of hell be confounded and put to shame, and may the servants of Satan place no hindrance in the way. May Christ, who was crucified for thee, deliver thee from all torments. May Christ, who vouchsafed to die for thee, deliver thee from eternal death. May Christ, the Son of the living God, conduct thee to the possession of the eternal joys of Paradise. May he, the true Shepherd, receive thee as his sheep. May he absolve thee from all thy sins, and place thee at his right hand among the number of his elect. Mayest thou see thy Redeemer face to face, and always in his presence behold, with happy eyes, the purest truth! Mayest thou, in the company of the blessed, eternally enjoy the sweetness of the divine presence. *R. Amen.*

PRAYER.

RECEIVE, O Lord, thy servant (handmaid) into the place of salvation, which he (she) hopes to obtain through thy mercy. *R. Amen.*

Deliver, O Lord, the soul of thy servant (handmaid) from all dangers of hell, and from all pain and tribulation. *R. Amen.*

Deliver, O Lord, the soul of thy servant (handmaid) as thou didst deliver Enoch and Elias from the common death of the world. *R. Amen.*

Deliver, O Lord, the soul of thy servant (handmaid) as thou didst deliver Noe from the flood. *R. Amen.*

Deliver, O Lord, the soul of thy servant (handmaid) as thou didst deliver Abraham from the midst of the Chaldeans. *R. Amen.*

Deliver, O Lord, the soul of thy servant (handmaid), as thou didst deliver Isaac from the hand of Abraham his father. *R. Amen.*

Deliver, O Lord, the soul of thy servant (handmaid), as thou didst deliver Lot from being destroyed in the flames of Sodom. *R. Amen.*

Deliver, O Lord, the soul of thy servant (handmaid), as thou didst deliver Moses from the hands of Pharaoh, king of Egypt. *R. Amen.*

Deliver O Lord, the soul of thy servant (handmaid), as thou didst deliver Daniel from the lion's den. *R. Amen.*

Deliver, O Lord, the soul of thy servant (handmaid), as thou didst deliver the three children from the fiery furnace, and from the hands of an unmerciful king. *R. Amen.*

Deliver, O Lord, the soul of thy servant (handmaid), as thou didst deliver Susanna from her false accusers. *R. Amen.*

Deliver, O Lord, the soul of thy servant (handmaid), as thou didst deliver David from the hand of king Saul and Goliath. *R. Amen.*

Deliver, O Lord, the soul of thy servant (handmaid), as thou didst deliver Peter and Paul out of prison. *R. Amen.*

And, finally, as thou didst deliver, O Lord, the blessed virgin and martyr, Thecla, from three most cruel torments, so vouchsafe to deliver the soul of this thy servant, and bring him (her) to share thy heavenly joys. *R. Amen.*

WE commend to thee, O Lord! the soul of thy servant, N. (thy handmaid N.), and beseech thee, O Lord Jesus Christ, the Saviour of the world! that thou wouldst admit into the bosom of thy Patriarchs this soul, for which, in thy mercy, thou didst come into the world. Acknowledge, O Lord, this thy creature; not made by any strange gods, but by thee, the only living and true God; for there is no other God but thee, and nothing equals thy works. Fill him (her), O Lord, with the joy of thy presence. Remember no more those sins and errors into which he (she) was led by the power of evil desires. He (she) has indeed sinned, but has never renounced his (her) faith in the Father Son, and Holy Ghost, and has had a zeal for the glory of God, and faithfully worshipped thee, the God and Creator of all things.

REMEMBER not, O Lord, the sins of his (her) youth and his (her) ignorance, but according to thy great mercy, be mindful of him (her) in the brightness of thy glory. May the heavens be opened to him (her), and may the angels rejoice in him (her). Receive, O Lord, thy servant (thy handmaid) into thy kingdom. May St. Michael, the Archangel of God, who has merited to be the chief of the heavenly host, conduct him (her). May the holy Angels of God come to meet him (her), and take him (her) to the city of the heavenly Jerusalem. May St. Peter, to whom God committed the keys of the kingdom of heaven, receive him (her). May St. Paul, who was worthy to be a vessel of election, assist him (her). May St. John, the chosen Apostle of God, to whom the secrets of heaven were revealed, intercede for him (her). May all the holy Apostles, to whom the Lord has intrusted the power of loosing and binding, pray for him (her). May all the Saints and chosen servants of God, who for the name of Christ in this world have suffered martyrdom, intercede for him (her), that he (she) being delivered from the bonds of the flesh, may merit to be received into the glory of the kingdom of heaven; by the mercy of our Lord Jesus Christ, who, with the Father and the Holy Ghost, liveth and reigneth forever. *Amen.*

AFTER THE SOUL HAS DEPARTED.

COME to his (her) assistance, ye Saints of God! Come to meet him (her), ye Angels of the Lord! Receive his (her) soul, and bring it into the presence of the Most High. May Jesus Christ, who has called thee, receive thee, and his Angels bear thee to Abraham's bosom.

Lord, have mercy on him (her)!

Christ, have mercy on him (her)!

Lord, have mercy on him (her)! Our Father, &c.

V. Eternal rest give to him (her), O Lord,

R. And let perpetual light shine upon him (her).

V. From the gates of hell,

R. Deliver him (her), O Lord.

V. May he (she) rest in peace.

R. Amen.

V. O Lord, hear my prayer,

R. And let my cry come unto thee.

PRAYER.

TO Thee, O Lord, we commend the soul of thy servant (handmaid), that having departed from this world, he (she) may live to thee alone, and that in thy infinite goodness and mercy thou wilt pardon him (her) whatever sins he (she) may have committed in this world, through human frailty. This we ask through Jesus Christ our Lord. *Amen.*

SPIRITUAL READING

SPIRITUAL READING

Familiar Lessons of Piety, in form of Narratives and Meditations.

THE SALVATION OF THE SOUL.

WE read in the history of the Church, that formerly many holy penitents, impressed with the belief of the nothingness of every thing earthly, and the importance of eternal truths, withdrew into solitary places, that they might give themselves up without distraction to the meditation of these holy truths. Separated from each other, and buried in gloomy caverns, as if already in their graves, they occupied themselves only with such thoughts as these:—that death is certain;—that no man knows when, where, or how he will die, and that any moment may be the last of our life;—that at the moment when a man dies, he is judged by God, and must give an exact account of all his thoughts, words, and deeds, which alone, of all he has, will follow him into the next world;—that after this life, which passes so quickly, comes eternity, which has no end, and which will be forever blessed, or forever miserable —that we come into this world only to work out our salvation, and if we fail in this, we cannot make good our loss in eternity;—that one mortal sin alone is enough to make us eternally miserable, and that sin is the only real evil, the only misfortune that we have to fear.

Penetrated by these solemn thoughts, they watched through whole nights, fasted, wore hair cloth, and used every instrument of penance to bring the body into subjection to the soul. They lived on roots and herbs or at best, on bread, moistened with their tears. Pale and emaciated, like living skeletons, they passed through a life which seemed more like a slow death, and after twenty, thirty, or forty years thus spent, having reached the end of their course, they asked each other, trembling and full of holy fear, with broken accents: "Think you, ah! think you, that God will have mercy on my soul, and will forgive my sins? Do you really think that there will be any consolation for me in death? that the Eternal Judge will soften the rigor of his judgment against me? Can I hope to escape the terrors of an eternity of misery, and share in the bliss of the elect?"

What dispositions! What an example! But also, what a condemnation, perhaps, for us! Let us weigh this well.

For if God does not call us to such extraordinary things, to which men are drawn only by a peculiar and powerful grace, we are all, without exception, called to a spirit of penance, without which, there is no salvation; for eternal wisdom has said: "*Except ye do penance, ye shall all likewise perish.*" (St. Luke, xiii.) We are called, first, to seek the kingdom of God, not to give our heart to the world, to mortify the body, subject it to the control of the spirit, and work out our salvation with fear and trembling. But why are we doing nothing of all this? These holy penitents, at whose life we wonder so much, had they another gospel to follow than ours, another religion to practise than we? Had they not the same God to serve, the same eternity to hope for or to fear? What, then, is the cause of so singular a difference? These saints possessed a degree of faith which we have not. And, therefore, they were careful to secure the salvation of their souls, while we neglect ours. They constantly meditated upon the greatness of God, the enormity of sin, the uncertainty of life, the fearful depths of divine judgment, an eternity of happiness or misery, approaching nearer at every moment; and we!—how much we fear to occupy ourselves with these high and holy subjects. In a word, they lived like saints, and we live like worldly-minded sinners.

Let us think of these things while there is yet time. What are we to expect, if we refuse to consider? What a consolation will it one day be to us, that we have reflected on these things! Let us occupy ourselves with them now, that in eternity, where these great truths will burst upon our minds with irresistible force, we may not despair, but rather may reap the eternal fruit of these salutary meditations.

A person who had passed his life in the service of an excellent prince, fell dangerously ill. His master, who loved him very much, visited him, and found him in great danger. There he lay, in his agony, just ready to breathe his last. Moved by this spectacle, the prince said to him: Can I do any thing for you? Ask freely whatever you wish, and do not fear that I shall refuse you any thing. My Lord! said the dying man, I know only one thing which, in my present condition, I would like to ask of you. Prolong my life for one quarter of an hour! Alas! said the prince, that is not in my power. Ask for something else; something that I can procure for you. See! said the dying man, for fifty years I have served this master of mine, and now he cannot prolong my life for one quarter of an hour. O! if I had only served my God as well, he would grant me not a quarter of an hour only, but a whole eternity of happiness! Very soon after that, he breathed his last.

Shall we not, by and by, have the same fate? We wear and wear ourselves out in the service of the world; we even sacrifice ourselves for it, and when our last hour comes, what will the world do for us, and what will remain to us after all we have done for it, if we have neglected the service of God, and the salvation of our soul? Let us consider this, and more sincerely and firmly than ever before, say: I am resolved to save my soul, and for this I will labor the remainder of my life! Hitherto I have neglected this too much! Have I not reason to look upon it as a great favor, that God still gives me the time and the grace to meditate seriously on these things?

THE MISERY OF SIN.

Arcadius, the heretical Emperor of Constantinople, was greatly enraged against St. John Chrysostom. He once exclaimed, in his anger, in the presence of his courtiers: "O, that I could take vengeance on this Bishop!" The courtiers immediately came forward with their advice. The first said: Send him into banishment, and never let him enter your presence again! Another said: Seize his property! A third: Throw him in chains, into prison! Are you not master? said a fourth; let him be put to death, and then you will be rid of him! At length, one who was wiser than the rest came forward, and said to the emperor: They are all mistaken; you cannot have your revenge in any such way. Where will you banish him? the whole world is his home. If you seize his property, you take it from the poor, not from him. If you throw him into prison, he will kiss his chains, and esteem himself happy. Condemn him to death, and you open heaven to him. No, my Prince, if you would revenge yourself on him perfectly, compel him to commit sin. I know this man; he fears nothing in the world but sin and nothing else can make him unhappy.

O, wonderful and sublime sentiments! Let us never forget them. No! nothing can harm us but sin. We cannot enter heaven, our true home, if we are sinners. If we are sinners we can never see God the author of our existence. By sin, and even by on mortal sin only, if not expiated in due time by pen ance, we become a prey to eternal torments, to ever lasting despair.

Let us consider this, and, if need be, forget ever, thing else, that we may meditate on it. "*Flee from sins, as from the face of a serpent, for if thou comest near them, they will take hold of thee. The teeth thereof are the teeth of a lion, killing the souls of men. All iniquity is like a two-edged sword, there is nc remedy for the wound thereof.*" (Eccli. xxi. 2.) Pray humbly also thus: "Father, I have sinned against heaven, and before thee. I know my iniquity, and my sin is always before me. Turn away thy face from my sins, and blot out all my iniquities." (Luke, xv. 18; Ps. l. 5, 11.)

ETERNITY.

A celebrated painter of antiquity was once visited by another painter, who asked him the following question: "How happens it that you, who are so great an artist, finish so few pictures, while I, wh am far inferior to you, complete so many in a shor time?"—"I can answer you that," said the other "you paint for time; I, for eternity."

A beautiful lesson! We all have a picture to paint; for, as Christians, if we would be numbered among the elect, we must restore in us the image of Jesus Christ, and our resemblance to him, who is the pattern and model of all the elect. Towards this great work, we may do something every day. A prayer offered to God, an alms given for his sake, a mortification sanctified by the spirit of penance, all these are so many strokes of the pencil, so many lines of resemblance to the divine pattern that is given us. But let us always remember that this painting is for eternity.

Penetrated by this great truth, we will, in future, live as men should live who are strengthened by the thought of eternity, cheered by the hope of eternity in a word, as men who are destined for eternity. O, that for us it may be an eternity of happiness!

Consider this well, and say incessantly to yourself: There is an eternity!—I am destined for eternity!—Perhaps I am at the gate of eternity! What will be my lot in eternity? Since I know not how much time is yet allowed to me here in this world, I will henceforth occupy myself with this great thought, and regulate my whole conduct by it.

DELAY OF CONVERSION.

"*Delay not to be converted to the Lord, and defer it not from day to day.*" (Eccli. v. 8.) We see every day in the world sinners who live in sin, are ingulfed in sin, but say all the while that at some future time they will convert; for they think that they shall always have time for that. But this is a delusion, a blindness, which has already destroyed, and will destroy a countless number of souls. Do not deceive yourself, O sinner! if you delay your conversion, you expose yourself to the danger of never being converted, and of dying as a reprobate. Certainly, your religion teaches you nothing which can sustain you in such a pernicious hope, but every thing warns you that you are in the most extreme peril. Yes, every syllable of our Faith ought to strike terror and distress to the conscience of a sinner who delays his conversion. Terrible are the judgments, the threats, the comparisons, the images, the histories, the examples of Holy Scripture. Every sound of the Gospel is an alarm-bell, every thing in the Church cries out in the name of God: *Delay no longer! Delay no longer!* Listen to these words, and weigh them well.

Terrible are the warnings, nothing more terrible than the passages of Holy Scripture on this point: "*Seek ye the Lord, while he may be found.*" [Is. lv 6.] "*Walk whilst you have the light, that the darkness overtake you not. He that walketh in darkness knoweth not whither he goeth.*" [John, xii. 35.] "*Be you also ready; for at what hour you think not the Son of man will come.*" [Luke, xii. 40.] "*To-day if you shall hear his voice, harden not your hearts.*" [Ps. xciv. 8.]

Terrible are the threatenings! "*You shall seek me, and shall not find me.*" [John, viii. 34.] "*Because I called and you refused, I also will laugh in your destruction; and will mock when that shall come to you which you feared, when sudden calamity shall fall on you, and destruction, as a tempest, shall be at hand, when tribulation and distress shall come upon you. Then shall they call upon me, and I will not hear.*" [Prov. i. 24, 26, 27, 28.] "*You shall die in your sin.*" [John, viii. 24.]

Terrible are the comparisons! "*The day of the Lord shall come as a thief in the night; for when they shall say, Peace and Security—then shall sudden destruction come upon them.*" [1 Thess. v. 2, 3.] "*As fishes are taken with the hook, and as birds are caught with the snare, so men are taken in the evil time, when it shall suddenly come upon them.*" [Eccl. ix. 12.]

Terrific are the figures! "*As the lightning cometh out of the east, and appeareth even unto the west.*" [St. Matt. xxiv. 27.] Behold the image of our lifetime! As the lightning appears for a moment, passes and disappears; so to-day we are in this world, to-morrow in eternity. And again: "*For now the axe is laid to the root of the trees. Every tree therefore that bringeth not forth good fruit, shall be cut down and cast into the fire.*" [Luke, iii. 91.]

Terrible are the parables! The foolish virgins slept, while the Bridegroom tarried, and at midnight he came; they hastened to meet him—but were rejected with those crushing words: "*I know you not!*" The servant who was surprised by the arrival of his master, was seized, bound, and thrown into the dark abyss. "*Cast the unprofitable servant out into the exterior darkness, there shall be weeping and gnashing of teeth.*" [Matt. xxv.]

Terrible are the examples! Esau sold his birthright. He wishes for it again, but it is too late; the blessing is forever lost. The dying Antiochus prayed, groaned, and sobbed; alas! miserable man, his heart was not right; he desired pardon, but obtained it not: "*This wicked man prayed to the Lord, of whom he was not to obtain mercy.*" [2 Mach. ix.]

O deluded sinner! What do all these words of thunder announce to those who delay their conversion to the last? What, after all these warnings, can those unhappy persons expect who are deaf to the voice of God during lifetime, who obstinately resist divine grace, stifle the voice that calls them to repentance, grieve the Holy Ghost within their hearts, dishonor the adorable blood of the Saviour, and harden themselves against all the stings of conscience? What can they expect, since they put off their conversion, but that their penance will never be done, or if done, will be done ill, without sincerity, without fruit, without pardon? "*You shall seek me, and you shall die in your sin.*" [St. John, viii. 21.] Woe to the sinner who will not take this to heart!

You say, perhaps, the prospect is not so gloomy as this: Did not the laborers who came even at the last hour to labor in the vineyard, receive their whole wages? That is true; but these laborers stood in the public place, and wishing and waiting for work. On the contrary, where are the sinners, who delay repentance to be found? At their gambling, their drinking, their amusements, in the midst of their disorderly sins. Are they preparing for a good death?

Or, it may be said: The penitent thief was converted in the hour of death: may we not hope for as much This was rather a miracle than an example, as St. Augustine has said: What! do you expect, sinner, such a miracle of mercy, such a miracle of conversion? Do you deserve it? True, the Good Thief was converted at death, but then he had never known the Saviour before; and besides, this is the only example of a conversion in the hour of death to be found in the Holy Scriptures. And where was he converted? By the side of the dying Jesus, sprinkled with his most holy blood! But turn, O sinner, turn your eyes to the other side; see and tremble! How did the wicked thief die? How? in despair, and yet before the very eyes of Jesus Christ. Instead of sleeping, then, in deceitful repose, tremble and live in fear all the rest of your life!

It is then true that the sinner who puts off doing penance, exposes himself to the danger of never being converted, and quieting himself with the thought of a future imaginary repentance, he casts himself into the abyss of a punishment as real as it is eternal. Consider this: repeat to yourself what the Holy Ghost is always repeating to your heart, "Delay not: begin to-day—to-morrow you will be too late!"

THE DEATH OF THE SINNER.

Now let us behold the sinner—the sinner—just as we have described him, persevering in sin, postponing his conversion from day to day, and flattering himself that he will be converted on his death bed;—now let us look at him, laid on his bed by dangerous sickness. At first he is not alarmed. He is told that it is nothing—nothing serious. Meantime the sickness increases; it is becoming serious. And then, what happens?—Physicians are called in consultation, all kinds of remedies are used, every thing brought to give relief to the body. And what becomes of the soul? There is yet time enough for that; that is not so pressing. The sick man must not be alarmed, let us wait till to-morrow; if the sickness increases, then he shall be informed. The sickness increases, and at last the physicians pronounce it mortal. Now, the members of the household look at each other; sorrow is read in every countenance; they speak in whispers; no one is willing to go to the patient; every one is afraid; no one knows how to tell it to him. O sinful love! O mistaken kindness!

At last the end of the sick man approaches, the faintness of death comes over him;—there he lies, unconscious, speechless, and insensible.—A Priest! a Confessor! they cry, in the greatest consternation. A Confessor!—He is sent for in haste; but, O wonderful justice! O frightful judgment of God! no Priest is to be found! Again he is sent for; he is expected; while the sick man dies. It is what Jesus Christ warned him of. "*You shall seek me, and shall not find me, and you shall die in your sins!*"

Perhaps a Priest is found immediately; he comes in haste, but at the moment he enters, the dying man breathes his last, and the Priest hears them cry: He is dead. Yes! "*You shall die in your sins.*"

Perhaps he finds the sick man still living: but what life is this? As to his soul's salvation, he might almost as well be dead. The drooping head is faint and giddy, his rolling eyes can see no more, his face is covered with the paleness of death, his limbs are stiffening, his breath is difficult and loud, he struggles feebly in the strong grapple of his merciless foe. The Priest speaks to him; no sign of contrition follows. What prospect of conversion is there here? He dies, and how? "*You shall die in your sins!*"

Yet we will allow to the sick man every possible advantage. Let us suppose that at the right time he is admonished of his situation, that the Confessor arrives in good time, and that the sick man is yet conscious and in possession of his faculties. Is he, with all that, in security? Come, let us place ourselves in spirit by his death-bed; let us witness a scene which outwardly, indeed, appears touching and edifying, and which, in fact, is most fearful and horrible. For, I ask you, what is usually the real state, on their death-beds, of those who have delayed their conversion? The judgments of God are terrible! I see there, for the most part, only impenitent sinners, differing in many respects one from the other, yet all equally impenitent. Slaves of sin were they in life; victims of God's vengeance are they now in death. "*You shall die in your sins.*"

O, impenitent sinner! thou who, in this last solemn hour, dost answer to every appeal with indifference, with deathlike insensibility; whom nothing touches, nothing moves any more! It is only too plainly seen, by this thy deadly distaste for all divine truths, that God has now deserted thee, that he has withdrawn himself from thy bed of death. "*You shall die in your sins.*"

O, impenitent sinner! thou, who now, on thy death-bed, regarding God only as a terrible Judge, and a merciless avenger, art casting thyself into the abyss of hopelessness and despair; thou who, at the sight of thy sins, of thy monstrous crimes, believest that for thee there is no more mercy; thou, who seest thy Lord only in the storm and lightning, thou dost condemn thyself, and dost thyself write thine eternal despair upon thine own soul. "*You shall die in your sins.*"

O impenitent sinner! thou who dost cast thyself

into another abyss, by giving thyself up to a rash confidence; thou, who dost imagine the God who created thee to be so full of love, that he cannot damn a being created by himself; that his compassion being infinite, he will therefore easily pardon every sin; thy confidence appears to thee beautiful and Christian, but it is devilish, and presumptuous, and delivers thee over to a reprobate mind, and impresses on thy hardened heart the seal of its damnation. "*You shall die in your sins.*"

O, impenitent sinner! thou who, having stifled all faith in thy heart, and having brought it by crime to the height of unbelief and impiety, wilt not now hear of conversion, of religion, of the sacraments; shuttest thine ear and eye to every thing, and diest, to the terror and horror of all around thee; so then thou dost complete the abomination of a godless and scandalous life by a most unblest and wicked death. "*You shall die in your sins.*"

It is over. The dying man breathes his last sigh. He is no more. Already sounds the sadly mournful toll of the bell. What does it announce? One member less in a family; one man less in the world; one reprobate more in hell. "*You shall die in your sins.*"

What a death! Can one think of it without a shudder?

This is the usual death, I will not say of all, but of most sinners who have put off penance for their death-bed. These are the dispositions of those hearts which they have hardened; this is the blow which then the terrible hand of God deals down upon them. A life of sin; a death accursed. A lifetime of guilt and presumption; an eternity of torment and despair. "*You shall die in your sins.*"

THE JUDGMENTS OF GOD.

Baltassar, the godless Baltassar, sat drinking at his licentious banquet, surrounded by his courtiers. Sunk, as it were, in sensuality and drunkenness, he blasphemed the Lord, abused the mercy of God, and even went so far as to profane the consecrated vessels of the temple. He considered this day as a day of joy and revelry. Unhappy man! it is thy judgment day! Suddenly, an awful hand was seen, writing on the wall these words: "*Mane: Thecel: Phares:*" I have numbered, I have weighed, I have divided! I have numbered thy days, they are ended: I have weighed thy deeds, they condemn thee: I have divided thy kingdom, and deliver thee to thine enemies. This was the verdict given, and the judgment pronounced against him. On the same night it was fulfilled; he who had lived a profligate, died a reprobate.

Let us fear the impenetrable judgments of God; let us think of them day and night, that we may always be prepared for them; let us tremble before the powerful arm of God, and never forget that even as God is a God of mercy, so also is he a God of justice.

St. Jerome was one of the greatest penitents in the Church of God. Disgusted by the tumult and grandeur of Rome, he retired into Palestine, and buried himself, so to say, in solitude. The austerity of his life and of his penance are not to be described nor the mortifications, discipline, and holy severity which he inflicted upon himself. He beat his breast with a stone, so that his body was always wounded and bathed in blood. With all this, he kept continually before his mind, in fear and trembling, the severity of the judgment of God. Absorbed in profound meditation on this thought, "Alas!" he exclaimed with a shudder, "I think I hear at every moment the dreadful trumpet, which will one day call us to judgment. Day and night it is sounding in my ears, and my troubled soul can find no rest, reflecting always upon the majesty of that God who is one day to judge it." Thus he passed his life in fear, and in the expectation of judgment. Happy was he, to anticipate that fearful trial by his constant and severe penance.

Let us also learn to reflect upon the judgment of God, for we must one day appear before it. Let us learn to fear it, for it will decide our fate for eternity. Let us learn to prepare for it, for our happiness or misery depends upon this preparation. Let us judge ourselves severely, that God may judge us in his mercy. Let us rise above the vain judgment of men, for this it is which turns us aside from the law of God. Finally, let us ask of God that he will be gracious to us on this dreadful day of retribution.

THE TIME OF GRACE.

How solemnly beautiful and interesting is that scene related in the Gospel, where Jesus, seeing before him the city of Jerusalem, began to weep over its fate. (St. Luke, xix.) Alas! said he, unhappy city, if thou also hadst known my purpose, full of compassion and mercy towards thee, what graces would have been thine! Thy enemies would have feared thee, thy inhabitants would have tasted the sweets of peace, in honor and glory thou wouldst have continued. Unthankful and guilty city! how often would I have gathered together thy children, as the hen gathereth her chickens under her wings, and thou hast not followed my tender call—and thou wouldst not. Behold, for the punishment of this thy infidelity, great distress shall come upon thee, thy enemies shall compass thee round; they shall lay waste thy fields, overthrow thy walls, slay thy children, and they shall not leave in thee one stone upon a stone! And therefore shall all this misery come upon thee, because thou hast not known the time of my visitation, because thou hast neglected the time of grace, because thou hast not responded to my invitations of mercy. All these prophecies were fulfilled: the ruin, the desolation of Jerusalem, and the long-continued miseries of the unbelieving Jews even in our day, fill the world with astonishment.

Of how many souls this guilty and unhappy City is an image! How many, by their obstinate resistance to grace, draw down upon themselves a sorrow which is all the greater, because it endures forever! Reflect upon it well! Grace urges you now: be true to it! Nothing is so terrible as the abuse of grace.

THE SUFFERINGS OF THIS LIFE.

It is related that when St. Peter was leaving Rome in the time of persecution, he met our Lord Jesus Christ, who was carrying a heavy cross upon his shoulders. St. Peter asked his Lord whither he was going in that sad condition, and our Lord answered him: I am going to Rome to deliver myself up to be crucified for you, because you refuse to suffer for me. St. Peter, ashamed of his weakness, and penetrated by a lively sorrow, returned to Rome, where, with great courage and joy, he suffered martyrdom for the name and honor of his Divine Master.

We have imitated St. Peter in his weakness; when shall we imitate him in his generosity? Alas, how often might our Lord Jesus Christ say to us: I am going to give myself up again to death for you, because you refuse to bear my cross! We would like to have nothing to suffer; we complain and murmur at the least trouble. Only the sound of the word "sufferings," nay, even the thought of it, makes us tremble. Is this to be a Christian, is this to be a disciple of a God who died for us on the cross? O suffering Saviour, teach us to suffer! help us to suffer! sanctify us through our sufferings, united with thine, and receiving all their merit from thine! Let us then be a little more considerate, and instead of bewailing our sufferings, let us praise God who gives us the means to atone for our sins.

A soul that cannot suffer cannot love. True love only shows itself in suffering. Jesus Christ has planted the cross in order to show us the way to heaven; He holds it before the soul to guide her there.

Many Saints would have been lost without suffering, and many lost souls would have been great saints through suffering. It is better to weep than to sin. Weep now with the penitent, that by and by you may rejoice with the elect.

THE LOVE OF OUR ENEMIES.

The brother of St. John Gualbert was assassinated. The murderer one day met John Gualbert unarmed; John was armed, and in a place where he could not possibly avoid him. When the murderer saw that there was no escape, he fell on his knees, and stretching out his arms in the form of a cross, implored his enemy, in the name of Jesus who had died on the cross, that he would spare his life. Gualbert, moved by these words, forgave and embraced him, and then went into a neighboring church to pray before a crucifix. From this moment he laid aside his armor, renounced the world, and retired to a cloister. Afterwards he became the founder of the order of Vallombrosa.

What an example, and what a disposition! Examine yourself and see if your dispositions are as Christian. Do you sincerely and from the heart forgive your enemies? Do you love your neighbor as yourself? Do you behold Jesus Christ in him? Reflect on this, and judge yourself in the presence of God.

Christians, children of one Father, let us love one another! Let us love each other in God and for God. Let us love each other sincerely, firmly, faithfully

Let us love one another in this world, that in the other we may be united forever!

WARNING TO PARENTS.

The High Priest Heli had two sons, who by their sinful lives, their injustice and profligacy, profaned the holy priesthood, and were the objects of complaint and scandal to all Israel.

Innumerable complaints were made to their father, but too great weakness and a sinful indulgence took from him the courage and strength to restrain them. At length, full of anger, God sent his servant Samuel, who announced to the unfaithful father that so dreadful a misfortune was about to fall upon him, that every one who heard it would be filled with horror. And so it happened; the moment for the divine punishment came. When the war broke out between the Israelites and Philistines, a battle took place in which twenty thousand Israelites were slain—left dead upon the field, the ark of the covenant fell into the hands of the enemy, and both the sons of the High Priest, Ophni and Phinees, were found on the battle-field swimming in their blood.

Trembling, the messengers brought this news to Heli, their unhappy father, and when he heard it he fell backward so suddenly, that his neck was broken and he died instantly. Thus in one day the punishment fell upon this wretched family, a terrible retribution upon the sinful weakness of the father and the evil conduct of his sons.

Fathers and mothers! reflect upon this, and teach your children to think of it also.

During a violent persecution which arose in Japan against the Christian religion, a Christian husband and wife were daily expecting martyrdom, and were preparing for it by fervent prayer. They had a son who was still very young, and on his account they were much troubled. As they sat together talking of him they said to each other: We hope, by the grace of God, to suffer martyrdom for our holy religion, but what then will become of our poor child? Will he have strength to endure the suffering? or, will he yield to the torture and deny his faith?

While they were talking, the child appeared to be at play, and not to take notice of what they were saying; he was heating an iron red hot in the fire by which they sat, and when it was entirely red, he drew it out and laid it with heroic courage upon his hand. The terrified parents asked him what he was doing, and why he did it? "I am doing it," calmly answered the child, "to show you that I have courage to suffer martyrdom, rather than to give up my faith." The parents were astonished—they tenderly embraced their child, burst into tears, and thanked God who had given him to them. All three were so happy as to receive the crown of martyrdom.

O! blessed results of that good education which these parents had given to that child of benediction. Happy parents! happy child! O, what will be the recompense of both in heaven!

Sentiments of Christian piety are sometimes as deep and lively in countries newly converted to the faith, as they were in the first Christians. In a distant and newly discovered country, lived a worthy Christian family. The father and mother led the life of saints; their sole occupation was the care of their salvation, and the duties of their condition. They daily assembled their whole house to listen to spiritual reading. One of their children, a boy of five or six years, who had heard them read of the sufferings of our Lord Jesus Christ, was so moved by them, that, from an earnest desire to imitate Jesus and to suffer something for love of him, he walked every day barefoot upon nettles, till his feet bled. He also made himself a crown of sharp thorns, upon which he laid his head at night, in honor of the crown of thorns of Jesus Christ. When his parents discovered this, they forbade him to do so any longer, but they well knew that God had particular designs of mercy with regard to this child. And, indeed, when he grew up, he entered into the priesthood, devoted himself to the labors of a missionary in a distant country, and there, by the grace of God, accomplished wonderful things, ending his life at last in these holy occupations.

In our days, certainly, parents have rather to see to that their children are kept from evil, than to restrain their pious zeal, for it rarely happens now, that the grace of God manifests itself so wonderfully in childhood. It is true that sometimes an especial inclination for prayer, love for invisible divine things, and an irresistible desire to imitate Jesus, are still to be found in the tender soul of children; but, alas, these beautiful buds of holiness are soon destroyed by bad principles, bad example, or the cold, foolish idea, that every thing is extravagant and objectionable, which is not to be seen every day, and does not follow the ordinary fashion of the world. Therefore, dear Christian parents, if you have a child which shows an extraordinary inclination to piety, thank God for it; and at the same time see that you do nothing to interfere with these dispositions. Do not, however, on the contrary, quench the Spirit of God by flattery and caresses, and thus teach your little children to be pious hypocrites. In fine, with regard to these matters, consult pious and well-instructed priests who thoroughly understand the ways of God.

WARNING TO CHILDREN.

One of the most wicked and miserable parents that perhaps ever lived, had a son who was as bad as himself. Sunk in every kind of vice, they both plunged deeper and deeper into the abyss of destruction. The son was disobedient, wilful, passionate, and violent, even to fury. They were always disputing and quarrelling, and lived in continual strife. Each cursed the other. One day, when the father rebuked the son, and reproached him with his bad behavior, the wretched child seized his father, who was already advanced in years, and in a rage threw him on the ground, and dragged him by the hairs of his head down the stairs, that he might throw him out of the house. When he had dragged him a little way, the father raised his voice and cried: Stop! wretch! when I was of your age I never dragged my father further than this! Thus, at last, the sinful father acknowledged the justice of God, who permitted his son to treat him as he himself had treated his own father.

O how terrible are the judgments of God, but also how guilty are you, ye disobedient and unnatural children! Learn to respect your parents always, even when you see them to be wicked. I know that excesses so dreadful as what I have related are not of every day occurrence, but still I know that great disorders happen every day, not only among people of low condition, of coarse sentiments, and without education, but also among the rich and refined; not always perhaps so publicly manifest to the eyes of men, but well known to God and detestable in his sight.

O then, children, be always kind and affectionate, respectful and obedient to your parents. Try in every possible way to make them comfortable and happy, and to repay them for the many cares and anxieties they have suffered for you. This is the will of God, and he will recompense you for it. Hear what a splendid promise is attached to the commandment which he gives you! "*Honor thy father and thy mother, that thou mayest be long-lived upon the land which the Lord thy God will give thee*"

THE LOVE OF GOD.

What a beautiful example is afforded us in the sublime action of a certain woman who lived in Alexandria! She appeared one day on a public place of that great city, holding in one hand a vessel of water, and in the other a burning torch, and when she was asked what she intended to do with them? she answered With this torch I would set the heavens on fire, and with this water I would extinguish the fire of hell, that henceforth man might love his God, not for the hope of reward or the fear of punishment, but only and purely for himself and because of his adorable perfections!

What a beautiful sentiment! worthy of a great soul that perceives what God is, and how much he deserves all our love for his own sake.

It is related of the Japanese, that when the Gospel was preached to them, and when they were instructed in the beauty, greatness, and infinite goodness of God, but especially when in the great mysteries of our religion they learned all that God had done for man—when it was represented to them, how from love to us and for our salvation he became man and died;—astonished and enraptured, they exclaimed: O how great, how good, how adorable is the God of Christians! But when they heard that there was an especial law, commanding us to love God, and threatening with punishment those who love him not, then they were still more astonished, and could not recover from their surprise. How is this? said they. Does a reasonable man need to be commanded to love a God like this God, who has so loved us? Is it not then the greatest happiness to love him, and the greatest misfortune not to love him? What! are not Christians always prostrate before the altar of their God, penetrated by his goodness, inflamed with holy love to him? And when they heard that there were Christians who not only did not love God, but who offended him and blasphemed him, they exclaimed with indignation: O unjust people! O ungrateful hearts! Is it possible that Christians are capable of such a sin, and in what accursed land do these senseless and heartless men live?

Christians, only too much do we deserve these just eproaches, and these people will one day be called p as witnesses against us, and will accuse us and condemn us before God!

Let us meditate on this. The precept to love God is the first and most essential of all the commandments. Love is the fulfilling of the whole law. Weigh this well, and let us imitate in this, as far as we can, what the saints are doing in heaven, and what we too hope to do in eternity. Let us love God with our whole heart.

Perhaps we have hitherto never loved God as we were bound. O distressing thought! Let us at least devote the rest of our lifetime to the holy love of God.

HEAVEN.

When King Assuerus would reward Mordechai for the important service which he had rendered to he State, he ordered him to be clad in royal appare., nd the crown placed upon his head; and thus adorned and surrounded with all the majesty and pomp of royal dignity, he commanded him to be placed in triumph on the King's own horse. The most illustrious nobleman of the whole court was then to conduct him through every part of the imperial city, preceded by a herald, who annou.ced in a loud voice to all the people: "Thus shall he be honored, whom the King hath a mind to honor."

Suppose that, at this very moment, God were to

open our eyes, and show us one of the Elect in the full splendor of that glory which surrounds him in heaven; could we thus behold him in all the joy and rapture wherein the blessed Saints are bathed in their heavenly home, and could we hear a celestial voice proclaiming, "Behold, ye mortals, and admire, thus God honors, thus God rewards his saints in glory!" How transported would we be at such a scene! "Ambitious man!" so would that blessed Saint address us, "what are all the honors of the world compared with the honor and glory which I now enjoy? Avaricious man! What are all your fleeting possessions and treasures, compared to these infinite and indestructible treasures prepared for the elect in Heaven? Ye dissolute and sensual sinners, what are all those base pleasures that you enjoy for a moment, compared to these pure and unspeakable raptures, which delight the elect of God for all eternity?" O how such a sight as this would fill us with disgust for all the false and deceitful goods of this world! What a longing would it excite in us for the enduring and never-ending treasures of a glorious immortality!

O Christians! what we cannot see with our bodily eye, religion manifests clearly to our faith, and offers to our hopes. Let us, then, by a holy life here, make ourselves worthy of an immortal life hereafter.

Heaven is waiting for us, let us detach ourselves on earth. We have here no dwelling-place, our true home is Heaven.

Let us ponder deeply on these things, and let our only endeavor be to merit Heaven. Happy are they who have striven for this their whole life long! Where shall we go when we die! What will be our fate? Heaven or Hell?

"Beautiful Heaven, I shall never see thee!" said once a famous heretic on his death-bed. What a death! "My son! look up to Heaven," said once a mother to her son, who was suffering martyrdom (2 Mach. vii.) The Church calls upon us all to look up to Heaven! Make yourselves worthy one day to enter there, and look well to it, that your way of life be such as will bring you there.

THE DISCIPLE OF JESUS.

A widow who possessed few of the goods of this world, but was therefore all the richer in piety and zeal for the education of her children, had a daughter, ten years of age, named Dorothy. She was lively and inclined to amusement, and her mother was obliged to take great care that she should not be spoiled by her playmates; and as she had not much leisure to devote to the little girl's education, she confided her, notwithstanding her poverty, to the care of a pious matron, in order that she might be brought up and educated in a religious manner.

The little Dorothy remained two years with her mistress, and during this time made wonderful progress in piety. She treasured up all the instruction of her beloved teacher, but more deeply than all the rest was this impressed upon her heart: namely, that in all our actions we must take Jesus for our pattern.

When Dorothy returned home to her mother, she was the example and consolation of the whole house. Patient, gentle, obedient, she never complained of any thing. She said little, but always spoke at the right time; she was always contented; whatever labor was imposed upon her, or whatever contradictions she met with, always she remained in the same cheerful disposition: pure-minded and modest, she was an enemy to every kind of vanity; she was respectful towards every one spoke no evil of any one, was useful to all, and always recollected and united to God.

Such conduct shortly procured for her the esteem of the whole parish. Nevertheless envy was not idle, but soon excited enemies against her. Some of her companions, stimulated by jealousy, calumniated her, and described her as a hypocrite and false devotee. Dorothy bore all this in silence for the love of Jesus Christ, and continued to treat all who spoke ill of her in the most friendly manner. In the end, the people acknowledged Dorothy's virtue, and the slanders of her enemies rebounded upon themselves to their own confusion.

The Priest of the parish, who saw with admiration the workings of divine grace in this young maiden, and also her good influence on all with whom she associated, once said to her: "Tell me, Dorothy, in confidence, how you pass the day, and how you conduct yourself towards your companions?" and Dorothy answered: "It seems to me, Father, that I do very little in comparison with what I ought to do. I have never forgotten the instruction which my teacher gave me when I was only eleven years old. She often said to me: In all your sufferings take Jesus Christ for your model. Now, this I endeavor to do, and I do it in this way:

"When I wake and arise in the morning, I imagine the infant Jesus before me and think how on awaking he offered himself as a sacrifice to God, his Heavenly Father. When I pray, I represent to myself Jesus praying, as he prayed to his Heavenly Father, and in my heart I unite myself to his divine devotion. When I am at work, I call to mind the sweat, the labor, and the pains which Jesus Christ endured for my soul's salvation, and so far from complaining, I unite my labor joyfully and submissively with his. If I am directed to do any thing difficult and painful, I immediately remember how Jesus Christ for my love suffered death on the cross, and this makes me glad to undertake any thing required of me, however arduous it may be.

"If any one speaks ill of me, or says to me cruel and insulting things, I answer nothing; I suffer in silence, and remember how Jesus Christ silently and without a murmur endured all false accusations, calumnies, tortures, and even the most cruel outrages; I remember that Jesus was innocent; that on the contrary, I am a sinner, and deserve far more suffering than can ever be inflicted upon me.

"If I eat, I represent to myself with what sobriety and temperance my Lord Jesus Christ took nourishment, that he might labor for the glory of his Heavenly Father. If I taste any thing disagreeable, I think of the gall which Jesus Christ tasted on the cross, and make a sacrifice of my sensuality to him. If I am hungry and have nothing to satisfy my hunger, I am not discontented, for I remember that Jesus fasted forty days and forty nights, and that he endured the most cruel hunger for love of me, and in expiation of the intemperance and gluttony of men.

"When I am present at any entertainment, or mingle in any conversation, I call to mind how gentle, kind, and holy was Jesus in the midst of his Apostles. If I hear any wicked language, or observe any sinful conduct, I instantly pray God to forgive it, and remember how deeply the most holy heart of Jesus was wounded whenever he saw any offence committed against his Heavenly Father. When I think of the innumerable sins which are committed in the world, and how much God is offended upon earth, then I mourn for them, and unite my sorrow to that of Jesus Christ, when, weeping, he cried to his Heavenly Father, '*Holy Father, the world hath not known thee.*'

"When I go to make my confession, I represent to myself the tears of Jesus Christ and his bitter agony in the garden, and on the cross. When I hear the holy mass, I unite my mind and heart with that most holy intention with which Jesus Christ offered himself upon the altar, for the glory of his Heavenly Father, in atonement for our sins, and for the salvation of all men. When I sing, or hear others sing the praises of God, I rejoice in the Lord, and think of that holy song of praise which Jesus Christ sang with his Apostles, that evening when he instituted the blessed Sacrament of the Eucharist.

"When I lie down to sleep, I represent to myself the sacred sleep of Jesus, who only allowed himself to repose that he might gain fresh strength to glorify his Heavenly Father; or I remember how different is my bed from the painful cross, whereon he lay extended like an innocent lamb, and offered to God his spirit and his life; then I fall asleep, repeating to myself the words of my crucified Jesus: 'Father! Father! into thy hands I commend my spirit.'"

The curate was surprised to find so much intelligence in a poor young village girl, and said to her: "O, Dorothy, how happy are you! What great consolations do you not enjoy in your humble condition!" "It is true," said Dorothy, "I enjoy great comfort in the service of God, yet I must not conceal from you that I have also endured great sufferings and struggles. I have been obliged to use great effort to bear the jests of those who ridicule me, and to conquer my extremely violent passions. God has indeed been gracious to me, yet he has permitted me to be assailed by many and great temptations; sometimes I have been almost overwhelmed with grief, sometimes I suffer great spiritual dryness, and sometimes I find myself quite downhearted, and ready to sink with weariness."

"And what do you do then," said the priest, "to free yourself from your troubles and temptations?" "Then," answered Dorothy, sweetly, "Then I think of my Saviour on the Mount of Olives, cast-down, distressed, and sorrowful even unto death; or I represent him to myself on the cross, forsaken and without consolation, and I unite myself with him there, and repeat to myself the words which he so often repeated in the time of his desolation: '*Father, thy will be done!*'

"And in my temptations I do thus: If I feel any secret inclination to go into certain kinds of company, to evening parties, dances, or other dangerous assemblies, which sometimes happens, when other decent girls who do not avoid such dangerous occasions invite me to go with them; or if I am urged by violent temptations to commit sin, or to allow myself a little more liberty, then I imagine Jesus Christ saying to me: 'What, my daughter! wilt thou quit me, to give thyself up to the world and its joys? Wilt thou take thy heart away from me, to devote it to vanity and the infernal enemy? Are there not enough already to offend me? Wilt thou go join them also, and leave my service?' And then I instantly answer Him with my whole heart: No, my God! never, never will I leave Thee. I will remain with thee until death. Where should I go, my Lord! if I leave thee? Thou alone hast the words of Lord!—and this thought immediately gives me strength and courage."

The pastor asked her further: "Upon what subjects do you speak with your companions when you are with them?" "I speak to them of just the same things as your reverence has just been good enough to listen to. I tell them that they must take our Lord Jesus Christ for their pattern in all their actions; they must, at prayers, at table, at work, in company, and in all the sufferings of life, remember what Jesus Christ did in the same circumstances, and unite themselves with his divine intention. I tell them that I make use of this holy practice, and find the advantage of it, that nothing can be higher, nothing nobler than to imitate a God, and nothing sweeter than to serve so good a Master."

"Well, Dorothy," said the good Priest to her, "go

on, and profit by the graces which heaven bestows upon you! The Lord has certainly great and merciful designs in regard to you. May he accomplish all his holy purposes to your satisfaction and happiness." O, happy souls, who are willing and ready to imitate Jesus Christ so closely!

Of the one only Saving Faith and Church

I. There is a true Religion.

From the foundation of the world religion has always existed, with its worship, its priests, its sacrifices, and its places consecrated to God. Among all the nations of the world from the beginning, there has been found a deep veneration for a great supreme divine Being, in other words, for God; while, on the other hand, those few who have been unwilling to acknowledge any respect for religion, worship, or sacrifice, were always regarded as worthy of detestation, and therefore called godless men, that is, men without God. Men who believe in no religion stand alone in the world, separated from all their race. The voice of mankind in all ages, and in all nations, condemns them. To say, a man without religion, a man without a God, sounds as strangely as to say, a man unlike other men, a man who is not a man, a man without a soul.

But if men who believe in no religion are few, those who believe in false religions are many, and it is not wonderful that it should be so.

As men removed themselves more and more from the restraints of religion, and became addicted to vice, particularly the vice of impurity, the most holy God, by a just punishment, abandoned them to their own perverse thoughts and imaginations, as the Apostle Paul tells us: "*For, professing themselves to be wise, they became fools, and they changed the glory of the incorruptible God into the likeness of the image of a corruptible man, and of birds, and of four-footed beasts and of creeping things.*" (Rom. i. 22.) In other words, they became idolaters, inventing strange, absurd, and unnatural religions for themselves, according to the desire of their corrupt hearts.

In this way, formerly idolatry sprung up, and in like manner, all other false religions have arisen. It is only through the sins of men, and their godless pride, that so many such are found in the world. All these false religions, however, only prove the more clearly the existence of a true religion, of which they are the separated and corrupted branches, just as the green tree is found in the midst of the withered boughs which lie around it.

II. There is only one true Religion.

Now, whoever says that, in the eyes of God, all the religions of the world are good, and that men can be saved in every religion, neither knows what God nor what religion is. There is only one true God, and consequently there is also one only true religion; for what is religion but the true way to serve and worship God? Two men, who contradict each other respecting one and the same thing, cannot both be right, neither can two contradictory religions both be true. All the various religions in the world contradict each other in the most important things; and yet among them all only one can be true.

Besides, God is always, and in all places, forever, and for all men, the same unchangeable God, who can neither practise deceit himself, nor be deceived by any other. God cannot, therefore, ever contradict himself, nor make contrary revelations at different times and places. What he reveals to men as true in one country, or one age of the world, must be true in every country and in all ages. Moreover, God is bound always to detest and reject every error and falsehood. It cannot, therefore, at one and the same time be true that Mahomet was the great Prophet of God, as the Turkish religion teaches, and that he was a great impostor and instrument of the devil, as every Christian is bound to hold. So, also, it cannot be equally true that the Pope is the Vicar of Jesus Christ on earth, as the Catholic religion teaches, and that he is Antichrist, as they say among the Protestants, for surely the God of truth would not have some men believe one thing true, and other men exactly the opposite.

Again, God is supremely good and wise; consequently, he cannot approve the vices and follies of men. But if God approves all religions, then he would have me live as a heathen among the heathen, like a Turk among the Turks, a Jew among Jews, a Christian among Christians. To believe this of an infinitely holy God, would be even more shocking than to believe that there is no God, because nothing can dishonor him so much as to impute to him a false and wicked spirit.

III. This one only true Religion, is the Religion of Jesus Christ.

In the first place, nothing can be more clear than that the true religion must be one revealed to us from Heaven. Eternal truth is known only to God, and to those to whom he chooses to reveal it, for as holy Scripture expresses it: "*God dwells in inaccessible light.*" (1 Tim. vi. 16.) No one, therefore, can be to us the Way, the Truth, and the Life, but God alone. For this reason it was that God spoke to men formerly by the Patriarchs and Prophets, and when the greater part had wandered away from that early light, in later times, he spoke to the world once more, teaching it again more clearly and more abundantly by his own Son Jesus Christ, whom, therefore, St. John calls so truly and significantly the Word of God.

Let us now examine for a moment the origin and

history of the Christian religion, and see if any room is left to doubt that it is the true faith, which comes from heaven and rests upon the authority of God.

Nearly 2,000 years ago, in the time of the Roman Emperor Tiberias Cæsar, and while Herod Antipas was reigning as the tributary king of the Jews, there appeared in that land which we now call Palestine, on the eastern borders of the Mediterranean Sea, an extraordinary person, whom the world has ever since known, and whom Christians adore by the name of Jesus Christ. The truth of his existence cannot be doubted, for we not only have his life and doctrines written out in full by his own friends and followers, but the great historians of those early days, both heathen and Christian, make frequent mention of him, and of the bitter persecutions raised against his disciples. After a struggle of 300 years, the religion of Jesus became dominant, and is found mingled ever since with all the important events of the civilized world. That he really lived, and is the founder of the Christian religion, none, therefore, but a madman can dispute. But what was his doctrine, and how did he establish its truth?

The account which this great Teacher gave of himself was startling and wonderful. While he acknowledged himself to have come into the world like other men, being born of a woman, he claimed to have for his Father no other than the eternal God himself. He declared himself to be older than Abraham, who had lived more than 2,000 years before, and that he had come from heaven, where he was reigning in glory with God his Father, before ever the world was created. (St. John, viii. 58; xvii. 5.) But the reason he gave for his coming into this world of ours was equally wonderful, and such as to melt the hardest heart to tears of tenderness. He came to suffer and die for sinners, that by the shedding of his innocent blood he might redeem and save all those who would believe in him, and keep his commandments.

But on what proofs did this extraordinary Preacher found his claim to be believed? How should men know that he was really, as he said, the Son of God, sent into the world to teach and to save mankind? He might easily appeal to the wisdom and holiness of his doctrine, which could only come from heaven; he might allege the voices of so many Prophets who had long before foretold his coming in the clearest terms: but he had arguments still more direct and convincing than these. He appealed confidently to the miracles which he wrought before the very eyes of his hearers. Go and relate, said he, what you have heard and seen: *the blind see, the lame walk, the lepers are cleansed, the deaf hear, and the dead rise again.* (St. Matt. xi. 4.) I do not bear witness of myself, nor do I ask the testimony of any man in my favor; these miracles which I do give testimony of me that God my Father hath sent me. By this you may know with certainty that my doctrine comes from God, if only you are willing to obey the word of God. (St. John, v.)

Such proofs were enough to convince the world. And the world has been convinced. It has believed that the doctrine of Jesus Christ is from God, that is, that Jesus Christ was himself the eternal Son of the eternal Father, and that his is the only true, holy, and saving religion. What is the history of the world since the time of Christ? Listen! On the Feast of Pentecost, the Holy Ghost, in the form of fiery tongues, descended upon the little company of Jesus' disciples. Then twelve simple and unlearned fishermen stood up before a great multitude assembled at Jerusalem, to celebrate the Feast, and preached that Jesus Christ, the crucified and despised Jesus Christ, who had been put to death as a criminal, was the Son of the living God, that he had arisen again from the dead, and was seated on a throne in heaven; that in his name alone was there any hope for the pardon of sins; that whosoever would believe and be baptized, should be saved, but that every one who refused to believe should be damned; and that, finally, a day was to come when all men, whether rich or poor, kings or beggars, should be brought before his throne to be judged. Wonderful doctrine, but what was its success?

Behold, before the doctrine of these twelve poor fishermen all the pomp and power of a heathen world fall prostrate! all kneel to adore the crucified Jesus, and that humble cross is planted in triumph throughout the world! In fact, no sooner does Peter, the Prince of the Apostles, begin to preach, than thousands throw themselves at his feet, crying, "What shall we do to be saved?" The sound of this apostolic trumpet fills the earth—the synagogues, the councils, the academies the doctors, the high priests, and the powerful rulers of the world all united together in a fury to overthrow this work of twelve poor fishermen; Peter, their chief and leader, comes at length to Rome, the most civilized of all cities, and the mistress of the world. There he preaches before Nero, the proudest of tyrants, who forbade men to listen to this stranger, under pain of death But in vain kings and people rage against Jesus, the anointed of the living God; Jesus is adored at the court of Nero: The Apostles are thrown into chains and prison; they are condemned to the most cruel tortures, and to the most dreadful sufferings; they are plunged in boiling oil; they are torn in pieces, pierced through with lances, flayed alive, but joyfully, for Jesus' sake, they suffer death in every cruel form. This even becomes an object of their most ardent desires. But behold a new wonder! Their very blood becomes the seed from which spring innumerable Christians over the whole earth! In spite of the rage of tyrants for three hundred years, the noblest and most learned men joyfully declare themselves the followers of Jesus Christ crucified, and confess, with the sacrifice of their blood, that the teaching of the twelve fishermen is true and divine. At length the time of persecution passes, and now emperors and kings, senators and pagan high priests, whole kingdoms and empires bow their heads before the crucified Jesus, and believing in the unfathomable mysteries of his religion. And such a religion! a religion which preaches a crucified God, and which commands its disciples to crucify the flesh and all its lusts; a religion that threatens with a terrible and eternal fire; a religion which names itself the only true and holy, the only saving religion; a religion which commands us to love our enemies, and requires the entire subjection of the understanding. And yet all bend their proud intellects and believe. Certainly all this can only be the work of the omnipotent God; it could not be done if Jesus were not in truth a GOD-MAN; this must be the work of the Holy Ghost, of a God in three persons. This religion must be the one true, holy, saving religion!

How blinded, then, are those proud men of our time, who venture to doubt a religion, which God has confirmed by so many prophecies and miracles, which has triumphed so wonderfully over a hostile world, which so many illustrious martyrs have sealed with their blood, which so many powerful minds have maintained, so many princes and distinguished men for so many ages have received, and which so many nations and heroes have defended with their life!

Surely, the truth of the Christian religion is clear enough! One is forced to exclaim with the royal Prophet, David, (Ps. 92): "*Thy testimonies, O God! are become exceedingly credible.*" But although the light of our holy faith shines clearer than the sun, yet that same faith remains dark for those who judge of divine things according to their low passions and carnal minds. Therefore the Holy Scriptures say

"*The sensual man perceiveth not the things that are of the spirit of God; for it is foolishness to him, and he cannot understand.*" (1 Cor. ii. 14.)

IV. The Infallible Word of God is the only True Ground of Faith.

Man, who is of the earth, can never by the sole power of his own understanding, comprehend that which is heavenly. Therefore does the holy Apostle, St. Paul, call faith a gift of God, because it is never attained through mere science or books, or by any long and deep search for it. Faith is a light, because it shows us with infallible clearness the truths which God has revealed to us. It is a supernatural light, because no one can come to the possession of faith by any mere natural effort of his own, neither by study nor reading, nor conversation with even the wisest of men, nor by disputes concerning religion. The reason of this is, because faith embraces truths which surpass the highest powers of our intellects, as far as heaven is raised above the earth, and therefore we can believe these truths on no other ground whatever, than simply because they are revealed by God himself, whose words are always true, whether we understand them or not.

Those who believe only so much of religion as they find clear and suitable to their own comprehension, and those who believe only in a printed book, or who follow the teaching of some man who pleases them best—such persons have no true saving faith—no faith pleasing to God, because they do not believe upon the only true grounds of a true faith, namely: because the eternal Truth, the infallible God himself, has spoken. But how can I know for certain what God has, and what he has not revealed?

V. The true Faith is that which St. Peter and the other Apostles taught.

I am sure that God speaks to me when I listen to those whom God has appointed for me to hear. In the first ages of the world God spoke to men through the Patriarchs, and after them through Moses and the Prophets; but when the appointed time had come, he spoke to us through his own and only begotten Son Jesus Christ, whom he appointed heir of all things, and by whom he created the world. Having sent this Son into the world, he gave him the clearest testimonials to his divine mission, once even speaking in a loud voice from a cloud of heaven, and saying: "This is my beloved Son, hear ye him." When the time came that our Lord Jesus Christ must return again to heaven, he left in his place, as teachers of the true faith, St. Peter and the other Apostles, who had been his most intimate friends and disciples. And this is the divine commission which he gave them: "*I will not leave you orphans,*" he said, "*I will send you a comforter, the Holy Ghost, and he will teach you all things. Go, therefore, and teach all nations, and baptize them in the name of the Father, and of the Son, and of the Holy Ghost. Teach them to observe every thing which I have commanded you.*" And that they might not be discouraged, he promised that he himself would always assist them, so that their doctrine should prevail and never be lost until the end of time. "*Behold, I am with you all days, even unto the consummation of the world.*" He gave them also very great power and authority, and threatened to punish in hell all those who would not believe their doctrine and follow it, saying: "*He that believeth and is baptized shall be saved, but he that believeth not shall be condemned. Receive the Holy Ghost; whose sins you shall forgive they are forgiven, and whose sins you shall retain, they are retained. He that heareth you heareth me; he that despiseth you despiseth me. As the Father hath sent me, so I send you.*" And to Peter in particular, he said: "*Thou art Peter* (that is, a rock), *and upon this rock will I build my church, and the gates of hell shall not prevail against it; and I will give to thee the keys of the kingdom of heaven, and whatsoever thou shalt bind upon earth, shall be bound also in heaven, and whatsoever thou shalt loose upon earth, it shall be loosed also in heaven; feed my lambs, feed my sheep.*" And then, again, he said to all of them: "*By this shall all men know that you are my disciples, if you love one another, as I have loved you.*" And then he prayed for them to his heavenly Father, and said: "*Sanctify them in truth. Thy word is truth; as thou hast sent me into the world, I have also sent them into the world. And not for them only do I pray, but for those also who through their word shall believe in me, that they may all be one, as thou, Father, in me, and I in thee, that they also may be one in us, that the world may believe that thou hast sent me. And the glory that thou hast given me, I have given to them, that they may be one as we also are one.*" (St. Matt. x. 40, xvi. 18; St. John, xiv. 16, xvii.; St. Mark, xvi. 15.)

How blind and wicked must that man be, who does not perceive in these clear and forcible words of Jesus Christ, that our Lord, before he left us, communicated his own power to his twelve faithful Apostles; that he conferred this power in a very marked and special manner upon St. Peter, and instituted him in his place as the Chief Pastor of all his sheep. That, furthermore, it was his will, and for this he prayed to his heavenly Father, that the same twelve Apostles should continue united to each other, in truth and love, and that all those who through them should believe in him, should continue inseparably united together under their ministry, and so form on earth a true spiritual kingdom of God, which, guided always by the Holy Ghost, should be perpetuated until the end of the world. Who does not discover, also, the infallibility of this Church in that solemn promise of Jesus Christ to remain with it himself until the end of the world, and that even the gates of hell should not prevail against it? This spiritual kingdom of Jesus Christ is called in the Holy Scriptures the Church of God, of which Jesus Christ himself says: "*Whosoever hears not the Church, let him be to thee as a heathen and a publican.*" It is this same Church which the Apostle calls "the pillar and ground of the truth."

VI. The true Faith is that which is taught by the Pope of Rome and the Catholic Bishops.

If the kingdom of Jesus Christ, which he has established by his blood, is to continue triumphant against the gates of hell, even to the end of days, then it must now, in the nineteenth century, be exactly the same kingdom as that which he established 1800 years ago. It must also now, in the nineteenth century, have true successors of the Apostles of Jesus Christ, and the true successors of St. Peter; and it must also remain now in the unity of truth and love, as unchangably beautiful and infallible, as it was when our Lord Jesus Christ established it upon the earth; else, how could these words be true: "*Behold I am with you all days, even to the consummation of the world!*"

But of all the spiritual kingdoms or Churches upon earth, there is only one that can boast of possessing the true successors of Jesus Christ, and also a true successor to St. Peter. That one is the *Roman Catholic Apostolic Church.* For, where did Peter, that "rock" of the Church, live, teach, and pour out his blood, but in Rome? Where repose the holy ashes of this prince of the Apostles of Jesus Christ, but in

Rome? Where is now to be found this rock, whereon the Church is built, this successor of St. Peter, to whom were given the keys of heaven? Nowhere but in Rome!

History, too, shows clearly how the whole body of orthodox Christians united never held any but the Bishop of Rome as the true successor of St. Peter. Yet, during the lifetime of St. John the Evangelist, St. Clement, the third successor of St. Peter in the Apostolic See at Rome, composed the differences of the Corinthian Christians, when St. John the Evangelist was still at Ephesus. These differences could, however, have been easily settled by St. John himself, who governed the Church of Asia. St. Clement, the Bishop of Rome, was therefore the man whom they acknowledged as the true successor of St. Peter, and supreme head of the whole united Christian Church.

As for the earliest successors of the Apostles in their Christian ministry, we have the clearest and most authentic proofs, that in the most important affairs of the Church they always appealed for a final decision to the Bishop of Rome, as the true successor of St. Peter. St. Polycarp, the disciple of St. John, journeyed to Rome on account of a dispute with regard to the celebration of Easter. To the same authority St. James had recourse concerning important affairs of the Church of Gaul. To the Bishop of Rome, in like manner, St. Cyprian, St. Athanasius, and St. Chrysostom addressed themselves. And who has not heard of the famous saying of St. Augustine? He says: "*Rome has spoken, the controversy is ended.*" But this is not all. The most ancient General Councils of the Church have received their sanction from Rome; one among the earliest, the third, styles Celestine I., who was the Bishop of Rome, the "Father of the General Council." Yes, all the General Councils, all the holy Fathers of the whole of orthodox Christendom agree in this, that in Rome the true successor of St. Peter has always his

Apostolic throne, and that he is endowed with just the same power to govern the Church of God as St. Peter himself.

These true successors of St. Peter have followed one another in an unbroken succession from the death of St. Peter even to the present Pope Pius IX.

Never has this true succession been interrupted never has this holy Chair of Peter perished, not even in the stormiest times and amid the most violent revolutions of empires. No! the more the spirit of the world, with all its power and cunning, the more the spirit of schism and heresy have arisen against this holy Chair of Peter, and threatened to overthrow it, only so much the more glorious and triumphant has it appeared in all ages, that all the world might clearly see how surely the Lord Jesus Christ has founded his true Church on the rock of Peter. There it has stood, and will stand immovable until the end of the world, according to the promise which he made: "*Thou art Peter, upon thee will I build my Church, and the gates of hell shall not prevail against it.*"

In the same manner as the Bishops of Rome (or Popes) are true successors of St. Peter, so are the other Catholic Bishops true successors of the other Apostles of Jesus Christ. For we read in the Holy Scripture itself, that even in the time of the Apostles, other pious men were appointed by them to the same Apostolic office. Thus they consecrated St. Paul and Barnabas to the Apostolic office, as told in the history of the Apostles, while they fasted and prayed, and laid their hands on them. St. Paul ordained St. Timothy and St. Titus to the Apostolic office by the laying on of hands; and to the Ancients of the Church at Ephesus he said: "*Take heed to yourselves and to the whole flock, wherein the Holy Ghost hath placed you Bishops, to rule the Church of God, which he hath purchased with his own blood.*"

Just as the Apostles ordained and consecrated their

successors, so did these in their turn consecrate and ordain other successors, who were named Bishops or Pastors; and in this way a true succession of Apostles has been continued and preserved until the Bishops of our own times.

Every open mind, then, which is candid and loves truth sincerely, can see where the true spiritual kingdom of Jesus Christ on earth is to be found; that kingdom which our Lord and Master established in this world. For it is there where for eighteen hundred years the true successors of St. Peter and the true successors of the holy Apostles are to be found in an uninterrupted succession, and where they have ever remained united in the same spirit of faith and charity for eighteen hundred years—that same spirit which held united the first Apostles of Jesus Christ with St. Peter in one holy and sacred society. Where, then, in our days, shall we look for this old and venerable Church of Christ? Who does not perceive at once, that all the world over, since the foundation of the spiritual kingdom of Jesus Christ, the Roman Catholic Church is that one which holds ever to the Pope or Bishop of Rome as the true successor of St. Peter, and to the other Bishops as true successors of the other holy Apostles, these Catholic Bishops continuing always united with the Pope of Rome, by the same holy bond of faith and charity which united the holy Apostles with St. Peter. Yes, this sacred bond, which holds all these Bishops in Catholic union with the Chief Bishop of them all, is the most beautiful, the surest, and brightest mark by which we may distinguish the true kingdom of Jesus Christ, his holy Church. Such was the meaning of Jesus Christ when he said to his Apostles: "*By this shall all men know that you are my disciples, if you have love for one another*" and also when he said in a particular manner to Peter: "*But I have prayed for thee that thy faith fail not; confirm thy brethren*;" and also when he prayed to his

Heavenly Father, as we have already seen, "*That they may be one, as we are one.*"

It is therefore quite evident that even a Bishop who is not united with the Pope and the other Bishops in faith and charity, is justly regarded as a heretic or a schismatic, and in fact those Bishops alone have always been considered as true successors of the Apostles, who have remained united with the true successor of St. Peter, the Pope, in faith and charity; all others have received the name of heretics and schismatics.

All the Catholic Bishops, thus united with the Pope of Rome, form through this holy union only one holy society, which is called the "Apostolic Ministry," or the "Teaching Church," (*Ecclesia Docens,*) of which our Lord Jesus Christ spoke when he said: "*If any man will not hear the Church, let him be to thee as a heathen and a publican.*" "*I am with you all days, even to the consummation of the world.*" "*He that heareth you, heareth me; he that despiseth you, despiseth me.*" It is this teaching Church of which St. Paul wrote that it is the pillar and ground of the truth, and that it is built on the foundation of the Prophets and Apostles, Jesus Christ himself being the corner-stone. This Church is consequently the only one which men ought to hear; she is infallible in her decisions and cannot deceive us, because the gates of hell can never prevail against her, and because Jesus Christ remains with her to the end of the world. Therefore that man only can be called a true Christian who listens to the infallible truth, to the pure doctrine of Jesus Christ, listens to Jesus Christ himself speaking ever through Peter and the Apostles,—who listens to the Pope of Rome and the Catholic Bishops united with him. He who thinks otherwise, or who teaches the contrary, is a heretic, because he despises the only true Apostolic ministry established by Jesus Christ himself.

VII. In what way can every Catholic become acquainted with the True Doctrines of the Apostles and of the Church.

The most simple Catholic Christian hears either his Bishop himself, or some Catholic Priest delegated by the Bishop, announce the Gospel of Jesus Christ. If he hears his Bishop preach, he listens to him as one whom he knows to be united in faith and in charity with the head of the Church, the Pope of Rome, and through him with all the other Catholic Bishops. He is certain, therefore, that what he hears from his Bishop are not the words and thoughts of a mere man, but the teaching of the true and infallible Church, the very Gospel of Jesus Christ. When, again, a Catholic listens to the preaching of a Priest whom he knows to be in union with his Bishop, he is sure that he hears from his lips the doctrine of his Bishop, which is the doctrine of the Pope, and of all the Bishops in union with the Pope, and therefore the doctrine of the Church.

If a Catholic Priest should err in faith and preach errors, the Catholic Christian is sure that the Bishop is watching over his flock, and will know how to deliver them from every wolf. But should the Catholic Bishop himself err, the Catholic Christian knows that the Pope of Rome, as the true successor of St. Peter, is ever watching with all the other Catholic Bishops, and ready to oppose at once any error in any quarter. In this way, in every parish and every diocese of the Catholic Church, each Catholic Christian hears not the voice and doctrine of a fallible man, but the doctrine of the whole Church, the sure Gospel of Jesus Christ.

In matters of Christian faith, the humblest Catholic is therefore as certain and confident as the wisest and most learned. He believes upon the authority of the same teacher, the Church, he relies upon the infallible word of God, that same living voice of the Apostolical Ministry, which for eighteen hundred years, in all places, in all parts, in all tongues and among all nations, has been sounding loudly through out the world, and still sounds in every city, village, or hamlet, where a Catholic Bishop or Priest can be found.

VIII. THINGS WHICH A TRUE CATHOLIC CHRISTIAN WILL NEVER BELIEVE.

1. No sound Catholic, however simple he may be, is simple enough to believe in what is called an "*invisible Church.*" He understands that this is only an idea of the imagination, invented and cherished by some who call themselves the elect of God, and say they are enlightened by the holy Ghost, but who in fact follow no guiding but their own, and will not submit to any authority, but that of the invisible Church which each one keeps and carries about in his own head.

2. The simple Catholic Christian never rests his faith upon *any book*, even if it were the most learned possible, because he knows that it is the fallible word of man. If he believes the Bible, he believes it only because this is a holy, a divine book, dictated by the holy Ghost, and because he is assured by the living and infallible Church that this book is really the Word of God. The Catholic Christian, moreover only receives that Bible from the hands of a Bishop or Priest of the Catholic Church, because he knows that they are united in faith and charity with the Pope of Rome and the other Catholic Bishops. H trusts no other, even if it has a Catholic title and i beautifully printed, for he knows only too well, that not every thing is true because it is printed or because many others think it so, and that even the Bible may be altered and corrupted by the wicked. What however he knows to be the true uncorrupted

Bible, the true written word of God,—this the good Catholic Christian esteems and reverences with his whole heart, although he does not trust himself to explain and interpret what he reads in it, and imagine that he can understand it by himself. He knows only too well, that what is contained in the Holy Bible is no word of man, but the word of the living God himself, and that for this reason no man has the right to interpret and explain the Holy Bible in his own way, according to his own mind, since Jesus Christ speaks to the Catholic Church by her Bishops and their associates, the Catholic Priests. It was to them alone he said, "*Go, teach all nations.*"

3. For the same reason the true Catholic does not trust to his *own reason*, and judgment in matters of faith, however learned he may be; he does not rely upon his own views, or his own talents, be they ever so brilliant. He is equally unwilling to put confidence in any teacher who is not sent by the one true Church of God; neither does he allow himself to be led away by those men who pass for something among the weak-minded, because they talk louder than others, know how to make a show of argument or of wit, and in this way try to throw ridicule upon holy things. No, the true Catholic Christian is perfectly confident that he has the only true faith of the living God, and therefore avoids the company of the godless, and despises their wisdom, which in the eye of God is folly.

The true Catholic Christian then does not trust to the vain words of men, nor to false teachers, nor his own understanding, nor to a mere book, nor to the so-called *inner light*, but he believes in the Holy Ghost alone, who dwells in the Catholic Church of Christ, and speaks to him through her Pope, and Bishops, and Priests.

This is the true foundation of Christian faith, and it is possessed alone by the Catholic, who is able to show a true, firm ground for his faith; hence no faith is wiser or more reasonable than the faith of a Catholic Christian. And whoever lays any other foundation, and builds not thus upon the Apostles, upon the true corner-stone, Jesus Christ, has a false faith and a false doctrine which Jesus Christ never taught, and which the Apostles never preached. He is heretical and blind, sitting in the shadow of death and shut out from the kingdom of Jesus Christ; for the truth alone can save, but error leads to destruction.

IX. THE CATHOLIC FAITH IS THE ONLY SAVING FAITH.

Jesus Christ alone is the Way, the Truth, and the Life; and St. Peter teaches that it is only in him that we can find salvation. Jesus Christ himself threatens with eternal damnation those who will not believe his Church; for just before his ascension into heaven, he says to the Apostles: "*Go ye into the whole world, and preach the gospel to every creature. He that believeth, and is baptized, shall be saved; but he that believeth not shall be condemned.*" He who does not believe the Apostles, does not believe Jesus Christ; he makes Jesus Christ a liar; he divides Jesus Christ, since he does not believe his whole doctrine, nor believe the word of his Apostles, and their true successors, nor believe in the true Church of Jesus Christ. Hence he is a real enemy of Jesus Christ, and, according to the declaration of St. John the Evangelist, a true Anti-christ, who has no part in eternal life, and is already judged, because he does not truly believe in Jesus Christ, the Son of the living God, although announced to him by his true heralds. As the holy Catholic faith is the only true faith, so it is also the only saving faith. Wherefore the great St. Cyprian says: "They (heretics and schismatics) may burn in fire and flames for their religion, they may be thrown to the wild beasts, they may be slain, but they will not be crowned. The holy Church is the body of Christ; he who is cut off from the body, has no longer any life. He cannot have God for his Father, who has not the Church for a mother."—(St. Cyp., Unity of the Church.)

X. Refutation of certain Errors of our Time.

It must appear clear and plain to any one who has read what we have already said, carefully, with a honest mind and without prejudice, how false, godless and ruinous are those principles of liberty and liberal ity (so called) of our time, widely diffused as they are, even among the most simple and uneducated class of men.

How foolish and wicked it is for one to say: "If I only act according to my conscience, it is no matter whether I am a Christian or a Turk, a Catholic or a Protestant." How foolish and wicked it is for one to say: "I can be a good man in any religion, and be saved too in any religion." "Every one must be left to believe what he likes." How foolish and wicked is it for one to complain, and to say: "If there is only one faith which can save us, then most men must be damned." What will they prove by this? Does the Church teach that any one will be damned who is innocent? How false and godless is it for a man to say: "Every one should remain in the faith in which he was born. I don't like to see one change his religion."

O the godlessness and blindness of our time, which, corrupted by Satan, the father of lies, is bold enough to utter such blasphemies! Is it not making the Apostles of Jesus Christ, and even Jesus Christ himself, a liar to say that all religions are the same, and that one ca save us as well as another, when the Apostles of Jesu Christ received the command from their Lord himself to preach to all nations the one Christian faith, and when these holy Apostles dispersed themselves throughout all parts of the world, in order to unite all nations, Jews and Heathens, in one holy faith, namely, the faith of Jesus the crucified? Wherefore did the holy Apostles, wherefore did the millions of Martyrs pour out their precious blood, if it were all one and the same thing what a man's faith is? Were the Apostles deceived, when they changed from Jews to Christians; were they still more wrong when they preached to other Jews and to the Heathen to change their faith for the one faith of Jesus crucified,—when they themselves avoided and directed others to avoid all fellowship with heretics,—and when even they threatened the Jews and Heathens with eternal fire, if they did not quit the faith in which they were born, and embrace the faith of Jesus Christ?

The Apostles of Jesus Christ were deeply penetrated by the truth that there was only one saving faith. Were they wrong?

XI. Exhortation to Perseverance in the Catholic Faith.

Dear Christian Brethren, do not be deceived by all the fine discourses of these false sages of our days, whose words are soft and full of honey, but poisonous and fatal to the heart which receives them. "*Try these spirits*," so I say to you with the Apostle St. John, "*try these spirits whether they be of God, for many false prophets are gone out into the world.*" Hold fast to that Church which is visible, one, holy, Apostolical, Catholic, and Roman. You are persuaded now, that she is the only true, the only saving Church, which can never lead you astray, because the Holy Ghost rules it, and together with Jesus Christ remains with it, even unto the consummation of the world. Be firm, be constant, and, as Jesus your Master warns you in the Apocalypse: "*Hold fast that thou hast, that no man take thy crown.*"

Yes, O my Lord, I hear thy voice, and I promise to remain until my last breath a faithful child of thy true and spotless Bride, The Holy, Roman Catholic Church. Amen!

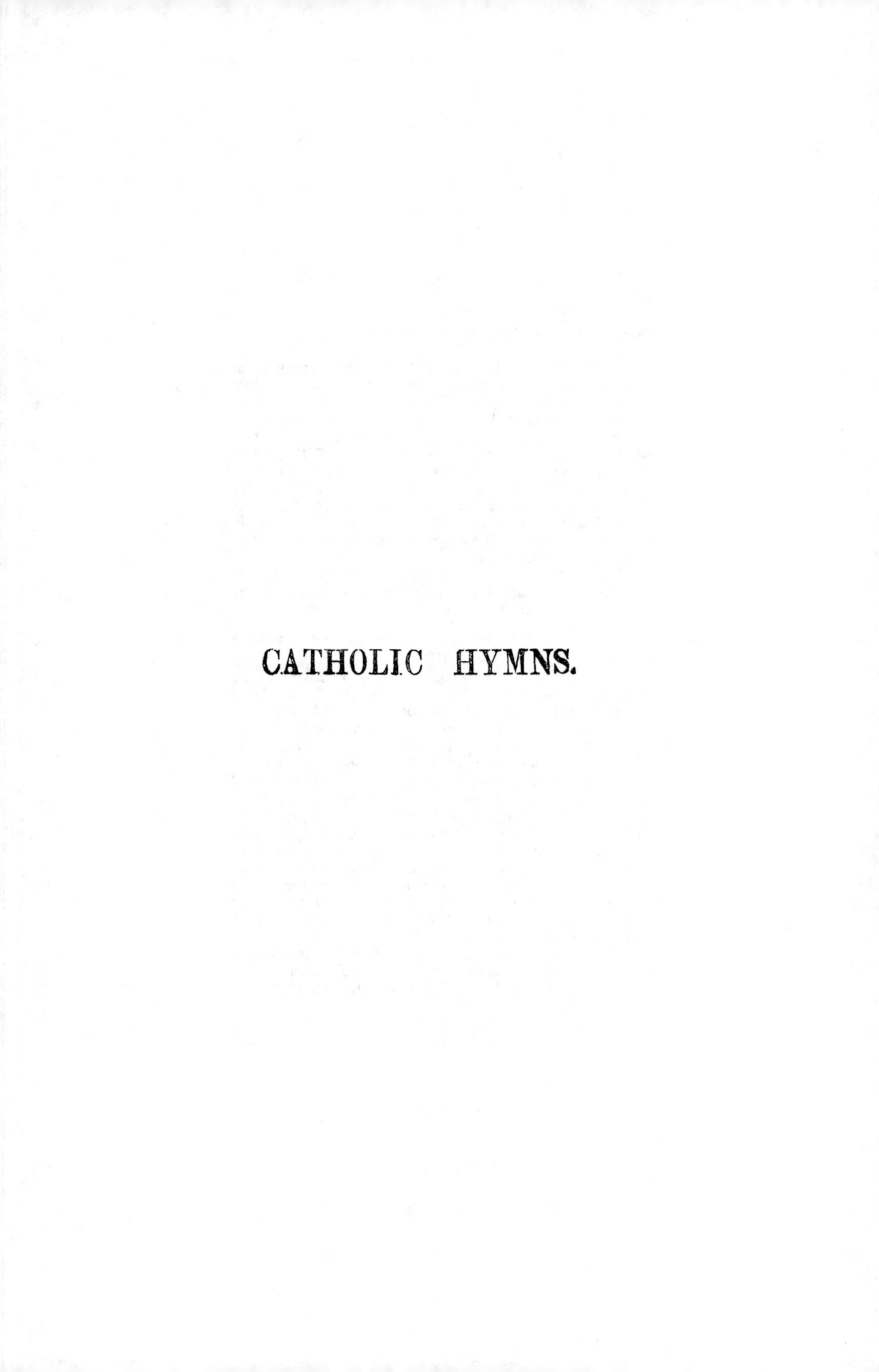

CATHOLIC HYMNS.

CATHOLIC HYMNS.

VENI CREATOR SPIRITUS.

SPIRIT, Creator of mankind,
Come visit ev'ry pious mind,
And sweetly let thy grace invade
Our hearts, O Lord! which thou hast made.

Thou art the Comforter, whom all,
Gift of the highest God, must call;
The living fountain, fire and love;
The ghostly unction from above;

God's sacred finger, which imparts
A seven-fold grace to faithful hearts;
Thou art the Father's promise, whence
We language have, and eloquence.

Enlighten, Lord, our souls, and grant
That we thy love may never want;
Let not our virtue ever fail.
But strengthen what in flesh is frail.

Chase from our minds the infernal foe,
And peace, the fruit of love, bestow;
And lest our feet should step astray,
Protect and guide us in the way.

Make us eternal truths receive,
And practise all that we believe:
Give us thyself, that we may see
The Father and the Son in thee.

Immortal honor, endless fame,
Attend th' Almighty Father's name:
To the Son equal praises be,
And, holy Paraclete, to thee. *Amen.*

MORNING HYMN.

Now with the rising golden dawn,
  Let us, the children of the day,
Cast off the darkness which so long
  Has led our guilty souls astray.

O, may the morn, so pure, so clear,
  Its own sweet calm in us instill;
A guileless mind, a heart sincere,
  Simplicity of word and will:

And ever, as the day glides by,
  May we the busy senses rein,
Keep guard upon the hand and eye
  Nor let the body suffer stain.

For all day long, on Heaven's high tower
  There stands a Sentinel, who spies
Our every action, hour by hour,
  From early dawn till daylight dies.

To God the Father glory be,
  And to his sole-begotten Son;
The same, O Holy Ghost! to Thee
  While everlasting ages run.

EVENING HYMN.

Now with the fast-departing light,
  Maker of all! we ask of Thee,
Of thy great mercy, through the night
  Our guardian and defence to be.

Far off let idle visions fly;
  No phantom of the night molest:
Curb thou our raging enemy,
  That we in chaste repose may rest.

Father of mercies! hear our cry;
  Hear us, O sole-begotten Son!
Who, with the Holy Ghost most high,
  Reignest while endless ages run.

JUDGMENT HYMN.

Lo! He comes with clouds descending
  Once for favor'd sinners slain:
Thousand—thousand saints attending,
  Swell the triumph of his train:
  Alleluia! Alleluia!
  Jesus Christ shall ever reign!

See the universe in motion,
  Sinking on her funeral pyre—
Earth dissolving, and the ocean
  Vanishing in final fire:—
  Hark, the trumpet! Hark, the trumpet
  Loud proclaims the Day of Ire!

Graves have yawn'd in countless numbers—
  From the dust the dead arise:
Millions, out of silent slumbers,

Wake in overwhelm'd surprise;
Where creation,—Where creation,
Wreck'd and torn in ruin lies!

See the Judge our nature wearing,
Pure, ineffable, divine:
See the great Archangel bearing
High in heaven the mystic sign:
Cross of Glory! Cross of Glory!
Christ be in that moment mine!

See Redemption,* long expected,
In transcendent pomp appear,—
All his saints, by man rejected,
Throng in gathering legions near:
Melt, ye mountains! Melt, ye mountains!
Into smoke,—for God is here!

Every eye shall then behold Him
Robed in awful majesty:—
Those that set at naught, and sold Him,
Pierced and nail'd Him to a tree,—
Deeply wailing,—Deeply wailing,
Shall the true Messiah see!

Lo! the last long separation!
As the cleaving clouds divide;
And one dread adjudication
Sends each soul to either side!
Lord of mercy! Lord of mercy!
How shall I that day abide!

Oh! may thine own Bride and Spirit
Then avert a dreadful doom,—
And me summon to inherit
An eternal blissful home:—
Ah! come quickly! Ah! come quickly!
Let thy second Advent come!

* Romans, viii. 23.

HYMN OF THE PASSION.

Yea, Amen! Let all adore Thee
 On thine amaranthine throne!
Saviour,—take the power and glory,
 Claim the kingdom for thine own!
 Men and angels,—Men and angels,
 Kneel and bow to Thee alone!

HYMN OF THE PASSION.

O'ERWHELM'D in depths of woe,
 Upon the Tree of Scorn
Hangs the Redeemer of mankind,
 With racking anguish torn.

See! how the nails those hands
 And feet so tender rend;
See! down his face, and neck, and breast,
 His sacred Blood descend.

Hark! with what awful cry
 His Spirit takes its flight,
That cry, it pierced his Mother's heart,
 And whelm'd her soul in night.

Earth hears, and to its base
 Rocks wildly to and fro;
Tombs burst; seas, rivers, mountains quake
 The veil is rent in two.

The sun withdraws his light;
 The midday heavens grow pale;
The moon, the stars, the universe,
 Their Maker's death bewail.

Shall man alone be mute?
 Come, youth! and hoary hairs!
Come, rich and poor! come, all mankind!
 And bathe these feet in tears.

Come! fall before His Cross,
  Who shed for us his blood;
Who died the victim of pure love,
  To make us sons of God.

Jesu! all praise to Thee,
  Our joy and endless rest!
Be Thou our guide while pilgrims here,
  Our crown amid the blest.

JESUS CRUCIFIED.

O come and mourn with me awhile;
  See, Mary calls us to her side;
O come and let us mourn with her,—
  Jesus, our Love, is crucified!

Have we no tears to shed for Him,
  While soldiers scoff and Jews deride?
Ah! look how patiently he hangs,—
  Jesus, our Love, is crucified!

How fast his Hands and Feet are nail'd;
  His blessed Tongue with thirst is tied,
His failing Eyes are blind with blood,—
  Jesus, our Love, is crucified!

His Mother cannot reach his Face:
  She stands in helplessness beside;
Her heart was martyr'd with her Son's,—
  Jesus, our Love, is crucified!

Seven times He spoke, seven words of love,
  And all three hours his silence cried
For mercy on the souls of men;—
  Jesus, our Love, is crucified!

What was thy crime, my dearest Lord?
By earth, by heaven, Thou hast been tried,
And guilty found of too much love;—
Jesus, our Love, is crucified!

Found guilty of excess of love,
It was thine own sweet will that tied
Thee tighter far than helpless nails;—
Jesus, our Love, is crucified!

Death came, and Jesus meekly bow'd;
His falling eyes he strove to guide
With mindful love to Mary's face;—
Jesus, our Love, is crucified!

O break, O break, hard heart of mine!
Thy weak self-love and guilty pride
His Pilate and His Judas were;—
Jesus, our Love, is crucified!

Come, take thy stand beneath the Cross,
And let the blood from out that Side
Fall gently on thee drop by drop;—
Jesus, our Love, is crucified!

A broken heart, a fount of tears,—
Ask, and they will not be denied;
A broken heart love's cradle is;—
Jesus, our Love, is crucified!

O Love of God! O Sin of Man!
In this dread act your strength is tried
And victory remains with love,
For He, our Love, is crucified!

ROCK OF AGES.

Rock of ages, rent for me,
Let me hide myself in Thee;
Let the water and the blood,
From thy riven side which flow'd
Be of sin the double cure;
Cleanse me from its guilt and power.

Nothing in my hand I bring,
Simply to the Cross I cling;
Naked come to Thee for dress,
Helpless look to Thee for grace,
Foul I to the fountain fly;
Wash me, Saviour, or I die.

While I draw this fleeting breath,
When my eyelids fold in death,
When I soar to worlds unknown,
See Thee on thy judgment-throne;
Rocks of Ages, cleft for me,
Let me hide myself in Thee.

JESUS, I MY CROSS HAVE TAKEN.

Jesus,—I my cross have taken,
All to leave and follow Thee;
I am poor, despised, forsaken,—
Thou henceforth my all shall be:
Perish every fond ambition,—
All I've sought, or hoped, or known;
Yet how rich is my condition,—
God and heaven may be mine own!

Let the world despise and leave me,
It has left my Saviour too;

Human hearts and looks deceive me,
Thou art not like them untrue;
Whilst thy graces shall adorn me,
God of wisdom, love, and might,—
Foes may hate, and friends may scorn me;—
Show thy face, and all is bright.

Go then, earthly fame and treasure,
Come disaster, scorn, and pain;
In thy service, pain is pleasure,—
With thy favor, loss is gain.
I have called Thee: Abba! Father!
I have set my heart on Thee:
Storms may howl, and clouds may gather,
All will work for good to me.

Man may trouble and distress me,
'Twill but drive me to thy breast,
Life with trials hard may press me;
Heaven will bring me sweeter rest.
Oh,'tis not in grief to harm me,
While thy love is left to me;—
Oh, 'twere not in joy to charm me,
Were that joy unmix'd with thee

Soul,—then know thy full salvation,
Rise o'er sin, and fear, and care:
Joy to find in every station,
Something still to do or bear.
Think what spirit dwells within thee,
Think what sacraments are thine;
Think that Jesus died to win thee:
Child of heaven, canst thou repine!

Haste thee on from grace to glory,
Arm'd with faith, and wing'd with prayer,—
An eternal day before thee
Waits for God to guide thee there.

Soon shall close thine earthly mission,
Patience shall thy spirit raise;
Hope shall change to glad fruition,
Faith to sight, and prayer to praise!

VIVA GESU.

Hail, Jesus! Hail! who for my sake
Sweet Blood from Mary's womb didst take,
And shed it all for me;
O blessed be my Saviour's Blood,
My life, my light, my only good,
To all eternity.

To endless ages let us praise
The Precious Blood whose price could raise
The world from wrath and sin;
Whose streams our inward thirst appease,
And heal the sinner's worst disease,
If he but bathe therein.

O sweetest Blood, that can implore
Pardon of God, and heaven restore,
The heaven which sin had lost:
While Abel's blood for vengeance pleads,
What Jesus sheds still intercedes
For those who wrong Him most.

O to be sprinkled from the wells
Of Christ's own sacred Blood, excels
Earth's best and highest bliss:
The ministers of wrath divine
Hurt not the happy hearts that shine
With those red drops of His!

Ah! there is joy amid the Saints,
And hell's despairing courage faints
When this sweet song we raise:
O louder then, and louder still,
Earth with one mighty chorus fill,
The Precious Blood to praise!

JESU DULCIS MEMORIA.

Jesus! the only thought of Thee
With sweetness fills my breast;
But sweeter far thy face to see,
And in thy presence rest.

No voice can sing, no heart can frame
Nor can the memory find,
A sweeter sound than thy blest name,
O Saviour of mankind!

O hope of every contrite heart,
O joy of all the meek,
To those who fall how kind thou art!
How good to those who seek!

But what to those who find? ah! this
Nor tongue nor pen can show:
The love of Jesus, what it is,
None but his loved ones know.

Jesus! our only joy be Thou,
As Thou our prize wilt be;
Jesus! be Thou our glory now,
And through eternity.

THE MEMORARE.

REMEMBER well, O Mother dear,
That none have had recourse to thee
Whose voice of prayer thou didst not hear;
O then to-day propitious be!

The chronicles of every age the tale repeat,
How every hour hath seen thy children at thy feet;
While thou hast shared their joy, or soothed their every pain,
Shall we the first of all invoke thy name in vain?
Remember well, &c.

MAGNIFICAT.

MAGNIFICAT! Inspired word,
From Mary's raptured bosom pour'd!
My soul, with Mary bless the Lord.
Magnificat!

Magnificat! O whence is this,
That God should heed my littleness?
Henceforward, all my name shall bless.
Magnificat!

Magnificat! Praise God alone,
The mercy of my Saviour own:
For He hath mighty wonders done.
Magnificat!

Magnificat! His wondrous grace
Is manifest from race to race
Of them who fear before His face.
Magnificat!

Magnificat! He hat rought down
The proud man from his lofty throne,
And lifted up the humble one.
Magnificat!

Magnificat! Grace for the Poor!
The Poor who plead at Mercy's door:
The scornful rich shall have no more.
Magnificat!

Magnificat! In me behold
Fulfill'd, the promises of old
To Abraham and the Fathers told.
Magnificat!

Magnificat! The Song of praise
To Father, Son, and Spirit raise!
One God, throughout eternal days!
Magnificat!

HAIL, HEAVENLY QUEEN.

HAIL, heavenly Queen! hail, foamy ocean's star,
O be our guide, diffuse thy beams afar.
Hail, Mother of God! above all virgins blest;
Hail, happy gate of heaven's eternal rest.
Hail, foamy ocean's star! hail, heavenly Queen!
O be our guide to endless joys unseen.

Hail, full of grace!" with Gabriel we repeat—
Thee Queen of heaven, from him we learn to greet;
Then give us peace, which heaven alone can give,
And dead through Eve, through Mary let us live.
Hail, &c.

O break our chains, our captive souls release,
O give us light, and let our blindness cease·
Let every ill that presses on our heart
Fly at thy voice, and every good impart.
Hail, &c.

Thy children save, O gracious mother hear,
From moisten'd eyes, O deign to wipe the tear;
Thy prayers, for us to God, thy Son, present,
Whose life and blood, to save mankind, were spent.
Hail, &c.

O Virgin meek, unmatch'd amongst mankind,
In whom nor stain, nor blemish God did find,
From Satan's chains our captive souls set free,
Make us like thee—meek, chaste, and sinless be.
Hail, &c.

Our lives unstain'd, in purity preserve,
Nor e'er permit our ways from truth to swerve,
That, when our time has roll'd its rapid round,
We may, with Christ, in heavenly bliss be crown'd.
Hail, &c.

Eternal praise to God, the Father, be,
Eternal praise to Christ's dread majesty,
And equal praise to God the Holy Ghost,
Here, as above, amongst the heavenly host.
Hail, &c.

HYMN TO ST. JOSEPH.

Hail! holy Joseph, hail!
Husband of Mary, hail!
Chaste as the lily flower
In Eden's peaceful vale.

Hail! holy Joseph, hail!
  Father of Christ esteem'd
Father be thou to those
  Thy Foster-Son redeem'd

Hail! holy Joseph, hail!
  Prince of the house of God,
May his best graces be
  By thy sweet hands bestow'd.

Hail! holy Joseph, hail!
  Comrade of angels, hail!
Cheer thou the hearts that faint,
  And guide the steps that fail.

Hail! holy Joseph, hail!
  God's choice wast thou alone;
To thee the Word made flesh
  Was subject as a Son.

Hail! holy Joseph, hail!
  Teach us our flesh to tame,
And, Mary, keep the hearts
  That love thy husband's name.

Mother of Jesus! bless,
  And bless, ye Saints on high,
All meek and simple souls
  That to Saint Joseph cry.

THE GUARDIAN ANGEL.

DEAR Angel! ever at my side,
  How loving must thou be,
To leave thy home in Heaven to guide
  A little child like me.

Thy beautiful and shining face
I see not, though so near;
The sweetness of thy soft low voice
I am too deaf to hear.

I cannot feel thee touch my hand
With pressure light and mild,
To check me, as my mother did
When I was but a child.

But I have felt thee in my thoughts
Fighting with sin for me;
And when my heart loves God, I know
The sweetness is from thee.

And when, dear Spirit! I kneel down
Morning and night to prayer,
Something there is within my heart
Which tells me thou art there

Yes! when I pray thou prayest too—
Thy prayer is all for me:
But when I sleep, thou sleepest not,
But watchest patiently.

But most of all I feel thee near,
When, from the good priest's feet,
I go absolved, in fearless love,
Fresh toils and cares to meet.

And thou in life's last hour wilt bring
A fresh supply of grace,
And afterwards wilt let me kiss
Thy beautiful bright face.

Ah me! how lovely they must be
Whom God has glorified;

Yet one of them, O sweetest thought!
   Is ever at my side.

Then for thy sake, dear Angel! now
   More humble will I be:
But I am weak, and when I fall,
   O weary not for me:

O weary not, but love me still,
   For Mary's sake thy Queen;
She never tired of me, though I
   Her worst of sons have been.

She will reward thee with a smile,
   Thou know'st what it is worth!
For Mary's smiles each day convert
   The hardest hearts on earth.

Then love me, love me, Angel dear!
   And I will love thee more;
And help me when my soul is cast
   Upon the eternal shore.

JERUSALEM.

JERUSALEM, my happy home,
   How do I sigh for thee!
When shall my exile have an end,
   Thy joys when shall I see!
      Jerusalem, Jerusalem,
      Jerusalem, my happy home,
      How do I sigh for thee

No sun, no moon, in borrow'd light
   Revolve thine hours away;

The Lamb on Calvary's mountain slain.
Is thy eternal day.
Jerusalem, &c.

From every eye He wipes the tear
All sighs and sorrows cease,
No more alternate hope or fear,
But everlasting peace.
Jerusalem, &c.

The thought of thee to us is given
Our sorrows to beguile;
T' anticipate the bliss of heaven,
In His eternal smile.
Jerusalem, &c.

BEFORE COMMUNION.

My God, my life, my love,
To Thee, to Thee I call;
O come to me from heaven above
And be my God, my All.

My faith beholds Thee, Lord!
Conceal'd in human food;
My senses fail, but in thy word
I trust, and find my God.

O when wilt Thou be mine,
Sweet lover of my soul!
My Jesus dear, my king divine.
Come o'er my heart to rule.

O! come and fix thy throne
Within my very heart;

make it burn for Thee alone,
And from me ne'er depart.

Begone ye, from my mind,
Vain, childish, earthly toys;
In Jesus, only, do I find
True pleasures, solid joys.

AFTER COMMUNION.

What happiness can equal mine,
I've found the object of my love—
My Jesus dear—my King divine,
Is come to me from heaven above!
He chose my heart for his abode;
There He becomes my daily bread;
There on me flows his healing blood,
There, with his flesh, my soul is fed.

I am my Love's, and He is mine;
In me He dwells; in Him I live;
What greater gifts could love combine?
What greater could e'en heaven give?
O sacred banquet, heavenly feast!
O overflowing source of grace!
Where God the food, and man the guest
Meet and unite in sweet embrace!

AFTER CONFIRMATION.

Soldiers of Christ! arise!
And put your armor on,
Strong in the strength which God supplies
Through his eternal Son;

Strong is the Lord of hosts,
 And in his mighty power,
Who in the strength of Jesus trusts,
 Is more than conqueror.

Soldiers of Christ! arise!
 The God of armies calls
Unto his mansions in the skies—
 His everlasting halls;
Behold! the angel host appears
 To welcome you to bliss!
Oh! what is earth, its sighs and tears,
 Its joys, compared to this!

Crush'd is the haughty foe,
 His might, his glory gone,
But ye, with victory crown'd, shall go
 To Christ's eternal throne.
There shall the conqueror rest,
 And in that blest abode,
Forever reign amid the blest,
 Triumphant with his God.

ADESTE FIDELES.

Adeste, fideles!
 Læti triumphantes,
Venite, venite in Bethlehem,
 Natum videte
Regem angelorum.
Venite, adoremus;
Venite, adoremus Dominum.

Deum de Deo,
 Lumen de lumine,

ASCENSION-DAY.

Gestant puellæ viscera,
  Deum verum
Genitum non factum.
  Venite, &c.

Cantet nunc Io!
  Chorus angelorum,
Cantet nunc aula
  Cœlestium, Gloria
In excelsis Deo;
  Venite, &c.

Ergo, qui natus
  Die hodierna,
Jesu tibi sit gloria.
  Patris æterni
Verbum caro factum.
  Venite, &c.

ASCENSION-DAY.

Rise—glorious Conqueror, rise,
Into thy native skies,—
  Assume thy right:
And where in many a fold
The clouds are backward roll'd—
Pass through those gates of gold,
  And reign in light!

Victory o'er death and hell,
Cherubic legions swell
  The radiant train:
Praises all heaven inspire;
Each angel sweeps his lyre,
And waves his wings of fire,—
  Thou Lamb once slain

Enter, Incarnate God!—
No feet, but thine, have trod
The serpent down:
Blow the full trumpets, blow
Wider your portals throw!
Saviour—triumphant—go,
And take thy crown!

Lion of Judah—Hail!—
And let thy name prevail
From age to age:
Lord of the rolling years,—
Claim for thine own the spheres
For Thou has bought with tears
Thy heritage!

Yet—who are these behind,
In numbers more than mind
Can count or say—
Clothed in mortal stoles,
Illumining the Poles—
A galaxy of souls,
In white array?

And then was heard afar
Star answering to star—
Lo! these have come,
Followers of Him, who gave
His life, their lives to save;
And now their palms they wave
Brought safely home.

O Lord! ascend thy throne
For Thou shalt rule alone
Beside thy Sire,

WHIT-SUNDAY.

With the great Paraclete,
The Three in One complete—;
Before whose awful feet
All foes expire!

WHIT-SUNDAY.

Holy Spirit! Lord of light
From thy clear celestial height,
Thy pure beaming radiance give:

Come, Thou Father of the poor!
Come, with treasures which endure!
Come, thou Light of all that live;

Thou of all consolers best,
Visiting the troubled breast,
Dost refreshing peace bestow;

Thou in toil art comfort sweet;
Pleasant coolness in the heat;
Solace in the midst of woe.

Light immortal! light divine!
Visit Thou these hearts of thine,
And our inmost being fill:

If Thou take thy grace away,
Nothing pure in man will stay:
All his good is turn'd to ill.

Heal our wounds—our strength renew;
On our dryness pour thy dew;
Wash the stains of guilt away;

Bend the stubborn heart and will;
Melt the frozen, warm the chill;
  Guide the steps that go astray.

Thou, on those who evermore
Thee confess and Thee adore,
  In thy sevenfold gifts, descend.

Give them comfort when they die;
Give them life with Thee on high:
  Give them joys which never end.

CORPUS CHRISTI.

SING, my tongue, the Saviour's glory,
  Of his Flesh the mystery sing;
Of the Blood, all price exceeding,
  Shed by our immortal King,
Destined, for the world's redemption,
  From a noble womb to spring.

Of a pure and spotless Virgin
  Born for us on earth below,
He, as Man with man conversing,
  Stay'd the seeds of truth to sow;
Then He closed in solemn order
  Wondrously his life of woe.

On the night of that Last Supper,
  Seated with his chosen band,
He the Paschal victim eating,
  First fulfils the Law's command;
Then, as Food to all his brethren,
  Gives Himself with his own hand

Word made Flesh, the bread of nature
  By his word to Flesh he turns;
Wine into His Blood he changes:—
  What though sense no change discerns!
Only be the heart in earnest,
  Faith her lesson quickly learns.

Down in adoration falling,
  Lo! the sacred Host we hail;
Lo! o'er ancient forms departing,
  Newer rites of grace prevail;
Faith, for all defects supplying,
  Where the feeble senses fail.

To the Everlasting Father,
  And the Son who reigns on high,
With the Holy Ghost proceeding
  Forth from Each eternally,
Be salvation, honor, blessing,
  Might, and endless majesty.

TE DEUM LAUDAMUS.

Holy God we praise thy Name!
  Lord of all, we bow before Thee!
All on earth thy sceptre claim,
    All in Heaven above adore Thee
      Infinite thy vast domain,
      Everlasting is thy reign.

Hark! the loud celestial hymn
  Angel choirs above are raising!
Cherubim and Seraphim
  In unceasing chorus praising,
    Fill the heavens with sweet accord:
    Holy! Holy! Holy Lord!

Lo! the Apostolic train
Join, thy sacred name to hallow!
Prophets swell the loud refrain,
And the white-robed Martyrs follow;
And from morn till set of sun,
Through the church the song goes on.

Holy Father, Holy Son,
Holy Spirit, three we name Thee,
While in essence, only One
Undivided God, we claim Thee;
And adoring bend the knee,
While we own the mystery.

Thou art King of Glory, Christ!
Son of God, yet born of Mary,
For us sinners sacrificed,
And to death a tributary:
First to break the bars of death,
Thou hast open'd Heaven to faith.

From thy high celestial home,
Judge of all, again returning,
We believe that Thou shalt come,
On the dreadful Doom's-day morning
When thy voice shall shake the earth,
And the startled Dead come forth.

Spare thy people, Lord, we pray,
By a thousand snares surrounded:
Keep us without sin to-day,
Never let us be confounded.
Lo! I put my trust in Thee,
Never, Lord, abandon me.

ALPHABETICAL INDEX.

www.ingramcontent.com/pod-product-compliance
Lightning Source LLC
LaVergne TN
LVHW020911110826
845150LV00004B/647

* 9 7 8 1 4 2 5 5 5 6 7 0 9 *